THE MIDDLE EAST IN 1958

THE MIDDLE EAST IN 1958

Reimagining a Revolutionary Year

Edited by
Jeffrey G. Karam
Lebanese American University

I.B. TAURIS
LONDON · NEW YORK · OXFORD · NEW DELHI · SYDNEY

I.B. TAURIS
Bloomsbury Publishing Plc
50 Bedford Square, London, WC1B 3DP, UK
1385 Broadway, New York, NY 10018, USA
29 Earlsfort Terrace, Dublin 2, Ireland

BLOOMSBURY, I.B. TAURIS and the I.B. Tauris logo are trademarks of Bloomsbury Publishing Plc

First published in Great Britain 2021
This paperback edition published 2024

Copyright © Jeffrey G. Karam and Contributors, 2021

Jeffrey G. Karam has asserted his right under the Copyright, Designs and Patents Act, 1988, to be identified as Editor of this work.

For legal purposes the Acknowledgments on p. xvi constitute an extension of this copyright page.

Cover design: Liron Gilenberg
Cover image © [top left] Bettmann/Getty Images; [top right] Keystone Pictures USA/Alamy Stock Photo; [bottom left] Photo 12/Alamy Stock Photo; [bottom right] Thomas J. O'Halloran/Library of Congress (LC-U9-1473D-11).

All rights reserved. No part of this publication may be reproduced or transmitted in any form or by any means, electronic or mechanical, including photocopying, recording, or any information storage or retrieval system, without prior permission in writing from the publishers.

Bloomsbury Publishing Plc does not have any control over, or responsibility for, any third-party websites referred to or in this book. All internet addresses given in this book were correct at the time of going to press. The author and publisher regret any inconvenience caused if addresses have changed or sites have ceased to exist, but can accept no responsibility for any such changes.

A catalogue record for this book is available from the British Library.

A catalog record for this book is available from the Library of Congress.

ISBN: HB: 978-1-7883-1942-3
PB: 978-0-7556-5687-5
ePDF: 978-0-7556-0680-1
eBook: 978-0-7556-0681-8

Typeset by Deanta Global Publishing Services, Chennai, India

To find out more about our authors and books visit www.bloomsbury.com and sign up for our newsletters.

To all the revolutionaries who fought bravely against injustice and cruelty, and the ones who are still daring to reimagine and create a better world.

CONTENTS

List of Figures	x
Foreword *Salim Yaqub*	xi
Acknowledgments	xvi
Note on Text and Translation	xix

Chapter 1
REIMAGINING 1958 THROUGH THE LENSES OF MULTILINGUAL
SOURCES AND INTERDISCIPLINARY PERSPECTIVES 1
    Jeffrey G. Karam

Part 1
THE REGIONAL AND INTERNATIONAL CONTEXT OF 1958: DECLINING AND RISING POWERS IN THE MIDDLE EAST

Chapter 2
THE POINT OF DEPARTURE: THE IMPACT OF THE REVOLUTIONARY
YEAR OF 1958 ON BRITISH POLICY 13
    Robert McNamara

Chapter 3
FRANCE AND THE MIDDLE EAST IN 1958: CONTINUITY AND
CHANGE THROUGH CRISIS 32
    Sofia Papastamkou

Chapter 4
CAUTIOUS REVISIONISM AND THE LIMITS OF HEGEMONY IN 1958: A
REVOLUTIONARY YEAR FOR THE UNITED STATES IN THE MIDDLE EAST 47
    Jeffrey G. Karam

Chapter 5
THE "PARTISANS OF PEACE" BETWEEN BAKU AND MOSCOW:
THE SOVIET EXPERIENCE OF 1958 65
    Elizabeth Bishop

Part 2
RIVALRY AND ALLIANCES BETWEEN ARAB AND NON-ARAB STATES: REGIONALIZING DYNAMICS OF THE COLD WAR

Chapter 6
SAUDI ARABIA IN THE CRUCIBLE OF 1958 — 79
Nathan J. Citino

Chapter 7
EGYPT'S REVOLUTIONARY YEAR: REGIME CONSOLIDATION AT HOME, PRAGMATISM ABROAD, AND NEUTRALISM IN THE COLD WAR — 92
Dina Rezk

Chapter 8
THE OUTSIDER INSIDE: TURKEY AND THE DOMINO EFFECT OF ARAB NATIONALISM IN 1958 — 113
Murat Kasapsaraçoğlu

Chapter 9
CREATING THE "ISLAND OF STABILITY": IRAN, THE COLD WAR, AND AMERICAN CULTURAL DIPLOMACY AT THE END OF THE 1950s — 125
John Ghazvinian

Part 3
CONNECTING THE LOCAL TO THE GLOBAL: REVOLUTIONS, WARS, AND COUPS IN THE MIDDLE EAST

Chapter 10
HOW ABOUT 1958 IN ALGERIA? A TRANSNATIONAL EVENT IN THE CONTEXT OF THE WAR OF INDEPENDENCE — 141
Sylvie Thénault

Chapter 11
THE IRAQI REVOLUTION OF 1958: ITS HISTORIC SIGNIFICANCE AND RELEVANCE FOR THE PRESENT — 153
Juan Romero

Chapter 12
NO TURNING BACK: SYRIA AND THE 1958 WATERSHED — 166
Fadi Esber

Chapter 13
THE CRISIS OF 1958 IN LEBANON: POLITICAL RIVALRIES 178
    Caroline Attie

Chapter 14
EVOLUTION AND REVOLUTION: JORDAN IN 1958 193
    Clea Hupp

Chapter 15
REFLECTIONS AND CONCLUSIONS FROM THE REVOLUTIONARY
YEAR OF 1958 204
    Jeffrey G. Karam

List of Contributors 213
Index 217

FIGURES

1. Map of Middle East, North Africa, and Europe — 106
2. Egypt's *al-Ahram* newspaper announcing the birth of the United Arab Republic — 106
3. Abd al-Hamid al-Sarraj meeting Gamal Abdel Nasser in Cairo — 107
4. A young Syrian helps an elderly man to vote for Gamal Abdel Nasser in the February 1958 plebiscite in Damascus — 107
5. Gamal Abdel Nasser addressing thousands of Syrians who came to greet him in 1958 — 108
6. US Marine sits in a foxhole and points a machine gun toward Beirut, Lebanon, in the distance — 108
7. American soldier reads a newspaper in the shade under a US Marine tank in Beirut, Lebanon — 109
8. Picture collage of the Algerian War of Independence — 109
9. Arab Federation talks between Jordan and Iraq in early 1958 — 110
10. US president Dwight D. Eisenhower meeting with Egyptian president Gamal Abdel Nasser — 110
11. President Eisenhower meeting with Secretary of State John Foster Dulles — 111
12. Leaders of the July 14, 1958, revolution in Iraq — 111
13. Chief of Staff of Arab Legion Glubb Pasha, King Hussein of Jordan, and Aide-de-camp Ali Abu Nuwar — 112

FOREWORD

On July 14, 1958, military officers proclaiming fealty to Arab nationalism forcefully overthrew Iraq's pro-Western regime. Over the next few days, US and British troops landed in Lebanon and Jordan, respectively, to help each country's government withstand dissident pressures that seemed linked to the upheaval in Iraq. These eye-catching events were the most conspicuous manifestations of a longer and deeper struggle unfolding in the Arab world, pitting an ascendant and at times radical pan-Arab movement against a conservative, Western-dominated status quo. Exemplifying those rival tendencies were two Arab mergers forged the previous February: the progressive United Arab Republic, consisting of Egypt and Syria, and the conservative Arab Union, combining the kingdoms of Iraq and Jordan. Due to the strategic, economic, and cultural importance of the Middle East, this inter-Arab contest was, at the time, a subject of consuming global interest.

The striking events of 1958 have also captivated scholars, generations of whom have explored, debated, and drawn connections among the crises and conflicts that perturbed the Middle East and reverberated more broadly during that fateful year. The essays in this volume form the latest contribution to this tradition, serving as imaginative reinterpretations of a topic of abiding relevance and fascination. Their authors survey a broad swath of nations, societies, and international actors, assessing their differing experiences of and interactions with the events of 1958. As often happens in historical reconstruction, a recurrent theme is the interplay of rupture and continuity.

Part 1 of this collection explores the outlooks and actions of what were then rather quaintly called the "great powers": Britain, France, the United States, and the Soviet Union. All of these nations took a keen interest in the Middle Eastern upheavals of 1958, though the first two were declining in the region while the second pair was ascending. In the case of each nation, the events of 1958 tended to reinforce or accelerate existing trends in its foreign policy, rather than cause abrupt changes of direction.

We are prone to see the Suez debacle of 1956 as the signal event in Britain's imperial decline, but Robert McNamara's contribution to this volume argues that the violent removal of Iraq's Hashemite regime, the lynchpin of London's strategy in the area, produced "a much more decisive shift in the attitude of Britain to Arab nationalism . . . than Suez ever did" (14). The result was a general scaling back of Britain's efforts to thwart Egypt's president Gamal Abdel Nasser and "a retreat to the oil rich emirates of the Persian Gulf"—protectorates Britain would maintain for another dozen years (24). Before beating this retreat, however, Britain did dispatch troops to Jordan to shore up its Hashemite throne. France, by contrast—distracted by the Algerian crisis and undergoing a change of government at home—found itself unable to play a central role in Lebanon, despite its prior domination of it. Not only did such impotence confirm France's imperial decline in the Middle East, writes Sofia Papastamkou; it was "symptomatic of a broader shift that occurred in France's relations with her major Western allies," ultimately taking the form of Paris's withdrawal from the North Atlantic Treaty Organization's military command (37).

The United States, as noted, was on the strategic upswing in the Middle East. In terms of policy, however, as Jeffrey G. Karam notes, it followed a geopolitical trajectory similar to Britain's: "from containing revolutionary Arab nationalists and shoring up pro-Western Middle Eastern regimes [in 1956–8] to accommodating Nasser and the growing nationalist trend" after 1958 (57). Over the two years preceding the marine landings in Lebanon, the Eisenhower administration tried to rally a coalition of pro-US Arab governments to combat Nasser's influence. The fact that military intervention ultimately proved necessary revealed the failure of Washington's *political* strategy, and in 1959 Eisenhower pragmatically sought improved relations with Nasser. Nonetheless, Karam writes, "the relative success of this military operation in Lebanon . . . set a dangerous precedent" for future US interventions, few of which would proceed so bloodlessly (58).

The other ascendant superpower was, of course, the Soviet Union, which since the mid-1950s had gained considerable influence in the region. As Elizabeth Bishop shows, the Soviets and their "partisans" had ample cause to celebrate the Iraqi revolution, which dealt a painful blow to their Western adversaries. The subsequent decision by Iraq's new president, 'Abd al-Karim Qassim, to align with Iraqi communists probably exceeded Soviet hopes. Unexpectedly, however, Nasser grew alarmed at the Soviet inroads into Iraq and began accusing Moscow of interfering in Arab internal affairs. Western observers had to acknowledge that Nasserism could be barrier to, and not simply an avenue of, Soviet encroachment on the region.

Part 2 is concerned with several Middle Eastern nations, geopolitical actors that were much closer to the upheavals of 1958 but that, with the exception of Egypt, were not directly caught up in them. In two of these countries, Turkey and Iran, we find the events of 1958 reinforcing or accelerating trends well underway. Murat Kasapsaraçoğlum argues that the Iraqi revolution, by prompting the Turkish government to consider military action to restore the ousted Iraqi regime, "widened the gap between the [Turkish] government and the opposition," paving the way for the military coup d'état in Ankara in 1960 (121). The overthrow of the Baghdad regime also significantly affected the government of Iran, causing it to seek protection in the form of closer strategic ties to the United States. "It was, ultimately, the events of 1958," writes John Ghazvinian, "that most clearly cemented Iran's pro-American, anti-Soviet and authoritarian foreign-policy orientation" (130). The "blowback" from that transformation occurred two decades later, yielding consequences that remain with us forty years after *that*.

Israel does not receive sustained attention in this volume, but its geopolitical history, too, bears the imprint of 1958. Like Iran, Israel forged closer strategic ties to the United States in the aftermath of that year. Previously, the administration of Dwight D. Eisenhower had kept Israel at arm's length, hoping to mitigate anti-Western sentiment in the Arab world. But in the post-intervention stocktaking in the summer of 1958, US officials viewed Israel in a fresh light. The issue was most sharply drawn in Jordan. Washington had long feared that Israel might respond to a Nasserist takeover in that country by seizing the Jordanian-controlled West Bank, in turn sparking an Arab-Israeli war. By 1958, there were indications that Nasser himself feared such an outcome and was thus urging restraint on his West Bank supporters. "It might be a good thing," US secretary of state John Foster Dulles mused in August, "that the UAR was afraid of Israel." At a time when pro-US Arab regimes seemed utterly incapable of containing Nasserism, the deterrent potential of Israeli power gained new value in American eyes. The United States modestly stepped up its military support of Israel.[1]

In the case of two other regional actors, Saudi Arabia and Egypt, one is powerfully struck by what did *not* happen. The year is rightly remembered as a time of revolutionary possibility, but that possibility went largely unfulfilled. Nathan Citino observes that the backdrop of pan-Arab agitation amplified calls by Saudi dissidents for a more equitable distribution of power in the kingdom. Ultimately, however, the status quo held firm. "Nineteen fifty-eight," he concludes, "was therefore a revolutionary year in the Middle East that created potential but ultimately unrealized opportunities for political reform in Saudi Arabia" (87). Nasserist pan-Arabism itself conspicuously failed to live up to its promise. In July 1958, the movement seemed unstoppable, but within months it had run aground and was even atrophying from within. Not only was Nasser feuding with Iraq's Qassim, but Syrian leaders had started to grumble about their subordinate status within the United Arab Republic; in early 1961, Syria seceded from the union. "Perhaps what was most revolutionary about 1958," Dina Rezk archly observes, "was . . . the spectacularly rapid deterioration of the pan-Arab vision [and] the clearly emerging dissonance between the dream and the reality" (99).

Part 3 focuses on Arab actors more directly caught up in the revolutionary upheavals of 1958. Of these, Iraq experienced the most immediate and momentous change. On a single day in July, it was violently transformed from a monarchy to a republic. The Iraqi line of the Hashemite dynasty was physically extinguished, and the nation's federation with Hashemite Jordan irrevocably severed. Iraq's close alliance with Britain and the United States gave way to a posture of formal neutrality in the Cold War, with a distinct tilt toward the East bloc. Iraq would remain more or less antagonistic toward the Western powers until 2003, when another violent event installed a pro-Western government in Baghdad. Juan Romero argues that the transformations of 1958 were not simply the result of elite maneuverings but reflected sentiments broadly felt across Iraqi society. As such, they qualify as "a genuine revolution" (153).

Lebanon and Jordan, too, were the sites of extraordinary tumult, if not the sort of fundamental rupture experienced by Iraq. In both Lebanon and Jordan, Western powers intervened to preserve the established order, though in the former case this was accomplished by placing limits on the political ambitions of Camille Chamoun, Lebanon's pro-Western president. Indeed, writes Caroline Attie, if 1958 events constituted a "watershed" for Lebanon, it was because they resulted in Chamoun's replacement by Fu'ad Shihab, who ushered in a decade of "administrative reform" featuring "more equitable economic expenditure by the state on infrastructure in hitherto neglected regions of Lebanon" (179). In Jordan, the upheavals of 1958 yielded starker ironies. Although Britain was the power sending troops to that country, the intervention was part of what Clea Hupp calls "a remarkable evolution" in Jordan's foreign relations, whereby "King Hussein bin Talal successfully negotiated the transition from an old patron (Great Britain) to a new one (the United States)" (193). In 1958, informed observers were deeply pessimistic about Hussein's chances of political survival, and even about Jordan's ability to endure as a nation. Few imagined his reign would continue for another four decades.

In Syria, too, a political actor powerfully entrenched itself for decades to come. The union with Egypt in February 1958, writes Fadi Esber, doomed Syria's traditional political parties and placed the nation's Ba'athist Party on the path to national ascendancy, a primacy it enjoys to this day. Esber adds that the party itself underwent a fundamental transformation after 1958, changing "from an organization led by intellectuals and civilian cadres to one commanded by a nucleus of restless and disillusioned military officers"—an observation that illuminates a good deal of subsequent Syrian history (167).

All of the Middle Eastern actors discussed so far enjoyed at least a semblance of national sovereignty. The Palestinians were not so fortunate, and they were growing less and less willing to accept this fate. While the Palestinian struggle does not receive extended coverage in this volume, it has its own 1958 pedigree. In the mid-1950s, Palestinian commandos had, with Cairo's support, launched raids into Israel from the Egyptian-administered Gaza Strip. Following the 1956 Suez War, United Nations peacekeepers occupied the strip, and Nasser was obliged to demobilize the commando organizations. No longer able to function in Gaza, several young Palestinian activists relocated to Kuwait, where they coalesced under the leadership of an engineer named Yasser Arafat and a schoolteacher named Khalil al-Wazir. Throughout 1958, the Kuwait activists met secretly and laid the groundwork for a new Palestinian organization. Publicly unveiled in 1959, al-Fatah championed themes that would become widely familiar to Arab audiences: the imperative of liberating all of Palestine, the primacy of the armed struggle, and the need for Palestinians to seize control of their destiny, fully independent of Arab regimes. Also contributing to the pent-up "liberationist" fervor were Palestinians residing in Syria who had been politically silenced by the crackdown on party activity there following the formation of the UAR in 1958, and Palestinians who had gained military experience fighting on the rebel side of Lebanon's civil war of that same year.[2]

Another struggle for national sovereignty, this one ultimately successful, raged two thousand miles to the west. Sylvie Thénault demonstrates that, although 1958 was not a decisive turning point in Algeria's war for independence, it was the year in which the struggle spilled over into neighboring Tunisia, dramatically aiding the independence movement's campaign to internationalize the conflict. Internationalization, in turn, would prove indispensable to Algeria's eventual achievement of independence. And, of course, Algerian events in 1958 did force a turning point back in the metropole: a political crisis resulting in the demise of the Fourth Republic—more than enough to tie France's hands over Lebanon.

Change versus continuity, revolutionary possibility versus the power of inertia—these themes defined the experiences, aspirations, collisions, and disappointments of 1958. With perceptiveness and authority, with impressive command of exciting new sources and methodologies, the essays collected here illuminate this six-decades-old history, establishing its resonance and relevance to a new generation of readers.

Salim Yaqub

Notes

1 Salim Yaqub, *Containing Arab Nationalism: The Eisenhower Doctrine and the Middle East* (Chapel Hill, NC: University of North Carolina Press, 2004), 263–4; Abraham Ben-Zvi, *Decade of Transition: Eisenhower, Kennedy, and the Origins of the American-Israeli Alliance* (New York: Columbia University Press, 1998), 77–83.
2 Yezid Sayigh, *Armed Struggle and the Search for State: The Palestinian National Movement, 1949–1993* (Oxford: Oxford University Press, 1997), 83–5, 92.

ACKNOWLEDGMENTS

Editing this book was harder than I thought but more rewarding than I could have ever imagined. Although my name is on the cover of this book, the volume is the product of deep and collective efforts between scholars residing and working at different institutions in various continents. None of this would have been possible without the authors of the chapters in this volume and the support of a legion of individuals and institutions.

Thanks to my home institution, the Lebanese American University, my colleagues in the Department of Social Sciences, the Dean's Office at the School of Arts and Sciences, and the Office of the Provost for supporting my research agenda and this book at different junctures. I have received several generous grants to present chapters from this volume at international conferences and prepare the book for production. I would like to thank all my colleagues in the Department of Social Sciences for their support, and especially Sami Baroudi and Bassel Salloukh, and Selim Deringil in the Humanities department, for participating in the conference on the book. I would also like to thank Lisa Salem at LAU for being a strong supporter of my scholarship and of my well-being.

Thanks to my alma mater, the American University of Beirut, and especially the diligent staff at the Center for Arab and Middle Eastern Studies and the Issam Fares Institute for Public Policy and International Affairs for organizing and hosting an international conference on this book in March 2019. I likewise thank the Center for American Studies and Research at AUB, especially its Director Robert Myers, for co-sponsoring Salim Yaqub's keynote address during the conference. This volume benefited immensely from the book workshop that most contributors participated in during that conference at AUB. The staff at AUB worked tirelessly to ensure that our invited guests had a pleasant stay in Beirut. I also thank my colleagues at AUB, especially Rayan El Amine and Carmen Geha, for participating in the conference and chairing different panel sessions. I also want to extend my deep gratitude to Nadya Sbaiti, Samir Seikaily, Tariq Tell, and Salim Yaqub for reading the entire manuscript and serving as discussants at our book workshop.

My deepest thanks go to Samer Frangie. Samer endorsed and encouraged the plan for the present volume back when I was a graduate student with preliminary ideas about the importance of 1958 in the political history of the modern Middle East. Samer read drafts of multiple chapters and proposals related to this book. The Center for Arab and Middle Eastern Studies, with Samer as Director, primarily supported the international conference, book workshop, and public roundtable. For being the primary supporter of this project and a sharp reader, but more importantly, for being a friend, I extend my gratitude to him.

Acknowledgments

A lot of the thinking and planning of this volume took place while I was living and working in Boston and Cambridge, Massachusetts. Therefore, I would like to extend my deep thanks to the Crown Center for Middle East Studies for their generous support during my doctoral journey and especially when the idea for this book developed during my research trips to the Middle East. I would like to thank the Pardee School of Global Studies for offering me the opportunity to design and teach innovative courses and providing a platform to discuss some of the book's preliminary research findings with the wider community at Boston University. I also extend my deep thanks to the International Security Program at Harvard University's Belfer Center for Science and International Affairs, particularly its co-directors Stephen Walt and Steven Miller, for offering me the support and space to think through many of the ideas in the volume at hand and my own research agenda. I also want to extend my warm thanks to the Middle East Initiative, particularly its director Tarek Masoud, for offering me the opportunity to remain affiliated as an associate with the Belfer Center and the Harvard Kennedy School of Government. I also thank the staff at the Belfer Center for actively sharing the fruits of my research to the wider community at Harvard and beyond.

Warm thanks to my colleagues who contributed chapters and made this volume possible. I am grateful that you have trusted me with your work. I have learned more about the Middle East by reading your chapters and by drawing on your esteemed scholarship in my work. I also want to offer my deep gratitude to Salim Yaqub for supporting this book in different ways, and I truly value his warm support and friendship.

I want to thank Sophie Rudland at I.B. Tauris and Bloomsbury for being a strong supporter of important books in the field of Middle East studies, and I am happy to have had the pleasure of working with her. The authors and I are grateful for the excellent and constructive feedback from several anonymous reviewers. Thank you for helping us get this volume ready for publication.

Warm thanks to my friends, near and far, for supporting this project in different ways. The idea for this book originated and concluded in Beirut, simmered in Boston and Cambridge, and then materialized between Amman, Ankara, Athens, Beirut, Berlin, Bowling Green, Damascus, Dublin, Houston, Istanbul, London, Mexico City, New Orleans, New York, Oran, Paris, Philadelphia, San Antonio, San Francisco, San Marcos, Santa Barbara, and Riyadh.

Warmest thanks to my family for supporting me over the years, and especially when I was constantly traveling between Boston and Beirut. I am forever thankful for having supportive parents, in-laws, and relatives who supported this project and continuously encourage me in different ways.

Finally, I want to extend my eternal gratitude to my partner, Sana Tannoury-Karam. Sana has read early and multiple drafts of my chapters in this volume, the book proposal, research articles emanating from this present volume, and every single piece of scholarly and policy writing that I have done so far. Sana consistently provided me with advice on every single aspect related to this volume, from the book cover to many of the arguments that I have raised in my chapters.

I would not have been able to edit this manuscript, write my own chapters, draft and finish articles and my book manuscript, teach my courses, and function as a human being without her love and support. Sana is my role model, and I thank her for always pushing me to work harder even when I am doubting myself. Thank you for everything that you are.

December 2019

NOTE ON TEXT AND TRANSLATION

Arabic and Turkish titles and names are spelled according to a simplified version of the transliteration system used by the *International Journal of Middle East Studies*. However, many familiar names such as "Chamoun," "Hussein," "Mosaddegh," "Nasser," and "Qassim" appear in their commonly used spellings. All translations from Arabic, French, Turkish, Russian, and other languages are by the authors of the respective chapters unless otherwise indicated.

Chapter 1

REIMAGINING 1958 THROUGH THE LENSES OF MULTILINGUAL SOURCES AND INTERDISCIPLINARY PERSPECTIVES

Jeffrey G. Karam

The year 1958 was a time marked by a series of transformative sociopolitical developments that shook the foundations of the existing Middle Eastern order and in various ways, sparked the beginning of a new sociopolitical landscape in the region. The year 1958 remains a vital, if not one of the most important, moments in the Middle East from the *Nahda* (Renaissance) to the Arab uprisings in 2010–11 and the most recent wave of protests in the region that erupted in 2019.[1] Against the backdrop of Egypt's nationalization of the Suez Canal Company and the ensuing crisis of 1956, the creation of the United Arab Republic with the merger of Syria and Egypt into one state on February 1, 1958, seemed the initial step toward greater Arab unity. As the present work shows, the repercussions of the union between Egypt and Syria had an impact both on the states in the Middle East and on the ones outside the region. The most visible impact manifested in three Arab states: first, the aggravation of the political crisis later turned civil war in Lebanon between May and July 1958; second, the attempted and foiled coups against Hussein in the Hashemite Kingdom of Jordan in June and July 1958; and third, the military coup turned revolution in Iraq on July 14, 1958, that ended the monarchy and created a republic.

The three seminal events constituted a turning point in the modern history of the Middle East and North Africa. However, this book considers that these sociopolitical developments were part of a larger series of events in a period marked by decolonization, revolutionary nationalism, internationalism, postcolonialism, imperialism, anti-imperialism, and state formation. Therefore, this book is a study that brings together these events, arguing for the importance of examining these moments in conjunction and in conversation with each other by using the time span of that seminal year of 1958. Existing scholarship, especially the edited volume *A Revolutionary Year: The Middle East in 1958*, by Roger Louis and Roger Owen, draws the connections between the events in Iraq and Lebanon. Other works examine the process of state formation in some states in the Arab Middle East and the importance of oil in the region.[2] However, these important contributions have mostly explored the experiences of a limited number of states and focused on collections of records and documents, while excluding a deeper appreciation of the role of non-Arab actors in the region and the multilayered connections between local, regional, and global developments in 1958.

This book remedies the fragmented nature of the scholarship on 1958 by bringing together, for the first time, scholars researching and writing about the wider context of critical events at the outset of the Cold War in the Middle East and particularly before and during the year 1958. Therefore, although the focus is on 1958 in the Middle East, the volume transcends, first, temporal limitations of one particular year to include pre- and post-1958 contexts, and second, the geographic scope of the Middle East to encompass global trends and processes. It, therefore, examines a series of momentous events in different Middle Eastern capitals and ones outside the region from a wide range of linguistic, geographic, historical, and academic specialties. Only by facilitating a dialogue between the many scholars and practitioners specializing in different aspects of the postcolonial moment in 1958 and its connections to broader revolutionary struggles, both failed and successful, can we appreciate the global, regional, and local experience of various Middle Eastern actors and states and the transnational nature of the twentieth-century world and the Cold War in the Middle East.

This book joins a multitude of interdisciplinary and multidisciplinary volumes that underscore the importance of studying critical junctures and sociopolitical developments in a particular year.[3] The present volume's focus is primarily on the revolutionary year of 1958. This is the result of three considerations. First, the authors control for and hold constant transformational events in 1958 and subsequently are able to focus their analysis on the connections between developments that preceded and proceeded vital and transformational moments in this particular year. This focused approach allows the authors to analyze similarities and differences within and across different states under the same temporal and conceptual considerations. Second, by focusing primarily on one year, the authors collectively demonstrate the methodological and conceptual merits of variation and in-depth analysis of turning points within and across different states in the region. This scholarly contribution is rarely found in works that either focus on the experiences of one particular state or adopt a larger temporal framework that must leave out many of the intricate details of important sociopolitical developments. Third, the authors' focus on the revolutionary year of 1958 through varied methodologies and archival sources is an important scholarly conversation that highlights the failed and successful experiences of different states within the same time period and in the context of similar transformational moments.

The book is primarily the product of two scholarly conversations. The first began in 2013, as I was conducting research for my doctoral dissertation in different Middle Eastern capitals. During this time, I established contact with a group of political scientists and historians that shared a common appreciation for the complexities of the events in the year 1958 and the need to address a number of cases, as well as records and sources, that were not fully analyzed in existing scholarship. The second phase was in early 2018, especially when plans for an international conference and the current volume started to materialize.

After correspondence with scholars in Europe, the Middle East, and North America, the authors of different chapters were invited to partake in an international conference at the American University of Beirut (AUB) in March 2019. For three consecutive days, the scholars discussed earlier versions of the chapters in this volume, and then consequently participated in a closed book workshop.[4]

Scope and Purpose of the Book

This book recovers the debates, introduces the personalities, and reveals the ideas central to the global revolutionary and postcolonial moment in the Middle East at the outset of the Cold War in the 1950s. It does so through a political, social, economic, anthropological, and historical study of the year 1958 to answer one broad question: to what extent were events in the year 1958 revolutionary and transformative for states in the Middle East and ones outside the region? And if we consider that year to be "revolutionary," in any given sense or definition of the term, how can an examination of 1958 enhance our understanding of revolutionary moments in the Middle East and the Third World more generally?

Besides the broader question that motivates this book, the chapters engage with many issues, including Egypt and Syria's perceptions of the United Arab Republic and internal motivations for merger into a single state; the linkages between the Algerian War of Independence and the collapse of the Fourth Republic in France; the extent to which states in the Gulf, such as Iran and Saudi Arabia, were affected by different crises and events in Iraq, Lebanon, and Jordan; the ability of Turkey and Jordan to weather the revolutionary wave at the time; the success of the military coup in Iraq and the failure of the different coup d'états in Jordan; Britain's coping strategies and actions with the ascendancy of the United States in the region; the introduction of US forces in Lebanon and the involvement of a superpower in a domestic political crisis; and the contributions of existing and newly declassified primary and secondary sources from different continents to inform novel discussions of the rivalry between the United States and the Union of Soviet Socialist Republics (USSR) in the region.

The authors examine these issues in a threefold manner. First, they collectively assert that important sociopolitical developments in the Middle East in 1958 were as transformative for Middle Eastern states as they were for outside powers, including Britain, France, the United States, and the USSR. By focusing on these states outside the region, the chapters explain how outside powers were equally impacted by the different military coups, uprisings, calls for reform, armed skirmishes, and crises in the region, the authors are both breaking the silence on the wider repercussions of the events in 1958 and drawing novel contributions on the interactions between local, regional, and global actors and movements at the time. While the chapters highlight the impact of the Cold War on events in the Middle East, they equally demonstrate that the sociopolitical developments in the Middle East had equal, if not stronger, repercussions on falling and rising powers at the time. They are specifically reversing the dominant and often assumed direction of impact between states in the twentieth century, by shifting the focus on the Third World global south and its agency in shaping Cold War history.

Second, the chapters move beyond the binaries and prevalent frames of reference, such as West versus East, capitalism versus communism, and the United States versus the USSR, that predominantly characterize the trajectory of many sociopolitical developments in the Middle East during that period.[5] The contributors to this volume contend that analyses along binary frames fail to properly account for the fluidity of different events and the complexity of alliances between and within Middle Eastern states and the two superpowers at the time. This again re-centers the conversation toward the agency and decision-making of local actors, notwithstanding the influence of ideology but rather without assuming actors' behavior as necessarily following these inhibiting binaries.

Third, almost all of the authors draw on multilingual sources, employ innovative methodologies that cut across disciplinary boundaries, and combine primary and secondary records to analyze the wider connections within and between revolutionary and transformative developments in the Middle East, North Africa, and beyond. Without such a holistic account, we are left with a biased and incomplete account of some of the most important critical junctures in the political history of the Middle East.

The Merits of Multilingual Sources

It is important to highlight two points regarding multilingual sources. First, almost all of the authors have surveyed documents and records in at least two languages in geographically diverse locations to produce novel, accurate, and inclusive scholarly accounts. In fact, most of the contributors to this volume have consulted documents in different languages that are available in archives based in France, the United Kingdom, the United States, and other Western countries. Many of the authors' proficiency in more than one language certainly allow them to thoroughly analyze Arab or French documents from archives and records in the West. This language proficiency has allowed many authors in the present volume to examine the original document, before it was translated, and in many ways to account for discrepancies or meanings that could be lost in translation across languages. Almost all of the contributors to this volume have analyzed both the original document and subsequent translations.

Second, almost all of the authors who have analyzed the experiences of non-Western states in 1958 have consulted a number of eyewitness accounts, primary records, newspaper and media reports, and secondary accounts authored and published by citizens of these countries. The availability of and access to archival documents in most non-Western states in the Middle East and North Africa is unlike what scholars experience in most Western archival locations and depositories. Many of the contributions to this present volume have scoured published and unpublished materials, drawn on previously conducted interviews with actors in various Middle Eastern capitals, and consulted *local* accounts to provide a holistic and culturally more sensitive account of important sociopolitical developments before, during, and after the revolutionary year of 1958.

Many of the contributors to this present volume have examined newly declassified and understudied archival records and documents to sustain arguments in their chapters. Other authors offer fresh perspectives and conclusions on previously available documents by employing interdisciplinary lenses and drawing connections between primary and secondary resources. Given that almost all contributors are proficient in more than two languages, they were able to extract records, interpret them, and translate parts of their findings to sustain assertions in their respective chapters. In some instances, the authors have not broken new ground by consulting existing archival sources. However, all the chapters are in effect providing revised interpretations from existing sources that center on drawing connections between several levels of analysis, ranging from domestic considerations to global ones. By inviting the contributors to "reimagine" the impact of the "revolutionary year of 1958" on different states during the wave of decolonization, nationalization, state formation, armed struggles, military coups, and rise of authoritarianism, the present volume does break new ground on the centrality of the Middle East and vital sociopolitical developments in 1958 that were a significant part of global trends and processes that unraveled in other regions.

Importance of the Volume and Contributions to Existing Scholarship

This book builds on existing scholarship, draws on a collection of primary and secondary sources, and makes novel contributions to different disciplines and subfields. In many ways, the present work continues the scholarly debates that began in A *Revolutionary Year* and so, deepens the analysis through the use of interdisciplinary methodologies and multilingual sources. The book's significance and contributions are manifold. I will briefly discuss four major ones.

First, the present work considers the significance of the year 1958 both in retrospect and in hindsight. While most scholarly works analyze important junctures that have occurred in the past and could often seem much more important in hindsight than when they transpired at the time, the authors analyzing events in the Middle East examine the commonality between different calls for reform and better economic opportunities in various societies at the time. The major uprisings in different states that began in the early 1950s shared a common purpose: the rejection of Western imperialism and the regimes they bolstered. Another common trend across most of the chapters is the profound distaste for Western-supported authoritarian leaders and regimes, and the slow economic development in different states. The mobilization of different actors and movements in various societies were sparked by the same triggers, a sense of alienation from the established status quo and the popular need to rebel. The volume explains how these struggles were an integral part of the wave of decolonization and state formation that transpired in the Middle East and other regions around the world.

Second, the book brings to the fore the voices of local political actors, movements, and institutions in the Middle East that have often been silenced in existing scholarship. Specifically, and while valuing the contributions that previous scholarship offer, the below chapters break away from the centrality of Western-centric records and sources to analyze the critical junctures in 1958. The authors collectively agree that scholarship that is informed by multilingual and diverse sources has been slow to develop, in large part because of the necessity for scholars to master multiple languages and work in different fields relevant to revisit and fully analyze significant turning points in the Middle East and other regions around the globe. While many of the authors draw on primary and secondary sources in Britain, France, and the United States, the authors collectively underscore the biases and confines of providing a narrow account of events in the year 1958 and the limitations of existing scholarship in bridging the gap between the existing scholarship and the growing field of postcolonial studies.

In this context, the book is a scholarly appreciation of the complexity of revolutionary struggles in Algeria and Iraq, state formation in Lebanon, Syria, and Jordan, the ascendancy of the United States and the USSR and fall of the British and French empires in the region, and the alignments and rivalry between Egypt, Iran, Saudi Arabia, and Turkey. It accordingly analyzes why and how these distinct and yet connected tracks are a manifestation of the intricacy of decolonization, anti-imperialism, and state formation.

Third, the present work is diverse along disciplinary, geographic, and gender lines. Although diversity along all these lines does not always appear at conferences, in academic departments and universities, and in publications, the volume's contributions emphasize the significance of fostering dialogue across various boundaries.

Besides the fact that the authors are based at different institutions of higher education in Europe, North America, and the Middle East, the chapters' assertions are supported by a meticulous survey of documents and records from state archives, depositories, libraries, and digitized collections in four continents: Africa, Asia, Europe, and North America. For brevity, I will not list the different archival locations and collections of primary and secondary records that were consulted. Instead, I invite readers to consult the extensive references to different collections at the end of each chapter.

Fourth, the authors of different chapters are at different stages of their careers, and so, include junior and senior faculty members and practitioners. Extending an invitation to both junior and senior faculty members and having the latter contribute to this volume has been an intellectually inspiring and rewarding endeavor. Many of the contributors, especially the junior faculty, have benefited from and drawn upon the scholarship of their senior colleagues.

The volume is partly the product of years of academic exchanges and discussions between the different contributors in their respective scholarship and the subsequent chapters. The common and overarching goal of the authors is to produce innovative scholarship in Middle Eastern studies that cuts across geographic boundaries, disciplines, and academic ranks.

A Note on Concepts and Outcomes

The authors jointly agree that revolutions are neither static events nor moments in time that have a clear beginning and end.[6] Revolutionary moments are usually ones characterized by radical change or extensive reform that paves the way for new beginnings.[7] However, revolutions are messy, and the consequences of such momentous events take time to materialize and could result in either positive or negative consequences. Both the positive and/or negative outcomes of revolutionary struggles are relative and dependent on how they are analyzed. A revolution that ushers in a new political regime, such as from monarchism to republicanism or from authoritarianism to theocracy or authoritarianism to totalitarianism, and any transition from a current form of government to another that results from challenging the status quo does not necessarily yield positive outcomes.[8]

The contributors are thus adopting a lenient, but inclusive, definition of "revolutionary" that considers different dimensions and phases of such processes. The authors of the below chapters are "reimagining" 1958 as a "revolutionary year" in three specific ways. First, the focus is on connecting the dots between a series of important sociopolitical events that led to a turning point that altered the status quo and existing order. Importantly, many of the authors in the subsequent chapters, such as Sylvie Thénault and Juan Romero, demonstrate that some of these turning points, including the internationalization of the revolutionary war in Algeria in spring 1958 and the successful Free Officers Revolt in Iraq in July, were the consequence of a long period of grievances, sociopolitical instability, and popular dissent. In fact, these consequences had wider repercussions beyond the moment of euphoria and exuberance that characterize revolutionary actions. In some instances, such as in Iraq, the revolutionary moment was followed by the establishment of a military dictatorship. In other cases, such as Iran, the repercussions of the wider revolutionary atmosphere in the region led the shah to adopt harsher authoritarian measures to undercut the possibility of significant political change.

The second way in which authors adopt the use of "revolutionary" relates to a shift in political strategy and a reassessment of policies in light of the repercussions of transformative developments outside the boundaries of their state. Some of the chapters, especially ones written by Robert McNamara, Sofia Papastamkou, and me, show that both rising and declining powers in the Middle East and North Africa, including Britain, France, and the United States, had to appraise the viability of policies and actions, and such an evaluation led to major shifts in state behavior. An accurate portrayal of these dynamics would be better framed as the unintended consequences of revolutions on states outside the geographic area where such momentous outcomes occurred.

The third way relates to understanding transformative and critical events that fall below the expectations of radical change, reform, or a new beginning, such as a new governing order or system of power. Some of the chapters, including the ones on Saudi Arabia and Jordan by Nathan Citino and Clea Hupp, respectively, analyze the limited sociopolitical opportunities that arose from the revolutionary atmosphere that swept across the Middle East and North Africa for a handful of states in the region. The focus is on how different revolutionary struggles and sociopolitical uprisings in different parts of the Middle East had repercussions on Iran, Jordan, Turkey, and Saudi Arabia. Yet, these states did not experience any revolutionary or enormous episodes of change. In such instances, the impact of the general atmosphere of revolutionary struggle in the Middle East led to some minor changes. However, these minor changes are analyzed in relative terms and thus explain that revolutionary moments could be limited but decisive in chartering a new, be it positive or negative, path.

Outline of the Book

The book's chapters examine the revolutionary year of 1958 at the crossroads of five interrelated junctures: (1) the general Cold War between the United States and the Soviet Union; (2) the waning power of colonial France and Britain and their repeated attempts at regaining power and influence in the Middle East and North Africa after the Suez Crisis and War of 1956; (3) the Arab Cold War between conservative regimes led by Iraq and Saudi Arabia and revolutionary ones led by Egypt; (4) the rise of non-Arab powers in the Middle East, including Iran and Turkey and their attempts at influencing Arab states; and (5) the myriad of domestic struggles, including wars, revolutions, domestic crises, and coups in Algeria, Iraq, Lebanon, Syria, and Jordan.

Based on these junctures, the book is divided into three parts and consists of fifteen chapters. In the foreword, Salim Yaqub provides a concise overview of the different chapters and draws important thematic connections across them. I will only discuss why and how the chapters were clustered under three main parts.

Part 1 focuses on the regional and international context of the year 1958. Specifically, the first two chapters in Part 1 focus on the decline of Great Britain and France as established powers and the crumbling of Anglo-French colonialism in the Middle East. The two subsequent chapters analyze the ascendancy of the United States in the Middle East and the growing influence of the Soviet Union in the region. These four chapters clearly demonstrate how the United States and the Soviet Union were competing, as rising powers, to fill the political vacuum created by the decline of Anglo-French hegemony in the Middle East.

Part 2 examines the role of and rivalry between revolutionary Arab states and pro-Western Arab and non-Arab countries. The first two chapters in this section focus on Saudi Arabia and Egypt, and analyze the wider repercussions of different crises in 1958 on the domestic politics of both Arab states. The two other chapters examine the role of Turkey and Iran as non-Arab actors and the unintended consequences of the revolutionary year of 1958 on their political regimes.

Part 3 focuses on the wars, military coups, domestic crises, and revolutionary struggles and the connections between local, regional, and global events in the

Middle East and North Africa. The first two chapters explain how the Algerian War of Independence and the Iraqi military coup had domestic, regional, and global repercussions in the Middle East and beyond. The three remaining chapters in Part 3 discuss how the revolutionary year of 1958 overhauled the political landscape in Syria, aggravated the political crisis turned civil war in Lebanon, and paved the way for the Hashemite Kingdom of Jordan to consolidate its close relationship with the United States, respectively.

The Conclusion discusses several takeaways across the chapters and provides a road map for future research avenues that could deepen the scope of analysis to include the experience of the revolutionary year of 1958 on states that were not addressed in the present volume.

Notes

1 For some recent articles on the protests in Iraq, Iran, and Lebanon, see Eskandar Sadeghi-Boroujerdi, "Between Solidarity and Absolution: An Interjection on the Western Left's Response to the Recent Protests in Iran," *Jadaliyya*, December 3, 2019, https://www.jadaliyya.com/Details/40321; Jeffrey G. Karam and Sana Tannoury-Karam, "The Lebanese Intifada: Observations and Reflections on Revolutionary Times," *Jadaliyya*, November 10, 2019, https://www.jadaliyya.com/Details/40218; Marsin Alshamary and Safwan Al-Amin, "Iraqi Protesters Demand Constitutional Change: Can They Make It Happen?" *The Washington Post: Monkey Cage*, November 7, 2019, https://www.washingtonpost.com/politics/2019/11/07/iraqi-protesters-demand-constitutional-change-can-they-make-it-happen/; Jeffrey G. Karam, "Lebanon's Government Resigned: Here Are Three Possibilities for What's Next," *The Washington Post: Monkey Cage*, October 31, 2019, https://www.washingtonpost.com/politics/2019/10/31/lebanons-government-resigned-here-are-three-possibilities-whats-next/.

2 William Roger Louis and Roger Owen, *A Revolutionary Year: The Middle East in 1958* (London; New York: I.B. Tauris, 2002); Malcolm Kerr, *The Arab Cold War: Gamal 'Abd al-Nasser and His Rivals, 1958–1970* (Oxford: Oxford University Press, 1971); Cyrus Schayegh, "1958 Reconsidered: State Formation and The Cold War In The Early Postcolonial Arab Middle East," *International Journal of Middle East Studies* 45, no. 3 (2013): 421–43; Reem Abou-Fadl, *Foreign Policy as Nation Making: Turkey and Egypt in the Cold War* (Cambridge: Cambridge University Press, 2019); Ivan L. G. Pearson, *In the Name of Oil: Anglo-American Relations in the Middle East, 1950–1958* (Eastbourne: Sussex Academic Press, 2010); Irene L. Gendzier, *Notes from the Minefield: United States Intervention in Lebanon and the Middle East, 1945–1958* (New York: Columbia University Press, 2006).

3 William Roger Louis and Roger Owen, *Suez 1956: The Crisis and Its Consequences* (Oxford: Clarendon Press, 1991); Simon C. Smith, ed., *Reassessing Suez 1956: New Perspectives on the Crisis and Its Aftermath* (New York: Routledge, 2016); Irene L. Gendzier, *Dying to Forget: Oil, Power, Palestine, and the Foundations of U.S. Policy in the Middle East* (New York: Columbia University Press, 2015); Elisabetta Bini, Giuliano Garavini, and Federico Romero, eds., *Oil Shock: The 1973 Crisis and Its Economic Legacy* (London: I.B. Tauris, 2016); Ervand Abrahamian, *The Coup: 1953, the CIA, and the Roots of Modern U.S.-Iranian Relations* (New York: The New Press, 2013); Eugene

L. Rogan and Avi Shlaim, eds., *The War for Palestine: Rewriting the History of 1948*, 2nd edn (Cambridge: Cambridge University Press, 2007); Avi Shlaim and William Roger Louis, eds., *The 1967 Arab-Israeli War: Origins and Consequences* (New York: Cambridge University Press, 2012); Asaf Siniver, ed., *The October 1973 War: Politics, Diplomacy, Legacy* (London: C. Hurst and Co., 2013).

4 The international conference and book workshop were organized and hosted by two research centers of the AUB: the Center for Arab and Middle Eastern Studies and the Issam Fares Institute for Public Policy and International Affairs. As mentioned in the acknowledgments, the international conference and workshop was also supported by a number of institutions and individuals in Lebanon and the United States.

5 Sana Tannoury-Karam, "Not Monolithic: Reflections on the Communist International in the Levant," *Rosa-Luxemburg-Stiftung*, July 2019, https://www.rosalux.de/en/publication/id/40817/not-monolithic/.

6 Hannah Arendt and Jonathan Schell, *On Revolution* (New York: Penguin Classics, 2006), 21.

7 For a recent and excellent discussion on classifying revolutionary change and varied processes, see Asef Bayat, *Revolution without Revolutionaries: Making Sense of the Arab Spring* (Stanford, CA: Stanford University Press, 2017).

8 For a comparison between positive cases of successful revolutions and negative ones, see Theda Skocpol, *States and Social Revolutions: A Comparative Analysis of France, Russia, and China* (Cambridge; New York: Cambridge University Press, 1979); for an excellent discussion of the connections between revolutions and wars, see Stephen M. Walt, *Revolution and War* (Ithaca, NY: Cornell University Press, 1996). For a wider discussion of different revolutions, outcomes, and actors, see James DeFronzo, *Revolutions and Revolutionary Movements* (Boulder, CO: Routledge, 2018).

Part 1

The Regional and International Context of 1958

Declining and Rising Powers in the Middle East

Chapter 2

THE POINT OF DEPARTURE

THE IMPACT OF THE REVOLUTIONARY YEAR OF 1958 ON BRITISH POLICY[1]

Robert McNamara

When the British foreign secretary, Selwyn Lloyd, announced on December 1, 1959, that Britain and Egypt would imminently restore relations broken since the Suez Crisis in late 1956, the opposition Labor Party's shadow foreign secretary, Aneurin Bevan, expressed his "appreciation of the fact that after a long and unnecessary journey the Right honorable and learned Gentleman has now returned us to the point of departure."[2] The failure of the Anglo-French—Israeli Suez intervention[3] to topple Nasser or even reverse his nationalization of the Suez Canal Company was, depending on one's point of view, a watershed moment in Britain's retreat from empire and global power after 1945 or just one of a sequence of crises in her spheres of influence which cumulatively had the effect of convincing politicians, diplomats, and the public that the cost of empire far outweighed its benefits.[4]

The archival record regarding British policy in the Middle East, from the denouement of the Suez Crisis to the restoration of relations with Egypt three years later, suggests a more complex story.[5] Elsewhere, I have argued that there are five distinct phases in the relationship between British governments and Nasser's Egypt between 1952 and 1967: the negotiated ending of British base rights in Egypt in 1952-4; successive crises over the Baghdad Pact and Suez in 1955-6; Macmillan's anti-Nasser strategy from Suez to the July 1958 Iraqi revolution; a gradual Anglo-Egyptian rapprochement from 1959 to September 1962; and lastly, a clash over Yemen and South Arabia down to the 1967 June war.[6] Suez, notably, did not provide a full stop to Britain's role in Middle East or her clash with Nasser, if one accepts this chronology.

Of course, structural factors—economic decline, domestic change, nationalism in the global south, and the diminished international position of the European empires due to the World Wars and Cold War—doomed them to wither at some stage. However, unexpected shocks or revolutions against the international system were important in influencing key decisions that accelerated imperial retreat. It is argued here that the revolutionary year of 1958 in the Middle East was one such shock; it assumes considerable, indeed arguably central, importance in recent readings of the period. According to this interpretation, it marked a much more decisive shift in the attitude of Britain toward Arab nationalism and its most visible exponent, Egypt's president Gamal Abdel Nasser, than Suez ever did.[7] The eighteen months after Suez provide plenty of evidence that senior British politicians, soldiers, and policy-makers saw opportunities for a rematch with Nasser, as well as evidence of a distinct lack of apology for previous policies. Indeed, Suez, contrary to earlier interpretations, may have actually delayed a much-needed reappraisal about Britain's position in the Middle East. The revolutionary year of 1958 is, with certain caveats, perhaps a greater watershed.

The British, well aware of their own increasingly limited coercive resources, were often deceived by the capriciousness of the United States, notably that of US secretary of state John Foster Dulles. Dulles and other American officials would, on the one hand, give the British hope, through loose talk, that they have come to see Nasser as a dangerous demagogue requiring "cutting down to size" while, on the other hand, simultaneously preparing to bargain with him when they considered him a bulwark against communism in the region. It was a pattern of capriciousness evident before Suez and would be replicated in spades in the next two years. Dulles's ability to talk out of both sides of his mouth at once to different audiences regarding the Middle East confused British decision-makers frequently.[8] Too often, though, they heard what they wanted to hear—which was that America shared their views on Nasser.

The collapse of the pro-British Iraqi regime on July 14, 1958, at the time apparently the only realistic pro-Western Arab counterweight to Nasser's pan-Arabism, ended serious hopes of challenging the Egyptian leader. Somewhat ironically, 1958 marked the high tide of Nasserism. Arab unity, apparently an unstoppable force in Middle Eastern politics that year, struggled thereafter. It would be persistently beset by personal rivalries among the secular nationalists of Egypt, Iraq, and Syria, and the resilience of the conservative monarchies (impoverished Jordan and oil-rich Saudi Arabia). Any hopes of it having real substance, under a secular leader like Nasser, would come to an end with the Israeli victory in the June 1967 war.[9]

Harold Macmillan, the British prime minister, was the central figure in British Middle Eastern policy-making, and he could not conceal his distaste for Nasser, which had been established while he was (relatively briefly) the foreign secretary in 1955. As the chancellor of the exchequer during the Suez Crisis, he was one of the most enthusiastic members of then prime minister Anthony Eden's cabinet for military action against Nasser though his panic over the drain on Britain's foreign currency reserves, and the threat to the position of the British pound as a reserve currency (caused by American selling of the pound on the currency exchanges) was one of the key factors behind the halting of the expedition without any of its objectives being met.[10] In spite of being the key bolter, his "soundness" on Nasser and Suez meant that he emerged as the Conservative Party leader and prime minister in January 1957, after Eden's resignation. It was a job that, due to his relatively advanced age, he would surely never have gotten if his predecessor had enjoyed anything like a normal span in office. That being said, unlike Eden,

Macmillan was prepared to consider the opinions of others.[11] He was also an almost obsessive believer in reviewing policy in the foreign and colonial sphere in an attempt to make it more rational and less costly.[12] It was, thereby, ironic that at times he could sound irrational on the subject of Nasser. In the early phase of his premiership, he remained determined to convert the Americans to the anti-Nasser cause, as he emphasized at the Anglo-American summit at Bermuda in March 1957. The bitterness of his rhetoric there, regarding the Egyptian leader, did not impress President Eisenhower.[13]

Macmillan was not alone in these views. There remained particularly strong anti-Nasser feelings among certain ministers, notably Minister of Defense Duncan Sandys, Commonwealth Secretary Lord Home, and, most vocally, Macmillan's son-in-law, and junior minister, Julian Amery. Influential British officials were moderating influences. Notably, cabinet secretary and Britain's most senior civil servant Norman Brook and certain diplomats (e.g., George Middleton, UK ambassador to Lebanon) were more open to new thinking and were realistic about British power in the Middle East and the need to come to terms with Arab nationalism, and especially with Nasser.[14] The British Joint Intelligence Committee (JIC), as during the Suez Crisis, offered considered and mainly non-alarmist threat assessments in the post-Suez era.[15] However, others, such as the ambassador to Iraq, Michael Wright, and the ambassador to Jordan, Charles Johnston, were reliably hostile to Nasser, who directly or indirectly threatened the governments of the states they were emissaries to.[16] The chief of the imperial general staff (CIGS), Field Marshal Gerald Templer, was a hawk on the Middle East but the influential naval chief, First Sea Lord Louis Mountbatten, had been a Suez skeptic and would oppose overly grandiose schemes for interventions in 1958.[17]

While there would be no apologies for the folly of Suez, Macmillan's initial few months in office were noticeable for his cautious approach to the region. Discussions by officials about Britain's future strategy in the Middle East in the early months of 1957 resulted in the conclusion that Britain should drop any pretense of regional dominance: let the Americans and the Eisenhower Doctrine take the strain. Protection of oil resources in Kuwait and the Gulf and maintenance of British influence in Iraq would take priority.[18] Doing little proved to be more successful than intervention as King Hussein of Jordan sacked his pro-Nasser prime minister in April 1957.[19] Jordan, together with Saudi Arabia, exited the Arab Solidarity Pact that they had formed with Egypt in January 1957. The British stood aside: their troops in Jordan, soon to be withdrawn after the recent abrogation of the Anglo-Jordanian alliance, ordered to keep their heads down.[20] Nonintervention had had its first success. Financial negotiations with Egypt to resolve claims for war damage and Egyptian seizures of British holdings, which began in May 1957, would drag on for the best part of the next two years, colored by a British determination, shared by Saudi Arabia and the Americans, not to strengthen Nasser financially by releasing the substantial blocked Egyptian sterling assets.[21] The British foreign secretary, Selwyn Lloyd, told the United States that the British had "no intention of giving up the policy of economic pressure on Nasser, or the process of cutting him down to size."[22]

The Syrian Crisis

The opportunity of cutting the Egyptian leader down to size came quicker than might have been expected. Its origins lay in the unstable politics of Syria—the central battleground between the two competing claims (the Hashemites Fertile Crescent/Greater Syria monarchist concept versus Nasser's secular all Arab vision) for Arab unity.[23] The Syrian masses, like the vast majority of Arabs, viewed Nasser as their lodestar from Suez.[24] Moreover, elite opinion in Syrian political and military circles shared this view. Therefore, Iraq could only win in Syria by subterfuge, coercion, disruption, and covert action backed by the British Secret Intelligence Service (SIS) and the Central Intelligence Agency (CIA). From Operation Straggle[25] in the autumn of 1956, both agencies cooperated on regime change in Syria. This involved deploying methods not dissimilar to the 1953 coup in Iran (i.e., suitcases full of cash for bribing military officers and politicians, and the fermenting of chaos on the streets and in the countryside) that would facilitate intervention by Iraq. Regime change in Syria was a major part of the Middle Eastern strategy for Britain and America that would not be finally abandoned until shortly after the creation of the United Arab Republic (UAR).

Covert action, notably Operation Straggle and subsequent plans, was almost entirely counterproductive as its uncovering pulled Syria closer to Nasser and the Soviet Union.[26] However, the evident growing links between Syria and the Soviets scared the Americans in the summer of 1957 and provoked renewed secret intrigue, Operation Wappen, which led the Syrians to expel three US diplomats on August 12 for alleged subversive activities.[27] This event, above all, convinced the Eisenhower administration of the imminent communization of Syria, increased their suspicion of Nasser, who appeared to be facilitating this process, and brought the United States to the brink of using force in the Middle East. From the British perspective it would, at least on the surface, align American views on Nasser with theirs and seemed to bring within reach joint Anglo-American military action in the Middle East.[28]

In late August 1957, Dulles informed Macmillan that action against Syria needed to be taken. Cooperation between the British and the Americans soon stepped into high gear. An Anglo-American Syrian Working Group was established to explore action against Syria.[29] The Syrian Working Group reported on September 18, 1957, urging the implementation of a covert plan to attack Syria. The essence of the plan, following "Straggle," was to incite internal unrest in Syria and to create border incidents that would justify an Iraqi-Jordanian invasion, which would be covered by Western military guarantees. Western intelligence agencies were to be heavily involved in sabotage and a vigorous propaganda campaign. The final section of the report is the most striking. Its title, "Elimination of Key Figures," leaves little to the imagination. As Matthew Jones notes, the British and American officials who drafted the report were advocating the liquidation of those they considered the most troublesome in the Syrian regime, namely, Abdel Hamid Sarraj, the head of Syrian intelligence, Afif al-Bizri, the army chief of staff, who was noted for his strong Communist sympathies, and Khalid Bakdash, the head of the Syrian Communist Party.[30]

It was little wonder that Macmillan and other government ministers were becoming increasingly intrigued about the possibilities that might emerge from the response of Egypt to an Iraqi attack on Syria. At a meeting in New York between Selwyn Lloyd and John Foster Dulles on September 16, Lloyd seemed most interested in what the United States would do if the Egyptians blocked the Suez Canal in response to allied action in Syria. Dulles replied that the United States "should use force to the degree necessary to secure the reopening of the Canal."[31] On September 21, Dulles told Lloyd that Egyptian military action in support of the Communist cause in the Middle East would see a favorable American response to any request for aid from Jordan. In a memorandum for Minister of Defense Duncan Sandys, Macmillan requested an exploration of Britain's military options against Nasser.[32] Sandys's assessment was that the Egyptian potential to intervene against Iraq would be limited to the air, but they could expect Nasser to close the Suez Canal.[33]

Macmillan's hopes, if they were ever serious, came to naught. The Arab coalition, which was never the most stable, began to have serious doubts about the wisdom of launching a military initiative against Syria. Only Turkey, a Muslim but non-Arab country, showed enthusiasm.[34] A parade of Arab leaders, including King Saud of Saudi Arabia and the Iraqi prime minister Ali Jaudat, whom the Anglo-Americans had been depending upon to act against Syria, arrived in Damascus pledging nonaggression. Macmillan, in response, referred to Jaudat's government as "weak and timid."[35] The Syrian Working Group completed its work sometime around the middle of October. With the Arab powers reluctant and Turkey under Soviet military pressure and with the obvious danger of regime change in Syria escalating into an East-West clash, it came out in favor of a less expansive policy called "containment plus," which had more modest goals of protecting pro-Western regimes against coups.[36]

The beneficiary of the crisis turned out to be Nasser. The Egyptian president successfully enhanced his prestige on October 13, 1957, when a contingent of Egyptian troops landed in Syria, ostensibly to protect Syria from Turkish aggression.[37] Nasser took the opportunity to increase his influence in Syria at the expense of his Arab enemies but also at the expense of his erstwhile allies: the Soviets and their Communist allies. The latter aspect led to a rapprochement with the Americans, who began to view Nasser as a possible tool against the Syrian Communists. Dulles and Eisenhower expressed interest in improving relations with Nasser at the end of October 1957 without telling the British. And in December, American diplomats confirmed, in response to overtures from Nasser, that provided he forestalled the Communists the United States would not oppose him in Syria.[38] Macmillan appeared to be utterly unaware of the American moves toward Nasser. He noted in his diary entry of December 19, 1957, that Eisenhower and Dulles "are now completely converted—too late—and wish devoutly that they had let us go on and finish off Nasser."[39]

The UAR and the Arab Union

The British lack of insight into the shifting views of the Americans was further demonstrated by their reaction to the announcement of Egyptian-Syrian union, the UAR, in January 1958—Nasser's greatest triumph in turning Arab nationalism from "mere shouts and slogans" to an actual reality.[40] The event was to destabilize most of the pro-Western Arab regimes. At a rather panicky meeting of the Baghdad Pact in Ankara at the end of January 1958, Nuri Said of Iraq demanded a strong response. He received strong backing from Lloyd who argued that the best option was "to oppose it [UAR] tooth and nail" and try to disrupt it immediately. Dulles agreed it required action, though he made clear that it had to be an Arab initiative.[41] On his return to Washington, more informed opinion in the State Department, arguing that the UAR was likely to be consolidated, changed the secretary of state's mind.[42] Lloyd, on his return to London, appears to have dusted down the "Preferred Plan" of the Syrian Working Group and considered covert action again.

Nuri Said, the Iraqi prime minister, moreover, appears to have come away from Ankara convinced of Anglo-American support for a renewed campaign against Syria and began to float much the same ideas. Nuri's plan, which he outlined to Macmillan, was that Syrian exiles and leaders would bombard the United Nations with complaints about the UAR claiming it was really an Egyptian occupation. This would be followed by an uprising and Iraqi intervention.[43] Macmillan, disingenuously, wrote in his memoirs, that he headed off Nuri's "more impossible or dangerous schemes, which are bound to fail."[44] Perhaps, but it does not sound all that different from what Lloyd was proposing to Harold Caccia a couple of weeks before. Nuri, moreover, appears to have made a serious blunder by claiming that he regarded "Mr. Dulles as having committed himself to support of the Iraqi plan and to the proposition that the American pilots of some squadrons should be ordered to fight as volunteers."[45] Dulles, when questioned, accepted that he had promised to support Arab action "but Nuri had built up an entirely fictitious picture of what he had agreed to do."[46] The Iraqis quickly realized that Western support was unlikely to be forthcoming and informed Ambassador Wright in Baghdad that it would be some months before a favorable opportunity would arrive to intervene in Syria.[47]

Subsequently, Nuri's Arab Union scheme (a union between Iraq and Jordan to oppose the UAR), with its need for Kuwaiti oil, became as much of a threat to British interests as Nasser.[48] Advice was torn between the need to support the Arab Union for Britain's strategic position in the region and the clear problem that pushing the Emir of Kuwait into the union could destroy his confidence in the British government, the payment for his oil in sterling, and his investment of the profits in Britain.[49] Worryingly, Nuri and King Faisal of Iraq pressed their scheme on Selwyn Lloyd in March. They advised that Kuwait should be declared independent and should accede to the Arab Union. The problem dragged on without much movement until June when the Iraqis demanded that the Kuwaitis hand over offshore islands and portions of territory—which Iraq believed to be oil rich. Nuri argued that he needed these to provide for increased defense expenditure.

He based Iraqi rights in the area on the old boundaries of the Ottoman Empire that suggested that Kuwait was part of the southern area of Iraq. Nuri Said, as one observer has noted, was by no means the "imperial flunkey" that Nasser made him out to be and unsurprisingly was committed to his regime's interests.[50] Sir Michael Wright in Baghdad argued for supporting the Iraqis, though he was skeptical of the whole Arab Union concept.[51] How much Nuri had upset the British (and the Americans) was evident when Macmillan went to Washington for consultations in June 1958 with Eisenhower. He foresaw "an acute crisis breaking out" over Nuri Said's demands for financial support for the liability that was the Arab Union, but whose breakup would be a "terrific blow to our side." Moreover, "Nuri had been difficult for some time and was now attempting a Nasser-type operation that 'out and out threatened' Kuwait." Dulles spoke of Nuri's "blackmail." Eisenhower decried that Nasser was much more effective than the West's Arab allies.[52]

The Lebanon Crisis and the British

The other problem in 1958 was the Lebanon crisis, when President Camille Chamoun's attempts to maintain a pro-Western stance, particularly after Suez, and unconstitutionally hold on to the office of president had broken the fragile political consensus. In May 1958, it culminated in anti-government riots, sabotage, and outright insurrection, aided by the UAR.[53]

"Containment plus," the policy that the Syrian Working Group had advocated, required that no more friendly Middle Eastern states fall under Nasser's or the Soviet's sway. From the autumn of 1957, "containment plus" had implied Anglo-American joint planning for military intervention in Lebanon and Jordan. There, however, remained reluctance on the part of many Americans to be drawn into intensive military cooperation in the region with the British. There were also reservations from the British chiefs of staff regarding placing British forces under American control on the basis of an "unrealistic operational plan."[54] The sudden deterioration in Lebanon in May 1958 transformed matters. The Americans and the British agreed that they would send troops if requested and stepped up joint planning for an operation codenamed Bluebat with some 2,000 British and 3,000 American troops earmarked for operations in Lebanon.[55] But differences soon emerged on the political side. The Americans were skeptical that Chamoun could run for a second term as president, while the British, considering the absence of other plausible pro-Western contenders and the pro-Chamoun views of Nuri and King Hussein, were reluctant to jettison him in the midst of a crisis.[56] Dulles, going against the State Department consensus, and deploying the kind of sweeping language that frequently confused, indeed misled, his listeners, told the British ambassador, Harold Caccia, that the failure to back Chamoun would be a prelude to further coups and "the final collapse of any Western position in the area."[57]

As it happened, the Lebanese crisis, like the crisis in Syria in late 1957, began to deescalate. On May 21, Harold Caccia learned that Nasser had informed the American ambassador that the Lebanese situation could be resolved constitutionally and the army commander, General Chehab, should become president at the end of Chamoun's term.[58] The situation began to improve, and on May 26, George Middleton was much more hopeful of compromise.[59] During the June 10 talks in Washington, Macmillan suggested that the United States tell Nasser to negotiate directly with the Lebanese and get the Egyptian leader "on a hook" as it would imply that he could bring the disorder to an end and would therefore demonstrate his complicity in its orchestration—something that could not then be withdrawn. Eisenhower demurred. Instead the American ambassador in Beirut was told to tell Chamoun of Nasser's proposal but to make it clear that the United States was not recommending he follow that course.[60]

A UN Security Council resolution of June 11, 1958, put in place an observation group to monitor alleged arms smuggling from Syria. The British government was aware that both the US government, especially their UN permanent representative Henry Cabot Lodge and Secretary General Dag Hammarskjold, suspected the British of desiring a military intervention that would allow Suez to be vindicated.[61] Chamoun, on the other hand, continued to do his best to bring about intervention, presumably to maintain his office.[62] Lloyd informed Hammarskjold that intervention was not British policy.[63] The British were forced to conclude toward the end of June 1958 that any resolution to the crisis—an end to UAR subversion via the UN observer group or military intervention—would need to be clearly presented in a UN framework.[64]

On the eve of Iraqi revolution, three points are worth noting: the Lebanese crisis was apparently nearly over; Britain was increasingly estranged from Iraq over Kuwait and Anglo-Egyptian financial negotiations were looking more hopeful.[65] One of Macmillan's private secretaries, Freddie Bishop, normally hostile to Nasser, suggested that an agreement with Egypt might form part of "a general settlement—so far as can be obtained of the Middle East at a Heads of Government meeting."[66] However, on July 14, 1958, news came through that the Iraqi government had been toppled in a bloody revolution, which saw the royal family, Nuri Said, and many others brutally murdered.

The Iraqi Revolution and Its Immediate Aftermath

British and American diplomats, while being well aware of the undercurrent of support for Nasser among the Iraqi population, believed that Iraq was safe from revolution. As Roger Louis notes as late as April 1958, British ambassador Michael Wright was "quite certain that today a revolutionary situation does not exist," though others in the Foreign Office were far less sanguine.[67] As Juan Romero, in this volume, convincingly argues, this was not the case, with strong opposition in the army and among the populace to the regime.[68] Indeed, the JIC later noted that Wright was informed throughout the spring by Nuri and the crown prince that "a permanent state of crisis prevailed." However, Nuri and the royal family had a strong faith in the army, which they had nurtured since the 1930s.[69] Some three months after the revolution, the JIC examined what had happened. They concluded that there was disaffection in the Iraqi army and that the Iraqi ministers who had been informed of this had failed to take effective action, as the evidence was in general terms. The military conspiracy, confined to a few officers and civilians, had provided too small a target for Iraqi military intelligence. The JIC concluded that the primary reason for the collapse was that the old regime was "in its failure to maintain confidence. Security measures could not have alone sufficed to counteract the ebb of allegiance."[70]

The revolution was a devastating blow to British regional influence.[71] Initial British reactions were understandably panicky and there were lots of unrealistic plans for intervention discussed in the immediate aftermath. The fundamental problem was that the available rapidly deployable British, indeed American, forces were wholly inadequate for a bold measure such as invading Iraq and would not be able to protect the large number of Western citizens there.[72] President Chamoun had responded to the coup with a plea for the deployment of Anglo-American forces to the Lebanon. To the British, the figure at the center of all this turmoil was President Nasser. Macmillan warned the Cabinet that the situation must be considered in a wide context and that a temporary intervention in the Lebanon alone would neither be to their advantage nor to their benefit. It would expose British interests to attack and offer "no prospect of a permanent solution to the political tension which is spreading through the Middle East." The Lebanese crisis was not caused by an internal situation but was "a form of covert aggression promoted by the United Arab Republic." British forces might be kept in reserve "against possible need to provide assistance to the governments of Iraq and Jordan." Furthermore, it was to be explained to the United States that the British government "should expect them to regard the whole enterprise of restoring political stability in the Middle East as a joint task which they should share with us." Eisenhower, would, however, demur, when Macmillan suggested a wider campaign in the Middle East.[73] The American deployment in Lebanon, moreover, was a unilateral action. Whether Eisenhower genuinely intended for the British to be kept in reserve, as he claimed, or whether it was an excuse to avoid a joint operation, with its overtones of Suez, is not fully clear.[74] Macmillan, in any case, was determined to do something. King Hussein was induced to appeal for Anglo-American aid and make clear that he faced a coup orchestrated from the UAR. Dulles was unenthusiastic, questioning the rationale for sending troops to Hussein and making clear that the United States would not do so.[75] Macmillan, however, made a persuasive case that the danger of the UAR taking control of Jordan was greater than the risks (i.e., only infantry could be deployed and Israel had not given guarantees of overflight rights) to the British Cabinet. It unanimously decided on July 16 that British troops should be deployed.[76]

The risk of sending infantry, lacking heavy weaponry, soon became apparent. The Israeli government turned out to be uncooperative in allowing overflight rights, and only the intervention of the Americans persuaded Israelis to relent and allow the completion of the deployment of the British Parachute Brigade. However, the Israelis continued to argue about the flights, seeing an opportunity to forge a tacit alliance with Britain similar to her arrangement with France. The British were cautious but could not dismiss the idea out of hand, and undoubtedly the subsequent supply of British Centurion tanks to Israel was closely related to the 1958 crisis.[77] A month later, rumors of an impending pro-Nasser coup in Jordan provoked near panic in Whitehall with the Chiefs of Staff (COS) concluding that in such an event, forcing overflights through Syria would be better than a clash with the Israelis should they prove uncooperative.[78]

Macmillan and British officials continued to believe that there was little basis for an understanding with Nasser.[79] As it turned out they were incorrect in their assessment. Nasser proved to be increasingly helpful. He claimed that he had little desire to get rid of King Hussein, as it would provoke Israel to seize the West Bank. At the United Nations in mid-August after the passage of an Arab sponsored resolution, the Egyptian foreign minister Muhammad Fawzi agreed with Selwyn Lloyd and Daj Hammarskjold that King Hussein ought to be maintained in power in Jordan for the foreseeable future and that the Egyptian propaganda war would cease.[80] There was also talk of ending the Anglo-Egyptian financial dispute and restoring relations.[81] Macmillan was even convinced.[82] It was all nicely timed from a British perspective, as the resolution of the Lebanon crisis meant the United States was able to begin to withdraw from the Lebanon rather more quickly than anticipated.[83] The calming of the situation allowed the British Cabinet to conclude in late September that a withdrawal from Jordan beginning within a month was now possible.[84]

In some ways, the 1958 crisis was a triumph of British statecraft. Jordan had been saved. A wider Middle Eastern war that might have broken out if Israel had taken the West Bank if Jordan had fallen under a pro-Nasser regime was avoided. However, this should not disguise that the end of the Iraqi monarchy was a huge blow to British regional influence. But every cloud has a silver lining and it facilitated a wide-ranging debate among British political and military elites that by early 1959 saw Britain decide to take a more detached view of Middle Eastern rivalries. It is to this debate that we should now turn.

Hawks and Doves

One policy thread that lasted until the end of 1958 was the Iraqi option. After spending a day or two pondering over reversing the Baghdad coup, Macmillan ruled out intervention. Indeed, he described rumors of a Turkish counterstroke as "criminal folly" just a couple of days later. He told his foreign secretary that we "must be realists in this affair" and he had not given up hope that the new government could be weaned off Nasser and brought over to the side of the West.[85] Indeed the prime minister wanted his foreign secretary to emphasize that the threat to Jordan was not from Iraq but from the UAR.[86] Not long afterward, ministers were in agreement that good relations should be established with Iraq and coming to terms with Arab nationalism did not necessitate friendliness to Nasser.[87] Indeed, the Cabinet Committee on the Middle East was, two weeks after the coup, talking about deploying the new Iraqi regime as a counterweight to Nasser.[88] And Selwyn

Lloyd told the new Iraqi foreign minister of Britain's desire for good relations in mid-August 1958.[89] Macmillan's analysis was correct in one way but wholly wrong in another. Brigadier Qassim, the new Iraqi leader, did prove to be an opponent of Nasser. But he ended up being a far graver threat to British interests in Kuwait than the Egyptian leader ever was. Egypt's suspicions of Britain's Iraq policy, moreover, would remain at the heart of problems in Anglo-Egyptian relations for much of 1958 and 1959. In December 1958, the British would warn Qassim of a plot against him much to the chagrin of the United States, particularly William Rountree of the State Department, who was absolutely convinced that Iraq was in danger of going Communist.[90] Macmillan, upon reading the report, suggested that Rountree seemed "easily alarmed."[91]

Some elements in the British military—the CIGS, Gerald Templer, and the undersecretary for war Julian Amery—favored a final confrontation with Nasser in the heat of July and August 1958. Papers generated by the COS in July and August were hawkish in the extreme. The first on July 28 is notable for the hyperbolic tone it takes about the effect of a premature withdrawal of the allied forces from Lebanon and Jordan, claiming not only Britain's Middle East position but also its global role was in peril. The paper went on to argue that this might be the last opportunity to secure long-term stability in the Middle East and this required the breaking of Nasser's leadership of Arab nationalism by force if necessary.[92] Julian Amery may well have encouraged the COS's belligerence arguing to his father-in-law, the prime minister, along such lines in July. In September, he returned to the topic.[93] Philip De Zulueta, the prime minister's private secretary, cautioned Macmillan that he doubted if "action [against Nasser] without the United States now has a chance of success."[94] Indeed, the Americans had already decided that coming to terms with Nasser was a necessary evil.[95]

The view that prevailed was that Britain needed to extract itself from intra-Arab rivalries. The British Foreign Office was dubious about a strategy to use Qassim as a weapon against Nasser.[96] The Iraqi revolution reinforced views among diplomats that Britain had to draw back from overcommitment in the Middle East. A committee of mainly Foreign Office officials led by cabinet secretary, Norman Brook, was tasked with rethinking British Middle East policy as early as July 22, 1958.[97] This then led to the drawing up of a weighty document entitled "Points for a Middle East Policy" which emerged after considerable discussion internally and with the Americans toward the end of 1958. Divided into two parts, Part I considered British actions on the assumption that the Middle East had entered a period of calm while Part II examined what to do in the event of a drastic deterioration in the Western position in the region. Part I was striking in its policy prescriptions. Britain should "confine our defense against [Nasserism] to certain key positions and see could [sic] we reach a *modus vivendi* with the Arab world."[98] There was little prospect of forging a new balance of power in the Middle East and the problem for the West was how to handle Arab nationalism in such a way as to thwart Soviet ambition while preserving Britain's basic interests in the region. British policy should not oppose Arab unity when it was in her interest, and even when it was not, she had to oppose cautiously as it would draw hostility toward the West. Britain should take a step back and allow the "likely fissiparous tendencies in the Arab world to rise to the surface."[99] This did not mean that Britain had to abandon the idea of "containing" Nasser, or that she "should recognize the inevitability of his pan-Arab empire." The paper reflected the change wrought by the Iraqi revolution and the recognition of the reality that Arab nationalism and Nasser were long term. Part II of the paper, which ranged through a number of different scenarios where coups took place against pro-Western regimes in the Middle East and North Africa, was bleak, concluding that without American support, Britain could not use force in the region. In any case, the use of force was inherently risky because unless Britain was willing to stomach a long-term occupation of a country, it was likely to have only a temporary effect. Macmillan personally voiced support for the views put forward in Points for a Middle East Policy at a meeting of the ministerial Middle East Committee on January 16, 1959.[100] Coming to terms with Nasser was by no means plain sailing. Indeed, while the restoration of relations with Nasser was noted as a priority in the paper, it would not happen until the end of 1959, thanks to Nasser's suspicions regarding British policy in Iraq. (Financial negotiations had concluded successfully in March 1959.)[101]

It should also be stressed that while Britain was anxious to contract out of the Arab Cold War, it was not about to leave the Middle East. Instead, it was beating a retreat to the oil-rich emirates of the Persian Gulf. In a meeting of British diplomats in Middle Eastern countries in July 1959, the Foreign Office deputy undersecretary Sir Roger Stevens summed up the new look to British strategy in the region, which was the pursuit of a policy of noninterference and noninvolvement in intra-Arab quarrels. However, he emphasized "it had never been contested that we should hold our position in Aden, the Aden Protectorate and the Persian Gulf. In any conflict between those positions and anything else it was paramount that we should hold on."[102] Therefore, while Britain withdrew from a more generalized involvement in anti-Nasser activities, she still remained committed to a presence in the Middle East. The determination to defend this presence explains the final phase of the Anglo-Egyptian antagonism (1962–7) that saw the return of adversarial relations centered on Nasser's intervention in Yemen's Civil War and the growing insurgency in the British-ruled Federation of South Arabia, fueled by British and Egyptian covert support for Yemeni Royalists and Aden nationalists, respectively.[103] Ironically, while a reconsideration of Britain's Middle Eastern position envisaged by Macmillan's endorsement of Points for a Middle East Policy was a harbinger of crucial decisions for imperial retreat in Africa that would soon follow later in 1959 and 1960, the last great British counterinsurgency campaign of empire would be fought against a Nasser-aided insurgency in the Aden protectorate from 1963 to1967. Escaping from the Middle Eastern Cold War was to prove easier said than done.

Conclusion

The revolutionary year of 1958 significantly shifted British policy in the Middle East from an unrealistic policy of remaining, despite Suez, a significant actor in the regional struggles of the Arab Cold War (between the secular pan-Arabism of

Nasser and the conservative pro-Western monarchies) and the Arab-Israeli conflict. The antagonistic relationship with Nasser that existed from 1955 continued for nearly two years after Suez. As this chapter has argued, at times in 1957 and 1958, the Macmillan government, in its desire to reduce or even eliminate the Egyptian leader's influence, was prepared to contemplate reckless actions and interventions, particularly if they could get the United States involved. Indeed, one can see how some of these schemes, if implemented, might have led to regional or even global conflict.

The loss of the most important British regional ally—Iraq—to the secular Arab nationalist tide of the 1950s, and the American decision to respond relatively cautiously, as Jeffrey G. Karam strongly argues in the present volume, made this policy fundamentally unsustainable. Afterward, British regional policy was much more pragmatic. There was a renewed focus on the vitally important interests of Britain—her oil interests in the thinly populated emirates of the Arabian Gulf, which lay on the periphery of the major Arab states. Britain increasingly sidestepped the great regional questions. This was not a simple and straightforward decision to make and, in the end, only the systemic shock to the Middle Eastern power balance caused by the July revolution in Iraq finally forced Britain to reluctantly acknowledge its greatly diminished regional influence and revise its policy. While one cannot draw a direct correlation between these events of 1958 and the rapid acceleration of British decolonization in Africa soon after, her failure against Nasser's brand of pan-Arabism in the Middle East certainly demonstrated the dangers of vigorously opposing powerful nationalisms in the global south. Perhaps, for Britain, that was the main lesson of the revolutionary year.

Notes

1 There is a growing literature on the 1958 crisis based on British official and private papers initially released in 1989. Occasionally, additional material, notably Joint Intelligence Committee assessments, minutes and reports, has surfaced since then. Stephen Blackwell, *British Military Intervention and the Struggle for Jordan: King Hussein, Nasser and the Middle East Crisis, 1955-1958* (London: Routledge) is the most up to date. William Roger Louis, "Britain and the Crisis of 1958," in *A Revolutionary Year: The Middle East in 1958*, ed. William Roger Louis and Roger Owen (London: Tauris, 2002), 15-76 is a very detailed account. Nigel John Ashton, "A Microcosm of Decline: British Loss of Nerve and Military Intervention in Jordan and Kuwait, 1958 and 1961," *The Historical Journal* 40, no. 4 (1997): 1069-83; Lawrence Tal, "Britain and the Jordan Crisis of 1958," *Middle Eastern Studies* 311 (1995): 39-57; Ritchie Ovendale, "Great Britain and the Anglo-American Invasion of Jordan and Lebanon in 1958," *International History Review* 16, no. 2 (1994): 284-303; Ivan Pearson "The Syrian Crisis of 1957, the Anglo-American 'Special Relationship' and the 1958 landings in Jordan and Lebanon," *Middle Eastern Studies* 43, no. 1 (2007): 45-64 are all reliable guides using British, and, sometimes American, archives. Harold Macmillan's memoirs provide detailed, if rather partial, coverage: see Harold Macmillan, *Riding the Storm* (London: Macmillan, 1971), 502-37.

Alistair Horne, *Macmillan 1957–86* (London, 1989), 92–8 is the official biographer's version. A skeptical military perspective can be found in Michael Carver, *Out of Step* (London: Hutchinson, 1989), 280–4; The Egyptian perspective on 1958 in briefly covered in Laura James, *Nasser at War: Arab Images of the Enemy*, (Basingstoke: Palgrave, 2006), 47–8 and given more comprehensive treatment with access to at least some of Nasser's personal documentation in Reem Abou-El-Fadl, *Foreign Policy as Nation Making: Turkey and Egypt in the Cold War* (Cambridge: Cambridge University Press, 2019), especially Chapter 9.

2 Hansard HOC Debs, 601, col. 1011-12, December 1, 1959.

3 A brief selection of the most useful books on Suez are K. Kyle, *Suez* (New York: St Martins, 1991), W. Scott Lucas, *Divided We Stand* (London: John Curtis, 1991), W. R Louis And Roger Owen, eds., *Suez 1956, The Crisis and the Consequences* (Oxford: Oxford University Press, 1989), and David Carlton, *Britain and the Suez Crisis* (Oxford: Blackwell, 1988).

4 On Suez as watershed, see Lucas, *Divided We Stand*, 324, David Reynolds, *Britannia Overruled: British Policy and World Power in the Twentieth Century* (London: Longman, 1991), 205, Bernard Porter, *The Lion's Share: A Short History of British Imperialism 1850–1995* (London: Longman, 1995), 334, John Darwin, *Britain and Decolonisation*, (London : Macmillan, 1988), 223. However, see also a more nuanced view where Darwin views the significance of Suez as "subtle" John Darwin, *The End of the British Empire: The Historical Debate* (London, 1991), 71. More emphatically, Rashid Khalidi, "Consequences of Suez in the Arab World," in *Suez 1956, The Crisis and the Consequences*, ed. Louis and Owen (Oxford: Oxford University Press, 1989) declares that it "destroyed any slim possibility that Britain and France would remain major powers in the Arab world," 380.

5 For the post-Suez British policy in the Middle East, see Robert McNamara, *Britain, Nasser and the Balance of Power in the Middle East 1952-67* (London: Frank Cass, 2003), Nigel John Ashton, *Eisenhower, Macmillan and the Problem of Nasser* (New York: Macmillan, 1996), and Ritchie Ovendale, *Britain, the United States and the Transfer of Power in the Middle East* (Leicester: Leicester University Press, 1996).

6 Robert McNamara, "The Nasser Factor: Anglo-Egyptian Relations and Yemen/Aden Crisis 1962–65," *Middle Eastern Studies* 53, no. 1 (2017): 51–68 is my most recent work on that phase of Anglo-Egyptian relations.

7 By example, the interpretations in Blackwell, *British Military Intervention*, Louis, "Britain and the Crisis of 1958," Ashton, *Eisenhower, Macmillan and the Problem of Nasser*, Ovendale, *The Transfer of Power*, McNamara, *Britain, Nasser*, would all broadly support the importance of 1958.

8 Macmillan was of course not oblivious to Dulles's modus operandi. He approvingly, I think, quotes Robert Murphy at the Bermuda conference, "You think you have got [Dulles] somewhere and then he slips out at the end." Macmillan Diary Bodliean Library [BL], March 23, 1957.

9 Khalidi, "Consequences of Suez in the Arab World," 381–5. On the Arab Cold War, the classic account is M. Kerr, *The Arab Cold War 1958–67* (Oxford, 1971). The 1967 war meant, as one scholar has noted, that the "sun, which had shown so brightly on Arab nationalism, had finally set." A. Dawisha, *Arab Nationalism in the Twentieth Century* (Princeton: Princeton University Press, 2003), 251.

10 Kyle, *Suez*, 465.

11 On this point, see Nigel John Ashton, *Eisenhower, Macmillan and the problem of Nasser: Anglo-American Relations and Arab Nationalism, 1955–59* (New York, 1997), 9.

12 S. Blackwell, "Pursuing Nasser: The Macmillan Government and the Management of British Policy towards the Middle East Cold War, 1957-63," *Cold War History* 4, no. 3 (2004): 85-104, 86. Important papers were produced over the first four years of his premiership upon such matters. See R. Hyam and Wm Roger Louis, eds., *BDEEP* (2000), Vol. A 4 Pt. 1, Doc. 3, UKNA CAB 134/1556, CPC (57) 30, "'Future constitutional development in the colonies': Memorandum for Cabinet Colonial Policy Committee by Sir N. Brook," September 6, 1957, UKNA, CAB128/98/9 Africa: The Next 10 Years Africa: The Next Ten Years, CAB 129/100/35 Future Policy Study, 1960-70, February 29, 1960.

13 Here, Macmillan appeared still determined to overthrow Nasser. "Let's make it clear that we'll get him sooner or later," he told a surprised Eisenhower. Indeed, he had not lost his enthusiasm for covert action. At the same meeting Eisenhower noted in his diary that the British spoke of "the existence of a secret Egyptian plot for executing a coup to dispose of Nasser. They apparently thought we knew a great deal about it and wanted us to make some public statement against Nasser in the hope that this would encourage the dissident Egyptians. Manifestly anything the British said against Nasser would only make him stronger in the area" *FRUS 1955-57* Vol. XVII, Doc. 239, March 21, 1957. TNA UK PREM 11/1838. British Minutes of 1st Plenary session of the Bermuda conference March 21, 1957. *FRUS 1955-57*, Vol. XXVII, Doc. 271, March 21, 1957. Among the British plots that there is some evidence for was *Salamander*. See J. Bloch and P. Fitzgerald, *British Intelligence and Covert Action* (Dingle: Brandon, 1983), 126. See also Dwight D. Eisenhower, *Waging Peace* (London: Heinemann, 1966), 12.

14 Brook was especially important, as he had created the modern Cabinet committee system in Britain. The system saw committees of officials shadowing and providing the papers for the ministerial Cabinet committees. By example, the Middle East committee of the British Cabinet made up of ministers had a shadow committee of officials. According to his ODNB entry, he destroyed most of the most controversial Suez documents, while considering the whole enterprise a "folly." He argued at the end of 1957 that our future policy "should be to harness these [Arab nationalist] movements rather than to struggle against them." TNA UK PREM 11/2418, Joint Intelligence Committee, Norman Brook-Macmillan, December 6, 1957.

15 This is not to suggest that they were blind to Nasser's intrigues. TNA UK CAB 158/34, JIC (58) 83, Lebanon and Jordan—Infiltration and subversion by the United Arab Republic, August 8, 1958, noted that "Indirect aggression by the [UAR] . . . has for several years threatened the internal security, the governments and the rulers of the other countries in the Middle East." See also TNA UK CAB 158/34, JIC (58) 112 (Final) Egyptian Activities in the Maghreb, December 4, 1958. The weekly reviews of intelligence in TNA UK CAB 179/4, 5 and 6 are models of generally dispassionate reportage.

16 Charles Johnston, *The Brink of Jordan* (London: Hamilton, 1972).

17 Carver, *Out of Step*, 280-4.

18 General British policy in the Middle East was discussed at the Middle East Committee made up of officials in TNA UK CAB 134/2338 OME (57), No. 3, February 1, 1957 & No. 14, April 29, 1957.

19 See the memoirs of C. Johnston, HMG's ambassador in Amman for an account of the monarchical coup. Johnston, *The Brink of Jordan*, 34-74, Richard H. Sanger, *Where the Jordan Flows* (Washington, DC: Middle East Institute, 1963), 381-7, Uriel Dann, *King Hussein and the Challenge of Arab Radicalism* (New York: Oxford University Press, 1991), 52-66.

20 By example, Andrew Rathmell, *Secret War in the Middle East: The Covert Struggle for Syria, 1949–1961* (London: Tauris, 1995), 132; *FRUS 1955–57*, Vol. XIII, Doc. 62, March 14, 1957.
21 TNA UK CAB 134/2340, OME (57) 27 (Revise), April 12, 1957.
22 These blocked sterling assets went back to the debts run up by the British during the North African campaign during the Second World War. The Egyptians were anxious to extract compensation for the war damage, which Britain was determined not to give. TNA UK FO 371/125444, J. H. A. Watson minute, May 20, 1957 & FO-Wash, No. 2263, May 19, 1957.
23 This is the theme outlined in Nuri Said, *Arab Independence and Unity* (Baghdad: Iraq Government Press, 1943).
24 Nasser's "direct and ever growing bond, with what became known as 'the Arab masses,' evolved into a highly personal admiration charged with emotional overtones," Youssef M. Choueiri, *Arab Nationalism: A History* (Oxford: Blackwell, 2000), 187. See also Dawisha, *Arab Nationalism*, 202.
25 On Straggle, see Anthony Gorsts and W. Scott Lucas, "The Other Collusion: Operation Straggle and Anglo-American Intervention in Syria, 1955–56," *Intelligence and National Security* 4, no. 3 (1989): 590, Rathmell, *Secret War*, 121.
26 Seale, *The Struggle for Syria* (London: Oxford University Press, 1965), 291.
27 Most accounts suggest that they were indeed plotting against the regime. Seale, *The Struggle for Syria*, 294, Rathmell, *Secret War*, 139, D. Little, "Cold War and Covert Action," *MEJ* 44, no. 1 (1990): 71. See also the memoirs of the US ambassador to Syria. Charles Yost, *History and Memory* (New York: Norton, 1980), 236–7.
28 Eisenhower, *Waging Peace*, (London: Heinneman, 1966) 199. A representative of Nasser, a Colonel Hatem, who was attempting back channel financial negotiations with the British in October 1957, was dismissive of American scaremongering as they were inclined "to exaggerate the extent of communism in Syria. In point of fact the Syrians were devoted followers of Colonel Nasser, who was more important to them than communism and who himself was anti-communist." This was hardly of much comfort to the British. TNA UK FO 371/125444, William Hayter Minute (not dated JE 1052/26).
29 The clearest account is Matthew Jones, "The 'Preferred Plan': The Anglo-American Working Group Report on Covert Action in Syria, 1957," *Intelligence and National Security* 19, no. 3 (Autumn 2004).
30 See the Working Group report as quoted in Jones, "The Preferred Plan," 408. Professor Jones was accidentally given access to this document in the Duncan Sandys papers at Churchill College. It has not been formally released and is not in the relevant files on the crisis in the British archives. Macmillan is presumably referring to this "formidable" document in his diary entry of September 22, 1957.
31 TNA UK PREM 11/2119, ROC between Secretary's Lloyd and Dulles, September 16, 1957, Top Secret.
32 The copy in the UK National Archives is in TNA UK PREM 11/2521, PM514/57; Horne, *Macmillan 1957–86*, 45.
33 TNA UK PREM 11/1899, Sandys-Macmillan, Note by COS, Possible British action to support Iraq against attack by Egypt, October 1, 1957, Top Secret.
34 Seale, *The Struggle for Syria*, 303–4, D. W. Lesch, "Nasser and an Example of Diplomatic Acumen," *Middle East Studies* 31, no. 2 (April 1995): 365, Rathmell, *Secret War*, 142.
35 Macmillan diary, September 22, 1957.

36 TNA UK PREM 11/2521, Morris (Washington) for Hood and Hayter. Working papers XVII & XIX (October 11, 1957), Completed drafts were contained in telegrams around this time, for example, TNA UK PREM11/2521, Lloyd—Macmillan NO. 2084. Prime Ministers Private Telegram /455/57 October 15, 1957.
37 See Lesch, "Nasser and an Example of Diplomatic Acumen," 367–8 and E. Podeh, *The Decline of Arab Unity* (Brighton: Sussex Academic Press, 1999), 35.
38 The key US correspondence can be found in *FRUS, 1955-57*, Vol. XIII, Doc. 392, 4 November 1957, Doc. 398, 13 November 1957, Doc. 420, December11, 1957, Doc. 421, December 12, 1957.
39 Macmillan Diary, December 19, 1957, cited in William Roger Louis "Macmillan and Middle East Crisis of 1958," *Proceedings of the British Academy*, 94 (1996), 214.
40 Hopwood, *Syria* (London: Unwin Hyman, 1988), 40.
41 This is quoted from the British account of the meeting TNA UK FO 371/134386 VY10316/10 (Lloyd (Ankara no. 195)) to Lord Privy Seal R.A.B. Butler (who was acting prime minister as Macmillan was away on a Commonwealth tour) January 28, 1958, which differs slightly but significantly from the American account. See USNA Memcom Ankara, January 28, 1958. Conference files (CF) 968. Ankara 1/27–30/58 Memcoms Box 143. USNA Memcom Ankara, January 28, 1958. CF 968. Ankara 1/27–30/58 Memcoms Box 143.
42 *FRUS 1958-60*, Vol. XIII, Doc. 194, February 8, 1958.
43 TNA UK PREM 11/2520, FO-Wash. No. 821, February 17, 1958.
44 Macmillan, *Riding the Storm*, 504.
45 TNA UK PREM 11/2520, FO-Wash. No. 820, February 17, 1958.
46 TNA UK PREM 11/2520, Wash-FO No. 395, February 18, 1958.
47 TNA UK PREM 11/2520, Baghdad-FO No.395, February 18, 1958.
48 USNA Memcom White House, June 9, 1958, MCT MC/5, CF120, Macmillan Talks Miscellaneous, Box 150. When the Parliament of the Arab Union met on February 18, 1958, all possible opposition was silenced. Deputies and speakers with anti-regime groups were not allowed to speak. Tal, "Britain and the Jordan Crisis of 1958," 45. In the account in Dann, *King Hussein*, 78–85, the whole federation had plenty of problems. See also Blackwell, *British Military Intervention*, 98.
49 Ovendale, *Transfer of Power*, 190.
50 Matthew Elliot, *"Independent Iraq": The Monarchy and British Influence, 1941-1958* (London: I.B. Tauris, 1996), 166.
51 TNA UK, FO371/132776, Wright to FO, June 8, 1958, Louis, "Britain and the Crisis of 1958," 24.
52 USNA Memcom White House, June 9, 1958, MCT MC/5, CF120, Macmillan Talks Miscellaneous, Box 150.
53 This crisis is dealt with detail Chapter 13, "The Crisis of 1958 in Lebanon: Political Rivalries," by Caroline Attie in this volume. Gendzier, *Notes from the Minefield* (New York : Columbia University Press, 1996), 80–91. See TNA CAB 158/34, JIC (58) 83, Lebanon and Jordan—Infiltration and subversion by the United Arab Republic, August 8, 1958.
54 Blackwell, *British Military Intervention*, 94.
55 TNA UK PREM 11-2386. Record of meeting of ministers held in the Cabinet room on Wednesday, May 14, 1958.
56 See for instance TNA UK PREM 11-2386, Caccia to FO, 1191 of May 17, 1958; Johnston (Amman) to FO, 538 of May 18, 1958, TNA UK PREM 11-2386, FO to Washington, 2799 of May 17, 1958.

57 TNA UK PREM 1/2386, Caccia to FO, 1225 of May 20, 1958.
58 TNA UK, Caccia (Washington) to FO, 1244 of May 21, 1958; ibid. 1252 of May 21, 1958.
59 He wrote: "In my opinion the position now reached is favourable to a compromise solution. Moderate opinion overwhelmingly recognizes that the country has been brought to the verge of the abyss and that common prudence demands a retreat. Chamoun cannot hope to be re-elected but U.A.R. intervention has been checkmated. A purely Lebanese answer to the crisis must now be sought. I see no reason to suppose that it will be unfavourable to western interests." TNA UK PREM 11/2386, Middleton (Beirut) to FO, 616 of May 26, 1958.
60 TNA UK PREM 11/2386, Macmillan—FO T 234/58 Wash to FO, No. 1483, June 10, 1958.
61 Richard Lamb, *The Macmillan Years 1957-63: The emerging truth* (London: John Murray, 1995), 34 For Cabot Lodge's views see USNA AmDelUN to State, No.1354, May 21, 1958, DOSCF 783A/00/5.2058.
62 TNA UK PREM 11/2386, Middleton (Beirut) to FO, 788 and 793 of June 17, 1958.
63 TNA UK FO371/134124, ROC between SOS Lloyd and UNSG Hammarskjold at London, June 18, 1958.
64 TNA UK PREM 11/ 2385, CRO-Ottawa, No. 1011, June 20, 1958.
65 TNA UK CAB 128/32 Cabinet Conclusions (58) 51, 4.
66 TNA UK PREM 11/2648, Bishop note—Macmillan n.d. July 1958.
67 William Roger Louis. "The British and the Origins of the Revolution," in *The Iraqi Revolution of 1958: The Old Social Classes Revisited*, ed. Robert A. Fernea and William Roger Louis (London: I.B. Tauris, 1990), 51-3.
68 Juan Romero, "The Iraqi Revolution of 1958: Its Historic Significance and Relevance for the Present," in Jeffrey G. Karam, *The Middle East in 1958: Reimagining A Revolutionary Year*, (London: I.B. Tauris, 2020).
69 TNA UK CAB 158/34, JIC (58) 102, Reasons for the failure of the Iraqi intelligence services to give warning of the revolution of July 14, October 8, 1958.
70 TNA UK CAB 158/34, JIC (58) 102, Reasons for the failure of the Iraqi intelligence services to give warning of the revolution of July 14, October 8, 1958.
71 See for instance the comments of Macmillan, *Riding the Storm*, 511.
72 *FRUS 1958-60*, Vol. XII, Footnote 1, 326.
73 TNA UK CAB 128/32, Cabinet Conclusions (58) 55, 1, July 14, 1958. See the more detailed account in Chapter 14 by Clea Hupp in this volume.
74 Nigel Ashton, *The Problem of Nasser*, 169-70 argues that it was to avoid a joint operation.
75 TNA UK PREM 11/2386. FO to Washington, tel. 4506, July 15, 1958, emergency top secret; Hood to FO, Tel 1916, July 15, 1958, top secret.
76 TNA UK CAB 128/32, Cabinet Conclusions, (58) 58, 1, July 16, 1958.
77 See Ovendale, *Transfer of Power*, 208. It is noticeable that Israeli requests for tanks suddenly started to receive a more favorable hearing in London.
78 TNA UK DEFE 4/110, COS (55) 71 Meeting, August 11, 1958. See also Tal, "Britain and the Jordan Crisis of 1958," 45.
79 TNA UK PREM 11/ 2953, FO-Belgrade, No. 359, August 8, 1958, TNA UK PREM 11/4056, Record of Conversation between Prime Minister and Robert Murphy, August 10, 1958.
80 TNA UK PREM 11/2381, Lloyd (New York TG 948), -to FO, August 22, 1958.
81 TNA UK PREM 11/ 2648, New York-FO, No. 944, August 21, 1958, The conversations are summarized for the Middle East Committee of the Cabinet in TNA UK CAB134/2342, OME 58 (43) meeting, September 11, 1958.

82 TNA UK DEFE 4/110, COS (55) 71 Meeting, August 11, 1958.
83 Eisenhower, *Waging Peace*, 199.
84 TNA UK CAB128/32 pt. 2, Cabinet Conclusions (58) 67, 1, September 29, 1958.
85 TNA UK PREM 11/2368, Macmillan-Lloyd PMPT 367/58, FO-Wash No. 4792, July 18, 1958.
86 TNA UK FO 371/134220, VG1051/28/G, Macmillan-Lloyd in FO to Washington, No. 4833, July 19, 1958.
87 TNA UK CAB130/153, GEN 658, 1st meeting, 22/7/58, cited in Ashton, *The Problem of Nasser*, 179. Ashton points out that "In hindsight, the speed with which the British government was to move in trying to establish close relations with Qassem does indeed appear extraordinary." Ibid., 179.
88 TNA UK CAB 134/32341, OME (58) 11th Meeting, July 31, 1958.
89 TNA UK PREM 11/ 2371, Record of Conversation between S. Lloyd and the Iraqi Foreign Minister, August 18, 1958.
90 Meeting of Ministers December 21, 1958, cited in Ashton, *The Problem of Nasser*, 199.
91 TNA UK PREM 11/2396, Roger Stevens meeting with Rountree, London Airport, December 20, 1958. His private secretary was much less sanguine. Philip De Zulueta-Macmillan December 29, 1958. See Ashton, *The Problem of Nasser*, 198, and Lamb, *Macmillan*, 44.
92 TNA UK DEFE 5/84, COS (58) 183, "Position in the Middle East," July 28, 1958.
93 TNA UK PREM 11/2397, Amery to Macmillan, September 8, 1958.
94 TNA UK PREM 11/2397, De Zulueta to Macmillan, September 10, 1958.
95 Some of the key US debates are covered in *FRUS, 1958-1960, Volume XII*, especially Doc. 35, July 29, 1958, Doc. 36, July 31, 1958, Doc. 42, August 19, 1958, Doc. 51, NSC Report, November 4, 1958.
96 TNA UK FO 371/134220, VQ 1051/33, Crawford Minute-Rose, July 23, 1958 Policy toward Iraq.
97 TNA UK CAB 130/153 GEN 657-667, Minutes of meeting held, July 22, 1958.
98 TNA CAB 134/2341, OME (58) 13, 1, 26 November 1958, Points for a Middle East Policy.
99 Points for a Middle East Policy.
100 TNA UK CAB 134/2230, ME(M) 59, 1st meeting, January 16, 1959.
101 TNA UK FO371/141922, VG1051/58, UKRep Cairo to FO, No.176, April 8, 1959; FO371/141925, VG1051/111, Crowe desp to Lloyd, June 26, 1959; FO371/141926, VG1051/117, Cairo to FO, No. 300, July 9, 1959, Meeting 10 Downing St July 13, 1959, FO to Cairo, No. 137, July 27, 1959; PREM 11/3266, Cairo to FO, No.414, 6 October 1959; Cairo to FO, No. 435, October 26, 1959.
102 See TNA UK FO 487/013, Record of Meeting of Heads of Middle East Missions Held in the Foreign Office, July 23–24, 1959.
103 For studies of the Yemen/ Aden conflict with Nasser very much at the center see Clive Jones, *Britain and the Yemen Civil War, 1962–1965: Ministers, Mercenaries and Mandarins: Foreign Policy and the Limits of Covert Action* (Brighton: Sussex Academic Press, 2004); Spencer Mawby, *British Policy in Aden and the Protectorates 1955–67: Last Outpost of a Middle East Empire* (London: Routledge, 2005); Peter Hinchcliffe, John T. Ducker, and Maria Holt, *Without Glory in Arabia: The British Retreat from Aden* (London: I.B. Tauris, 2006). Also important is the recent published work of Jesse Ferris, *Nasser's Gamble* (Princeton: Princeton University Press, 2012). R. J. Gavin, *Aden under British Rule, 1839–1967* (London: Hurst, 1975), has held up very well.

Chapter 3

FRANCE AND THE MIDDLE EAST IN 1958
CONTINUITY AND CHANGE THROUGH CRISIS

Sofia Papastamkou

In 1958, the famous French historian Fernand Braudel theorized his conception of the multiplicity of social times, arguing that each immediate reality was the outcome of confluent movements with different origins and rhythms. "The same is true for this difficult year 1958 in France," Braudel noted on the spot,[1] as France was shaken by a series of chain reaction events that eventually led to a change of regime that same year. Laying on the long time of the colonization, these events were a by-product of a particular conjuncture of the decolonization era, the Algerian War of Independence, as much as of an internal one, the institutionally weak regime of the Fourth Republic.[2]

Integrated to France since 1848, Algeria became the theater of a bitter war, after the Front de Libération Nationale (FLN; National Liberation Front), the Algerian nationalist movement, launched in 1954 its struggle for independence.[3] As part of the war's strategical aims, in autumn 1956 a series of French actions essentially defied international legality: first, the Sudanese-flagged *Athos* ship (and its Egyptian arms cargo) was seized in international waters; then a Moroccan plane carrying the external delegation of the FLN was intercepted and forced to land at French territory; and, finally, France colluded with Israel and the UK against Egypt in the Suez operation. If the aim was to cut short the transnational dimension of the war in Algeria and have hands free for a French solution, the outcome of these actions was the exact opposite. Eventually, 1956 was a milestone for the war turning into an international affair.[4] In 1958, this trend further accentuated, after the French military forces of Algeria bombed the border Tunisian village of Sakiet-Sidi-Youssef, causing civilian losses and the strong reaction of Tunisian president Habib Bourguiba. The bombardment proved to be a turning point for France, as it triggered a chain reaction of events: first, an Anglo-American mediation through the "Good Offices Mission," then the fall of the government of Félix Gaillard, a subsequent regime crisis, and the May 13 rebellion of the *ultras* of a French Algeria in Algiers. The generalized crisis opened the way to General Charles de Gaulle's political comeback and transition from the Fourth to the Fifth Republic.[5]

In 1958, crisis was on the agenda in the Middle East as well, where a series of events seemed to defy and threaten the established system: Egypt's merger with Syria to form the United Arab Republic (UAR), the Lebanese crisis, and finally the Iraqi revolution.[6] Louis and Owen's edited volume that focuses on this year considers 1958 as the culminating point of a broader period that began in 1956 with the Suez Crisis, even a year earlier with the formation of the Baghdad Pact.[7] Before this present volume, this collective work by Owen and Louis remains the most comprehensive study of the events that marked this period and the interactions between them, focusing on the regional and major international actors in the new context of the postcolonial early Cold War. Perhaps because of her secondary postwar role in the Middle East, with the sole exception of the Suez Crisis, France was nothing but sporadically evoked. Yet, as this book demonstrates, recent approaches propose to revisit decolonization as a global, connected process and to shift focus from sequences of events toward interactions with the Cold War dynamics.[8] This brings France wholly into the scene: a former mandatory power in Syria and Lebanon—the French Levant or Near, rather than Middle, East—and a colonial power at war in Maghreb, France found herself in the intersection of these global dynamics in action in the whole MENA region.

Overview of the Position of France in the Middle East up to 1958

The postwar position of France in the Middle East was largely refashioned by her defeat in the Second World War that challenged her status as a great power. Deprived of special positions in Syria and Lebanon after their independence and suspicious of Iraqi intentions, France put high stakes in the preservation of the Syrian independence, through support to the Syrian Army that had come out of the French-trained Troupes spéciales du Levant, and consequently to the military regimes of Colonel Husni al Zaim and Colonel Shishakli.[9] Up to 1953, this was one of the main guiding principles of the French policy, in addition to joining the 1950 Tripartite Declaration, a status-quo guarantee that France had joined at the invitation of the United States and Great Britain, and maintaining cautious relations with Israel.[10]

In 1954, the end of the Indochina war enhanced a more active policy in the Middle East, which was also responsive to the initiation of the US New Look policy and regime change in Syria. This policy, essentially a form of arms sales diplomacy, was initiated by Premier Pierre Mendès France and placed development of relations with Syria, Egypt, and Israel at its core. This scheme persisted with mitigated success up to 1956 and was eventually blown by the Suez debacle. During this period, relations with Syria did not bear fruit as the country turned toward neutralism. Once more, the French diplomacy stuck to the preservation of Syrian independence through a fundamental opposition to the Baghdad Pact, which happened to be the basis of the British and US policy in the Middle East and the fruit of concertation between them. This attitude persisted even after Syria, following the Egyptian example, turned to the Soviet camp for arms supplies in 1956 and transcended France's post-Suez eclipse.[11] On the other hand, relations with Egypt gained in strength precisely because of a common opposition to the Baghdad Pact and a will to keep Syria out of it. They did, however, disintegrate from 1955 on, under the combined weight of the war against Algerian nationalists, who had Nasser's support, and the development of the French-Israeli ties.[12] Indeed, relations with Israel evolved to a de facto alliance against pan-Arabism between the defense establishments and intelligence of the two countries, contrary to the imperatives of the general French policy that became literally invaded by the war led in Algeria.[13]

An accessory in this war, the military operation in Suez against Nasser, put in contact the temporalities of the Cold War and those of the decolonization. Its failure costed France a prolonged diplomatic—and political—isolation in the Arab Middle East, with Lebanon being the only country maintaining diplomatic relations with Paris. France's positions in North Africa were further mined, in the newly independent countries (Tunisia, Morocco) included. Furthermore, the Suez debacle had lasting consequences on France's relations with the United States and Great Britain.[14] After Suez, France seemed more concerned by the fracture of East-West relations and was receptive to the Eisenhower Doctrine, though wary of its possible consequences on her—much pursued—primacy in the Maghreb.[15] The combination of this global policy that covered the whole MENA region with the internationalization of the Algerian war and the strength of the pan-Arabism, all of them consequences of the Suez debacle, created new dynamics with France in their intersection.

France and the 1958 Lebanon Crisis: Perception, Position, and Constraints

In May 13, 1958, the insurrection of the *ultras* of French Algeria in Algiers triggered a political crisis in France. In an electric atmosphere, in what was no less than a constitutional coup d'état, General Charles de Gaulle was called to form on June 1 the last government of the Fourth Republic with full powers to work on a new constitution. Almost immediately, de Gaulle finished settling the pending crisis with Tunisia: on June 17, an agreement provided for the retreat of the French forces from the country, with the exception of the Bizerte zone.[16] During this troubled period, the immediate priorities of de Gaulle were to reestablish the state's authority, albeit continuing the military operations in Algeria to eventually allow for a French solution; to pursue economic reforms in Algeria; and to prepare for the regime transition.[17]

Turmoil in France coincided with a troubled summer in the Arab Middle East. The Lebanese crisis, in particular, questioned both the French will and capacity to act. After the assassination on May 8 of the *Al Telegraph* newspaper editor Nassib al-Matni, an insurrection erupted in the major cities of Lebanon and along the frontier with Syria. The uprising, led by a coalition of President Camille Chamoun's political adversaries, came as a reaction to the latter's intention to seek for a second mandate, contrary to the provisions of the National Pact. The recently formed UAR was quickly pointed by Chamoun as guilty of interference in Lebanon's domestic affairs and, on May 13, he subsequently asked the United States, the United Kingdom, and France assistance in the name of the 1950 Tripartite Declaration.[18] Thus, the Lebanese crisis raised the issue of a possible deployment of French forces in the region for the first time since 1956, while the country was at war in North Africa, and at the very moment, lived its own regime crisis.

Notwithstanding the internal turmoil, French diplomacy had a clear perception of the crisis in Lebanon that remained unaffected by governmental change even after de Gaulle's comeback. The Quai d'Orsay did not underestimate either the regional dimension of the crisis or the appeal Nasser's pan-Arab ideology exercised on Lebanese Muslims. However, the conviction was that a crisis would not have occurred had the problem of the presidential election not arisen.[19] Already after the formation of the UAR, in February, the French ambassador in Beirut, Louis Roché, had expressed fears for the forthcoming presidential election interacting with this important regional evolution, albeit not considering Lebanon to be among Nasser's immediate priorities.[20] Roché, who reasoned largely in terms of clash of civilizations between the West and the Orient, could hardly be considered a sympathizer of Nasser's pan-Arabism.[21] But, once the crisis burst out, he did not give particular credit to Chamoun's claim about Syrian-Egyptian interference in Lebanon, considering that he was seeking to internationalize the election and force himself as the champion of the West.[22] Furthermore, the French diplomacy had no particular attachment to the Lebanese president, although his attitude during the Suez Crisis had been appreciated. A former champion of the Lebanese independence, Chamoun was perceived as much too Anglophile.[23]

The preferred solution for Paris was a consensual candidate, able to rally both the partisans of Chamoun and the opposition. In this sense, France was tied to the attitude of Vatican, which did not favor Chamoun's reelection in fear of the divisive effect it could have for the country. Internal notes of the Africa-Levant Department and correspondence with the French Embassy of Beirut show, moreover, a mixed feeling of confidence for France's positions, on the one hand, and a necessity to keep a restrained attitude, on the other hand. Indeed, the country's soft power (*influence culturelle*), via her ties with the Maronite community and the presence of cultural establishments, was thought to be a sufficient means to preserve her presence as long as Lebanon's political evolution would be in accordance with Western interests. But, simultaneously, France's past as a mandate power, the war in Algeria, and the French-Israeli ties admittedly suggested discreetness out of fear to compromise, rather than serve, any preferred political solution.[24]

Essentially, the French had no means to push for a solution on their own, even so since several undefined variables were at play. To begin with, the United States and the United Kingdom remained ambiguous about Chamoun renewing his candidacy. Furthermore, the governmental vacuum in Paris further impeded taking a powerful stance on the Lebanese crisis, especially in the middle of the Algiers uprising. Finally, all available military forces were busy in Algeria, not to mention that their top leaders' loyalty to Paris at this very moment was far from granted. In these conditions, Chamoun's request on May 13 seemed to rather embarrass the French.[25] Interestingly, the British Embassy in Paris reported exchanges with French officials, such as former premier (then vice president of the short-lived Pflimlin government) Guy Mollet and Africa-Levant director in the Quai d'Orsay Pierre de Sébilleau, who seemed haunted by the Suez experience.[26] Nevertheless, it was also clear that it was out of question for France not to participate, even in a symbolic way, in a joint Anglo-American intervention, if any. Thus, just like the United States and the British, France replied positively to Chamoun, while plans for a limited military contribution and evacuation of some 3,000 French nationals were underway. Moreover, between May and July—while the US attitude eventually pushed Chamoun toward a political solution of the crisis—France delivered light armament and munitions of half a billion francs to Lebanon.[27]

The contours of the French attitude along these lines became more perceptible after the comeback of de Gaulle in the beginning of June. Fearing that the prolonged political trouble in Lebanon could provoke an economic crisis and cause harm to French interests, Paris was favorable to a political compromise around the personality of Lebanese chief of staff general Fuad Chehab.[28] Actually, this was also the solution pursued by Nasser and UN secretary Dag Hammarskjöld since mid-May but was resisted by the United States, eager to not comply to a political victory of the Egyptian leader.[29] In any case, the Chehab solution existed in the French thinking since the presidential election crisis of 1952, which ended with Chamoun succeeding Bechara al Khoury.[30] For the French, ideally, Chamoun should publicly declare that he would not seek reelection, while General Chehab would act to reestablish the public order for elections to be held. For Paris, Chehab should be a candidate for the election, and it was considered necessary to rally the Maronite Patriarch, the moderate opposition, and the partisans of Chamoun around this solution.[31] Nevertheless, the constraints the French faced before remained pretty much the same: they did not have the weight to make their views prevail against the United States and the UK, and they recognized that the war in Maghreb did not allow them to play an important role in Lebanon.

This brings into play the question of the tripartite concertation on the Lebanon crisis and whether France actually weighed on the resolution of the latter. The appeal of France on the Lebanese Christian communities was taken seriously by both the UK and the United States. In this sense, John Foster Dulles favored concertation between the ambassadors of the three countries in Beirut, in terms of alignment to the US position: consider the presidential election as a Lebanese domestic affair, without either dissuading Chamoun from seeking reelection or promising him any support.[32] No other direct US-French cooperation was established at any level, whereas it was the case at all levels between the United States and the British (Beirut Embassies, governmental, and, since 1957 and the Syrian crisis, intelligence[33]) in spite of the previous Suez hardship. The sole exchanges at a higher level came about during the general talks Dulles held with de Gaulle in Paris, on July 5, only to express doubts on the Chehab solution, because it was also Nasser's solution, and to exclude France from being a part of a military intervention, if any, because of her situation in Algeria and her ties with Israel.[34] As we shall see below, the British were also adamant against French participation in a military operation. But, in condition that the United States would agree, they were interested in using any possible French contribution to a political solution.

Although the British disliked the Chehab solution for the same reasons as the United States, the prolonged crisis and the fear of a civil war in Lebanon made them keen on reaching a political solution.[35] On June 29 and 30, British prime minister Harold Macmillan and foreign secretary Selwyn Lloyd held general talks in Paris with General de Gaulle and his foreign minister Maurice Couve de Murville. Both sides agreed on sending common instructions to their ambassadors in Beirut to suggest that Chamoun make a clear declaration excluding his reelection. The US Embassy in Paris was informed and similar instructions were sent to Ambassador McClintock in Beirut.[36] On July 1, McClintock, Middleton, and Roché met with Chamoun and essentially suggested that he publicly declare that he will not seek reelection, propose the formation of a national unity government, and give his views on a possible candidate. Chamoun got furious at the first two points—the essence of the French suggestion.[37] Eventually, the United States were not happy either with the approach, which had gone further than they had wished, or with the British, to whom they expressed their misgivings. And the French were critical of the United States for not exercising real pressure on Chamoun.[38] However, the crisis in Lebanon was essentially on its way toward a political solution by the moment the Iraqi revolution rushed US intervention in Lebanon and British intervention in Jordan. The preferred solution for the French happened to be the most realist as well, and also the one pursued by local and supranational actors such as Nasser and the Hammarskjöld's mission. The general détente that followed the resolution of the crisis was also profitable for France in that it saw a first normalization of the relations with Egypt, albeit limited to cultural, financial, and economic aspects.[39]

France, a Reluctant and Embarrassing Military Ally in the Middle East

Perhaps the most important aspect of the 1958 Middle Eastern crises, in relation to France, carried on the question of the country's involvement in a military operation following Chamoun's demand. The position of France appears puzzling, even contradictory; whereas the one of her allies was perfectly clear. Eventually, the question appears symptomatic of a broader shift that occurred in France's relations with her major Western allies, and NATO, in the early Cold War and materialized in the following decade with France's retreat from the military instances of the Atlantic Alliance.

As seen earlier, France was essentially embarrassed by Chamoun's demand to honor the guarantees of the Tripartite Declaration, arriving as it did at a moment of power vacuum in Paris and while the main commanders of the military forces in Algeria, such as generals Salan and Massu, led the dissident movement in Algiers. As also shown, the preferable solution for the French was the political resolution of the crisis in Lebanon, not least because it was also a way to spare

France from any action with its allies in this complicated moment. The immediate difficult conjuncture put apart, there seems to have been a sincere reluctance to have to act militarily with the United States and the UK.[40] One should see there a profound impact of the Suez debacle that had laid bare France's political weakening in the Middle East and necessarily led to a general policy reorientation, albeit momentarily in standby because of the troubled decolonization in Maghreb. At least in the sphere of the French diplomacy, it was recognized that, rather than acting in concertation with only the United States and the UK, France's interests would be best served through concertation with European partners such as the Federal Republic of Germany and Italy, who were also economic players in the Middle East, and with expansion of its economic and cultural positions.[41] For all reasons, de Gaulle reiterated to Dulles, during the July 5 talks, France's unwillingness to see a military operation actually taking place in the Middle East.[42] But what was equally clear was that if an intervention was to happen, France would be a part of it, even in a symbolic way and regardless of her allies associating her or not.[43] International prestige seems to have been the main motivation behind the French resolution to send a naval force, in case there were joint Anglo-American operations, which later occurred.

France was definitely perceived as a compromising ally by the United States and the UK, once the option of a military operation was under consideration. Upon Chamoun's request on May 13, the British Cabinet quickly approved a positive response, as it placed high stakes on the independence of Lebanon. Three main ideas dominated the British thinking, apparently haunted by the Suez experience: first, a British intervention could only be part of a US one; second, it should be acceptable to Britain's Middle Eastern allies, especially Iraq; third, the French should not participate, given their involvement in Algeria would alienate any Arab support.[44] The specter of de Gaulle was not absent from this thinking, as the British feared "a blood row" with him, if an intervention occurred without France's participation.[45] This was one of the reasons they favored a political solution for the Lebanese crisis and cooperated with the French in this sense. But as long as the possibility of a military intervention remained open, the best solution the UK and the United States could think of was to keep the French in the dark about the preparation of military operations, if any.[46] Nuri al-Said was also encouraged to let Chamoun know he would be unable to support a Western military operation if the French were involved, which he did.[47]

While the Lebanese crisis was definitely headed to a political solution on the basis of the candidature of Fuad Chehab, the Iraqi revolution of July 14 actually made the joint intervention happen. The French were kept informed of the imminent US operation in Lebanon but were indeed in the dark as for the British one in Jordan on July 17. Once the former took place, the French did not rush at first to send a naval force, the *De Grasse* cruiser, albeit the French Marine was eager to have it sent by July 17. The Beirut Embassy recommended to delay until there was a better view of the political situation in Lebanon.[48] A neutral communiqué underlined the attachment of France to the independence of Lebanon, the existence of French moral and material interests in the country, and the will to defend these interests in agreement with the Lebanese government and the UN Chart.[49] Two days later, British intervention in Jordan came about. *De Grasse* finally appeared in the port of Beirut on July 18: although the French and the US commanders met, there was clear opposition from the latter to any French forces landing in Beirut.[50] In any case, French ambassador Roché and the chief of the naval force Admiral Jozan agreed that no further demonstration of the French ship was necessary except in case of aggravation of the situation.[51]

Although there were three distinct operations with only two of them constituting concerted action, as a result of previous joint planning between the Americans and the British, one could read in *Le Monde* a neutral description of the events leaving the impression of unity: according to the newspaper, the Western powers, the "Occident," had acted in defense of their interests in the Orient and in the world.[52] In his memoirs, de Gaulle presents France's limited action as a sign of an independent policy already.[53] Up the degree that France was left with no other choice, this was only half true. Nevertheless, wariness about the impact of a common action was a sincere, yet paradoxical, preoccupation: regardless of the damage the Algerian war caused to France's prestige, in the Middle East it was now the United States and the British that embodied the imperialist West. The French diplomacy and de Gaulle were perfectly aware of this.[54] Reporting from Paris on the state of mind of the public opinion, according the French press, the British Embassy noted there was both embarrassment and relief for France not being closely associated to the Anglo-US action.[55]

Finally, it is worth noting that the Iraqi coup and the violent overthrow of the Hashemite monarchy do not seem to have had a decisive impact, or indeed any, on the French thinking. Some 600 French nationals, working mainly in the public construction domain, as well as French holdings, were kept safe.[56] Otherwise, France had only indirect contacts with Baghdad via the Swiss diplomatic mission, after the rupture that had followed the Suez Crisis. De Gaulle kept a reserved attitude declaring that the coup was an internal affair in which the West should not get involved.[57] Although there were indirect exchanges between Paris and Baghdad on the possibility of restoring diplomatic relations, the continuing war in Algeria and the French-Israeli ties eventually postponed any further development in that direction.[58]

1958, a Watershed or a Milestone?

At the end of the troubled summer of 1958 in the Middle East, France found herself with a first normalization of the relations with Egypt, a political solution in Lebanon that had been her preferred solution, and even reserved, yet not fruitful, openings on behalf of the new Iraqi regime. Pending the full restoration of diplomatic relations with the Arab Middle Eastern countries, which would not occur until after the Algerian independence, the germs for a (future) policy of influence in the Middle East, as opposed to a policy of power, seem to be actually present. The burden of the war in Algeria, as well as the French-Israeli connection, were still hiding the fact that, without the cost of a military operation in the Middle East, France was on its way to becoming a potential alternative Western partner, casting somewhat aside the superpowers' rivalries.[59]

There was, however, another level where the 1958 Middle Eastern crises had apparently an impact: the general policy of de Gaulle and his efforts to bring about a shift in the interallied relationship. The joint, although internally hesitant, US/UK military intervention in Lebanon and Jordan had not come out of the total blue. Studied for the first time by a joint planning group set after the 1957 Bermuda talks, the 1958 interventions were partly the outcome of the restoration of US and UK relations in the Middle East after Suez, and the product of a secret machinery that somewhat formalized bilateral consultation and joint planning.[60] In other words, it was a symptom of close Anglo-American cooperation on international matters. It was this last dimension that de Gaulle immediately targeted after his advent, as it had already been clear during his June and July talks with Macmillan and Dulles, respectively. Although after the interventions in Lebanon and in Jordan France refrained from publicly criticizing US and UK action in the UN and NATO instances, de Gaulle handed immediately a diplomatic memorandum to Washington and London. Referring specifically to the British action taken in Jordan, de Gaulle briefly explained he did not consider urgency to justify any lack of previous exchanges with France and asked for tripartite concertation on the Middle East. He also raised the issue of the Atlantic Alliance being concerned by any action undertaken in this part of the globe, although the Atlantic Pact did not cover the Middle East zone.[61] This last issue was the main subject of the famous memorandum of September 17, with which de Gaulle asked Eisenhower and Macmillan a tripartite informal instrument in charge of a common policy on world matters. In this document, the 1958 crises in the Middle East, and in the Taiwan straits, were evoked to demonstrate the interconnection of the theaters of global responsibility and to argue there was discrepancy between the risk-sharing and the decision-making process in the Atlantic Alliance.[62]

The September memorandum was sent right after the formation of a "provisional government of the Republic of Algeria" (Gouvernement provisoire de la République algérienne) in Cairo—soon to move to Tunis. Historical research has convincingly interpreted the memorandum not only as a prelude to the future policy of independence of de Gaulle, the *grandeur* politics, but also as part of a diplomatic activity that aimed at neutralizing any legitimation of the Algerian initiative and, at term, assuring support for French primacy in the Maghreb.[63] The preparatory notes for the talks de Gaulle held with Dulles in the summer, where the idea for a tripartite informal machinery had been presented, show the French had no illusions about the chances of such a demand being accepted. What they were essentially after was to assure a certain primacy in time of peace for the African theater.[64] It is important to note that the war in Algeria was parallel to the country's efforts at defining privileged relations with the newly independent states of Morocco and Tunisia. Especially in the latter, France resented the US (and UK) support to Habib Bourguiba after the Syrian 1957 crisis and Nasser's openings toward the Tunisian leader.[65]

From this point of view, de Gaulle's receptiveness to the Soviet proposal for a summit on the Middle East, addressed to the United States, Great Britain, France, and India on July 19, offers a valuable insight into the general French thinking. Contrary to Eisenhower, who rejected having direct conversations with the USSR, and Macmillan, who proposed keeping the dialogue at the level of the Security Council, de Gaulle accepted the principle of a conference in a letter he addressed to Khrushchev on July 22. The French were open to the idea because it assured them a place, which shows how precarious they felt their chances were to be part of a global Western policy, if any, that could be decided jointly by the United States and Britain, with France being marginalized. Furthermore, they sought for a modus vivendi that would, ideally, prevent the Arab states from exploiting Cold War rivalries and could possibly diminish the Maghreb-Levant interactions. In this sense, the crises of 1958 in the Middle East were perceived as part of a larger crisis generated by the overlap between Arab nationalism and external powers' rivalries.[66] Once Khrushchev privileged the UN framework, rather than a summit, de Gaulle lost interest for the proposal, as he was clearly after a trickled multilateralism that would assure France a special place.[67]

In other words, France found herself in the very intersection between the growth of Arab nationalisms, as one of the aspects of global decolonization, and the Cold War rivalries. In the summer of 1958, de Gaulle's comeback into politics, crisis in France, turmoil in the Middle East, and the evolution of the Algerian war with all its impact in North Africa, weighed on the formation of imbricated dynamics. If 1958 constitutes a watershed in France's political life, it appears as a milestone for both her Middle Eastern policy and her place in the international system. From the first point of view, France was on her way to invent a more realistic Middle Eastern policy; from the second, she headed toward a readjustment of her position inside the Western camp. In both cases, decolonization played a key role.

Conclusion

How to understand the connections between the events experienced in France, Maghreb, and the Middle East in 1958? Through 1955 to 1958, the French experience of decolonization in Maghreb appears as part of a transnational configuration that gradually linked Cold War dynamics with policies based on perceived national interest: of disintegrating empires in a quest for an international position of influence, of superpowers, and of new nonaligned actors. Indeed, as a first internationalization of the Algerian War of Independence in the Third World subsystem, the 1955 Bandung Conference interacts with the 1956 Suez Crisis, which placed the Algerian combat in a global context through an overlap between the Cold War and the decolonization process, and ended up reinforcing the nonaligned movement. Subsequently, it was the 1957 Cairo Conference that first echoed the Algerian demand of France respecting the Geneva Conventions on the Laws of War in regard to captured fighters.[68] As Sylvie Thénault's chapter shows, this was a strategic aim of the FLN in 1958 and the actions of reprisal it generated, combined with the political crisis in Paris, triggered the 1958 insurrection of the French ultras in Algiers.

What was the significance of 1958 in the Middle East for France in this context? For many scholars, especially historians, 1958 demonstrates the polysemous nature of the historical event: although it first seemed as the culminating point of pan-Arabism, it soon revealed Nasser's pragmatism and will to deal with the West, as Salim Yaqub's previously cited work has shown and Dina Rezk's chapter further consolidates. The détente allowed France and Egypt to restore their cultural relations, although full diplomatic relations would not be resumed until 1963. Furthermore, French positions in Lebanon were preserved and further consolidated during Chehab's presidency. France's position in the Middle East was not normalized until after the independence of Algeria and, equally, the readjustment of the French-Israeli relations after the 1967 Six-Day War by de Gaulle, which opened the way to further development of France's relations with the Arab countries and particularly with Iraq, mainly in the cultural and economic domains. France's stance as an alternative Western partner of the Arab states during the Cold War and beyond, compared to the United States, was indeed rooted in the orientation its policy was already taking in the difficult year of 1958. What was essentially at stake was France's place in the postcolonial world and a complicated transition toward a policy of cooperation.

Notes

1 Fernand Fraudel and Immanuel Wallerstein, "History and the Social Sciences: The Longue Durée," *Review* (Fernand Braudel Center) 32, no. 2 (2009): 171–203. Original article: Fernand Braudel, "Histoire et Sciences sociales: La longue durée," *Annales* 13, no. 4 (1958): 735.
2 For the deconstruction of the historical time in relation with the 1958 crises see Michel Winock, *L'agonie de la IVème République. 13 mai 1958* (Paris: Gallimard, 2006), and René Rémond, *1958, le retour de De Gaulle* (Brussels: Complexe, 1998). The former is more interested in the long time of the colonization; the latter adopts the scope of the regime crisis in the *longue durée*. See also Sylvie Thénault's chapter in the present volume that considers the 1958 crisis in relation with the Algerian actions in the international political arena.
3 Sylvie Thénault, *Histoire de la guerre d'indépendance algérienne* (Paris: Flammarion, 2005), 47–52; Alistair Horne, *A Savage War of Peace: Algeria 1954–1962* (New York: New York Review of Books, 2011).
4 Matthew Connelly, *A Diplomatic Revolution: Algeria's Fight for Independence and the Origins of the Post–Cold War Era* (New York: Oxford University Press, 2002), 115–16; Martin S. Alexander et J. F. V. Keiger, "France and the Algerian War: Strategy, Operations and Diplomacy," in *France and the Algerian War 1954–1962: Strategy, Operations and Diplomacy*, ed. Martin S. Alexander and J. F. V. Keiger (London: Frank Cass, 2002), 18. See also Sylvie Thénault's chapter in the present volume.
5 Irwin Wall, *France, the United States, and the Algerian War* (Berkeley: University of California Press, 2001), 99–133. See also Geoffrey Barei, "The Sakiet Sidi Youssef

Incident of 1958 in Tunisia and the Anglo-American 'Good Offices' Mission," *The Journal of North African Studies* 17, no. 2 (2012): 355–71. For the 1958 crises in France see Rémond, *1958*, and Michel Winock, *L'agonie de la IVème République*.

6 See the chapters of Dina Rezk on Egypt and Fadi Esber on Syria for detailed perspectives on the first event, Caroline Attié on the Lebanese crisis and Juan Romero on the Iraqi revolution in this volume.

7 William Roger Louis and Roger Owen, eds., *A Revolutionary Year: The Middle East in 1958* (London: I.B. Tauris, 2002), 1, 289.

8 Martin Thomas and Andrew S. Thompson, "Rethinking Decolonization: A New Research Agenda for the Twenty-First Century," in *The Oxford Handbook of the Ends of Empire*, ed. Martin Thomas and Andrew S. Thompson (Oxford: Oxford University Press, 2018), doi: 10.1093/oxfordhb/9780198713197.001.0001.

9 Ministère des affaires étrangères (hereafter MAE), Levant 1944–1952, Syrie-Liban 319, 982 AL, Paris au MAE, A/s Coopération militaire franco-syrienne, November 6, 1950: Syrie. Aide-mémoire sur l'évolution de la question des fournitures de matériels de guerre par la France à la Syrie, October 15, 1950.

10 MAE, Levant 1953–1959, Généralités 545, Conférence des diplomates français du Moyen-Orient tenue à Beyrouth du 22 au 30 Mai 1953.

11 Sofia Papastamkou, "La France au Proche-Orient, 1950–1958: un intrus ou une puissance exclue?" (Unpublished doctoral thesis supervised by Professor Robert Frank, University Paris 1-Sorbonne: 2007), chapters 5 and 9.

12 Sofia Papastamkou, "French-Egyptian Relations before the Suez Crisis (1954–1956)," in *Les Occidentaux et la crise de Suez: une relecture politico-militaire*, ed. Philippe Vial, Georges-Henri Soutou, Robert Frank, Martin Alexander (Paris: Publications de la Sorbonne, 2015), 77–94.

13 For a recent contribution see Charles Cogan, "Part One: Paris," in *Suez Deconstructed*, ed. Philip Zelikow and Ernest R. May (Washington: Brookings InstitututionPress, 2018), 58–69; see also Frédérique Schillo, *La politique française à l'égard d'Israël: 1946–1959* (Brussels: André Versaille, 2013).

14 For an overview of the consequences of the Suez debacle for France in relation with the Cold War see Georges-Henri Soutou, *La guerre froide de la France 1941–1990* (Paris: Tallandier, 2018), 279–84.

15 *Documents diplomatiques français* (DDF) 1957, t. I, 460–1, Telegram 395/402, Pineau aux représentants diplomatiques de France à Tel Aviv, Beyrouth, Ankara, Téhéran, Tripoli, Khartoum, March 14, 1957. MAE, Amérique 1952–1963, États-Unis 438, Telegram 871, Direction Générale to Ambafrance Tunis, February 23, 1957.

16 The foundations of this settlement were already decided by the previous government, see MAE, Tunisie 1956–1972, 429/1, Compte-rendu de la réunion tenue dans le bureau du Président Pleven, le Samedi 24 mai 1958 de 15h à 16h; Telegram of Direction Générale des Affaires Marocaines et Tunisiennes (Joxe) to New York 2318/22, Washington 5944/48, Londres 5411/15, Rabat 2854/15, May 26, 1958; La Documentation française, *Bulletin d'Informations et de Presse internationale*, No. 0668, June 24, 1958.

17 Rémond, *1958*, 100–3.

18 For further context regarding the Lebanese crisis, see chapters of this volume written by Caroline Attié for the internal and regional aspects of the crisis, Jeffrey G. Karam for the US factor, and Robert McNamara for the British attitude. From an extensive bibliography, see also Erika G. Alin, *The United States and the 1958 Lebanon Crisis: American Intervention in the Middle East* (Lanham, MD: University Press of America

19. MAE, Liban 1953–1959, L626, Direction Afrique-Levant, Note A/s La crise au Liban, May 14, 1958.
20. MAE, Liban 1953–1959, 616, Note 421 AL, Roché, March 20, 1958.
21. See Stéphane Malsagne, *Sous l'oeil de la diplomatie française, le Liban de 1946 à 1990* (Paris: Geuthner, 2017), 63.
22. MAE, Liban 1953–1959, 626, 654 AL, Roché au MAE, May 9, 1958; MAE, Liban 1953–1959, 625, Telegram 548/51, Roché (Beyrouth), May 7, 1958.
23. MAE, Syrie-Liban 1953–1959, 292, 1182 AL, Balaÿ to Schuman, October 1, 1952.
24. MAE, Liban 1953–1959, 628, Service du Levant, Note, January 22, 1958; Liban 626, Service du Levant, Note, October 24, 1958; Letter of Roché to de Sébilleau, March 7, 1958; Letter of Roché to de Sébilleau, March 21, 1958.
25. As Jean Chauvel, ambassador in London, admitted, see The National Archives (hereafter TNA), FO 371/134117, 912, FO to Paris, Top Secret, May 14, 1958.
26. TNA, FO 371/134118, Paris to FO, 10631/20/58.
27. MAE, Liban 1953–1959, 626, Note, May 15, 1958; MAE, Levant 1953–1959, Généralités 727, July 2, 1958, Livraison de matériels au Liban (par voie aérienne); État-Major des Forces Armées, 431 3 BTMA TS, May 20, 1958.
28. MAE, Levant 1953–1959, Liban 626, Direction Afrique-Levant, Note, June 13, 1958.
29. Yaqub, *Containing Arab Nationalism*, 215.
30. Malsagne, *Sous l'œil de la diplomatie française*, 42–3.
31. MAE, Liban 1953–1959, 626, Direction Afrique-Levant, Note, June 13, 1958.
32. *FRUS, 1958–1960*, vol. XI, 17: State Department to American Embassy in Lebanon, March 18, 1958.
33. Matthew Jones, "Anglo-American Relations after Suez, the Rise and Decline of the Working Group Experiment and the French Challenge to NATO, 1957–1959," *Diplomacy & Statecraft* 14, no. 1 (2003): 49–78.
34. MAE, Secrétariat Général, Entretiens et Messages, 1956–1966, vol. 5, CR des entretiens franco-américains à Matignon, le 5 juillet 1958; Entretien de Couve de Murville et de John Foster Dulles, Quai d'Orsay, 5 juillet 1958.
35. Ritchie Ovendale, "Great Britain and the Anglo-American Invasion of Jordan and Lebanon in 1958," *The International History Review* 16, no. 2 (1994): 284–303.
36. MAE, Secrétariat Général, Entretiens et Messages, 1956–1966, vol. 5, Entretiens franco-britanniques des 29 et 30 juin à la Présidence du Conseil, CR de la première séance le 29 juin à 19 h; Entretiens franco-britanniques des 29 et 30 juin à la Présidence du Conseil, CR de la troisième séance le 30 juin à midi. MAE, Secrétariat Général, Entretiens et Messages, 1956–1966, vol. 5, Entretien de M. Couve de Murville et de M. Selwyn Lloyd, Quai d'Orsay, 30 juin 1958. PRO, TNA, FO 371/134128, VL 1015/42, Minute by Hayter, July 1, 1958. *FRUS, 1958–1960*, vol. XI, 190: note 3.
37. *FRUS, 1958–1960*, vol. XI, 190–2: Telegram From the Embassy in Lebanon to the Department of State, 1 juillet 1958; MAE, Levant 1953–1959, Liban 625, Telegram 1193/1201, Roché (Beyrouth), July 1, 1958; Telegram 1207/09, Roché (Beyrouth), July 1, 1958.
38. *FRUS, 1958–1960*, vol. XI, 198–9: Memorandum of a Conversation Between the Minister of the British Embassy (Lord Hood) and the Assistant Secretary of State for Near Eastern, South Asian, and African Affairs (Rountree), Department of State,

Washington, July 3, 1958. MAE, Liban 1953–1959, 626, Direction Afrique-Levant, Note A/s Derniers développements de la crise libanaise, July 3, 1958.
39 See Zurich Agreement of August 22, 1958.
40 MAE, Liban 1953–1959, 626, Direction Afrique-Levant, Note, June 13, 1958.
41 MAE, Levant 1953–1959, 545, Note établie par Baudet, du Chayla, Charpentier, Lalouette, juin 10, 1958.
42 MAE, Secrétariat Général, Entretiens et Messages, 1956–1966, vol. 5, CR des entretiens franco-américains à Matignon, le 5 juillet 1958.
43 MAE, Levant 1953–1959, Liban 625, Telegram 969/72, Roché (Beyrouth), June 13, 1958; Liban 626, Direction Afrique-Levant, Note, June 26, 1958; TNA, FO 371/134117, 203, Paris to FO, May 14, 1958; 913, FO to Paris, May 14, 1958.
44 TNA, FO 371/134118, Record of meeting of Ministers held in the Cabinet Room on Wednesday, May 14, to discuss the situation in the Lebanon. PRO, FO 371/134117, 925, FO to Beirut, May 15, 1958. TNA, CAB 128/32, 1, Cabinet Conclusions (58) 42, May 13, 1958.
45 TNA, FO 371/134125, 1699, Washington to FO, June 24, 1958; Letter of Sir Jebb to Sir Hoyer-Millar, June 19, 1958; Letter of Sir Hoyer-Millar to Sir Jebb, June 20, 1958.
46 TNA, FO 371/134117, 2738, FO to Washington, Top Secret, May 16, 1958. See also Yaqub, *Containing Arab Nationalism*, 213.
47 TNA, FO 371/134125, Letter of Sir Hoyer-Millar to Sir Jebb, June 20, 1958.
48 MAE, Levant 1953–1959, Liban 625, Telegrams 1384/85, 1386/87 and 1389, Roché (Beyrouth), July 16, 1958.
49 *Le Monde*, July 17, 1958.
50 Cited in Malsagne, *Sous l'œil de la diplomatie française*, 59.
51 MAE, Levant 1953–1959, Liban 625, Telegram 1413/18, Roché (Beyrouth), July 18, 1958.
52 *Le Monde*, "Du bon usage de la force," July 18, 1958.
53 Charles de Gaulle, *Mémoires d'espoir: Le renouveau, 1958–1962* (Paris: Plon, 1970), 216–17.
54 See the exchanges between Dulles and de Gaulle on July 5, in Paris, as reported in Connelly, *A Diplomatic Revolution*, 189.
55 TNA, FO 371/133793, 353, Paris to FO, July 18, 1958.
56 *Le Monde*, July 18, 1958.
57 MAE, Irak 1953–1959, 566, Bucher, Légation de Suisse en Irak, au Chef de la division des Organisations internationales, Département politique fédéral, October 1958.
58 MAE, Irak 1953–1959, 566, Service du Levant, Reconnaissance éventuelle du nouveau gouvernement irakien et reprise des relations diplomatiques, July 28, 1958; Service du Levant, Attitude de la France à l'égard de l'Iraq, January 15, 1959.
59 For the example of the development of French-Lebanese relations see Malsagne, *Sous l'œil de la diplomatie française*, 67–70; for the rest of the Arab countries after 1967 see Maurice Vaïsse, *La puissance ou l'influence? La France dans le monde depuis 1958* (Paris: Fayard, 2009), 368–70.
60 Ritchie Ovendale, "Great Britain and the Anglo-American Invasion," 285–6; Jones, "Anglo-American Relations after Suez," 50, 61–9.
61 MAE, NUOI 161, Note A/s La crise libanaise devant le Conseil de Sécurité, August 2, 1958; MAE, États-Unis 1952–1963, 432, Telegram 100, REPAN Chaillot, July 17, 1958; États-Unis 432, Telegram, Cabinet du Ministre to London 7492/7500 and Washington 8011/19, July 17, 1958.

62 MAE, Secrétariat général, Entretiens et messages, 1956–1966, vol. 5, Mémorandum du 17 septembre 1958.
63 For the first trend, see mainly Maurice Vaïsse, "Aux origines du mémorandum de septembre 1958," *Relations internationales* 58 (1989): 253–68 and Jones, "Anglo-American Relations after Suez," 61–73. For the second, see mainly Edward Kolodziej, *French International Policy under de Gaulle and Pompidou: The Politics of Grandeur* (Ithaca London: Cornell University Press, 1974); Connelly, *A Diplomatic Revolution*, 192–3; Wall, *France, the United States, and the Algerian War*, 168–70, 196–9.
64 MAE, Cabinet du Ministre, Maurice Couve de Murville 1958–1968, 10, Direction Politique / Service des Pactes, Note A/s Réorganisation de l'Alliance. Rôle de la France, July 3, 1958.
65 In November 1957, while France attached strings to its arms sales to Tunisia, Great Britain and the United States had delivered the country arms to cut short the pressure Nasser put on Habib Bourguiba to accept Egyptian deliveries. See details in Connelly, *A Diplomatic Revolution*, 150–4. See also Samya el Mechat, *Les relations franco-tunisiennes. Histoire d'une souveraineté arrachée* (Paris: L'Harmattan, 2005) for a larger view of French-Tunisian relations after the independence.
66 MAE, Levant 1953–1959, Généralités 540, Service du Levant, Note, July 22, 1958.
67 Thomas Gomart, *Double détente. Les relations franco-soviétiques de 1958 à 1964* (Paris: Publications de la Sorbonne, 2003), 227–9.
68 Reem Abou-El-Fadl, "Building Egypt's Afro-Asian Hub: Infrastructures of Solidarity and the 1957 Cairo Conference," *Journal of World History* 30, no. 1–2 (2019): 117.

Chapter 4

CAUTIOUS REVISIONISM AND THE LIMITS OF HEGEMONY IN 1958

A REVOLUTIONARY YEAR FOR THE UNITED STATES IN THE MIDDLE EAST

Jeffrey G. Karam

The revolutionary year of 1958 remains one of the most important watersheds in the history of the modern Middle East. The union between Egypt and Syria in 1958 marked the zenith of Arab nationalism. The short-lived United Arab Republic was in part the result of the Arab Cold War, the competition between pro-Western conservative regimes, led by Iraq, and revolutionary Arab governments, led by Egypt. Intra-Arab and non-Arab alignments in the Middle East were further aggravated by bipolar competition between the United States and the Soviet Union in the region and elsewhere. This competition in the Middle East resulted from the growing interest of the United States in the rich oil fields in the Gulf and its grand strategy to deny the Soviet Union access to the resources and strategic position of the region.

By looking through the lenses of diplomacy, covert action, and military intervention, I explain how and why 1958 was revolutionary for the United States in the Middle East. The political vacuum that ensued after the Suez War bolstered the United States to become the new Western hegemon in the Middle East and launched the beginning of a new US-led order.[1] However, I argue that the United States acted as a cautious revisionist power by attempting to reshape the decaying Anglo-French imperial order in an orderly and slow manner rather than quickly and completely overhaul it.[2] Specifically, the cautious and gradual rise in US power in the Middle East was based on the Eisenhower administration's ability to leverage its economic, diplomatic, and covert power to achieve political goals and shape developments in different states. Yet, a number of significant sociopolitical developments in various Middle Eastern states, including Iraq, Jordan, Lebanon, and Syria, between the Suez Crisis of 1956 and the revolutionary summer of 1958 exposed the limits of the emerging US order and its growing hegemony. Weeks after the Syrian crisis of 1957, the Eisenhower administration was well aware that diplomacy, economic aid, and covert action were insufficient to maintain the rising US-led order in the Middle East. In response to the Iraqi Free Officers coup in July

1958, the United States launched its first large-scale military operation in Lebanon and wider Middle East. In many ways and especially against the background of the Eisenhower administration's decisions to increase the involvement, though still limited in the 1950s, of the US military involvement in Vietnam, this military operation became a model of "success" for US "limited wars" around the world.[3] In fact, such limited interventions demonstrated the willingness of the United States to use force to protect its commercial and strategic interests while attempting to minimize the possibility of getting immersed in a long and costly war. In this context, the revolutionary year of 1958 brought an end to the limited success and ability of the United States to leverage its economic and diplomatic power and ushered in a phase marked by coercion and the use of force.

The chapter draws on US declassified records and secondary accounts. It proceeds in the following manner. First, it addresses the legacy of the Suez Crisis and the beginning of the Eisenhower Doctrine. Second, it considers the stipulations of and reactions to the Eisenhower Doctrine. Third, it focuses on the first phase of events that tested the limits of growing US power and hegemony by analyzing on sociopolitical developments in Jordan, Lebanon, and Syria. Fourth, it focuses on a second phase of developments that likewise tested the limits of growing US power starting with the creation of the United Arab Republic and ending with the Anglo-American interventions in Jordan and Lebanon respectively. The final section concludes with a discussion of four takeaways on how and why the year 1958 was revolutionary for the United States in the Middle East.

Legacy of Suez and the Foundations of the Eisenhower Doctrine

The Eisenhower administration opposed the joint British, French, and Israeli aggression against Egypt partly because it wanted to keep some distance from the practices of their allies to ensure that most states in the Middle East would not tilt toward the Soviet Union.[4] By openly shunning the region's former colonial powers and Israel for their bellicosity against Egypt, the Eisenhower administration, at least for a short period of time, signaled to the international community and many revolutionary Arabs that it opposed Western intervention and Israeli aggression.[5] However, the Eisenhower administration had to strike a balance between two concerns: redeeming the declining Anglo-French position in the Middle East, and shoring up its alliances with oil-producing Arab and non-Arab states to deny the Soviet Union access to Gulf oil and limit their expansion in the region.[6]

The growing tension between the United States, Britain, and France during and after the Suez War forced the Eisenhower administration to adopt a clearer foreign policy in the Middle East.[7] The clearest form of such a foreign policy emerged in November 1956 and, thus, set the foundations for the Eisenhower Doctrine in January 1957.[8] It is important to highlight that the United States was supportive of the Baghdad Pact of 1955, the defensive pact and organization between Turkey, Iraq, Great Britain, Pakistan, and Iran to limit, prevent, and contain the growing influence of the Soviet Union in the Middle East.[9] However, the United States did not formally join the Baghdad Pact but was rather a participant in committee meetings. It also signed bilateral agreements with the states that formed the Baghdad Pact. In brief, it had to find an alternative to the collapsing Western order, including military pacts and arrangements such as the Baghdad Pact, and the political vacuum that resulted from the ill-conceived Anglo-French-Israeli military aggression in the Middle East.[10]

In mid-November 1956, the Eisenhower administration was still attempting to build on its newfound popularity in the Arab world. Nonetheless, this popularity would soon be eclipsed by stronger Arab demands for the United States to reconsider its Middle East policy, especially on Palestine and its commitments to protecting and securing Israel.[11] Specifically, many Arab leaders concurred that the United States must adopt a harder line with Israel and ensure its compliance with the 1947 UN Resolution that if implemented would lead to an independent Arab state in Palestine. Moreover, most revolutionary Arab leaders, primarily Gamal Abdel Nasser, expected that a new phase in US-Arab relations was only possible through a reassessment of US relations with its Western allies in the region.[12] Such a reconsideration centered on the termination of European strategic and commercial interests in the Middle East and support for an independent Arab state in Palestine.

Toward the end of November and in part due to repeated Arab demands on and propaganda campaigns against the Eisenhower administration and pro-Western states in the Middle East, the newfound popularity of the United States with Arab revolutionary regimes was waning. According to US policy-makers at the time, the future of US policy in the Middle East and preservation of the new order was possible by adopting a three-prong strategy: First, the denial of the region's massive oil reserves to the Soviet Union and preserving those resources for the West. Second, the dire need for the United States to restore and maintain the Western position in the Middle East due to the large inability of the French and British to play a constructive role in the region. The US belief of restoring the Western position was undoubtedly imperial in scope and nature. Third, the determination to create and support a federation of pro-Western states in the Middle East to weaken the influence and prestige of Nasser and other revolutionary Arabs.[13]

The heart of the Eisenhower administration's conceptualization of a new Middle East policy was to contain Soviet expansion and build on the Arabs' positive perception of the US role in opposing Anglo-French and Israeli aggression against Egypt in 1956.[14] Moreover, the Eisenhower administration wanted to maintain good relationships with conservative and revolutionary regimes in the region, primarily Egypt.[15] While both policy considerations were compatible, the events that followed between 1957 and 1958 forced the Eisenhower administration to view them as mutually exclusive. The ability of the United States to adopt flexible and ambiguous policies in the Middle East, such as establishing working channels with different conservative and revolutionary states, before the Suez Crisis and the War of 1956, was becoming limited. As the new rising Western power, the United States was caught in the regional rivalry between revolutionary and conservative regimes in the Middle East and was determined through covert action and economic inducements to keep most Middle Eastern states in the Western orbit. Clearly, the US involvement in the Arab Cold War was not passive. The Arab Cold War was also aggravated by growing US-USSR competition in the Middle East, and the two superpowers were supporting the Iraqi and Egyptian blocs, respectively, while the United States was still attempting to placate Nasser and Egypt following Suez.

The Eisenhower Doctrine: A Policy in Practice

The discussions before the formal declaration of the Eisenhower Doctrine in early 1957 centered on the belief that US offers of economic aid and military support to different Arab states, including a reconsideration of financial assistance for Egypt's Aswan Dam project, could lure Arab governments away from the Soviet Union and bring them in line with the new US order in the Middle East.[16] While the Eisenhower administration knew that the failure to finance the Aswan Dam sparked the Suez Crisis of 1956, deliberations of a new US policy and approach in the region called on providing economic inducements, before coercion and use of force, to attract Arab allies, and by extension, secure their allegiance.[17]

On January 5, 1957, Eisenhower unveiled his administration's Middle East policy to the Eighty-Fifth Congress. This "new" Middle East policy was about the willingness of the United States to support the independence and territorial integrity of "freedom-loving nations of the area."[18] A clearer provision in this Middle East policy was the employment of US armed forces to protect "freedom-loving nations" in the Middle East from "any overt armed aggression from any nation controlled by International Communism."[19] The new Middle East policy, later dubbed the "Eisenhower Doctrine," received sharp scrutiny in Congress. While Eisenhower attempted to portray his administration's Middle East policy as a model of bipartisanship, many Democratic Senators, including ones gearing up for their party's nomination, such as John F. Kennedy and Lyndon B. Johnson in the presidential elections of 1960, criticized different aspects of this policy. Following a month of deliberations between members of Congress, the Senate Foreign Relations and Armed Services committees passed an amended version of the Eisenhower Doctrine.[20] Among the different amendments, Senator Mike Mansfield introduced and pushed for a stipulation that stressed the preservation of the independence and integrity of the nations of the Middle East was vital to US national interests. The Senate approved the Middle East Doctrine on March 5, and two days later, Eisenhower signed the bill that became the law of the land.[21]

Besides internal criticism and back-and-forth deliberations in the United States for close to nine weeks, a handful of foreign governments had their own reactions to the Eisenhower Doctrine. British prime minister Harold Macmillan, Anthony Eden's successor, endorsed the Eisenhower Doctrine. However, the British government had come to terms with the fact that the US Middle East policy would eventually replace the British sponsored Baghdad Pact.[22] The French government equally endorsed the Eisenhower Doctrine. Yet, they had some reservations on the scope of the Doctrine and whether it would entail any unilateral decisions on North

Africa, the mainland of French colonies that were undergoing transformative changes, and in some cases, such as Algeria, a revolutionary war. In brief, British and French support of the Doctrine signaled their apprehension of the new role of the United States in the Middle East.[23]

Reactions among Arab and non-Arab states in the Middle East varied on the Eisenhower Doctrine. On the one hand, members of the Baghdad Pact, including Iran, Iraq, Pakistan, and Turkey, strongly supported the Eisenhower Doctrine for different political and military ends.[24] Pro-Western Arab states, including Lebanon, Jordan, Tunisia, Libya, and Saudi Arabia, equally voiced their support for the new role of the United States in the region and consequently, its new Middle East policy.[25] On the other hand, Egypt and Syria showed no support for the Doctrine.[26] Nasser did not outright reject the new US policy; however, he was worried about the implicit objectives of the Eisenhower Doctrine, mainly the containment of revolutionary Arab governments.[27] Israel was concerned with the prospects of increased military aid to different Arab states and the extent of support it could muster from the United States under the Doctrine.[28]

Testing the Limits of the Eisenhower Doctrine and the New US Order in 1957

The Eisenhower administration was strongly convinced that its Middle East policy was instrumental in shoring up unpopular pro-Western regimes. In fact, the successful show of force and the provision of covert assistance to Jordan and Lebanon convinced members of the Eisenhower administration of the vital need of such a policy to repress Arab revolutionary nationalist elements and limit Soviet influence, respectively. However, the third test of the Eisenhower Doctrine in Syria during the summer and fall of 1957 was a more challenging endeavor. The inability of the Eisenhower Doctrine to prevent the consolidation of a pro-nationalist government in Syria that moved closer to the Soviet Union demonstrated the limits of the new Middle East policy.[29] Between July and December 1957, the Eisenhower administration discussed how and whether its Middle East policy to guard against the threat of International Communism was in some way applicable to Syria.

The first major test of the Eisenhower Doctrine materialized weeks after the Senate approved it. The domestic crisis in the Hashemite Kingdom of Jordan that was brewing before and after the Suez Crisis of 1956 had finally reached its apex in the first few months of 1957.[30] In brief, the domestic crisis resulted from divisions over power and competition between King Hussein, Suleiman al-Nabulsi, the leader of the National Socialist Party and later prime minister, and Major General Ali Abu Nuwar, commander of the Jordan Arab Army. One of the main contentions was on Jordan's pro-Western orientation and the endorsement of the Eisenhower Doctrine.[31] Hussein wanted to maintain Jordan's orientation toward the West, while the Nabusli government and other members of the opposition pushed for better relations with the Soviet Union and China.[32] In early April 1957 and against the backdrop of an alleged military coup against the monarchy, the

Eisenhower administration was eager for the young king to shore up his regime and maintain its pro-Western orientation. Hussein was politically savvy in enlisting US support against the opposition by playing the "Communist card."[33] By taking measures to crack down on pro-Communist movements in Jordan, he was able to demonstrate his commitment to America's grand strategy to contain and limit the influence of the Soviet Union in the Middle East. On April 24, the United States responded favorably by ordering the Sixth Fleet to the Eastern Mediterranean.[34] This demonstration of power served as a clear warning to Arab states that were planning to support the opposition against the monarchy and deterred Israel from attempting to occupy the West Bank.[35] The US resolve dissuaded Jordan's Arab and non-Arab neighbors from any military intervention, and as a result, the Kingdom survived and Hussein remained in power.

The second major test of the Eisenhower Doctrine occurred in June 1957.[36] This came in the form of the parliamentary elections in Lebanon that served as a referendum on the popularity of the pro-Western president Camille Chamoun and the regime's ability to maintain its tilt toward the United States[37] The elections were crucially important for the continuation of the president's pro-Western regime because the elected parliament would be responsible for electing Chamoun's successor. A few Arab states, including Egypt and Syria, tried to influence the outcome of the elections by providing economic assistance and small shipments of arms to several opposition leaders.[38] However, Egypt and Syria were not the only states that attempted to influence the course of the elections. The US government, through arranged funds for the CIA Station and US Embassy in Lebanon, ensured that pro-Chamoun candidates won over two-thirds of the parliamentary seats.[39] For a moment, it seemed that the Eisenhower administration could use covert economic inducements to ensure the loyalty of key individuals in various governments. There was limited need for active military engagement and thus, pro-Western regimes in the Middle East were in fact rewarded for their allegiance.

The third major test of the Eisenhower Doctrine ensued in July 1957. In late July 1957, and against the backdrop of tense US-Syrian relations, a delegation of Syrian political and military officials headed to the Soviet Union.[40] One of the goals of this visit was for the Syrian government to secure Soviet assistance to counter the growing Western, mainly US-led, influence in the Middle East.[41] At the time that members of the Syrian government were courting the Soviet Union for economic support, some accounts suggest that US Embassy officials in Syria were actively recruiting Syrian officers to plan and execute a coup that would overthrow the pro-left and Communist-leaning military with one that was favorable to the West.[42] Nonetheless, some of these recruited officers reported to their Syrian superiors of ongoing US-backed plans to remove the existing regime, and these officers were instructed by their commanders to maintain close contact with US officials to retrieve operational details on any US-backed coups.[43] Even though many US records related to its preparations and sponsorship for a coup within the Syrian military remain classified, there is preponderant evidence of US collusion with some officers to overthrow the pro-left and Soviet-leaning government.[44] On August 12, 1957, Syrian authorities announced, through the Syrian Broadcasting

Station, that the regime services had just foiled an "American plot to overthrow the present [Syrian] government."[45] This announcement increasingly worsened US-Syrian relations and ushered in a new phase in Syrian politics that was marked by massive repression of Syrian officials that espoused pro-Western sentiments.[46] The Eisenhower administration contemplated for weeks whether they could invoke any of the provisions in the Middle East policy to remove the pro-leftist and Soviet-friendly government.[47] In October 1957, US officials discussed the possibility of sponsoring an alliance of pro-Western Arab governments to use force against the government in Syria.[48] A larger consideration for the Eisenhower administration was to steer away from a serious diplomatic and possible military showdown with the Soviet Union over Syria that could engulf the entire region.

In stark contrast to quick and favorable outcomes in Jordan, and Lebanon, the Eisenhower administration was limited in its ability to shape the course of events in Syria. The Syrian crisis of 1957 had in effect exposed the limits of the Eisenhower Doctrine and the new US-led order. The complexities of the Syrian situation and the involvement of regional players, as well as the Soviet Union, revealed US political weakness in the Arab world. This weakness was evident in the limits of US economic aid, covert action, and diplomacy to compel the Syrian government from shifting closer toward the Soviet Union.[49] Moreover, the Eisenhower administration's support for Jordan and Lebanon to repress revolutionary Arab nationalist elements and opposition movements in the first half of 1957 aggravated the tenuous and deteriorating relations between Syria and the United States[50] The inability of the Eisenhower administration to find a reliable and strong faction in Syria largely explains the rationale for sponsoring coups. As a result, between November and December 1957, the United States, in deliberations with Britain, discussed the need for contingency plans that centered on joint military intervention in the Middle East to shore up pro-Western allies against the growing wave of Arab revolutionary nationalism and the possibility of closer ties with the USSR.[51]

Testing the Limits of the Eisenhower Doctrine and the New US Order in 1958

On February 1, 1958, Egypt and Syria formed a union that was revolutionary and transformative for Arab nationalists across the Middle East. The union, known as the United Arab Republic (UAR), enhanced Nasser's political and strategic leadership in the region, as well as expanded Egypt's borders beyond North Africa. The reactions of the Eisenhower administration to Nasser's growing popularity and the UAR varied between deep concern for pro-Western Arab governments and encouragement for the emergence of an Arab bloc that could be drawn closer to the United States[52] Accordingly, some US officials viewed an Arab alliance as useful to limit the influence of the Soviet Union in the region. However, it was difficult for the Eisenhower administration to simultaneously support the UAR and contain its persuasive and revolutionary nationalist sway in pro-Western regimes.[53] The United States was limited in its ability to pursue an ambiguous and flexible policy that accommodated the UAR and still upheld its commitments to pro-Western Arab governments. The Eisenhower administration had mutually exclusive policy choices and, thus, had to choose between either accommodating Nasser's growing popularity or disrupting the UAR.[54] However, the turning point that ended the ability of the United States to pursue contradictory policies was the Iraqi Free Officers coup and later revolution in Iraq in 1958.[55] This revolutionary event was followed by the introduction of US forces in Lebanon for upholding US credibility and safeguarding oil interests in the region. Both strategic and political concerns were meant to limit Nasser's political sway in the region and deny the Soviet Union the ability to increase its influence and gain access to the rich oil fields in the Gulf.

The first challenge to the US-led order in early 1958 emerged from the pro-Western Arab bloc. In response to the UAR, Iraq and Jordan announced the Arab Union, a federation between the Hashemite monarchies, to counter the growing influence of Nasser. While Hussein of Jordan extended an invitation to King Saud of Saudi Arabia to join the Arab Union, the latter refused to be part of a pro-Western bloc as long as Iraq remained in the Baghdad Pact.[56] The Eisenhower administration, specifically the State Department, welcomed the formation of the UAR and the declaration of the Arab Union. By issuing identical statements toward both blocs, the Eisenhower administration presented itself as a supporter of any drive toward Arab unity in the Middle East and thus, avoided criticisms that could have pointed to the Iraq-Jordan Federation as a Western-supported initiative.[57] The United States had privately supported the formation of the Arab Union as a counterweight to the UAR; yet, the Eisenhower administration was aware of the unpopularity of a bloc of pro-Western regimes in the streets of Amman, Baghdad, and other Arab states.[58]

Against this background, Eisenhower and some members at a National Security Council Meeting in mid-March 1958 viewed that the loss of Western access to Middle East oil and the collapse of pro-Western regimes would enhance the Soviet position and further contribute to Nasser's popularity. While still considering the merits of pursuing a double-edged policy of accommodating and disrupting the UAR, US officials at the NSC found a pretext for possible Western intervention in the Middle East by conflating between "International Communism" and revolutionary Arab nationalism.[59] Moreover, Nasser's consolidation of power in Syria, particularly his growing sway over the main avenues through which Arab oil was shipped to the West, such as Lebanon, and growing popularity in the Arab world, convinced US officials of the urgent need to disrupt the UAR and contain Nasser. The Eisenhower administration focused on bolstering pro-Western Arab regimes against Nasser while still attempting to avoid public criticism of its covert plans to undermine revolutionary Arab regimes. Put differently, the Eisenhower administration simultaneously supported a handful of pro-Western Arab regimes and tried to appease Nasser by relaxing some US restrictions on exports and cultural exchanges. However, declassified US records strongly suggest that in late March, the Eisenhower administration shifted US policy more toward containing the UAR rather than accommodating it.[60] But the prospect of placating Nasser and improving US-UAR relations remained a policy priority, especially that the Eisenhower administration was trying to avoid a military showdown and diplomatic controversy in the Middle East.[61]

The second challenge that likewise complicated the delicate and double-edged policy that the Eisenhower administration was pursuing materialized in Lebanon and particularly from pro-Western President Chamoun.[62] In the first three months of 1958 and against the wills of a strong opposition movement, composed of both Christian and Muslim leaders, in a country where domestic crises took sectarian overtones, Chamoun was determined to introduce an amendment to the constitution to be able to stay in office for another term.[63] The Eisenhower administration faced another dilemma as to whether support Chamoun against an opposition movement that was supported by Nasser and other Arab nationalist forces in the region or to abandon a staunch pro-Western ally and by extension endanger US credibility to pro-Western regimes in the region.[64] For the first half of 1958, the Eisenhower administration delicately pursued simultaneous options. On the one hand, it attempted to dissuade Chamoun from seeking office for another term while still attempting to appease Nasser.[65] On the other hand, it provided economic assistance and military aid to bolster Chamoun and other pro-Western allies in the regime to maintain US credibility.[66] The assassination of Nassib al-Matni, a pro-left and Arab nationalist journalist who was critical of Chamoun, on May 8, 1958, triggered a new phase between the president and the cross-sectarian opposition movement. Immediately after the murder of al-Matni, opposition leaders called for a general strike in which they denounced Chamoun and asked for the president's immediate resignation.[67] A political crisis over Chamoun's intent to succeed himself in office turned into the first civil war in Lebanon after independence in 1943.

On May 13, 1958, Chamoun conveyed to US, British, and French officials that he was considering the option of requesting Western military intervention.[68] Members of the Eisenhower administration discussed Chamoun's possible plea and concluded that military action could lead to the sabotage of oil pipelines and the resurgence of anti-Western feeling.[69] Eisenhower and other officials also concluded that military inaction would suggest that the United States was not prepared to defend its pro-Western allies and by extension allow both adversaries and friends to question the credibility of its Middle East policy and other commitments.[70] The more serious dilemma for the Eisenhower administration to justify intervention under the provisions of the Middle East policy was to muster convincing evidence that the UAR attacked Lebanon and that the Egyptian-Syrian union was controlled by International Communism. The needed evidence was dubious, and thus, the Eisenhower administration then considered whether the Mansfield Amendment that stressed "the preservation of the independence and integrity of the nations of the Middle East" could be used as a pretext for military action.[71] In contrast to the Eisenhower administration's success in Lebanon in 1957, the United States was unable to resolve the crisis turned civil war through economic aid, covert action, or diplomacy. Specifically, the United States was hesitant to use force and sustain a pro-Western president that lacked popular support. However, the risk of military inaction and subsequent loss of US credibility in the Middle East outweighed the costs of use of force and intervention.

The third challenge to the US-led order in the Middle East that compelled the Eisenhower administration of the dire need to adopt a clearer policy and one that advocated military action rather than diplomacy materialized in Jordan and Iraq. The first crisis occurred in late June 1958, when Jordanian security officials unveiled a conspiracy among army officers to assassinate Hussein and overthrow the monarchy.[72] With US, primarily CIA, support, Hussein was able to arrest the conspirators and repress the nationalist officers from executing their coup.[73] Nonetheless, Hussein was still worried about other revolutionary cells within the officer's corps that might likewise attempt to assassinate him and thus, requested Iraq's support to shore up the monarchy.[74] The government of Iraq positively responded and dispatched the army's Twentieth Infantry Brigade from Baghdad to Amman. The Brigade never reached Amman, but instead marched on Baghdad and executed a swift coup.[75]

The second major crisis that rattled Western intelligence agencies, embassies, and governments unraveled in the early hours of July 14, 1958.[76] The Iraqi Free Officers exploited the window to bolster Jordan's monarchy by seizing Iraq's Ministry of Defense, police station, royal palace, and residence of notorious Premier Nuri al-Said. Within hours, tens of thousands of Iraqis took to the streets and cheered for the end of the Hashemite monarchy and the beginning of a Republican government.[77] Pro-Western leaders in the Arab world and Western governments were caught by surprise with the coup turned revolution in Iraq.[78]

In response to the swift Iraqi coup, the Eisenhower administration was again confronting two hard and distinct policy choices. First, it considered the consequences of and possible reactions to the introduction of US forces in the region. Second, it contemplated whether US intervention would shore up pro-Western Arab governments and consequently, reverse the Iraqi Free Officers and reinstate a loyalist and friendly Western-oriented regime.[79] The Iraqi revolution and the possibility of similar revolts in other pro-Western states convinced the Eisenhower administration that military action and use of force outweighed the costs of inaction. The Eisenhower administration felt that military inaction would jeopardize US credibility in the Middle East and access to the strategic resources and position of the region. As a result, the Eisenhower administration was very constrained in its ability to leverage economic aid, covert action, and diplomacy to both preserve its role as dominant Western hegemon in the region and contain the Soviet Union from expanding in the region. In retrospect, Operation Blue Bat, the codename of the US military operation, was successful in the sense of ensuring the continuation of the pro-Western regime in Lebanon, demonstrating US resolve in the region, and signaling to the Soviet Union the extent to which the United States was willing to go to uphold its commitments. The quick sequence of events in the revolutionary summer of 1958 and particularly in Jordan, Iraq, and Lebanon demonstrated the limits of US hegemony and the need of using force and coercion to maintain the US-led order.

Conclusion

This chapter has argued that the United States acted as a cautious revisionist power by attempting to reshape the decaying Anglo-French imperial order in a slow manner rather than quickly overhauling it. By drawing on extensive declassified records and documents, I have demonstrated that the cautious and gradual rise in US power in the Middle East was based on the Eisenhower administration's ability to leverage its economic, diplomatic, and covert power to achieve political goals. However, a number of significant sociopolitical developments in Iraq, Jordan, Lebanon, and Syria between the Suez Crisis of 1956 and the revolutionary year of 1958 exposed the limits of the emerging US order. It is important to highlight that the events from the Suez Crisis to the revolution in Iraq were as revolutionary for the Middle East as for the United States and four key considerations support this concluding thought.

First, the shift from containing revolutionary Arab nationalists and shoring up pro-Western Middle Eastern regimes to accommodating Nasser and the growing nationalist trend was an involuntary policy choice for the Eisenhower administration. While the Eisenhower administration was determined to undercut Nasser's growing appeal and influence, it later realized that its support for unpopular regimes, mainly pro-Western conservative monarchies and governments in the area, was in effect jeopardizing the new Western order that the United States was trying to create and uphold. The friction between the UAR and the Soviet Union also convinced the Eisenhower administration that support for revolutionary Arab nationalists was antithetical to US goals and interests, primarily Middle Eastern oil, in the region.[80]

Second, the success of the United States in both supporting Hussein of Jordan against Arab nationalists and rigging the parliamentary elections in Lebanon to ensure a pro-Western chamber in 1957 demonstrated the utility of the Eisenhower Doctrine as a channel for economic assistance, covert action, and diplomacy. However, the same channels of economic assistance and covert action failed miserably in Syria in the second half of 1957. While US officials recruited Syrian officers and promised economic inducements to remove the pro-left and nationalist government, the available documentary evidence points to the operational, strategic, and diplomatic weaknesses of the Eisenhower Doctrine in states that were farther from the West. The three events in 1957 clearly pointed to the positives and negatives of the Eisenhower Doctrine, at least from the vantage point of the administration at the time. Yet, the Syrian crisis of 1957 demonstrated that the United States as the emerging Western power in the Middle East that is attempting to fill a political vacuum and build a new US-led order was politically weak in the region. As the emerging Western power, the United States failed through diplomacy and covert action to dissuade Syria from moving closer to the Soviet Union, which consequently suggested its limited ability to counter revolutionary Arab nationalist governments. This stark finding was revolutionary for an emerging power that was determined to redeem the Western position in the Middle East after the Suez War and Crisis of 1956.

Third, the introduction of US forces in Lebanon twenty hours after the Free Officers coup in Iraq was the first large-scale US military operation in the Middle East and what in retrospect became a model for US "limited wars" around the world.[81] In fact, the relative success of this military operation in Lebanon, especially that it faced minimal resistance, set a dangerous precedent.[82] The United States could use military power to ensure favorable diplomatic outcomes and weaker states had limited means to resist and oppose such military exploits. However, this belief was radically challenged in Southeast Asia and the Middle East a few years after 1958.[83]

Fourth, Eisenhower's decision to introduce US forces in Lebanon was partly related to maintaining US credibility in the Middle East and beyond.[84] This equally set a dangerous precedent which President Lyndon Johnson used as a pretext to plunge US forces in Vietnam and increase America's involvement in Vietnam after 1964.[85] In retrospect, both precedents and the revolutionary year of 1958 demonstrated the limits of growing US power in the Middle East and the world. But such a realization at different intervals in the Cold War and beyond was hard to come by and often too late to recognize.

Notes

1 For a discussion of Britain and France in 1958 see Robert McNamara, "The Point of Departure: The Impact of The Revolutionary Year of 1958 on British Policy," and Sofia Papastamkou, "France and the Middle East in 1958: Continuity and Change through Crisis," in Jeffrey G. Karam, ed., *The Middle East in 1958: Reimagining a Revolutionary Year* (London: I.B. Tauris, 2020).

2 Scholarship on the rise and fall of great powers and power shifts in the international system remains a central debate in the field of international relations. Much of the literature focuses on the dichotomy between revisionist and status-quo powers. Broadly, revisionist actors seek to alter the status quo and create a new governing order that suits their preferences, while status-quo actors are determined to maintain the existing order that benefits their interests and share of power. See Randall L. Schweller, *Maxwell's Demon and the Golden Apple: Global Discord in the New Millennium* (Baltimore, MD: Johns Hopkins University Press, 2014); Randall L. Schweller, *Deadly Imbalances: Tripolarity and Hitler's Strategy of World Conquest* (New York: Columbia University Press, 1998); Jason Davidson, *The Origins of Revisionist and Status-Quo States* (New York: Palgrave Macmillan, 2006). Recent scholarship focuses more closely on the concept of "reluctance" in international politics. Specifically, some studies contend that rising powers are not always inclined to subvert an existing order. Instead, revisionist powers can sometimes seek to reform international orders in a gradual manner with the aim of consolidating their status as a status-quo state. See Joshua R. Shifrinson, Rising Titans, Falling Giants: How Great Powers Exploit Power Shifts (Ithaca, NY: Cornell University Press, 2018) and Sandra Destradi, "Reluctant Powers? Rising Powers' Contributions to Regional Crisis Management," *Third World Quarterly* 39, no. 12 (2019): 2222–39; Sandra Destradi, "Reluctance in International Politics: A Conceptualization," *European Journal of International Relations* 23, no. 2 (June 2017): 315–40 for revisionist accounts on the divergences in rising state strategies.

3 It is important to highlight that US involvement in Vietnam occurred much earlier than the manufactured Gulf of Tonkin incident in 1964. For important works on different aspects of decision-making, especially as it relates to the doctrine of "limited wars" and the Vietnam War see Spencer D. Bakich, *Success and Failure in Limited War: Information and Strategy in the Korean, Vietnam, Persian Gulf, and Iraq Wars* (Chicago; London: University of Chicago Press, 2014); Fredrik Logevall, *Embers of War: The Fall of an Empire and the Making of America's Vietnam* (New York: Random House, 2014); Fredrik Logevall and Campbell Craig, *America's Cold War: The Politics of Insecurity* (Cambridge: Belknap Press, 2012); James M. Carter, *Inventing Vietnam: The United States and State Building, 1954–1968* (New York: Cambridge University Press, 2008); Thomas Preston, *Pandora's Trap: Presidential Decision Making and Blame Avoidance in Vietnam and Iraq* (Plymouth: Rowman & Littlefield Publishers, 2013). For a discussion of US involvement, both political and military in the Middle East, see Douglas Little, *American Orientalism: The United States and the Middle East since 1945* (Chapel Hill: University of North Carolina Press, 2008). For a brief discussion of the legacy of the Vietnam War and the notion of limited wars see Dennis Ricci, *Presidential Decision Making and Military Intervention in the Post-Cold War Era: Go or No-Go* (London: Lexington Books, 2019), 249.

4 Memorandum of Discussion at the 302d Meeting of the National Security Council, Washington, November 1, 1956; Memorandum From the Counselor of the Department of State (MacArthur) to the Acting Secretary of State, Washington, November 14, 1956. See also Salim Yaqub, *Containing Arab Nationalism: The Eisenhower Doctrine and the Middle East* (Chapel Hill: University of North Carolina Press, 2004), 3, 51.

5 During the Suez Crisis, the United States opposed aggression against Egypt and was consequently viewed as the defender of Egypt's sovereignty. Telegram from the Department of State to the Embassy in Egypt, November 1, 1956. Department of State, Central Files, 684A.86/11-156; Yaqub, *Containing Arab Nationalism*, 54–5. Telegram from the Department of State to the Embassy in Egypt, November 1, 1956. Department of State, Central Files, 684A.86/11-156.

6 Memorandum from the Acting Secretary of State to the President, Washington, November 21, 1956, Eisenhower Library, Whitman File, Dulles-Herter Series.

7 For an overview of US declassified records on the Suez Crisis of 1956 see Nina J. Noring, ed., *Foreign Relations of the United States, 1955–1957, Suez Crisis, July 26– December 31, 1956, Volume XVI* (Washington: United States Government Printing Office, 1990). See also Peter L. Hahn, *Caught in the Middle East U.S. Policy toward the Arab-Israeli Conflict, 1945–1961* (Chapel Hill: The University of North Carolina Press, 2006), 223–4.

8 Document 139, Memorandum from the Counselor of the Department of State (MacArthur) to the Acting Secretary of State. Paul Claussen et al., eds., *Foreign Relations of the United States, 1955–1957, Near East Region; Iran; Iraq, Volume XII* (Washington: United States Government Printing Office, 1991).

9 Behcet Kemal Yesilbursa, *Baghdad Pact: Anglo-American Defence Policies in the Middle East, 1950–59* (New York: Routledge, 2005). See also Murat Kasapsaraçoglu, "The Outsider Inside: Turkey and the Domino Effect of Arab Nationalism in 1958" in this volume.

10 For declassified US records on deliberations before and after the Suez Crisis see Paul Claussen et al., *FRUS, Vol. XII, 1955–1957, Near East Region*.

11 Paper Prepared in the Bureau of Near Eastern, South Asian, and African Affairs and the Policy Planning Staff, Washington, December 5, 1956, Department of State, Central Files, 661.80/12-556; Telegram 1007, US Embassy in Baghdad to Department of State, December 6, 1956.
12 Telegrams 1725 and 1843, US Embassy in Egypt to Department of State, November 29 and December 10, 1956.
13 Document 178, Operations Coordinating Board Report and Document 182, Memorandum of a Meeting, White House, Washington, January 1, 1957, Claussen et al., *FRUS, Vol. XII, 1955–1957, Near East Region*. FRUS, Vol. XII.
14 Documents 148, Memorandum From the Acting Secretary of State to the President and 161, Paper Prepared in the Bureau of Near Eastern, South Asian, and African Affairs and the Policy Planning Staff in Claussen et al. *FRUS, Vol. XII, 1955–1957, Near East Region*; Memorandum of a Meeting, White House, Washington, January 1, 1957, Eisenhower Library, Whitman File, Legislative Meetings. Yaqub, *Containing Arab Nationalism*, 54.
15 Yaqub, *Containing Arab Nationalism*, 58.
16 Document 556, Memorandum by the President in Noring, *Foreign Relations of the United States, 1955–1957, Suez Crisis, July 26–December 31, 1956, Volume XVI*. Document 175, Memorandum of a Conference With the President, Washington, December 20, 1956, Claussen et al., *FRUS, Vol. XII, 1955–1957, Near East Region*. FRUS, Vol. XII.
17 Document 574, Memorandum of a Telephone Conversation Between the President and the Acting Secretary of State, Washington, November 13, 1956 in Noring, *FRUS, Vol. XVI, 1955–1957, Suez Crisis*. Document 178, Operations Coordinating Board Report, Claussen et al., *FRUS, Vol. XII, 1955–1957, Near East Region*. FRUS, Vol. XII.
18 Document 183, Editorial Note, Claussen et al., *FRUS, Vol. XII*.
19 Ibid.
20 Document 193, Editorial Note, Claussen et al., *FRUS, Vol. XII, 1955–1957, Near East Region*. FRUS, Vol. XII.
21 Ibid.
22 Telegram from the Embassy in the United Kingdom to the Department of State, London, March 7, 1957, Department of State, Central Files, 611.41/3-757. For a wider discussion of Anglo-American relations and overview of the "Special Relationship" after Suez, see documents on "the Bermuda Conference," particularly "Conference Proceedings" documents 263–84, and "Conference Documents" documents 285–293 in *Foreign Relations of the United States, 1955–1957, Western Europe and Canada*, vol. XXVII (Washington: United States Government Printing Office, 1992).
23 For a wider discussion of events in Algeria see Sylvie Thénault, "How about 1958 in Algeria? A Transnational Event in the Context of the War of Independence," in *The Middle East in 1958: Reimagining A Revolutionary Year*, ed. Jeffrey G. Karam (London: I.B. Tauris, 2020).
24 Memorandum from the Assistant Secretary of State for Near Eastern, South Asian, and African Affairs (Rountree) to the Acting Secretary of State, Washington, April 16, 1957, Department of State, Central Files, 120.1580/5-1057.
25 Memorandum from the Assistant Secretary of State for Near Eastern, South Asian, and African Affairs (Rountree) to the Acting Secretary of State, Washington, April 4, 1957, Department of State, Central Files, 120.1580/5-1057.
26 Peter L. Hahn, "Securing the Middle East: The Eisenhower Doctrine of 1957," *Presidential Studies Quarterly* 36, no. 1 (March 2006): 41.

27 Telegram from the Embassy in Egypt to the Department of State, Cairo, January 10, 1957, Department of State, Central Files, 611.80/1-1057.
28 Telegram from the President's Special Assistant (Richards) to the Department of State, Tripoli, May 4, 1957, Department of State, Central Files, 120.1580/4-1957; Memorandum from the Assistant Secretary of State for Near Eastern, South Asian, and African Affairs (Rountree) to the Acting Secretary of State, Washington, May 8, 1957, Department of State, Central Files, 120.1580/5-1957.
29 For earlier discussions of US and Turkish fears of "a leftist-oriented Syria" and needed steps to rectify the "current situation" (growing leftist and pro-Soviet sentiments) see Instructions from the Department of State to the Embassy in Syria, Washington, September 21, 1956, Department of State, Central Files, 783.00/9-2156.
30 For a wider discussion of events in Jordan see Clea Hupp, "Evolution and Revolution: The Survival of the Jordanian Hashemite Regime in 1958," in *The Middle East in 1958: Reimagining a Revolutionary Year*, ed. Jeffrey G. Karam (London: I.B. Tauris, 2020). See also Clea Lutz Hupp, *The United States and Jordan: Middle East Diplomacy during the Cold War* (London: I.B. Tauris, 2014).
31 Telegram from the Embassy in Jordan to the Department of State, Amman, February 13, 1957, Department of State, Central Files, 685.00/2-1357.
32 Ibid.
33 Telegram from the Department of State to the Embassy in Jordan, Washington, February 6, 1957, Department of State, Central Files, 685.86/2-657; Letter from King Hussein to President Eisenhower, Amman, May 12, 1957, Eisenhower Library, Whitman File, International File. Secret.
34 Telegram from the Joint Chiefs of Staff to Unified and Specified Commanders, Washington, April 24, 1957, National Archives and Records Service, Joint Chiefs of Staff Records, CCS 381 EMMEA 11-19-47, SSC.57.
35 Telegram from the Department of State to the Embassy in Jordan, Washington, April 25, 1957, Department of State, Central Files, 785.00/4-2257.
36 For a wider discussion of events in Lebanon see Caroline Attie, "The Crisis of 1958 in Lebanon: Political Rivalries," in *The Middle East in 1958: Reimagining A Revolutionary Year*, ed. Jeffrey G. Karam (London: I.B. Tauris, 2020). See also Caroline Camille Attié, *Struggle in the Levant: Lebanon in the 1950s* (London; New York, NY: I.B. Tauris in association with the Centre for Lebanese Studies, 2004).
37 Telegram from the Department of State to the Embassy in Lebanon, Washington, February 2, 1957, Department of State, Central Files, 783A.56/1-1857; Memorandum of Conversation, Department of State, Washington, February 5, 1957, Department of State, Central Files, 680.00/2-557.
38 Document 139, Editorial Note in Will Klingman, Aaron D. Miller, and Nina J. Noring, eds., *Foreign Relations of the United States, 1955–1957, Volume XIII, Near East: Jordan-Yemen* (Washington: United States Government Printing Office, 1988).
39 Wilbur Eveland, *Ropes of Sand: America's Failure in the Middle East* (London; New York: W.W. Norton, 1980); Irene L. Gendzier, *Notes from the Minefield: United States Intervention in Lebanon and the Middle East, 1945–1958* (New York: Columbia University Press, 2006).
40 Sami Moubayed, *Syria and the USA: Washington's Relations with Damascus from Wilson to Eisenhower*, Reprint edition (London; New York: I.B. Tauris, 2013), 157.
41 Memorandum from the Assistant Secretary of State for Near Eastern, South Asian, and African Affairs (Rountree) to the Acting Secretary of State, Washington, August

13, 1957, Department of State, Central Files, 783.00/8-1357; Special National Intelligence Estimate No. 36.7-57, Washington, September 3, 1957.
42 David W. Lesch, *Syria and the United States: Eisenhower's Cold War in the Middle East* (Boulder: Westview, 1992), 119, 138–40.
43 Ibid., p. 138.
44 For a wider discussion of events in Syria see Fadi Esber, "No Turning Back: Syria and the 1958 Watershed," in *The Middle East in 1958: Reimagining A Revolutionary Year*, ed. Jeffrey G. Karam (London: I.B. Tauris, 2020); Moubayed, *Syria and the USA*.
45 Memorandum From the Assistant Secretary of State for Near Eastern, South Asian, and African Affairs (Rountree) to the Acting Secretary of State, Washington, August 13, 1957, Department of State, Central Files, 783.00/8-1357.
46 Lesch, *Syria and the United States*, 119–20.
47 Telegram From the Department of State to the Embassy in Saudi Arabia, Washington, August 21,1957, Department of State, Central Files, 683.00/8-2157; Memorandum from the Secretary of State to the President, Washington, August 20, 1957, Eisenhower Library, Whitman File, Dulles-Herter Series.
48 Telegram from the Department of State to the Embassy in Israel, Washington, September 10, 1957, Department of State, Central Files, 783.00/9-1057; Telegram From the Department of State to the Embassy in Turkey, Washington, September 10, 1957, Department of State, S/S Files: Lot 66 D 123.
49 Special National Intelligence Estimate No. 36.7-57, Washington, September 3, 1957; Letter From the Chargé in Syria (Strong) to the Assistant Secretary of State for Near Eastern, South Asian, and African Affairs (Rountree), Damascus, October 16, 1957, Department of State, Central Files, 783.00/10–1657.
50 Despatch No. 18 (Dispatch) from the Embassy in Syria to the Department of State, Damascus, July 15, 1957, Department of State, Central Files, 611.83/1-1557; Despatch No. 43 (Dispatch) from the Embassy in Syria to the Department of State, Damascus, July 29, 1957, Department of State, Central Files, 611.83/7-2957; Special National Intelligence Estimate No. 36.7-57, Washington, September 3, 1957.
51 Memorandum Presented to the National Security Council Planning Board, Washington, November 4, 1957, Department of State, S/P–NSC Files: Lot 61 D 167, NSC 5801 File; Letter From the Acting Assistant Secretary of Defense for International Security Affairs (Irwin) to the Deputy Under Secretary of State for Political Affairs (Murphy), Washington, February 6, 1958, Department of State, Central Files, 785.00/2-658.
52 Telegram From Secretary of State Dulles to the Department of State, Ankara, January 29, 1958, Department of State, Central Files, 396.1–AN/1–2958; Memorandum From Acting Secretary of State Herter to President Eisenhower, Washington, January 30, 1958, Eisenhower Library, Herter Papers, Chronology File.
53 National Intelligence Estimate 36–58, Washington, June 5, 1958, Department of State, INR–NIE Files. Secret.
54 Special National Intelligence Estimate 30-58, Washington, February 20, 1958, Department of State, PPS Files: Lot 67 D 548, Near and Middle East 1958. Secret.
55 For a wider discussion of events in Iraq see Juan Romero, "The Iraqi Revolution of 1958: Its Historic Significance and Relevance for the Present," in *The Middle East in 1958: Reimagining A Revolutionary Year*, ed. Jeffrey G. Karam (London: I.B. Tauris, 2020); Juan Romero, *The Iraqi Revolution of 1958: A Revolutionary Quest for Unity and Security* (Lanham, MD: University Press of America, 2010).

56 Telegram From the Department of State to the Embassy in Jordan, Washington, February 13, 1958, Department of State, Central Files, 685.87/2-1358.
57 Yaqub, *Containing Arab Nationalism*, 193-4.
58 Telegram from the Embassy in Iraq to the Department of State, Baghdad, February 21, 1958, Department of State, Central Files, 786.00/2-2158; Telegram From the Embassy in Jordan to the Department of State, Amman, February 24, 1958, Department of State, Central Files, 786.00/2-2458.
59 Memorandum of Discussion at the 358th Meeting of the National Security Council, Washington, March 13, 1958, Eisenhower Library, Whitman File, NSC Records.
60 Memorandum from the Assistant Secretary of State for Near Eastern, South Asian, and African Affairs (Rountree) to Secretary of State Dulles, Washington, March 24, 1958, Department of State, Central Files, 780.00/3-2458; Memorandum from the Assistant Secretary of State for Near Eastern, South Asian, and African Affairs (Rountree) to Secretary of State Dulles, Washington, April 16, 1958, Department of State, Central Files, 611.80/4-1658.
61 Memorandum from the Assistant Secretary of State for Near Eastern, South Asian, and African Affairs (Rountree) to Secretary of State Dulles, Washington, March 24, 1958, Department of State, Central Files, 780.00/3-2458.
62 Attie, "The Crisis of 1958 in Lebanon: Political Rivalries."
63 Telegram from the Embassy in Lebanon to the Department of State, Beirut, February 21, 1958, Department of State, Central Files, 783A.00/2-2158.
64 Memorandum of a Conversation, White House, Washington, June 15, 1958, Eisenhower Library, Whitman File, Eisenhower Diaries; Memorandum of a Conference With the President, White House, Washington, July 14, 1958, Eisenhower Library, Whitman File, Eisenhower Diaries.
65 Telegram from the Department of State to the Embassy in Lebanon, Washington, February 27, 1958, Department of State, Central Files, 783A.00/2-2158; Telegram from the Embassy in Lebanon to the Department of State, Beirut, March 5, 1958, Department of State, Central Files, 783A.00/3-558.
66 Memorandum of a Conversation between the President and the Secretary of State, Washington, May 2, 1958, Eisenhower Library, Dulles Papers, Meetings with the President; Memorandum of a Conversation, White House, Washington, May 13, 1958, Eisenhower Library, Dulles Papers, Meetings with the President.
67 Fawwaaz Traboulsi, *A History of Modern Lebanon* (London: Pluto, 2007), 134-6.
68 Telegram from the Embassy in Lebanon to the Department of State, Beirut, May 13, 1958, Department of State, Central Files, 783A.00/5-1358.
69 Memorandum of a Conversation, White House, Washington, May 13, 1958, Eisenhower Library, Dulles Papers, Meetings with the President.
70 Special National Intelligence Estimate 36.4-58, Washington, June 5, 1958, Department of State, INR-NIE Files.
71 Memorandum of a Conversation, White House, Washington, May 13, 1958, Eisenhower Library, Dulles Papers, Meetings with the President.
72 Telegram from the Embassy in Jordan to the Department of State, Amman, June 28, 1958, Department of State, Central Files, 785.00/6-2858.
73 Jack O'Connell, *King's Counsel: A Memoir of War, Espionage, and Diplomacy in the Middle East* (New York: W. W. Norton & Co., 2011).
74 Telegram from the Embassy in Jordan to the Department of State, Amman, July 11, 1958, Department of State, Central Files, 785.00/7-1158.

75 Jeffrey G. Karam, "Missing Revolution: The American Intelligence Failure in Iraq, 1958," *Intelligence and National Security* 32, no. 6 (January 8, 2017): 693–709; Romero, *The Iraqi Revolution of 1958*.
76 Karam, "Missing Revolution: The American Intelligence Failure in Iraq, 1958."
77 Hanna Batatu, *The Old Social Classes and the Revolutionary Movements of Iraq: A Study of Iraq's Old Landed and Commercial Classes and of its Communists, Ba'thists, and Free Officers* (Princeton: Princeton University Press, 1978).
78 Karam, "Missing Revolution: The American Intelligence Failure in Iraq, 1958."
79 Memorandum of a Conference With the President, White House, Washington, July 14, 1958, Eisenhower Library, Whitman File, Eisenhower Diaries.
80 Special National Intelligence Estimate 30-3-58, Washington, August 12, 1958, Department of State, INR–NIE Files.
81 Little, *American Orientalism*, 235–7. For a discussion of US decision-making, especially as it relates to the doctrine of "limited wars" and the Vietnam War see Bakich, *Success and Failure in Limited War*; Logevall, *Embers of War*; Logevall and Craig, *America's Cold War*; Carter, *Inventing Vietnam*; Preston, *Pandora's Trap*.
82 John H. Kelly, "Lebanon: 1982–1984," in *U.S. and Russian Policymaking with Respect to the Use of Force*, ed. Jeremy R. Azrael and Emil A. Payin (RAND Corporation, 1996), https://www.rand.org/pubs/conf_proceedings/CF129.html.
83 Ibid. It is also important to mention that the experience of 1958 for many Lebanese, especially Christian Maronites and their allies across other sectarian groups, convinced them of US support and readiness to intervene militarily to assist them at the beginning of the civil war in 1975. For a good discussion of US decision-making and the beginning of the Lebanese Civil War see James R. Stocker, *Spheres of Intervention: US Foreign Policy and the Collapse of Lebanon, 1967–1976* (Ithaca, NY: Cornell University Press, 2016).
84 Memorandum of a Conversation, White House, Washington, June 15, 1958, Eisenhower Library, Whitman File, Eisenhower Diaries; Memorandum of a Conference With the President, White House, Washington, July 14, 1958, Eisenhower Library, Whitman File, Eisenhower Diaries.
85 As mentioned earlier, US involvement in Vietnam occurred much earlier than the manufactured Gulf of Tonkin incident in 1964. Logevall, *Embers of War*; Logevall and Craig, *America's Cold War*; Douglas Little, "His Finest Hour? Eisenhower, Lebanon, and the 1958 Middle East Crisis," *Diplomatic History* 20, no. 1 (January 1, 1996): 53.

Chapter 5

THE "PARTISANS OF PEACE" BETWEEN BAKU AND MOSCOW

THE SOVIET EXPERIENCE OF 1958

Elizabeth Bishop

Twenty years ago, William Roger Louis and Roger Owen co-convened a conference, "The Revolutionary Year," at the University of Texas at Austin, with specialists on different jurisdictions addressing a single moment, and the contributions were published in an edited volume.[1] Our collective project returns to 1958 as "a revolutionary year," drawing primarily but not exclusively on the year's *14 Tammuz* (July) coup in Iraq. This chapter addresses the Soviet Union's role during the period of time leading up to "the revolutionary year" as well as Soviet acts surrounding *14 Tammuz*.

As a general observation, this is relevant because some Soviet-era narratives regarding the Middle East remain in circulation,[2] uniting a set of discussions regarding Moscow's relationship with Arab capitals.[3] Specialists agree on the common threads, including N. S. Khrushchev's responsibility (as general secretary of the Soviet Union's Communist Party) for new policies. While Paul Rivlin acknowledges the Second World War and nationalism exercised an effect on policies in the USSR,[4] Guy Laron contrasts Khrushchev's openness toward countries of the Middle East with the Stalinist "Socialism in One Country."[5] William Ochsenwald and Sydney Nettleton Fisher further classify Khrushchev's policy as "strategic" (to break through American alliances), rather than "ideological"; by implication, foreign policies of his predecessor I. V. Stalin were "ideological" rather than "strategic."[6]

Acknowledging these, the Soviet census following the "revolutionary year" enumerated more than 209 million people, and it's helpful to acknowledge facts anomalous to the "Khrushchev was the USSR" narrative as well. During the Second World War, the USSR's 1936 ("Stalin") constitution established Republic-level commissariats for defense and foreign affairs. Azerbaijan's oil fields had been Nazi Germany's objective during its military campaign, and Azerbaijan's capital, Baku, remained the Soviet Union's fifth most populous city. Fifteen Union Republics— including Azerbaijan—gained sovereign-states status in international law during the war, making Baku a legal equivalent to London, Paris, and Washington, DC.

In Azerbaijan, the Muslim-majority community represents both Sunni and Shi'a in approximately equal numbers. As historian David Motadel points out, Transcaucasia's Shaykh al-Islām Ali Zade was elected during May 1944, pledging allegiance to Stalin (whom he called "God-sent and wise head of the Soviet government").[7] As Ali Zade told a reporter: "I was born in Baku, and received a higher spiritual education in the school at the Tusa mosque [the pride of] the city of Najaf."[8] This chapter addresses Azerbaijani Shi'a Muslims, including Transcaucasia's Shaykh al-Islām Ali Zade, as Soviet citizens.

Of Najaf in Iraq, historian Chibli Mallat identifies the city to be at the center of what he calls a "Shi'i International."[9] In the USSR, the imam enjoyed government support. Performing hajj at the war's end, he arrived in Jeddah with a delegation of religious leaders by air.[10] Leaders of Azerbaijan's *Ahlul Bayt* community then re-established connections with co-religionists outside the USSR when, after the fall of Berlin, Ali Zade's recorded speeches in Persian were broadcast over Iranian national radio.[11] Similar exchanges, established during the war, strengthened Soviet Shi'a Muslims' connection with the Shi'a in Iran, Iraq, and Lebanon.

After the war, USSR urban reconstruction funds went to "Hero Cities" (a bureaucratic designation for a collective Order of Lenin, awarded to thirteen cities). These "Hero Cities" with predominantly Russian-speaking populations had enjoyed a high level of public services before the war; Moscow had a subway system since 1935, Kiev since 1938, and Leningrad since 1941. An Order of Lenin for the "Hero Cities" denied Baku a meaningful portion of reconstruction funds. Without a subway, Baku's residents depended on buses and taxis for daily transportation. On a daily basis, they read the *Bakinskij Rabochij* (*Baku Worker*) newspaper for news from Moscow and from Shi'i communities outside the USSR.

French was regularly taught in Soviet secondary schools (including in Azerbaijan, where most people spoke a Farsi-inflected dialect of Turkish at home) because France's Communist Party had more members than any outside the Eastern Bloc. Like Chibli Mallat's idea of a Shi'i International, global Francophonie connected people living in the USSR (among them, the Azerbaijani Shi'a) with French speakers outside the USSR and the Shi'a homelands. Soviet citizens knew French, as did colonial populations in *les outre-mer,* as well as people in the British Empire. Native speakers of Farsi (such as Mohammad Mossadegh, the lawyer who became Iran's finance minister and prime minister) and of Arabic (such as Taha Hussein, the poet who became Egypt's minister of education) communicated in French.[12]

This chapter documents how information regarding Baghdad's *14 Tammuz* coup arrived in Moscow via the Shi'i International and global Francophonie.[13] In this volume, McNamara proposes a shift toward 1958. If there is a "lesson of 1958," it is that Iraq's coup merely succeeded in removing King Faisal II, his uncle, Crown Prince Abdul Illah, and Hashemite henchman Nuri el-Said.[14] Soviet diplomats, with support from the Shi'i International and global Francophonie, organized a publicity campaign to protect the new government.

Origins

Historians of the 1950s dismiss "peace" as a ploy.[15] "Ostensibly led by prominent scientists and intellectuals,"[16] the World Peace Council was "a Communist front."[17]

In Syria, Partisans were "dedicated to propagating and disseminating pro-Soviet propaganda."[18] In Iraq, they functioned "openly and freely" for the underground Communist Party;[19] in Iran, they emerged after the Tudeh party lost its legal identity.[20] To this, I reply that the origins of the "Peace Partisans" were unofficial, informal, and local. Certainly, during the 1950s, the UK outlawed the Communist Party,[21] as did India,[22] and Jordan.[23] Law no. 51 of Iraq's 1938 penal code specified imprisonment (or a fine) for propagation of "communism, anarchism, or immorality." These laws denied Communist parties the legal identity necessary to open a bank account for party funds, to rent office premises, and so on.

At first, vague opposition to conventional warfare held the Partisans together, as when Polish Communist Jerzy Borejsza's attempt to frame the Eastern Bloc members as supporters of peace (against the West as conventionally armed warmonger). A liaison bureau formed to continue international work.[24] The group held second meetings simultaneously in Paris and, when French authorities threatened to deport activists, in Prague.

Two members of the Shi'i International—Yusuf Ismail (a citizen of Iraq, living in Paris) and Khalid al-Salam (also Iraqi, just beginning university in Paris)— attended the Prague conference. At the same time, a Soviet Peace Committee (SPC, also known as Soviet Committee for the Defense of Peace) (SCDP, in Russian: Sovetskij Komitet Zashhity Mira) formed. Radio Moscow's news service announced this committee to domestic audiences, using Borejsza's vague definition of "peace" introduced in Paris and Prague.[25]

When another Partisans conference was held in Warsaw (1950), Mohammed Mahdi Al-Jawahiri was elected to its World Council. Born in Najaf during the preceding century, trained in Islamic law, al-Jawahiri turned to poetry. Jawahiri's poem "Wings of Peace" served as a catalyst for other Iraqis to form their own Partisans groups.[26] Lutfi Bakr Sedqi's *Al Alam Al Arabi* (*Arab World*) newspaper attracted writers responding to this poem, among them Hussein Marwa, Jassim Mohammed Rajab, and Mohammed Sharara.

Distinguishing their concerns from European activists' loose opposition to conventional warfare, members of the Shi'i International enunciated new goals for Partisans. Al-Jawahiri responded to contemporary affairs in French:

> In the name of war, the imperialists and their agents justify their plans, chaining our country with aggressive blocs serving their expansionist interests and bringing to our beloved homeland nothing but slavery, misery and the destruction; it is in the name of war and for war that Anglo-American imperialists strive to undermine the resistance of peoples and to subject their economies to the demands of rearmament; it is for war that they constantly attack democratic freedoms and popular and patriotic organizations.[27]

"Chaining our country" remained a valid metaphor for a subsequent mutual-defense agreement between Iraq and Turkey (February 1954), with its umbrella clause permitting the UK's later accession to a bilateral agreement. While the poet avoided the specific words *atomique* and *nucleare*, his remaining "aggressive blocks" was a clear reference to Iraq's then-ongoing relationship with the UK. Baghdad residents' *Al-Wathbah* uprising repudiated the Anglo-Iraqi Treaty of January 1948. In short, "peace" emerged as an antinuclear stance as France, the USSR, and the UK emerged as atomic powers.[28]

Meanwhile, Muslim leaders from Soviet Azerbaijan expanded their connections with the "Shi'i international." Originally, Iran's prime minister Qavam es Sultaneh scheduled direct air travel from Tehran to Moscow. Called "the old fox" for his diplomatic skills, Qavam claimed inclement weather forced his delegation to make an unscheduled stay in Baku.[29] Soviet Azerbaijan radio subsequently reported "a very warm welcome to [Qavam] and to members of the Iranian Mission which has seldom been given a foreign delegate. . . . [which] illustrates the affection and sincerity of the great Soviet nation towards the Iranian nation and its representatives."[30] Prime Minister Qavam and his party planned a stop in Soviet Azerbaijan on their return trip.[31]

While historian Jamal Hasanli argues, "Turkey closely watched Qavam's Moscow visit," and Turks assessed the "failure" of the Moscow visit to have indicated "bankruptcy of the Soviet-Iranian talks,"[32] the subsequent success of Qavam's Baku visit merits mention. It was during his term in office—as Roman Krakovsky points out—Turkey's signature to a nuclear-enabled NATO coincided with "a new phase" for the emerging peace movement.[33] Historian John Jenks agrees that "massive destruction and death brought about by the Second World War, and the arrival of the atomic bomb, gave strong incentives to avoid further wars."[34] Popular resistance developed among the "Shi'i international."

Informal Peace Movement

Soviet "Intellectuals for Peace" contributed an editorial to *Pravda* (lit. *Truth*, daily newspaper of the Soviet Union's Communist Party) specifying plans to hold an All-Union congress, to advance *their* "proposal that atomic weapons should be prohibited and made illegal as weapons of mass destruction."[35] Despite the apparent political visibility of the *Pravda* editorial, the National Archives of Azerbaijan's sole surviving "Partisan" document from 1949 is a survey of mosque communities.[36] From surviving broadcast media and archival collections, it seems a "peace campaign" functioned as a continuation of informal wartime collaboration between existing trade union councils, writers' unions, the Pedagogical Academy, the Academy of Sciences, and anti-fascist committees of Soviet Youth and Women, in both Baku and Moscow.

In Moscow, no documents survive from the "Soviet Committee for the Defense of Peace" before 1955. During these early years, Partisans were active in Azerbaijan, and a series of Turkish-language broadcasts updated shortwave listeners as to the anti-Partisan legislation in the US Congress.[37] Archival records in the Republican and All-Union collections suggest "Partisan" and "Peace" activities were decentralized and under-institutionalized.[38]

During March 1950, a World Peace Committee met in Sweden;[39] there, a series of speakers warned of the atomic arms race and condemned weapons of mass destruction.[40] This meeting's "Stockholm resolution" was recognized as "one of the cleverest political documents this century has seen."[41] Its language ("we demand unconditional prohibition of the atomic weapon as a weapon of aggression and mass annihilation of the people, and strict international control for the implementation of this decision be established") was phrased in terms both precise ("unconditional prohibition of the atomic weapon") and vague ("international control"). Cleverly avoiding the legality of colonial rule, the Stockholm resolution called on decolonizing states to renounce their pursuit of this new weapon. Individuals living in British and French colonies and former colonies "signed on to Stockholm" to indicate their support for multilateral nuclear disarmament,

A "Preparatory Committee for Supporters of Peace" formed in Baghdad under Jawahiri's leadership. While representing the Shi'i International, the Partisans included Iraqi and Lebanese citizens of different faiths. Sheikh Abdul Karim al-Mashati extended his support for the Stockholm petition, and its signatories included Abdulwahab Mahmood, artist Youssef Al-Ani, Dr. Abdullah Ismail Al Bustani. Dr. Khaleda Al-Qaisi, journalist Abdul Jabbar Wahbi, lawyers Amer Abdullah and Tawfiq Munir, and poets Bader Shaker Al-Sayyab and Mohammed Saleh Bahr Al-Uloum.[42] In Beirut, poet Kazem al-Samawi, engineer Antoine Thabet (leader of the Lebanese Communist Party) and Dr. George Hanna (representing Lebanon) met to share "peace" publications. In this way, Partisans" were connected to Kazem Dujaili (of Iraq's Federation of Trade Unions), Dr. Safa Al-Hafiz, poet Mohammed Saleh Bahr Al-Uloum, and Dr. Khalil Jameel Al-Jawad (both members of the Iraqi Communist Party).

Moscow Radio's shortwave service reported 500 million signatures to the cleverly phrased Stockholm resolution.[43] People in Sunni Arab communities signed the petition to protest plans for nuclear tests in North Africa. During the six-month period after Stockholm, Algerian Partisans collected 266,000 signatures calling for France to renounce nuclear weapons; Moroccan Partisans, 19,581; and Egyptian Partisans, 12,000. Sunni and Shi'i Muslims alike signed the petition against NATO atomic weapons at military bases in Turkey and Iran.[44]

In the USSR, passage of the *Zakon o zashchite mira* ("in defense of peace") law during 1951 remains a sole piece of evidence indicating Soviet support for a peace movement at this early date. This was so broadly written as to be virtually meaningless in the context of Soviet domestic politics; rather, the law brought together a loosely gathered coalition of activists developing their own international connections. Held in Vienna, a World Peace Congress convened the same year.[45]

Together, the Stockholm resolution, Soviet law, and the Vienna congress resolution established terms for a new semantic field. "Peace" was equivalent to the UN Charter, and "democratic forces" in support of it, opposing "defense of peace" to "atomic bombs," with nuclear radiation threatening human health, and multilateral agreements facilitating proliferation. With the 1951 law, Soviet Partisans gained a downtown Moscow office, a seal signifying official status, and letterhead stationery, and at the same time as Turkey joined NATO.[46]

In Baghdad, semantic tension opposed law-abiding citizens to diplomats at the US Embassy. To the embassy staff, items in the window of the USIS library were innocuous: "there is, for example, an electric light burning with the notation that so much atomic stuff will cause it to burn for an astronomical number of years, also the size of a pound of uranium illustrated by a block of wood." Editors of the *Al Alam Al Arabi* newspaper further confused American diplomats. The editorial listed threatening items from the window display: a mushroom cloud explosion, a squadron of bomber aircraft, and field artillery in action. Querying, "What kind of service is the atom rendering to humanity?" *Alam Al Arabi* editors enjoined fellow citizens not to "pay any attention to such harmful propaganda."[47] Americans didn't understand why an unidentified person pasted a paper note to the USIS library window, "we want the destruction of atomic and germ warfare," signed "Partisans of Peace."

In the USSR, a *Bakinskij Rabochij* cartoon shows how the Anglo-American relationship was understood among the Shi'i International. In this, a hefty American GI rested his ample rear on a wooden crate marked "Atom Bombs" (in Russian) and "Made in USA" (in English). This wood crate pins John Bull—with lion claws, side whiskers, and top hat, yet a desiccated, patched, and moth-eaten rug—to the floor.[48] Local intellectuals of the Shi'i International demonstrated a sophisticated appreciation for international affairs, evident in this Russian cartoon in the intersection between Arabic, Azerbaijani Turkish, and English.

Azerbaijan's neighbors Iran and Turkey joined Iraq and the UK, expanding what had been a bilateral defense agreement into a collective security agreement, the cartoon's lower caption serves as a humorously rhetorical question posed to John Bull, "Where could they possibly be misplaced, these atomic bombs?" This new Baghdad Pact gave U-2 planes access to bases in Pakistan, and to fly over the USSR.[49]

"Revolutionary Year" among Peace Partisans

English-language documents dating from the Cold War dismiss the Partisans as a "front organization," hiding Communist parties.[50] This point of interpretation is well established, and even present in the archival evidence; it appears among British imperialism's documents, as well as those of the UK's allies. Description of the Partisans as a "front organization" appears in Foreign Office file 1110/609 (1953), and FO 371/110992 (1954). Deep within the documents of the Iraq Petroleum Company, Ian G. MacPherson called Partisans a "communist-front organization,"[51] as did the British-edited *Iraq Times*.[52] This equation—between Partisans and Communist parties—reappears in the records of the US executive branch,[53] and, later, in the legislative branch as well.[54]

In Azerbaijan (where a Communist party required no "front" organization), Partisans had access to government media. In Baku, the *TASS (Telgrafnoye agentstvo Sovetskogo Soyuza*, Telegraph Agency of the Soviet Union) broadcast a diplomatic note about the Soviet people's solidarity and sympathy with Europeans alarmed by American bombers carrying atomic and hydrogen bombs over NATO member countries.[55] The Italian delegation of Partisans and the Soviet committee were in full communication.[56] Radio Moscow reported on French citizens' pressure on the National Assembly, forcing a referendum on the deployment of atomic weapons.[57]

Leaders in the Gray Zone

Partisans of the Shi'i International were more prominent, more numerous, and better-funded Communist parties and Soviet diplomats. Through signature campaigns and local organizations, Partisans of different jurisdictions prepared for the events of 1958.[58] Posed against them was the diplomat representing Iraq on the UN Security Council, Abdul Majid Abbas. When a Hashemite Arab Union united Iraq and Jordan, Abdul Majid Abbas represented that as well.[59]

Article 51 of the Arab Union's new constitution had empowered the union's head by appointing diplomatic representatives, and rule 15 of the UN Security Council's provisional rules of procedure required any reappointment to be routed through the secretary general. The year of the Arab Union, the USSR conducted thirty-six nuclear tests. Recently re-established as one of the USSR's most prestigious awards, the "revolutionary year's" Lenin Prize was awarded *both* to the I. V. Kurchatov Institute of Atomic Energy, responsible for atomic and hydrogen weapons in the USSR,[60] *and* Louis Aragon, who dedicated his Prize to Peace Partisans.[61]

Diplomacy among the Shi'i

In her review of Louis and Owen's edited volume, *A Revolutionary Year*, Amy Zalman asked: "To what extent were the troubles in Lebanon and the *coup d'état* in Iraq externally inspired?"[62] Certainly, Partisans played a role in Baghdad events of July 14, 1958. Coup planners liberated political prisoners from Baquba early that morning;[63] and British diplomats later reported a crowd "being addressed by a speaker on some kind of raised platform."[64] Even though Soviet deputy premier (and Baku native) Anastas Mikoyan declined to comment on initial reports from Iraq, the USSR, too, played a role in the revolutionary events of July 14, 1958,[65] as the Partisans conveyed information about the *14 Tammuz* coup in Baghdad to Moscow.[66]

That Monday evening, Cairo's Voice of the Arabs shortwave radio station was the first government news media to announce recognition of a new Republic of Iraq at 8:00 p.m. In Iraq, the Communist Party's central committee pledged its allegiance to the new government, "for the sake of an honorable, free, democratic life for the Iraqi people and for the sake of Arab unity, *peace*, and progress,"[67] and Radio Bagdad promised the new government would "adhere to its former political and economic undertakings and will endeavor to promote them *by peaceful means*."[68] The Partisans organized a multinational campaign to recognize the "rebel government in Iraq," granting it (and its domestic allies) diplomatic recognition.

When Iraq's new cabinet met on Tuesday, the coup's ministers sent a cable recalling Abdul Majid Abbas from the UN, appointing Hashim Jawad in his place. The telegram failed to meet the requirement for communications by "letter, duly signed" and until such a letter reached New York, the new government's fate hung in the balance. Soviet diplomats raced against time to out-maneuver the Hashemites in Amman, coordinating an effort among allied political movements and states to recognize the new Republic. Both *Pravda* and *Izvestia* published the army's "communiqué no. 1," as the *Literaturnaia Gazeta* (*Literary Newspaper*) announced "The End of Iraq's Black Regime."[69] Wednesday, centers of Partisan activity around the world stepped into this gap in parliamentary requirements. First, the Soviet Union and Yemen announced diplomatic recognition of the new government in Baghdad over Radio Moscow.[70] TASS broadcast the French Communist Party's statement recognizing "the rights of Iraq and Lebanese peoples."

As the UN awaited a "letter, duly signed" from Baghdad, a cable reached the Secretariat from Amman, stating,

> Representation of the state of Iraq in the Security Council or in any other United Nations body must be authorized by His Majesty [King Hussein in his capacity as head of the Arab Union] and any persons purporting to represent rebel government in Iraq have not any constitutional basis to do so and that any credentials they may present to your Excellency from rebel government in Baghdad are not legally valid.[71]

As the cable, too, failed to meet the requirement for communications by "letter, duly signed," editors of *Izvestiya* and *Pravda* placed a "Statement of the Government, In Connection with Events in the Near and Middle East" on its front page, with *Pravda* adding Khrushchev's greeting to "His Excellency Mr. Abdel Karim Qassim, Prime Minister of Iraq" and *Izvestiya* reporting from the UN Security Council. A series of independent declarations of diplomatic recognition served to stall any external move to gain control of Arab Union representation at the UN.

Two days after the coup, North Korea extended diplomatic recognition to the new government in Baghdad, broadcasting over its national radio's domestic service; Bulgaria's followed; then East Germany's. North Vietnam—invoking the name of the standing secretariat of the Afro-Asian People's Solidarity Organization—extended its recognition the following morning.

Friday, UN secretary Hammarskjold convened a second meeting, to report that he had received a "letter, duly signed" from the Republic of Iraq. Dated three days previously, it had reached him on Thursday. He thereby transferred Abbas's credentials to Hashim Jawad. The Republic of Iraq's new ambassador flew to New York where he told reporters: "Our main interest is to establish a good welfare state." Had Baku received funding for a subway, global coordination between antinuclear activists of many faith communities and the Soviet Union's Ministry of Foreign Affairs might not have recognized the 1958 coup in a timely manner.

Conclusion

While N. S. Khrushchev (as general secretary of the Soviet Union's Communist Party) is held responsible for new directions of Soviet policy in the Middle East, and while Paul Rivlin acknowledges the significance of "nationalism," and while Guy Laron considers the USSR's Communist Party's openness toward the Middle East, the substance of this strategic direction became clear during the "revolutionary year" of 1958. Azerbaijan, which had enjoyed something akin to a sovereign-nation status during the Second World War, was denied reconstruction funds after the war. During the war, Azerbaijani Muslims' spiritual leaders re-established diplomatic relations with co-religionists in neighboring jurisdictions, building on secular communications within global Francophonie.

Information transmitted through these networks and in this language addressed the nature of "Peace," and influenced the direction of a new nongovernmental organization, the Peace Partisans, from conventional warfare toward opposition to nuclear-enabled regional alliances. This was particularly the case for Iraq; when its Shi'i and Sunni citizens refused bilateral agreements with the UK, its legislators were tricked into a multilateral "Baghdad Pact," and then a parliamentary union with the Hashemite Kingdom of Jordan. While at first this peace movement was loosely organized in Moscow, the activities of Azerbaijani Partisans gave the organization direction.

The success of the "Stockholm resolution" in the Arab and Islamic world justified greater organization within the USSR. Partisan-based communication networks were pressed into service the day of the July *14 Tammuz coup*, when international coordination was needed to stall Jordan's Hashemite monarchy's claims to represent Iraq at the UN. While Egypt's Voice of the Arabs was the first to announce recognition of Iraq's new Republic, a series of Soviet-connected entities (North Korea, Bulgaria, East Germany, North Vietnam, and the Afro-Asian People's Solidarity Organization) acknowledged the coup d'état, while diplomats raced to secure its recognition at the UN in New York.

Notes

1 William Roger Louis and Roger Owen, *A Revolutionary Year: The Middle East in 1958* (New York, NY: I.B. Tauris, 2002).
2 Elizabeth Bishop, review of Alexei Mikhailovich Vasiliev, *Russia's Middle East Policy: From Lenin to Putin*. In *Cairo Review of Global Affairs* (Fall 2018).
3 I'm grateful to Malouka Arabi (Université Hassiba Benbouali de Chlef), Shannon Duffy (Texas State University, San Marcos), Jeffrey G. Karam (Lebanese American University and Belfer Center for Science and International Affairs), Nabil Al Tikriti (University of Mary Washington), and Salim Yaqub (University of California, Santa Barbara), as well as participants in "The Middle East in 1958" workshop at the American University in Beirut, for helpful comments. Any remaining errors are of course my own.

4. Paul Rivlin, *L'Économie Russe et. Exportations d'Armes au Moyen-Orient*. Mémorandum n 79. Centre Jaffee d'études stratégiques (November 2005), 15.
5. Guy Laron, "Cutting the Gordian Knot: The Post WWII Egyptian Quest for Arms and the 1955 Czech Arms Deal," *Cold War International History Project*, working paper #55 (Washington DC: The Woodrow Wilson International Center for Scholars, February 2007), 6.
6. William Ochsenwald and Sydney Nettleton Fisher, *Le Moyen-Orient: Une Histoire* (Boston MA: McGraw Hill Humanities, 2010), 720.
7. David Motadel, *Islam and Nazi Germany's War* (Cambridge MA: Harvard University Press, 2014), 175.
8. The National Archives of the Republic of Azerbaijan, in Azerbaijani, *Azərbaycan Respublikasının Milli Arxiv İdarəsi* (hereafter *Milli Arxiv İdarəsi*), fond 3188, opis 1, delo 38.
9. Chibli Mallat, *The Renewal of Islamic Law: Muhammad Baqer as-Sadr, Najaf and the Shi'i International* (Cambridge UK: Cambridge University Press, 1993).
10. *Milli Arxiv İdarəsi, f.* 3188, *op.* 1, *dd.* 15, 17.
11. *Milli Arxiv İdarəsi, f.* 3188, *op.* 1, *d.* 15, see also Elizabeth Bishop, "'Lofty and Precipitous Chains,' The Roles of the Zagros Mountain Region during the Cold War," *Tunisian-Mediterranean Review of Historical, Social and Economic Studies* (Béja, Tunisia) (May 2013), 27–67.
12. See Sofia Papastamkou "France and the Middle East in 1958: Continuity and Change Through Crisis" in this volume.
13. Elizabeth Bishop, "American Atomic Policy and Hashemite Iraq, 1954–1958," in *US Foreign Policy in the Middle East: From American Missionaries to the Islamic State*, ed. Tugrul Keskin and Geoffrey Gresh (London: Taylor & Francis, 2018).
14. Elizabeth Bishop, "'Day-to-Day Politics': Iraq's Development between Bilateral and International Organizations," *Studia Europaea* 2 (2013): 5–21.
15. Geoff Simons, *Iraq: From Sumer to Saddam* (New York NY: Palgrave Macmillan, 1996); Stephen C. Pelletière, *Losing Iraq: Insurgency and Politics* (New York, NY: Praeger Security International, 2007); Julia C. Strauss, *Staging Politics: Power and Performance in Asia and Africa* (London: I.B. Tauris, 2007).
16. Tony Judt, *Postwar: A History of Europe since 1945* (New York NY: Penguin, 2005).
17. Patrick Iber, *Neither Peace Nor Freedom: The Cultural Cold War in Latin America* (Cambridge, MA: Harvard University Press, 2015).
18. Rami Ginat, *Egypt's Incomplete Revolution: Lutfi al-Khuli and Nasser's Socialism in the 1960s* (London: F. Cass, 1997/2013).
19. Tareq Y. Ismael, *The Rise and Fall of the Communist Party of Iraq* (Cambridge, UK: Cambridge University Press, 2008).
20. Tomas B. Phillips, *Queer Sinister Things: The Hidden History of Iran* (London: Lulu, 2012).
21. Tony Shaw, *British Cinema and the Cold War: The State, Propaganda and Consensus* (London: I.B. Tauris, 2006), 13.
22. K. D. Gaur, *Textbook on the Indian Penal Code* (New Delhi: Universal Law Publishing, 1988), 212.
23. Robert B. Satloff, *From Abdullah to Hussein: Jordan in Transition* (Oxford, UK: Oxford University Press, 1994), 77.
24. Donald McLachlan, "The Partisans of Peace," *International Affairs* 27, no. 1 (1951): 10–11.
25. "All-Union Peace Conference Planned," FBIS-FRB-49-130, July 7, 1949.

26 Mohammed Shafi Agwani, *Communism in the Arab East* (Calcutta, India: Asia Publishers, 1969); Robin Ostle, *Sensibilities of the Islamic Mediterranean: Self-expression in a Muslim Culture from Post-classical Times to the Present Day* (London: I.B. Tauris, 2008).
27 "Mohamed Medhi Al-Jawahiri," *Revue Mondiale de la Partisans de la Paix* 14 (1950): 14.
28 Elizabeth Bishop, "'Atoms for Peace': Hashemite Iraq and the Baghdad Pact during the Cold War," in *War and Geography; The Spatiality of Organized Mass Violence*, ed. Frank Jacob and Sarah Danielsson (Paderborn, Germany: Ferdinand Schöningh, 2017), 263–96.
29 "Iranian Moscow Mission Stops at Baku," FBIS-FRB-46-035.
30 "Iranian Papers Praise Soviet Cordiality," FBIS-FRB-46-040.
31 "Qavam to Stop at Baku on Way Home," FBIS-FRB-46-045.
32 Jamil Hasanli, *Stalin and the Turkish Crisis of the Cold War, 1945–1953* (Lanham, MD: Lexington Books, 2011), 183.
33 Roman Krakovsky, "The Peace and the War Camps. The Dichotomous Cold War Culture in Czechoslovakia: 1948–1960," in *Cold War Cultures: Perspectives on Eastern and Western European Societies*, ed. Annette Vowinckel, Marcus M. Payk, and Thomas Lindenberger (London: Berghahn Books, 2012), 217.
34 John Jenks, "Fight against Peace? Britain and the Partisans of Peace, 1948–1951," in *Cold War Britain: 1945–1964*, ed. M. F. Hopkins (London: Palgrave Macmillan, 2003), 55.
35 "For Peace—Against the Instigators of War," FBIS-FRB-49-165, August 26, 1949.
36 *Milli Arxiv İdarəsi, f.* 3188, *op.* 1, *d.* 8, "Servitors of religious cults."
37 "Imperialists Launch 'Peace' Campaign," FBIS-FRB-50-114, June 12, 1950.
38 State Archive of the Russian Federation, in Russian, *Gosudarstvennyj arhiv Rossijskoj Federacii* (hereafter, *GARF*), *f.* R-9518, *op.* 2, *d.* 96; *f.* R-9576, *op.* 12, d. 10; also see Russian State Archive of Contemporary History, in Russian, *Rossijskij gosudarstvennyj arhiv novejshej istorii* (hereafter, *RGANI*), *f.* 5, *op.* 28, *dd.* 96, 449.
39 "Swedes Cool to Parley," *New York Times*, March 18, 1950.
40 "Communists: Isn't It Clear?" *Time*, July 24, 1950.
41 McLachlan, "Partisans," 12.
42 http://www.almadasupplements.com/news.php?action=view&id=14425.
43 "July Stockholm Congress to Boost Peace," FBIS-FRB-58-100, May 14, 1958.
44 Elizabeth Bishop, "'Lofty and Precipitous Chains,' The Roles of the Zagros Mountain Region during the Cold War," *Tunisian-Mediterranean Review of Historical, Social and Economic Studies* (Béja, Tunisia) (May 2013), 27–67; see also Samia Henni, "*Empreintes toxiques de Bleu, Blanc, Rouge—Les bombes nucléaires françaises en Algériem*" *Funambulist* (December 2017); Murat Kasapsaraçoglu. "The Outsider Inside: Turkey and the Domino Effect of Arab Nationalism in 1958" in this volume; and Sylvie Thénault, "How about Algeria in 1958?: A Transnational Event in the Context of the War of Independence" in this volume as well.
45 US House of Representatives, *Report on the Communist "Peace" Offensive; A Campaign to Disarm and Defeat the United States*, 1951; 165, 114.
46 Hasanli, *Stalin and the Turkish Crisis*, 265; see Dina Rezk, "Egypt's Revolutionary Year: Regime Consolidation at Home, Pragmatism Abroad, and Neutralism in the Cold War" in this volume.
47 US National Archives, Record Group 59. Records of the Department of State. Decimal Files, 1950–1954. United States Embassy, Iraq Dispatch from Burton Berry to the Department of State. "Partisans of Peace Object to Atomic Display," October 18, 1952.

48. *Bakinskii Rabochii*, December 26, 1954.
49. Elizabeth Bishop, "'Dogs of Wall Street, Let Us Alone'; Graffiti in Cold War Baghdad, 1953," in *Making of Arab Spring: Assessing Role of Civil Society through Cases of Innovative Activism*, ed. Cenap Çakmak (London: Palgrave Macmillan, 2016), 17–33.
50. Matthew Elliot, *"Independent Iraq": The Monarchy and British Influence, 1941–1958* (London: I.B. Tauris, 1996), Ismael, *Rise and Fall*, 79; Walter Laqueur, *Communism and Nationalism in the Middle East* (London: Routledge & Paul, 1956).
51. BP Archive, ArcRef: 242183, barcode Z01603936; "Ian McPherson," *The Telegraph*, January 12, 2011.
52. "Communists Led," *Iraq Times*, February 1, 1954; "Peace Partisans Arrested by Police," *Iraq Times*, May 7, 1954.
53. US National Archives, General Records of the Department of State, 1950–1954, central decimal file, box no. 6121, file 987.61/1-3153 et al.
54. US House of Representatives, *Strategy and tactics of world communism*, 1955, 863.
55. "Text of Bulganin Note to Macmillan," FBIS-FRB-58-007, January 10, 1958.
56. "Italy's Inclusion in 'Atom Zone' Urged," FBIS-FRB-58-009, January 11, 1958.
57. "French Protests," FBIS-FRB-58-041, February 21, 1958.
58. Juan Romero, "The Iraqi Revolution of 1958: Its Historic Significance and Relevance for the Present" in this volume.
59. UN Archives and Records Management Service, box S-0189-0002-01, May 18, 1958.
60. Arkadii Kruglov, *The History of the Soviet Atomic Industry* (New York, NY: Taylor and Francis, 2002), 24.
61. "Lenin Award Winner Aragon," FBIS-FRB-58-986, April 28, 1958.
62. Amy Zalman, review of *A Revolutionary Year*. Arab Studies Journal, 11/12, 2/1 (Fall 2003/Spring 2004).
63. Gerald de Gaury, *Three Kings in Baghdad: The Tragedy of Iraq's Monarchy* (London: Hutchinson, 1961), 190.
64. United Kingdom National Archives, FO 371/134199. Events of Monday, July 14, 1958: British Embassy Staff Report, Baghdad, July 27, 1958. Printed in *Records of Iraq, 1914–1966*, volume 12, 2001, 261.
65. Elizabeth Bishop, "The Local and the Global: The Iraqi Revolution of 1958 Between Western and Soviet Modernities," *Ab Imperio* 4 (Kazan, Russia) (December 2011): 172–202.
66. Abd al'-Aziz Nur, "Revoljucija v Irake," *Sovremennyj Vostok* (October 1958): 34.
67. Ismael, *Rise and Fall*, 79; Fukuyama, Francis, *The Soviet Union and Iraq since 1968* (United States Air Force N-1524-AF. July, 1980), 23 (emphasis mine).
68. "Foreign Policy Reviewed," FBIS-FRB-58-136, July 15, 1958; emphasis added.
69. Directly above, "The Atomic Bomb and Neutrality" on the printed page.
70. "USSR, Yemen recognize Iraqi Republic," FBIS-FRB-58-138, July 16, 1958.
71. UN Archives and Records Management Service, box S-0189-0002-01, July 18, 1958.

Part 2

Rivalry and Alliances between Arab and Non-Arab States

Regionalizing Dynamics of the Cold War

Chapter 6

SAUDI ARABIA IN THE CRUCIBLE OF 1958

Nathan J. Citino

In 1958, the kingdom of Saudi Arabia faced a combined domestic and regional crisis. This crisis represented the greatest threat to the Saudi ruling dynasty since the death of its founder, 'Abd al-'Aziz ibn Saud, five years earlier. On the most basic level, it involved a political struggle between 'Abd al-'Aziz's sons King Saud and Crown Prince Faysal. But Saud and Faysal contended for power at a time when revolutionary Arab nationalism, and the influence of Egyptian president Gamal Abdel Nasser, mobilized popular support across the Arab region.

As Juan Romero and Clea Hupp explain elsewhere in this volume, the revolutionary movements of 1958 extinguished one branch of the rival Hashemite dynasty in Iraq and threatened to bring down another in Jordan. Revolutionary and leftist movements also organized in Saudi Arabia. Unlike in Iraq, however, they did not reach beyond a relatively narrow base of support, nor did they achieve the strength needed to overthrow the Saudi dynasty. Rather, revolutionary nationalism inspired dissidents within the ruling family, government officials, and labor leaders in the oil sector. These groups demanded reforms including radical measures to establish a constitutional monarchy and protect individual rights. They also sought a diminished role for the US military and the Arabian American Oil Company (Aramco). Political dissent intensified with the succession struggle, but ultimately Faysal, backed by the United States, defeated even modest political reforms and asserted his claim to legitimacy as a "modernizer." Precipitated by revolutionary nationalism, the crisis and its counter-revolutionary resolution established the basis for the kingdom's governing institutions, foreclosed political alternatives, and introduced discourses of religious legitimacy that carried important implications for the future. It is therefore not much of an exaggeration to interpret the 1958 crisis as the crucible that forged modern Saudi Arabia.

Reexamining the 1958 crisis using primary and secondary materials, including neglected Arabic sources, not only offers the opportunity for a fuller understanding of one especially pivotal year in Saudi history. Such a reexamination also places that history in an Arab regional setting and injects contingency into Saudi historiography, which has too often been characterized by determinism centering on personalities such as 'Abd al-'Aziz and religious essentialism associated with "Wahhabi" Islam. For instance, some accounts portray the kingdom principally as the heroic achievement of its founder or as the product of reforms enacted by Faysal.[1] Debates about this era in Saudi history are often narrowly framed between accounts that praise Faysal and those that seek to rehabilitate Saud.[2] Following 9/11, in the context of "the war on terror," analysts produced polemics and counter-polemics.[3] Yet Faysal initially wrested power from King Saud in March 1958 following the publication of an alleged plot by the king to have Nasser killed and as part of a political struggle in which junior princes and nonroyal dissidents held the balance of power. Recent scholarship by Madawi al-Rasheed, Robert Vitalis, and Toby Craig Jones has reexamined Saudi history in the contexts of social change, global capitalism, and technological development.[4] Through interviews and extensive research conducted in the kingdom, Rosie Bsheer has recovered the buried history of the Saudi Arabian Left.[5] This chapter draws from these accounts and my own published work. It also incorporates select primary materials into a reinterpretation of the 1958 crisis. By focusing on neglected dissident sources in Arabic, I emphasize the Arab nationalist opposition to Saudi rule that existed in 1958. This emphasis highlights the political alternatives that critics of the ruling family articulated then and enriches our understanding of that year's events beyond the Cain-and-Abel story of rival Saudi heirs. My reinterpretation considers the possibilities for reforming Saudi Arabia created by a revolutionary year in the Middle East. "Multiple futures were possible at the time," writes Bsheer, "contrary to what the historiography would have us believe."[6] The chapter concludes by considering how the crisis influenced subsequent religious discourses. Such discourses evolved in a transnational context that reveals how dissent against the ruling family, in both its Arab nationalist and its Islamist forms, transcended the borders of the kingdom itself.

To the March Crisis

The March 1958 crisis is best understood as the culmination of three, interrelated domestic and regional challenges facing the Saudi kingdom since the end of the Second World War. The first of these challenges concerned Saudi Arabia's role in what scholars have called the "postwar petroleum order."[7] This phrase refers to the set of political and economic relationships, as well as the physical infrastructure, by which petroleum from the Gulf was produced, transported, and sold by major Western oil companies to markets in Europe and beyond. The postwar petroleum order represented a new historical phase in the integration of the Middle East region into the global economy. For Saudi Arabia, it involved a politically fraught relationship with Aramco, the consortium of major US companies that developed the oil fields of the kingdom's Eastern Province. In order to extract oil resources, Aramco built workers' communities and infrastructure and played an important role in the kingdom's finances, advancing the Saudi government monies against future royalties as a lender of last resort. The government contended with Aramco over royalties and other payments, as well as over the treatment of workers and the company's investments in the kingdom. King Saud even attempted unsuccessfully to establish a shipping company to transport the country's oil exports, through an aborted deal with Greek magnate Aristotle Onassis, which would have operated outside of Aramco's control.[8] The postwar petroleum order structured Saudi Arabia's relationships not only with Aramco but also with other Arab states and major Western powers. The export of Saudi oil depended on agreements with transit states whose territory was crossed by Tapline, the pipeline administered by a sister company of Aramco, including Jordan, Syria, and Lebanon, and with Egypt, which controlled the Suez Canal that served as the major tanker route to Europe.[9] Since the end of the war, the United States had maintained an airbase at Dhahran near Aramco's facilities to provide security. The United States also subsidized Aramco, and therefore the Saudi government, through its tax policies and loans provided to finance projects needed by the company. As the result of its integration into the postwar petroleum order, Saudi Arabia earned oil revenues of $236 million in 1953, the year of 'Abd al-'Aziz's death and his succession as king by Saud.[10]

The second challenge came in the form of revolutionary Arab nationalism and its association with Nasser, who had emerged as the Egyptian leader following the 1952 Free Officers' coup. For about a decade following the war, Saudi and Egyptian foreign policies were strategically aligned against Britain and its allies, the Hashemite monarchies in Iraq and Jordan. Concerned over historic Hashemite claims to the Hijaz and the British threat to the Buraymi oasis on the kingdom's contested eastern frontier, 'Abd al-'Aziz had complained about "Anglo-Hashemite encirclement" of Saudi Arabia.[11] When Britain and the United States sponsored a "northern tier" anti-Communist alliance based on Iraq and known as the Baghdad Pact, Saudi Arabia and Egypt responded by pledging support for a federal union together with Syria. But the Saudi leadership, including both Saud and Faysal, recognized that Nasser's growing popularity and the rise of revolutionary nationalism threatened the ruling family. As Nasser became the leader of Arab resistance against Israel, accepted Soviet aid, and promoted Cold War nonalignment, Saudi Arabia's dependence on the United States increasingly seemed to constitute a neocolonial relationship based on Aramco's pervasive role in the kingdom. In 1955, Saudi military officers who had been trained in Egypt attempted to organize a coup against the ruling family.[12] The following year, Nasser's visit to the oil city of Dammam attracted enthusiastic crowds that served to underscore his popularity among Aramco's Arab workers.[13] When Britain, France, and Israel invaded Egypt during the 1956 Suez Crisis, Saud pledged his support for Nasser. During the war, however, Nasser scuttled ships to block the canal. Its closure depressed Saudi oil revenues, which dropped from $340 million in 1954 to $290 million in 1956 at a time when the kingdom owed hundreds of millions of dollars in debts.[14] By disrupting the postwar petroleum order, Nasser presented Saudi Arabia with an economic as well as a political threat.

The third challenge involved establishing a stable government structure and succession mechanism for the kingdom to ensure the continuity of Saudi family rule beyond the life of its founder. In a "now legendary scene," wrote Gary S.

Samore, 'Abd al-'Aziz on his deathbed had reportedly made Saud and Faysal "vow not to quarrel after his death" and established the succession principle of the "eldest able" heir.[15] A Council of Ministers formed prior to 'Abd al-'Aziz's death offered a basis for power sharing between King Saud and Crown Prince Faysal, who became the prime minister in August 1954.[16] But several factors caused a breakdown in this arrangement. The kingdom's debts forced Saud to cut imports and royal family stipends, which alienated younger princes and provided an opportunity for Faysal to attract political supporters. The king eventually submitted to austerity measures imposed by the International Monetary Fund after Aramco refused to advance the government additional monies following the Suez Crisis.[17] Saud also appointed ministers personally loyal to him and promoted his own sons within the kingdom's military and government structure, raising concerns that he planned to preempt Faysal's succession.[18]

But the most serious differences arose over how to address the challenges posed by revolutionary nationalism. Within Aramco's labor force, nationalism had fueled strikes against the company in 1953 and in 1956. Government ministers and Aramco employees who participated, such as 'Abd al-'Aziz ibn Mu'ammar, employed in the Finance Ministry's Labor Office in Dammam, and Nasser al-Sa'id, who sought to represent Aramco workers through the Federation of Arab Trade Unions, criticized Saudi Arabia's close ties to the United States and Aramco and demanded constitutional reforms.[19] After Suez, Saud drew closer to the United States by accepting an invitation to Washington to meet President Dwight Eisenhower and by appearing to endorse the Eisenhower Doctrine. Eisenhower pledged to support Middle Eastern states that were resisting "International Communism," and sought to build up Saud as an alternative regional leader to Nasser on the basis of the king's religious role as the guardian of the holy cities of Islam.[20]

Saud tried to use US support, in the form of weapons, aid, and a renewal of the lease agreement for the Dhahran airbase, to overcome Faysal's challenge to his authority. Saud even adapted religious themes to cultivate his own nationalist credentials—for instance, by proclaiming that Israel's access to the Gulf of Aqaba threatened maritime routes to the Hijaz and therefore the safety of the Muslim pilgrimage.[21] He also pursued a rapprochement with the Hashemite monarchies in Jordan and Iraq, vilified by Nasser's propaganda and by many nationalists as Anglo-American clients.[22] Although Faysal recognized the dangers of Arab nationalism for the ruling family, he maintained a more cooperative approach to Nasser and a less deferential attitude toward the United States. This proved to be the more realistic policy after the exposure of an unsuccessful US covert operation to overthrow Syria's government.[23] Nasser landed Egyptian troops at the Syrian port of Latakia, upstaging Saud and confirming Nasser's unassailable position as Arab leader. By this time, Faysal had already left the kingdom on an extended absence for medical treatment beginning in June 1957.[24] In September, he visited with Eisenhower and US officials in Washington. Faysal spent January 1958 in Cairo, meeting with Nasser who was in the process of negotiating a political union between Egypt and Syria.[25]

The Fire beneath the Ashes

Faysal's return to the kingdom in February heralded a major crisis for Saud. A new budget published in the newspaper *al-Bilad al-Saudiyya* revealed the extent of Saud's austerity, alienating junior princes and those who profited from the import trade. On February 1, Nasser proclaimed the establishment of the United Arab Republic (UAR) with Syria, which Saud had strenuously opposed. In response, Jordan and Iraq announced plans for a union of their own.[26] Saud therefore faced a choice between joining his Hashemite rivals, including the Baghdad Pact member Iraq, or accepting Saudi Arabia's isolation between the two Arab unions. Then, in a speech given on March 5, Nasser revealed that he had foiled a plot in which his military intelligence chief in Syria, Colonel 'Abd al-Hamid al-Sarraj, had been offered bribes to support the "overthrow [*inqilab*]" of the government and to disrupt Arab unity. Although Nasser did not mention Saud by name, his reference to "oil money [*fulus al-bitrol*]" left little doubt as to the source of the bribes.[27] Nasser had already withdrawn Egypt's military mission to the Saudi kingdom. More specific accusations against Saud followed from al-Sarraj himself and in articles published by the Cairo daily *al-Ahram* and the Damascus newspaper *al-Nasr*. These accounts charged Saud with using his Syrian wife Umm Khalid and father-in-law As'ad Ibrahim as go-betweens in offering bribes to al-Sarraj to kill Nasser by bringing down his plane. Reports also implicated Saud's politically unpopular Syrian adviser Yusuf Yasin. The US government was said to have approved of Saud's plan. *Al-Nasr* published photos of checks drawn on the Arab Bank of Riyadh allegedly provided to al-Sarraj as well as other incriminating documents.[28]

The truth of these accusations and their relationship to Saud's conflicts with both Nasser and Faysal remain the subject of dispute. Certain accounts justifiably question whether Saud sought to "assassinate" Nasser.[29] One eyewitness claimed that Umm Khalid had grasped Saud's left hand and cautioned him against any assassination. The king did not insist on it but wanted Syria to remain independent and to retain influence over its government.[30] Regarding Faysal's role, Sarah Yizraeli suggests that US secretary of state John Foster Dulles, together with Aramco, may have decided to promote Faysal's seizure of power.[31] But declassified US sources show that officials regarded Saud's crisis with alarm. On March 6, CIA director Allen Dulles told the National Security Council that Saud was "gravely endangered" by the charges "although we had tried to warn Saud, vainly, that he was falling into a trap."[32] Turning to Eisenhower, the CIA director declared that "unless the trend were reversed," pro-Western regimes in the Middle East "may well collapse, and we may find that the USSR will take over control of this whole oil-rich area. The situation was extremely grave."[33] Indeed, months before Eisenhower dispatched troops to Lebanon, he first raised the possibility of intervening militarily in support of Saud.[34] Samore, for his part, argues that "there is no good evidence for proving a secret deal between Nasser and Faisal" to cooperate against Saud.[35] While there is no hard evidence, the CIA was aware that as Saud faced pressure to relinquish authority, Faysal was "playing a double game." Secretary Dulles asked cryptically "whether King Saud knew what we know about Faysal."[36] In any event, the charges against Saud were widely believed because of his association with the Eisenhower Doctrine.[37] On March 22, following an intervention by the king's uncle 'Abdullah ibn 'Abd al-Rahman, Saud issued a royal decree ceding executive power to Faysal.[38]

More than just a ruling-family quarrel, the March crisis raised fundamental questions about Saudi Arabia's place in the postwar petroleum order. As Bsheer has shown, leftist movements, such as the Front for the Liberation of the Arabian Peninsula, organized against Saudi family rule and Aramco. The Front denounced "the traitors and agents of colonialism, and those who are corrupt like Saud and Faisal... their descendants and their lineage."[39] But such revolutionary forces were incapable of overthrowing the ruling dynasty, as would occur in Hashemite Iraq. Rather, the succession struggle and the specter of revolution indirectly created opportunities for political reformers. In the wake of Nasser's speech, a group of junior princes assembled at the home of Prince Talal, who was sympathetic to Nasser and favored reforms. They "agreed that Saud should no longer be allowed to run the country."[40] Aramco sources reported that 'Abd al-'Aziz ibn Mu'ammar, the supporter of labor strikes against the company, attended the meeting.[41] The Front of National Reforms, established during the 1953 strike by officials, military officers, and Aramco employees, published an open letter to Faysal calling for a constitutional government.[42] What Lebanese intelligence called a "Saudi cell" met in Beirut to praise Nasser and the UAR and to denounce the Eisenhower Doctrine and Saud. Addressing the meeting, Lebanese opposition figure 'Abdullah al-Machnouk explained that he was not "against monarchy but against the henchmen of colonialism [*adhnab al-isti'mar*]." He praised Yemen's adherence to the UAR and called for the liberation of the Arabian Peninsula. The rich oil resources of the region, he declared, belonged to the Arabs.[43] These Arab nationalist voices echoed ideas expressed in this era's most important Saudi dissident source, Nasser al-Sa'id's *Risala ila Su'ud min Nasser al-Sa'id* (Letter to Saud from Nasser al-Sa'id).

The reemergence of Nasser al-Sa'id, the labor leader and former Aramco employee from the Nejdi town of Ha'il, has been attributed to opportunism on the part of Nasser and Saud's opponents. Indeed, al-Sa'id's *Risala*, originally dated June 1957, was published during the crisis as part of the Egyptian propaganda offensive. Al-Sa'id also appeared in an exposé of the king published by *al-Nasr* on March 29.[44] But these accounts neglect the significance of the *Risala*'s content. Polemical and marred by exaggeration, the *Risala* nevertheless delivers a powerful structural criticism of Saudi integration into the postwar petroleum order. It connects Saudi Arabia's relationships with the United States and Aramco to Saud's corruption and a lack of democracy in the kingdom. Al-Sa'id describes Saud as "yielding to his American masters" as a "servant of the dollar." The king's lavish palace at Nasseriyya, allegedly paid for by the United States, with its slaves, cinema, and electric lights, symbolizes the king's corruption. There on June 9, 1956, al-Sa'id writes, demonstrators brought Saud petitions protesting the renewal of the Dhahran base agreement and demanding labor reforms. The petitions denounced members of Saud's circle of advisers, whom al-Sa'id accused of accepting secret salaries from Aramco. They included Saud bin Jiluwi, the Eastern Province governor responsible for the violent suppression of labor strikes, and Yusuf Yasin, the Syrian figure later implicated in the Nasser plot. Jiluwi reportedly told Saud that the petitioners represented a revolution rather than a labor demonstration. Al-Sa'id alleges that arrests and killings followed, including those of labor leaders named by Aramco.[45] But al-Sa'id warns that this repression cannot extinguish "the fire [burning] beneath the ashes [*al-nar taht-al-ramad*]." Rather, "the pressure will create an explosion [*infijar*]."[46] Al-Sa'id associates Saud's corruption with his support for the Eisenhower Doctrine, which led him to sacrifice the sovereignty of his country in the name of the "alleged communist threat." After visiting the United States as the guest of American Zionists and his "beloved Dulles Eisenhower [sic]," Saud renewed the lease for the airbase at Dhahran, where al-Sa'id claimed the Americans enjoyed the right to stockpile nuclear weapons.[47] In protest, al-Sa'id argues that the kingdom faced an "American" rather than a "communist" threat.[48] He attacked the king for reconciling with the Hashemites and cooperating with agents of imperialism. According to him, Saud had witnessed Nasser's popularity during his visit to the kingdom in 1956 and had then concocted the "crazy [*jununiya*]" scheme against Nasser's life.[49] Al-Sa'id demanded an Arab nationalist and neutralist foreign policy, which Saudi Arabia would pursue from Buraymi to Palestine to Algeria.

The *Risala*'s principal charge is that Aramco exploited the kingdom and Saudi laborers. As Bsheer shows, figures such as Muhammad Saeed Ba'shen, editor of the publication *al-Adwa'*, combined similar charges against Aramco with demands for individual rights.[50] Aramco attempted to mute such criticisms. The company's public affairs director W. Paul Butler went so far as to confront the editors of *al-Adwa'* in Jidda before offering to contribute to their purchase of a new printing press, which Aramco would presumably control.[51] But al-Sa'id condemns King Saud directly for abetting Aramco's exploitation while pursuing "useless ['*aqima*]" programs in education and economic development.[52] Over a decade, Aramco had reaped a profit of some $8 billion by exploiting the toil of its workers and avoiding taxes. As an agent of American imperialism, the company had "occupied" the kingdom "economically, politically, culturally, and socially." Saud had even surrendered to Aramco regarding the short-lived Onassis tanker company.[53] Ending this exploitation required political reforms that limited the ruler's power. Rather than despotic rule by one person over some 8 million Saudis, al-Sa'id called for a constitutional government.[54] Concluding his letter with an Arabic wordplay based on a Qur'anic verse, he warned King Saud that he would be overthrown.[55]

Nasser al-Sa'id's *Risala* helps to illustrate how domestic and regional challenges to Saudi family rule converged in 1958. Providing perspective, Madawi al-Rasheed explains that dissidents such as al-Sa'id "remained scattered voices," representing an educated elite who had been exposed to Arab nationalist politics. Activists were "motivated by a desire to overcome their marginality," she writes, "in a society that still defined people's status and achievements along the old tribal lines."[56] Nevertheless, technocrats, Aramco employees, labor leaders, military officers, and junior princes such as Talal identified political alternatives to the status quo in the form of constitutional rule and greater alignment with Nasserism. These elements sought to reform the kingdom from within through means short of revolution. As Arab nationalism threatened pro-Western governments across the region during mid-1958, King Saud and Crown Prince Faysal pursued contrasting responses. Saud maintained close contacts with the Eisenhower administration through his envoy 'Azzam Pasha. When Free Officers overthrew the Hashemite monarchy in Iraq, Saud demanded that "the Baghdad [Pact] powers intervene in Iraq" and declared that "American and [British] troops should be sent to Jordan." Otherwise, he warned, Saudi Arabia "will not stand alone against the UAR" and will have to "go along with UAR foreign policy."[57] For his part, Faysal declared that Saudi Arabia would follow a neutral foreign policy. During the Anglo-American interventions of July in Jordan and Lebanon, Faysal refused to allow troops to receive supplies from Saudi territory. At his insistence, the US flag was lowered at the Dhahran airfield.[58] In contrast to Saud, Faysal vocally opposed the interventions and sympathized with those who overthrew the Iraqi government. While "the coup was initiated by military officers," the crown prince told the US ambassador, "it was really a popular revolt reflecting popular hatred" of the government and its pro-Western policies.[59] In August, Faysal met with Nasser and reportedly agreed not to renew the American lease at Dhahran.[60]

The Best Hope for Modernization

The March 1958 crisis opened the door to political reforms in the kingdom. Talal, who led the group of younger princes, proposed the creation of a National Council. This body was conceived as "the first step towards a constitutional monarchy." Mu'ammar and other nonroyal reformers, including future oil minister 'Abdullah al-Tariqi, supported this proposal.[61] Saud shifted his policies and used an alliance with the reformers as an avenue back to power. He appointed Mu'ammar to his royal *diwan* at the end of 1959 and a year later even endorsed the formation of a committee to draft a constitution. Talal told the US attaché in Jidda that the family dispute was one of "divergent principles not personalities." In Talal's words, Saud rejected "the policies of the reactionary group led by Faysal to maintain all power in the hands of [the] royal family and deny people [a] voice in government."[62] According to accounts compiled by Saudi journalist Sultan al-Jumayri, al-Tariqi's statement that the kingdom would "become a constitutional monarchy" angered Faysal, while Aramco vice president James Terry Duce accused Mu'ammar of being a Communist.[63] Talal was forced to leave his ministerial position in 1961, and shortly after Faysal regained power as acting prime minister. Faysal's cooperative relationship with Nasser ended following the collapse of the UAR and the outbreak of civil conflict in Yemen, which intensified into a Saudi-Egyptian proxy war. Having dismissed al-Tariqi and other reformers who continued their opposition from exile in Egypt, Faysal took credit for a ten-point program that prescribed economic development and the "complete abolition of slavery."[64] The program closed the door to political liberalization while burnishing Faysal's reputation as a modernizer. One of President John Kennedy's top foreign-policy advisers proclaimed Faysal as the "best hope for modernization in Saudi Arabia."[65] Faysal therefore created the template for a modernizing crown prince, in the context of war in Yemen, who assumed leadership of the royal family while suppressing opposition and bids to limit his power.[66] Muʻammar was arrested in 1963.[67] The next year, Faysal replaced Saud as king with the support of senior princes and religious leaders. Saud's reign was subsequently written out of the kingdom's past. Although there have recently been attempts at historical revision, those revisionist accounts do not directly address the charges against Saud raised by al-Saʻid nor the king's pro-US stance during the revolutionary crises of 1958.[68]

While not apparent at the time, 1958 was also important in terms of transnational religious influences that would hold implications for the future. That year in Iraq, Muhammad Baqir al-Sadr founded the Islamic Daʻwa Party to counter Communist appeals to marginalized Shiʻa. The Daʻwa Party would later play a role in the political mobilization of Shiʻa from the Gulf to Lebanon. The figure who would become the leading Shiʻa cleric in Saudi Arabia, Shaykh Hasan al-Saffar, was born in Qatif in 1958. Al-Saffar would adhere to the rival Shiʻa movement to al-Daʻwa, the Shiraziyyin, which organized Shiʻa resistance in the Saudi Eastern Province.[69] According to Michael Farquhar, 1958 also marked the origins of the Islamic University of Medina (IUM), a "Saudi-led counter-project" to Nasserism "grounded in claims to religious authenticity and calls for Islamic solidarity." Drawing on existing transnational Sunni networks, plans for IUM materialized just as Faysal "seized effective power from his brother Saud and the conflict between the two became particularly fractious." Indeed, Faysal would utilize IUM, along with institutions such as the Muslim World League and the Organization of the Islamic Conference, in his struggle against Nasser. Among those with ties to IUM was Juhayman al-ʻUtaybi, who following Faysal's assassination led the seizure of the Grand Mosque in Mecca.[70] Al-ʻUtaybi made similar charges against the royal family of corruption and subservience to the United States as Nasser al-Saʻid had, although al-ʻUtaybi couched his accusations in Islamist rather than Nasserist ideological terms. The Saudis regarded Islam as a "means for pursuing their worldly interests," Juhayman wrote, while they "consorted with Christians (America)."[71] In 1979, another revolutionary year regionally that directly threatened the Saudi dynasty, al-ʻUtaybi led his attack in Mecca, a revolution toppled the shah, and a Shiʻa uprising challenged Saudi authority in the Eastern Province. From his exile in Beirut, Nasser al-Saʻid praised the Grand Mosque seizure as part of a "People's Revolution." He was kidnapped on December 17, "allegedly by agents of the Saudi government." He was never heard from again.[72]

Conclusion

Nineteen fifty-eight was therefore a revolutionary year in the Middle East that created potential but ultimately unrealized opportunities for political reform in Saudi Arabia. King Saud and Crown Prince Faysal struggled over political power in the context of a clash between the kingdom's role in the postwar petroleum order and the revolutionary Arab nationalism that inflamed the entire region. Although the succession struggle and the threat of revolution opened the door to a constitutional monarchy, Faysal successfully promoted modernization as a counter-revolutionary strategy with US support. He also utilized Islamic institutions to counter Nasser's Arab nationalist ideology. Meanwhile, revolutionary opposition to the Saudi dynasty continued to burn within and beyond the kingdom's borders. The 1958 crisis served as a crucible for modern Saudi Arabia, which is the product not only of ruling-family politics and modernization programs but also of the opposition that has always smoldered beneath them.

Notes

1. See Robert Lacey, *The Kingdom: Arabia & the House of Saud* (New York: Avon Books, 1981); Richard Johns and David Holden, *The House of Saud* (London: Sidgwick and Johnson, 1981); Gerald De Gaury, *Faisal: King of Saudi Arabia*, Rev ed. (Louisville, KY: Fons Vitae, 2007); and Joseph Kéchichian, *Faysal: Saudi Arabia's King for All Seasons* (Gainesville: University Press of Florida, 2008). See also Joseph Kostiner, *The Making of Saudi Arabia, 1916-1936: From Chieftancy to Monarchical State* (New York: Oxford University Press, 1993).
2. See Madawi al-Rasheed, *A Most Masculine State: Gender, Politics, and Religion in Saudi Arabia* (Cambridge, UK: Cambridge University Press, 2013), 91.
3. For examples, see Robert Baer, *Sleeping with the Devil: How Washington Sold Our Soul for Saudi Crude* (New York: Three Rivers Press, 2003); and Rachel Bronson, *Thicker than Oil: America's Uneasy Partnership with Saudi Arabia* (New York: Oxford University Press, 2006).
4. Madawi al-Rasheed, *A History of Saudi Arabia*, 2d edn (New York: Cambridge University Press, 2010); Robert Vitalis, *America's Kingdom: Mythmaking on the Saudi Oil Frontier* (Stanford, CA: Stanford University Press, 2007); and Toby Craig Jones, *Desert Kingdom: How Oil and Water Forged Modern Saudi Arabia* (Cambridge, MA: Harvard University Press, 2010).
5. Rosie Bsheer, "A Counter-Revolutionary State: Popular Movements and the Making of Saudi Arabia," *Past & Present* 238 (February 2018): 233–77.
6. Ibid., 257.
7. See Daniel Yergin, *The Prize: The Epic Quest for Oil, Money, and Power* (New York: Simon & Schuster, 1992), 409–30; Nathan J. Citino, *From Arab Nationalism to OPEC: Eisenhower, King Saud, and the Making of U.S.-Saudi Relations*, 2d edn (Bloomington: Indiana University Press, 2010); and David S. Painter, "Oil and the American Century," *Journal of American History* 99 (June 2012): 24–39.
8. See Nathan J. Citino, "Defending the Postwar Petroleum Order: The US, Britain, and the 1954 Saudi-Onassis Tanker Deal," *Diplomacy & Statecraft* 8 (March 1997): 96–136.
9. See Asher Kaufman, "Between Permeable and Sealed Borders: The Trans-Arabian Pipeline and the Arab-Israeli Conflict," *International Journal of Middle East Studies* 46 (February 2014): 95–116.
10. Al-Rasheed, *A History of Saudi Arabia*, 102.
11. Quoted in Citino, *From Arab Nationalism to OPEC*, 26.
12. Al-Rasheed, *A History of Saudi Arabia*, 111–12.

13 Citino, *From Arab Nationalism to OPEC*, 106.
14 Al-Rasheed, *A History of Saudi Arabia*, 102–3.
15 Gary S. Samore, "Royal Family Politics in Saudi Arabia, 1953–1983" (Ph.D. diss., Harvard University, 1983), 84.
16 Sarah Yizraeli, *The Remaking of Saudi Arabia: The Struggle between King Saud and Crown Prince Faysal, 1953–1962* (Tel Aviv: Moshe Dayan Center for Middle Eastern and African Studies, 1997), 54.
17 See Citino, *From Arab Nationalism to OPEC*, 138.
18 See Yizraeli, *The Remaking of Saudi Arabia*, 59; and Al-Rasheed, *A History of Saudi Arabia*, 104–5.
19 See Vitalis, *America's Kingdom*, 161–2; and al-Rasheed, *A History of Saudi Arabia*, 95–6.
20 See Salim Yaqub, *Containing Arab Nationalism: The Eisenhower Doctrine and the Middle East* (Chapel Hill: University of North Carolina Press, 2004).
21 See Saud's message to Eisenhower in Madrid to State Department, February 17, 1957, Saudi Arabia, King Saud 1957 (1), box 46, International Series, Dwight D. Eisenhower Papers as President of the United States, 1953–1961 (Ann C. Whitman File) [ACW], Dwight D. Eisenhower Library [DDEL], Abilene, Kansas.
22 See Yaqub, *Containing Arab Nationalism*, 140–2.
23 Ibid., 147–80.
24 See Yizraeli, *The Remaking of Saudi Arabia*, 57.
25 See Samore, "Royal Family Politics in Saudi Arabia," 111.
26 On these negotiations, see Tawfiq al-Suwaydi, *Mudhakkirati: nisf qarn min ta'rikh al-Iraq wa-l qadiya al-'Arabiya* (Beirut: Dar al-Katib al-'Arabi, 1969), 580.
27 "Speech by Gamal Abdel Nasser on the Occasion of the Announcement of the Interim Constitution for the United Arab Republic in Damascus," (Arabic) March 5, 1958, http://nasser.org/Speeches/browser.aspx?SID=606&lang=ar (accessed May 3, 2019).
28 See *al-Nasr* (*Dimashq*), March 8, 11, 13, 1958.
29 See Samore, "Royal Family Politics in Saudi Arabia," 111–14; and Yizraeli, *The Remaking of Saudi Arabia*, 69.
30 See *al-Nasr*, March 8, 1958, 4.
31 See Yizraeli, *The Remaking of Saudi Arabia*, 66–7.
32 "Memorandum of Discussion at the 357th Meeting of the National Security Council, Thursday, March 6, 1958," March 7, 1958, box 9, NSC Series, ACW, DDEL.
33 Ibid.
34 See "Memorandum of Discussion at the 358th Meeting of the National Security Council, Thursday, March 13, 1958," March 14, 1958, box 9, NSC Series, ACW, DDEL; and Caccia to the Foreign Office, March 13, 1958, PREM 11/5068, UK National Archives [UKNA], Kew, England.
35 Samore, "Royal Family Politics in Saudi Arabia," 111.
36 "Memorandum of Discussion at the 359th Meeting of the National Security Council, Thursday, March 20, 1958," March 21, 1958, box 9, NSC Series, ACW, DDEL.
37 See al-Rasheed, *A History of Saudi Arabia*, 112; and Ghassan Salamah, *Al-Siyasa al-kharjiyya al-Saudiyya mundhu 'am 1945: Dirasa fi al-'Alaqa al-Dawliyya* (Beirut: Mahad al-Inma' al-'Arabi, 1980), 633–4.
38 See Yizraeli, *The Remaking of Saudi Arabia*, 70–1. For the Arabic text of the decree, see Salman bin Saud bin 'Abd al-'Aziz, *Ta'rikh al-Malik Saud bin 'Abd al-'Aziz* (Beirut: Dar

al-Saqi, 2005), 1: 214–15. See also Caccia to Foreign Office, March 25, 1958, PREM 11/5068, UKNA.
39 See Bsheer, "Counter-Revolutionary State," 266.
40 Yizraeli, *The Remaking of Saudi Arabia*, 69. See also Samore, "Royal Family Politics in Saudi Arabia," 115.
41 See Caccia to Foreign Office, March 26, 1958, PREM 11/5068, UKNA.
42 See Alexei Vassiliev, *The History of Saudi Arabia* (New York: New York University Press, 2000), 339, 356.
43 "*Akhbar*," March 9, 1958, 3, Emir Farid Chehab Collection, Woodrow Wilson Center, https://digitalarchive.wilsoncenter.org/document/177307 (accessed May 3, 2019).
44 See Vassiliev, *The History of Saudi Arabia*, 354–5; and De Gaury, *Faisal*, 91. On the origins of the *Risala*, see Nasser al-Saʻid, *Risala ila Suʻud min Nasser al-Saʻid* (Cairo: al-Dar al-Qawmiya, 1958), 4 [*tamhid*].
45 *Al-Risala*, 4, 12, 16, 20–1.
46 Ibid., 22.
47 Vitalis rightfully questions this dubious claim. See *America's Kingdom*, 193. But see also Strategic Air Command, "Report of a Session of the Commanders Conference," April 25–27, 1950, Ramey Air Force Base, Puerto Rico, 60, U.S. Declassified Documents, CK2349592568.
48 *Al-Risala*, 24, 28.
49 Ibid., 34.
50 Bsheer, "Counter-Revolutionary State," 251.
51 ʻAbd al-Fattah Abu Mudin, *Wa Tilka al-Ayyam* (Jidda: Dar al-Bilad, 1985), 69, 72–3.
52 *Al-Risala*, 23.
53 Ibid., 36–7.
54 Ibid., 22–4.
55 Ibid., 49 (*munqalab/yanqalibun*); see *al-Qurʼan* 26:227.
56 Al-Rasheed, *A History of Saudi Arabia*, 109.
57 See attachment, Allen W. Dulles to Goodpaster, July 18, 1958, ME Lebanon [1] (July 16–23, 1958), box 11, International Series, Office of the Staff Secretary, Records 1952–1961, DDEL.
58 See Samore, "Royal Family Politics in Saudi Arabia," 146; and Citino, *From Arab Nationalism to OPEC*, 142.
59 Embassy in Saudi Arabia to the Department of State, July 25, 1958, *FRUS, 1958–1960*, 12: 730–3. See also Dulles to Eisenhower, n.d. [July 1958], Saudi Arabia [1], box 46, International Series, ACW, DDEL; and "*balagh rasmi*," *al-Bilad al-Saudiyya*, July 20, 1958, 1.
60 See Samore, "Royal Family Politics in Saudi Arabia," 125.
61 Al-Rasheed, *A History of Saudi Arabia*, 105.
62 See Smith to State Department, June 17, 1960, 786A.00/6-1660, Box 2065, Record Group 59, National Archives and Records Administration, College Park, Maryland. See also Weir to Walmsley, January 12, 1960, FO 371/148871, UKNA; and Mulligan to Mandis, February 8, 1960, folder 64, box 2, William E. Mulligan Papers, Special Collections, Georgetown University, Washington, DC.
63 Sultan al-Jumayri, *ʼAn al-tajriba al-nidaliyya al-ʻummaliyya fi al-Saudiyya*, https://docs.google.com/document/d/1IwuBr-E4sM6-Nk4Wdt__pdZ_ZTfozQCTXh91iu7opcg/edit, 7–8, accessed May 3, 2019.
64 See Vassiliev, *The History of Saudi Arabia*, 364–5.

65 Komer to Bundy, November 9, 1962, United Arab Republic, General 9/62-12/62, box 168A, National Security File, John F. Kennedy Library, Boston, Massachusetts.
66 On "The Myth of Faisal's Reforms," see Vitalis, *America's Kingdom*, 241–6.
67 Ibid., 250.
68 See al-Rasheed, *A History of Saudi Arabia*, 119; and Salman bin Saud bin 'Abd al-'Aziz, *Ta'rikh al-Malik Saud bin 'Abd al-'Aziz*.
69 See Laurence Louër, *Transnational Shia Politics: Religious and Political Networks in the Gulf* (London: Hurst & Co., 2008), 84, 145–6; and Toby Craig Jones, "Rebellion on the Saudi Periphery: Modernity, Marginalization, and the Shi'a Uprising of 1979," *International Journal of Middle East Studies* 38 (May 2006): 215.
70 Michael Farquhar, *Circuits of Faith: Migration, Education, and the Wahhabi Mission* (Stanford: Stanford University Press, 2017), 70, 73 (on al-'Utaybi, see 83).
71 Rif'at Sayyid Ahmad, *Rasa'il Juhayman al-'Utaybi, Qa'id al-Muqtahimin lil-Masjid al-Haram bi-Makkah* (Cairo: Maktabat Madbuli, 1988), 14.
72 Thomas Hegghammer and Stéphane Lacroix, "Rejectionist Islamism in Saudi Arabia: The Story of Juhayman al-'Utaybi Revisited," *International Journal of Middle East Studies* 39 (February 2007): 13; and al-Rasheed, *A History of Saudi Arabia*, 96. See also "Saudi Opposition Leader: 'The Mosque Incident Was Part of a People's Revolution,'" *MERIP Reports* 84 (February 1980): 17–18.

Chapter 7

EGYPT'S REVOLUTIONARY YEAR

REGIME CONSOLIDATION AT HOME, PRAGMATISM ABROAD, AND NEUTRALISM IN THE COLD WAR

Dina Rezk

On January 11, 1958, as a self-appointed Syrian delegation of army officers arrived in Cairo to negotiate an unprecedented political union with Egypt, Nasser had his sights set far beyond the Arab world. He was entertaining his friend and ally Indonesian president Sukharno in the temperate climate of Aswan. It took a month of heated negotiations with the Syrians before Nasser was able to exact terms he considered favorable for union, following which he declared: "Today Arab nationalism is not just a matter of slogans and shouts; it has become an actual reality."[1]

The formation of the UAR seemed to mark the pinnacle of the Arab world's anti-colonial politics in the postwar era. Early hopes that Nasser could be courted as an ally of the West were thwarted by tense negotiations over the British evacuation of the Suez Canal base and the Western preoccupation for a regional anti-Soviet alliance, eventually culminating in the ill-fated Baghdad Pact.[2] The Israeli raid on Gaza in February 1955, French arms sales to Israel, and Egypt's inability to secure weapons from the United States led to an unprecedented arms deal with the Soviet Union via Czechoslovakia in September 1955. As Nasser endorsed "positive neutralism" with his attendance at Bandung and recognition of the People's Republic of China, the US government withdrew their offer to fund the Aswan Dam.[3]

The subsequent nationalization of the Suez Canal and the tripartite invasion that ensued marks a historical "turning point" over which much ink has been spilled. Scholars have told a tale of woe replete with the West's failure to understand Arab nationalism, their neglect of regional opportunities to harness Arab nationalism at the expense of Cold War preoccupations and fundamental misperceptions of President Nasser.[4] At the time, and subsequently, the events of 1958 were regarded by many as the culmination of a political victory for Egypt following the Suez debacle, which in turn symbolized an unprecedented triumph of nationalism against Britain's last throw of the imperial dice: never again would the UK's prestige and authority be so directly and publicly challenged on a global scale. In Egypt and the Arab world more broadly, Nasser was elevated to the status of an ideology rather than simply a leader.

Due to its strategic position across oil pipelines, connecting the Persian Gulf with NATO member, Turkey, Syria occupied a geopolitical pride of place in the region. In the enthusiasm for Western covert action that marked this era, the British SIS and the American CIA conspired to execute a coup in Damascus in 1956, which was foiled by Syrian intelligence. In 1957, a second CIA plot codenamed "Operation Wappen" tried and failed to engineer another military overthrow in Syria, eventually forcing the notoriously weak President Quwatli to seek support from the Soviet Union. In turn the Syrian Ba'ath Party appealed to Nasser for salvation from Communist infiltration of the Syrian government.[5]

Historians remain divided about the motivations and significance of 1958 for Egypt. Scholars such as McNamara have identified the union as a "turning point" in Middle East affairs which seemed to mark the "complete success of the Nasserite project in Syria" going on to "unleash a chain of events that were to destroy what was left of Britain's power in the Middle East."[6] Podeh's work was among the first to examine the union based on declassified documents, suggesting that Nasser received an informal green light from Washington before proceeding.[7] Others such as James Jankowski and Salim Yaqub have highlighted the pragmatism which underlay Nasser's moves toward Arab nationalism.[8] This builds on an older and more established literature that argues that Nasser's pan-Arabism was an instrumental addition to the Free Officer's objectives, enabled by the political victory of the Suez Crisis rather than an ideological commitment to Arab unity.[9] A more recent wave of scholarship deploying Arabic language sources argues that pan-Arabism was more deeply rooted within the Free Officer's vision, convinced by the experience of defeat in the 1948 Arab-Israeli War that only unity could truly defeat imperialism.[10] These Egypt-centered studies have also highlighted the domestic and internal politics around this historic moment, upon which this chapter will further build.[11]

On the face of it, 1958 appeared to place Nasser's brand of pan-Arabism in the ascendancy, marking a revolutionary moment that formed a pinnacle of the political victory and popularity Nasser had enjoyed since the Suez Crisis. However, deploying a range of Anglo-American declassified documents and Arab sources, this chapter argues that a closer look at this revolutionary moment reveals that in fact, the events of 1958 showcase Nasser's overriding pragmatism at the domestic, regional, and global level. Domestically, the formation of the UAR presented an opportunity for Nasser to dispense with his primary rival in the military corps, Abdel Hakim Amer, in the attempt to unseat his minister of defense from the helm of his expanding power base in the security services. Regionally, while of course publicly capitalizing on the propaganda opportunities afforded by the union to rally the support of the Arab masses, in private Nasser proceeded with caution, reluctance even, and initially at least, sought to de-escalate the "Arab Cold War" the union risked exacerbating. Finally, at the global level, perhaps the most revolutionary dimension of 1958 was the clear rift that emerged between Cairo and Moscow as a result of the events of that year. While the American intelligence community was aware that an anti-Communist drive was behind Egypt's union with Syria, the course of this revolutionary year revealed just how far Nasser was willing to break with his Soviet patrons.

Domestic Politics

A brief look at the great icons of Egyptian popular culture at the time alludes to the significance of Arab unity and its appeal at the domestic level. Songs by nationalist singers Abdel Halim Hafez and Mohammad Qandil captured the sentimental and emotive appeal of the union with Syria. Indeed, black-and-white films from the 1960s are replete with images of Egyptians gathered around coffee shops across major cities of Cairo, Alexandria, and Suez, tuned in to hear the latest nationalist proclamations.[12]

However, scholars have also highlighted how divided the Egyptian political elite was in the run up to 1958. In one of the few Western studies that have looked at the Suez Crisis from the Egyptian perspective, Crowcroft suggests that on the eve of the union with Syria, the business community was troubled by the country's drift toward socialism and the Soviet Union. Thousands of military officers who had been forced into early retirement were resentful of Nasser's reforms, and the vast majority of Egypt's poorest peasants remained under the stronghold of wealthy landowners.[13] Contemporaneously, American analysts noted in 1958 that "despite strides which state socialism has made in Egypt, private enterprise still remains deeply rooted" and was even viewed "with [a] sort of schizophrenic favor [sic] by [the] government."[14] The much hailed Aswan Dam, designed to end the cycle of flood and drought of the Nile and bring electric power to Egypt's rural areas, had rendered Egypt, "increasingly in [the] position of [a] man very busy laying foundation for future wealth but in the meantime nearly starving."[15] Nasser's popularity was by no means to be taken for granted.

Indeed, the most threatening domestic opposition Nasser faced was from his longtime friend and then defense minister Amer. This rivalry is well documented in Egyptian sources.[16] Nasser would refer to Amer as his brother and the two men were indeed related by marriage. Sadat remembers Nasser telling him that Egypt "was run by a gang . . . I am responsible as President but it is Amer that rules."[17] The roots of this internal conflict also have their origins in Nasser's political success during the Suez Crisis. As Crowcroft argues, nationalization of the Canal was as much about "domestic political consolidation" as an expression of Egypt's struggle to secure full national freedom.[18] In particular, the way in which the decision to nationalize the Canal had been made alienated his rival, with Amer asserting that as commander of the military it was he who would "have to defend this decision."[19] Thus Nasser only informed Amer on the day before the public announcement that the Canal would be nationalized, leaving his top military commander and minister of defense outraged.[20] According to Egyptian accounts, Amer had allegedly wanted to surrender in the face of the

Anglo-French forces. Nasser had apparently retorted, "I don't want you issuing any orders. . . . If you can't do better than mope around like an old hag then you will be court martialed."[21]

With this confrontation, the scene was set for a power struggle between the two men.[22] In 1957, Amer's protégé, spy chief Salah Nasr, took control of the civilian sector of the intelligence services which helped consolidate Amer's power and presented a more concerted challenge to Nasser. Amer was well known for shoring up support within the officer corps through a system of financial incentives, benefits, and promotions that offered a marked contrast to Nasser's austere incorruptibility. In 1957, Amer promoted himself to the rank of Field Marshal and devoted himself to transforming the military into "a state within a state." He treated the military as a personal fiefdom, promoting officers based on their loyalty to him, rather than to Nasser.[23] Amer's security men were keen to ensure that Nasser would not carry out a military shake-up against their will.[24] They provided him with a regular stream of attempted plots they claimed to have foiled and by 1958, the vast majority of military and civilian security organs were under Amer's control. On the eve of the union with Syria, Nasser's position within the security community had considerably deteriorated.

The formation of the UAR thus presented Nasser with a golden opportunity to dispense of his rival. As Kandil puts it, "The expansion of Egyptian influence abroad was critical to the consolidation of his power at home and so he kicked his friend-turned-rival upstairs" appointing him governor of Syria, now renamed the Northern Sector of the United Arab Republic.[25] The Field Marshal agreed, believing he would now have his own country to run. Nasser was thereby relieved of the most urgent domestic challenge to his powerbase within Egypt.

Regional Politics

At the regional level, Nasser found himself navigating two countervailing trends. On the one hand, the union with Syria appeared to fulfill a pan-Arab agenda to which he had devoted much rhetorical energy. On the other hand, when faced with the realization of these goals, Nasser revealed a certain moderation that seemed to run contrary to his public proclamations. The year 1958 ultimately revealed the pragmatism of Nasser's foreign policy in the region, over his ideological commitments to Arab nationalism.

Publicly of course, Nasser had long made the case that Arab unity was the only mechanism of defeating imperialism. In *Philosophy of the Revolution*, he wrote,

> The Arab circle in my eyes had become a single entity. . . . I have followed developments in the Arab countries, and I find they match, point for point. What happened in Cairo had its counterpart in Damascus the next day, and in Beirut, Amman, Baghdad and elsewhere. . . . It is a single region. The same circumstances, the same factors, even the same forces, united against all of it . . . the foremost of these forces was imperialism.[26]

Nasser's spy chief Sami Sharaf also articulated the Free Officers' "recognition and conviction that Egypt's security was inseparable from the security of the Arab nation."[27] Similarly, the Syrian elite had long peddled a narrative that reinforced the importance of an expanding, pan-Arab movement. As Syrian Ba'athist Salah Aldin Bitar had put it in 1956, the Syrian-Egyptian union "could not be solid, strong and lasting if other Arab regions, with their Arab people and their immense material and spiritual capabilities, were not joined to it."[28] In a speech before the great sultan and military commander Saladin's tomb, Nasser himself pledged to follow the hero's example "to realize total Arab unity" against Western oppression.[29]

Moreover, Nasser devoted tangible resources to this endeavor. In particular, the appeal of nationalism was propagated through the Sawt el Arab (Voice of the Arabs) radio station.[30] Ahmed al-Said, the radio station's best-known presenter and general manager, remembers that the mandate of promoting Arab unity was clearly laid out in the original plans of the station's founding.[31] Cairo committed military support to the nationalist front in Algeria in 1954, with the Algerian revolution declared on the station. Through Ben Bella, Cairo offered similar support to nationalist groups in Morocco and Tunisia.[32] According to al-Said, Sawt el Arab played a crucial role in fomenting upheaval in the Arab world, particularly Jordan, Iraq, and Lebanon. Representatives of the station would contact members of pro-Egyptian organizations in other Arab countries, whereupon Mukhabarat officers, sometimes disguised as students doing doctoral research, would call upon the trustworthy ones for situational reports.[33] Unsurprisingly, the subversive potential of Sawt al Arab was well recognized by Nasser's enemies.[34]

However, the first tangible indication of a specifically Egyptian-Syrian union was the signing of a military pact in October 1955. Significantly, this was a direct response to the infamous pro-Western "Baghdad Pact."[35] Syria was from the outset more enthusiastic about the possibilities for this kind of cooperation with Egypt.[36] While there had also been talk of an economic union, as the seasoned British ambassador to Egypt, Sir Harold Beeley, put it in 1958, despite "considerable emotional support for the idea" it was merely "propaganda" and as unlikely as "other Arab nationalist dreams."[37] American analysts agreed that while "the mystique" of Arab unity had "become a basic element of Arab political thought" in fact "the tendency" of the area was "towards fragmentation."[38]

Little surprise, therefore, that the realization of this nationalist dream, provoked panic in the Western world. As Roger Louis writes, "Most British officials . . . shared the idea of Nasser as a latter-day dictator of 1930s vintage."[39] The British intelligence community feared that Nasser sought to establish an Islamic empire based on Arab oil wealth. The Joint Intelligence Committee (JIC) argued that this was backed up by Nasser's "own pronouncements" according to which it was "fair to say that his long-term aims are that Egypt should control the Arab world."[40] Indeed, the Egyptian weekly *Akhar Sa'a* [last hour] published a map envisaging the newly established union after thirty years: Lebanon and Israel had disappeared as political entities, and the Arab world and portions of Black Africa were included within the shaded area of the new Egyptian empire.[41]

In reality, however, the historical record demonstrates the pragmatism with which Nasser approached the prospect of unity. In particular, Arab accounts have emphasized the extent to which the union was forced upon Nasser.[42] According to Nasser's closest confidante Haykal, as late as January 1958, Nasser remained convinced that any Egyptian-Syrian union would require at least five years' preparation. Haykal offers the most substantial firsthand account of Nasser's discussions with the Syrian officers and claims that the Egyptian president was clear that despite his public proclamations, his priority was strengthening Egypt for the foreseeable future.[43] Nor were these doubts about the formation of the UAR exclusively Nasser's. Ba'ath party literature indicates that even those Syrian Ba'athists advocating union had their doubts about the Egyptian partnership.[44] As the Syrian chief of staff Afif al-Bizri more cynically put it, "No one wanted unity. Even Abdel Nasser didn't want it. . . .Who at that hour could dare say we do not want unity? The people would tear their heads off."[45]

Nasser's pragmatism was similarly evident in his regional approach in the months after the UAR was formed. Even once the union was declared, his immediate response was to allay fears that the UAR would expand its borders across the Arab world. For example, he urged his nationalist supporters in Lebanon and Jordan to moderate their celebration of the Egyptian-Syrian merger. When the rival Iraqi-Jordanian union was announced in mid-February, Nasser sent his congratulations to King Faisal and refrained from criticizing the monarchies. As the Lebanese crisis threatened to set off a civil war, the Egyptian Foreign Ministry's Arab Bureau urged that the Egyptian news media should work "not to arouse confessional strife" in Lebanon but, rather, to calm the situation there. As Yaqub writes, "All these recommendations were in keeping with Egypt's general strategy of avoiding unnecessary controversy with the conservative Arab states during the crucial weeks in which the UAR was being consolidated."[46]

Within a month, however, revolution in the West's most important regional ally, Iraq, seemed yet another exemplification of the Arab nationalist fervor spreading through the Middle East. The end of the Hashemite monarchy established by the British in 1921 was brutish and short, bringing yet another young and zealous military officer, General Abdul Karim Qassim, to the helm of power. It appeared as if Nasser's brand of Arab nationalism was now in power in Egypt, Syria, and Iraq. Onlookers feared that Nasser's revolutionary fervor could easily spread to Lebanon and Jordan. As Nasser himself put it in a speech to an enthusiastic Syrian audience, "We see today America occupying Lebanon and Britain occupying Jordan. I say to them . . . : there was an occupation in the past. There was the French occupation of Damascus and the British occupation of Baghdad and Cairo and Amman. Where are they now? Their occupation ended, it turned to dust."[47]

In actuality, however, despite Nasser's rhetoric, Egypt's role in this latest Arab revolution was limited. It soon became clear that while Nasser declared his support for his Iraqi counterparts, the Egyptian leader had certainly not orchestrated this most recent expression of Arab nationalism. The director of the CIA, Allen Dulles, noted contemporaneously that the timing of the move seemed "a little out of gear with what might have been expected, as well as the manner and brutality of carrying out the coup."⁴⁸ The British intelligence community similarly conceded that Nasser could not, as "the self-appointed leader of Arab nationalism," have refused General Qassim's support.⁴⁹ Indeed the British ambassador in Baghdad, Michael Wright, was a veteran hand in the Middle East and argued from the outset that the revolution was Iraqi led rather than driven by the Egyptians.⁵⁰ Scholars have since concluded that although "the Egyptian revolution was an influence [in Iraq], as the fount of pan-Arab feeling and as a model of successful defiance of the West . . . it may be more nearly correct to speak of 'convergent development' in closely similar situations."⁵¹

Far from being a Nasserist stooge, General Qassim proved to be a force of nature in his own right. He quickly demonstrated his desire to resist local Nasserists such as his deputy Abd al-Salam Arif, utilizing the support of the Iraqi Communist Party (ICP). In fact, the Iraqi Ba'ath mistrusted Nasser and were more concerned with capitalizing on the Egyptian president's prestige than accepting his leadership. The Ba'athist view of pan-Arabism certainly was not to be "under the domination of one country."⁵² Perhaps for this reason, as Arif suggests in his memoirs, Nasser had reacted cautiously to his suggestions that Iraq accede to the UAR.⁵³ Tensions between Nasser and Qassim became increasingly public, with Nasser playing on Qassim's name to denounce him as "divider of Iraq." According to the pronouncements of the Egyptian president, Qassim was "following the example of Nuri-al-Said, and the example of the enemies of Arab nationalism."⁵⁴

Similarly, there were early indications that Nasser would also face real challenges in Syria. Syrian president Quwatli had reputedly warned Nasser that absorbing Syria would be no easy task. Apparently, he said: "You don't know what you're getting into, Mr. President. You have taken a people, all of whom consider themselves politicians, fifty percent of whom think that they are leaders, twenty-five percent of whom think they are prophets, and at least ten percent of whom think that they are divine."⁵⁵ Nasser's conditions for the union were draconian, demanding that the Syrian political landscape be obliterated, much in the way the Free Officer regime had clamped down on Egyptian politics: political parties would be dissolved and replaced with a "National Union" as in Egypt. The Syrian cabinet requested a federal union that would give Syria more autonomy, but Nasser was insistent that the union be either total or not at all.⁵⁶

Scholars have since concluded that "ultimately there was a clash of cultures between the dark-skinned bureaucrats from the Nile Valley and the free-wheeling Syrians."⁵⁷ American analysts described Syrians as "a people of remarkable commercial enterprise whose traditional way of life is founded upon personal and economic freedom."⁵⁸ Analysts suggested that "possibly the most pertinent difference" between the two cultures was "Syrian laissez-faire and zealotry, as opposed to Egyptian submissiveness to state authority" as a result of Egypt's dependence on a centralized irrigation system.⁵⁹ As Heikal would later put it, Syria was a "'rain society' and Egypt a 'river society.'"⁶⁰

At the time, certain prescient Western observers, such as the American ambassador to Egypt, Raymond Hare, also presented a more sober view of the recent moves toward pan-Arab unity. Hare reminded American policy-makers that Nasser had "scored his greatest successes outside Egypt as irresponsible champion of Arab nationalism." This was the first time, Hare argued, that "he must assume responsibility outside Egypt and it remains to be seen whether [the] result will be increased prestige or disenchantment." The ambassador seemed to suggest that the latter was more likely, "in which case, it was possible to foresee [the] deflation of Nasser's ego to the point where he would be more amenable to reason and impelled [to] deal more constructively with us." This was the potential silver lining: the possibility of Nasser "coming down a bit from his high horse under [the] compulsion of events and consequently being more tractable."[61] Hare believed that increased responsibility was having a "sobering rather than inflating effect."[62] At the regional level, therefore, perhaps what was most revolutionary about 1958 was actually the spectacularly rapid deterioration of the pan-Arab vision, the clearly emerging dissonance between the dream and the reality, and the opportunity this offered for Egypt's global politics.[63]

Cold War Politics

Nasser's pragmatism was nowhere more evident than in his dealings with the Soviet Union. As it became clear that Nasser was neither able nor particularly eager to expand an Arab empire across the region, and indeed that the motivation for his intervention in Syria was in fact to counter Communist forces there, the opportunities for a rift between Nasser and the Soviets and a rapprochement with the Western world became increasingly viable.

Egypt was the largest recipient of Soviet support and yet had managed to maintain its autonomy. Nasser received almost half of all Soviet aid to the Third World between 1954 and 1961.[64] Indeed he was offered a hero's welcome in the Soviet Union in 1958, and was photographed standing beside Lenin's tomb.[65] But American ambassador Raymond Hare recalled Nasser saying, "If they (the Russians) ever make the mistake of getting into the Middle East politically, you'll see what will happen, we will show them." According to Hare, it was clear that "the Egyptians and others weren't about to get rid of the British only to inherit the Russians."[66] The CIA confirmed at the time that they "do not believe that Nasser is a Communist or sympathetic to Communist doctrine."[67]

In fact, the prospect of a Soviet-controlled Syria fundamentally undermined Nasser's commitment to nonalignment in the Middle East.[68] It was therefore almost secondary that "extending the Egyptian revolution to Syria fitted in conveniently with Nasser's own conception of Arab unity."[69] American analysts recognized that Nasser agreed to the proposed union "because he was convinced that it was necessary in order to forestall a Communist takeover in Syria, as well as because he saw a propitious moment for realization of long-laid plans on his own terms." Syrian fears of communism dovetailed with Nasser's own concerns on this front.[70] Nasser ultimately saw Syria as an "unstable ally" but came to believe that he could only maintain a dominant influence in the country by acceding to President Quwatli's demands. Nasser had been effectively "put on the spot."[71]

Nasser's anti-Communist imperatives also expressed itself in Iraq where the rift between Nasser and Qassim revealed deeper geopolitical roots. Qassim quickly demonstrated that he was willing to empower Iraqi Communists in order to quash Nasserists such as Arif, whom he arrested in November 1958. The Communists in Iraq were among the best organized of all the political groups and Qassim was quite willing to use their political prowess to resist the desires of army officers like Arif to merge with the UAR.

By 1959, sharp exchanges between Cairo and Moscow came to public light over the airwaves. Nasser declared, "Whether the Communists go from Damascus to Baghdad to organise a plot against their native land . . . the conspiracy by the Communists against our country will not succeed."[72] Clashes between Nasser and Khrushchev led the British intelligence community to aver that "the fundamental contradiction between the objectives of Moscow and President Nasser" were coming to fruition. While the Soviet Union would "continue the process of healing their rift with Nasser" through, for instance, aid for the Aswan Dam, they estimated that "if Nasser were to mount a new campaign against Qassim . . . the Soviet Union would be expected to support Qassim, even at the cost of Nasser's goodwill."[73] In fact research into Iraqi police records shows that the Soviet Union held back the ICP precisely so as not to alienate Nasser.[74] As the British intelligence community put it, Nasser was "now more outspoken against the methods of international communism and the dangers of communist imperialism than would have seemed possible even a few months ago." This was partly to protect his leadership of the Arab world alongside what was now recognized to be a "genuine desire" to resist the spread of Communist influence.[75]

New opportunities therefore presented themselves for reconciliation with Nasser on the part of the West. The events of 1958 had revealed that Nasser's power and appeal were such that it would be folly not to try and work with him. Attempts to cultivate conservative Arab opposition in the form of the rival Jordanian-Iraqi union had clearly failed. Surveying the main currents in the Arab world in 1959, the CIA asserted: "Nasser once considered the most radical advocate of social change, now appears a moderate reformer in comparison to certain elements in Iraq."[76] Nasser had demonstrated sufficient moderation and anti-Soviet credentials to be considered a statesman with whom the US administration could, and indeed should, do business. The events of 1958 therefore led to a rapprochement with the United States that lasted into the Kennedy era, thwarted only by Nasser's next, and final, pan-Arab adventure: the Yemeni Civil War.

Conclusion

The events of 1958 clearly had important reverberations for Egypt at the domestic, regional, and global level. Domestically, the union with Syria presented an opportunity for Nasser to tackle one of the most significant internal challenges he faced: the rapidly expanding power base of Defense Minister Amer. Regionally, the union with Syria, the Lebanese crisis and the Iraqi revolution revealed the preeminence of pragmatism over revolutionary ideology in Nasser's foreign policy. At the global level, Nasser's challenges in Iraq and Syria, combined with an increasingly evident anti-Soviet posture, brought to the forefront for the West the possibility of cooperation with the Egyptian nationalist. In 1959, the UK began negotiations to reopen its embassy in Cairo, and Nasser enjoyed a rapprochement with the United States that, while tumultuous, lasted well into the 1960s.

Ultimately, the aftermath of this revolutionary year appeared to play out Nasser's private fears that neither Egypt nor his regional counterparts were ready for Arab unity in practice. Syrians came to refer to Egyptian behavior in reproachful terms that had primarily been directed at the West, including *"isti'imar"* (imperialism) and *"tassalut"* (dominion).[77] At the highest political level, this manifested in a split with the Ba'ath Party which had advocated union in the first place. Ba'athist Michel Aflaq later recounted his hopes that "our role would be both practical and theoretical since it was we who began practicing socialist ideas."[78] Indeed the Ba'ath reasoned that the "ideology and the discipline" of their regional movement would furnish the "political rationale for Nasser's revolutionary regime in Egypt."[79] However, Nasser quickly demonstrated that he was not willing to take direction from Syria: the terms of the union clearly indicated his desire for absolute hegemony. In mid-1959, Syrian Ba'athists were purged from the military and reassigned to postings in Egypt where their subversive activity could be limited. One Ba'athist of note was a young air force pilot named Hafez Al Asad who formed a "secret military committee" with other reassigned Syrian military officers. The committee would have an important role in the aftermath of secession, and of course, Asad would eventually rise to the Syrian presidency approximately a decade later.[80]

Ultimately, however, it was Nasser's experience in Iraq that, as Devlin puts it, finally "shattered the psychological impetus to unity."[81] The public acrimony with General Qassim set aside any illusory ideas about the possibility of a pan-Arab union. In Iraq, Nasser was called a "fascist dog" and "agent of imperialism" by the people who just months earlier had called for Iraq to accede to the UAR.[82] In March 1959, a group of nationalists in the northern city of Mosul began plotting to overthrow Qassim. With Egyptian support, and most likely that of the United States, the Mosul revolt was the closest Nasser came to eliminating his Iraqi rival.[83] Qassim defeated the Nasser-inspired coup with the help of his Communist allies who rallied their supporters to the streets. The failed Mosul revolt was arguably Nasser's greatest setback thus far. As McNamara puts it, "Never again would he be as close to dominating the Middle East."[84] Nasser's clashes with the Iraqi Communists brought to the forefront his fears of Soviet domination of the Middle East. While he would continue to deploy Soviet aid over the next decade, his adventures in the Arab world made clear that the nationalist was no Communist and would seek to maintain Egyptian power and primacy above all else.

Notes

1. R. McNamara, *Britain, Nasser and the Balance of Power in the Middle East, 1952–1967: From the Egyptian Revolution to the Six Day War* (London: Frank Cass, 2003), 117.
2. N. J. Ashton, "The Hijacking of a Pact: The Formation of the Baghdad Pact and Anglo-American Tensions in the Middle East, 1955–1958," *Review of International Studies* 19, no. 2 (1993): 123–37.
3. R. Abou-El-Fadl, "Neutralism Made Positive: Egyptian Anti-colonialism on the Road to Bandung," *British Journal of Middle Eastern Studies* 42, no. 2 (2015): 219–40.
4. See for example, W. R. Louis, "The Tragedy of the Anglo-Egyptian Settlement of 1954," in *Suez 1956: The Crisis and Its Consequences*, ed. W. R. Louis and E. Owen (Oxford: Clarendon, 1991). In the same volume Shimon Shamir attributes the failure of "Project Alpha" to the British, "low awareness of the authenticity, intensity and autonomy of the Arab anti-Western posture." See S. Shamir, "The Collapse of Project Alpha," in *Suez 1956: The Crisis and Its Consequences*, ed. Louis and Owen, 89. For further examples see S. Yaqub, *Containing Arab Nationalism: The Eisenhower Doctrine and the Middle East* (Chapel Hill, NC: The University of North Carolina Press, 2004), 8: the Eisenhower doctrine "rested on a basic misunderstanding of the Nasserist movement, on a drastic underestimation of its power and independence." See also E. Podeh, "The United States and the Baghdad Pact," in *The Middle East and the United States*, ed. D. Lesch (Boulder: Westview Press, 1996), 100: "The greatest mistake of the United States was its failure to comprehend Arab psychology in the postcolonial era and the depth of Arab rivalries."
5. D. Little, "Cold War and Covert Action: The United States and Syria, 1945–1958," *Middle East Journal* 44, no. 1 (1990): 51–75.
6. McNamara, *Britain, Nasser and the Balance of Power*, 117.
7. E. Podeh, *The Decline of Arab Unity: The Rise and Fall of the United Arab Republic* (Brighton: Sussex, 1999).
8. J. Jankowski, *Nasser's Egypt, Arab nationalism and the United Arab Republic* (Boulder, CO: Lynne Rienner, 2002). Jankowski persuasively argues that "Nasser's involvement in specific Arab controversies or crises was often initiated reluctantly, in response to external stimuli rather than as part of a grand desire for regional dominance."
9. A. Dawisha, *Egypt in the Arab World: The Elements of Foreign Policy* (London; New York: Macmillan, 1976), 107–9; M. Kerr, "Egyptian Foreign Policy and the Revolution," in *Egypt since the Revolution*, ed. P. J. Vatikiotis (New York: Praeger, 1968).
10. R. Abou-El-Fadl, "Early Pan-Arabism in Egypt's July Revolution: The Free Officers' Political Formation and Policy-making, 1946–54," *Nations and Nationalism* 21, no. 2 (2015): 289–308.
11. See for example, H. Kandil, *Soldiers, Spies and Statesmen: Egypt's Road to Revolt* (New York: Verso Press, 2012); and B. Crowcroft, "Egypt's Other Nationalists and the Suez Crisis of 1956," *The Historical Journal* 59, no. 1 (2016): 253–85; For more recent scholarship that sheds detailed light on Egyptian internal politics see Reem Abou-Fadl, *Foreign Policy as Nation Making: Turkey and Egypt in the Cold War* (Cambridge: Cambridge University Press, 2019).
12. For a rare scholarly exploration of this, see for example, Chapter 2 of D. Mostafa, *The Egyptian Military in Popular Culture: Context and Critique* (London: Palgrave, 2017).
13. Crowcroft, "Egypt's Other Nationalists," 265.

14 Telegram from UAR embassy to State Department, April 17, 1958, FRUS 1958-1960, Vol. XIII.
15 Telegram from UAR embassy to State Department, October 26, 1958, FRUS 1958-1960, Vol. XIII.
16 Mohamed Abdel Ghani El-Gamasy, *The October War: Memoirs of Field Marshall Al Gamasy of Egypt* (Cairo: The American University of Cairo Press, 1993), 41.
17 Anwar al Sadat, *Al-Bahth'an al-zat* (In Search of Identity) (Cairo: al-Maktab al-Misri al-Hadith, 1978), 220.
18 Crowcroft, "Egypt's Other Nationalists," 284.
19 'Abd al-'Azim Ramadan, *Al-Haqiqah al-tarikhiyah hawla qarar ta'amim sharikat qanat al-suways* (The Historical Truth about the Decision to Nationalize the Suez Canal Company) (Cairo, 2000), 21–3, 27.
20 Crowcroft, "Egypt's Other Nationalists," 263.
21 S. Aburish, *Nasser: The Last Arab* (New York: St Martin's Press, 2004), 267.
22 In addition to Kandil's book and thesis, for further detail on this rivalry within Egypt's security state see D. Rezk, "Egypt's Spy Chiefs: Servants or Leaders," in *Spy Chiefs Volume 2: Intelligence Leaders in Europe, the Middle East and Asia*, ed. P. Maddrell, C. Moran, I. Iordanou, and M. Stout (Washington: Georgetown, 2018).
23 H. Kandil, "Power Triangle: Military, Security, and Politics in the Shaping of the Egyptian, Iranian, and Turkish Regimes" (Unpublished UCA PhD thesis), 147–9.
24 A. Al-Rafe'i, *Thawrat23 Yulyu 1952: Tarikhnaal-qawmifeisaba'sanawat, 1952–1959* (The Revolution of July 23, 1952: Our National History in Seven Years, 1952–1959) (Cairo: Dar al-Ma'aref, 1989), 269.
25 Kandil, "Power Triangle," 150.
26 G. A. Nasser, *Falsafat al-Thawra* (The Philosophy of the Revolution) (Cairo: Madbuli, 2003), 69.
27 S. Sharaf, *Sanawat wa Ayam ma'a Jamal Abd al-Nasser: al-Juz' al-Awwal* (Years and Days with Jamal Abdel Nasser: I) (Cairo: Al-Fursan, 2005), 171.
28 S. Bitar, *Al-Siyasa al-Arabiyah bayn al Mabda aw al Tatbig* (Arab Policy in Principle and Practice) (Beirut: Dar al-Tali'ah, 1960), 48.
29 A. Alexander, *Nasser: His Life and Times* (Cairo: Cairo University Press, 2005), 109.
30 Rezk, "Egypt's Spy Chiefs: Servants or Leaders," 231.
31 Ahmed al-Said, cited in L. James, "Whose Voice? Nasser, the Arabs, and 'Sawt al-Arab' Radio," Arab Media and Society, June 1, 2006, https://www.arabmediasociety.com/whose-voice-nasser-the-arabs-and-sawt-al-arab-radio/ (accessed July 17, 2019).
32 F. Al-Deeb, *Abdel Nasser wa Thawrat al-Jaza'ir* (Abdel Nasser and Algeria's Revolution) (Cairo: Dar al-Mustaqbal al-'Arabi, 1984), 33–42.
33 James, "Whose Voice? Nasser, the Arabs, and 'Sawt al-Arab' Radio."
34 D. Rezk, *The Arab World and Western Intelligence: Analysing the Middle East 1956–1981* (Edinburgh: EUP, 2017), 84.
35 The Baghdad Pact, a regional defense organization linking Britain to Iraq, Turkey, Iran, and Pakistan was ostensibly designed to protect the Middle East from Communist incursions but was regarded by Egyptian regime as an attempt by the British to pursue its enduring imperial interests in the Arab world. The United States famously refrained from joining the Pact.
36 Memorandum from Acting Assistant Secretary of State for Near Eastern, South Asian and African Affairs (Berry) to Acting Secretary of State, January 25, 1958, FRUS 1958–1960, Vol. XIII, No. 187.

37 Memorandum from Beeley to Middleton, August 13, 1957, TNA, FO 371/128224.
38 NSC Report 5801/1, "Note by the Executive Secretary to the National Security Council on Long Range U.S. policy toward the Near East," January 24, 1958, FRUS Vol. XII, No. 5.
39 R. Louis, *Ends of British Imperialism: The Scramble for Empire, Suez and Decolonization: Collected Essays* (London: I.B. Tauris, 2006), 793.
40 JIC memorandum (58) 25, "The Implications of the United Arab Republic and the Arab Union," April 30, 1958, TNA, CAB 158/32.
41 *Akhar Sa'a*, March 12, 1958, quoted in Keith Wheelock, *Nasser's New Egypt* (London: Stevens, 1960), 262.
42 Podeh, *The Decline of Arab Unity*, 177.
43 Yaqub, *Containing Arab Nationalism*, 184–6.
44 J. Devlin, *The Ba'ath Party: A History from Its Origins to 1966* (Stanford, California: The Hoover Institution Press, 1976), 88.
45 Jankowski, *Nasser's Egypt*, 106.
46 Yaqub, *Containing Arab Nationalism*, 207.
47 Nasser quoted in Alexander, *Nasser*, 112.
48 Briefing Notes by DCI Dulles, July 14, 1958, FRUS 1958–1960, Vol. XII, No. 110.
49 JIC memorandum (58) 77, "Nasser's probable policy and aims over the next six months," August 1, 1958, TNA, CAB 158/33(emphasis added).
50 Memorandum by Ambassador Wright in Iraq, "The Immediate Outlook," July 24, 1958, TNA, FO 371/134201. Wright had also served in Sir Miles Lampson's Cairo embassy during the Second World War.
51 N. Daniel, "Contemporary Perceptions of the Revolution," in *The Iraqi Revolution of 1958: The Old Social Classes Revisited*, ed. Robert A. Fernea and Wm. Roger Louis (London: I.B. Tauris, 1990), 26.
52 JIC memorandum (58) 76, "The Immediate Outlook in Iraq," August 5, 1958, TNA, CAB 158/33.
53 Alexander, *Nasser*, 114.
54 Ibid., 115.
55 Jankowski, *Nasser's Egypt*, 114.
56 Ibid., 107.
57 T. Ismael, J. Ismael, and K. Jaber (eds.), *Politics and Government in the Middle East and North Africa* (Miami: Florida International University Press, 1991), 196.
58 Despatch from Clarke in at British Consulate General Damascus to FO, July 31, 1961, TNA, FO 371/158797.
59 Intelligence report, "The Outlook for the UAR," March 11, 1960, OSS/SDIRR, The Middle East 1950–1961, Microfilm, Reel 2, SOAS Library.
60 H. M. Heikal, *Matar, Bisaraha 'an Abd al Nasser* (Beirut: al-Dar al-Muttahida li al-Nashr, 1972), 157.
61 Telegram from Embassy in Cairo to State Department, February 10, 1958, FRUS 1958–1960, Vol. XIII, No. 195.
62 Telegram from Embassy in Cairo to State Department, February 18, 1958, FRUS 1958–1960, Vol. XIII, No. 197.
63 Hare also argued that the union provided "'opportunities to undercut' Nasser in his 'newly extended and more vulnerable' position."
64 C. Andrew and V. Mitrokhin, *The Mitrokhin Archive II: The KGB and the World* (London: Allen Lane, 2005), 150.
65 Ibid., 149.

66 Interview with Raymond Hare, available at https://adst.org/wp-content/uploads/2018/02/Egypt.pdf, 10.
67 SNIE 30-3-58, "Arab nationalism as a factor in the Middle East situation," August 12, 1958, FOIA Reading Room.
68 For more detail on this see Rezk, *The Arab World and Western Intelligence*, Chapter 2.
69 JIC memorandum (58) 25, "The Implications of the United Arab Republic and the Arab Union," April 30, 1958, TNA, CAB 158/32.
70 SNIE 30-58, "Prospects and Consequences of Arab Unity Moves," February 20, 1958, FOIA Reading Room.
71 Memorandum from Acting Assistant Secretary of State for Near Eastern, South Asian and African Affairs (Berry) to Acting Secretary of State, January 25, 1958, FRUS 1958–1960 Vol. XIII, No. 187.
72 Nasser quoted in Alexander, *Nasser*, 117.
73 JIC memorandum (59) 61, "Possible Trouble Spots in the Middle East over the Next Six Months," August 7, 1959, TNA, CAB 158/37.
74 Sluglett and Sluglett, "The Social Classes and the Origins of the Revolution," in *The Iraqi Revolution of 1958*, 69.
75 JIC memorandum (59) 50, "A re-examination of the likely consequences of military intervention in Iraq," June 8, 1959, TNA, CAB 158/36.
76 NIE 30-59 "Main Currents in the Arab world," August 25, 1959, FRUS 1958-1960, Vol. XII, No. 71.
77 Podeh, *The Decline of Arab Unity*, 55.
78 Jankowski, *Nasser's Egypt*, 118.
79 Telegram from Embassy in Damascus to State Department, February 8, 1958, FRUS 1958–1960, Vol. XIII, No. 192.
80 Jankowski, *Nasser's Egypt*, 129.
81 Devlin, *The Ba'ath Party*, 127.
82 Telegram from Embassy in Baghdad to State Department, March 26, 1959, FRUS 1958–1960, Vol. XII, No. 166.
83 K. Osgood, "Eisenhower and Regime Change in Iraq: The United States and the Iraqi Revolution of 1958," in D. Ryan and P. Kiely (eds.), *America and Iraq: Policy-Making, Intervention and Regional Politics* (Abingdon: Routledge, 2009), 20. Although the documentary record remains incomplete, Osgood concludes: "At the very least, the United States gave its tacit approval to the scheme. Knowing of the plot beforehand, the Eisenhower administration did nothing to thwart it and did not alert Qassim to the danger."
84 McNamara, *Britain, Nasser and the Balance of Power*, 150.

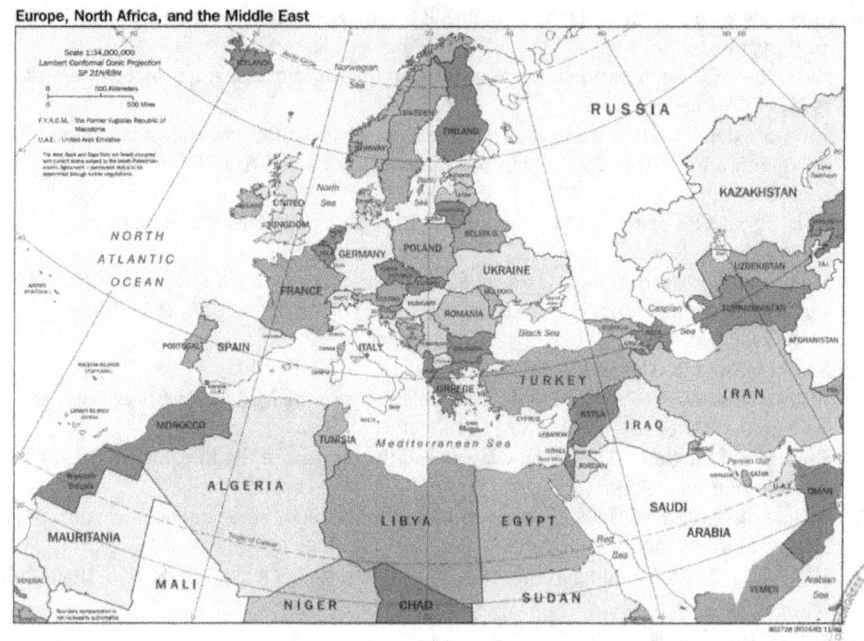

Figure 1 Map of Middle East, North Africa, and Europe.
Source: Creative Commons Attribution, Public Domain.

Figure 2 Egypt's *al-Ahram* newspaper announcing the birth of the UAR on February 23, 1958, following the plebiscites that took place in Syria and Egypt.
Source: Damascus History Foundation. Courtesy of DHF chairman Dr. Sami Moubayed.

Figure 3 Abd al-Hamid al-Sarraj meeting Gamal Abdel Nasser in Cairo after he was smuggled out of the Mazza prison in May 1962. He was jailed following the September 1961 coup in Damascus that ended the UAR.
Source: Damascus History Foundation. Courtesy of DHF chairman Dr. Sami Moubayed.

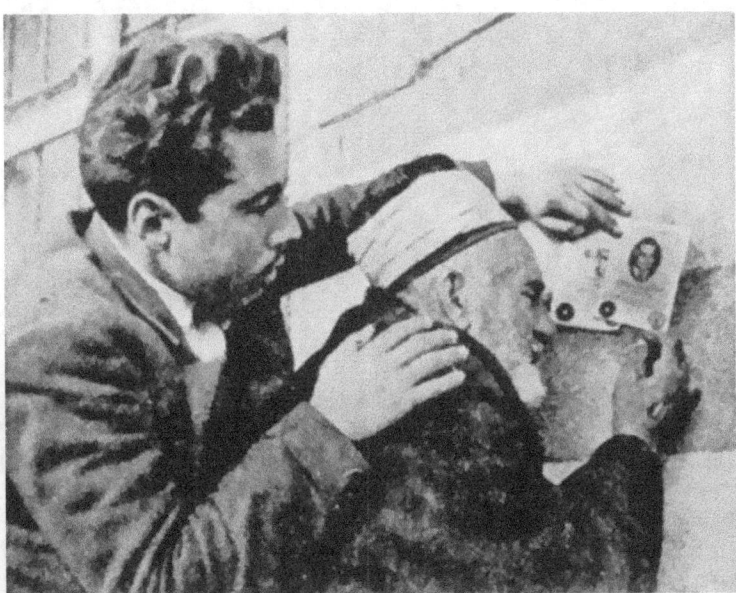

Figure 4 A young Syrian helps an elderly man to vote for Gamal Abdel Nasser in the February 1958 plebiscite in Damascus.
Source: Damascus History Foundation. Courtesy of DHF chairman Dr. Sami Moubayed.

Figure 5 Gamal Abdel Nasser (now president of the UAR) addressing thousands of Syrians who came to greet him on his first visit to Damascus in February 1958.
Source: Damascus History Foundation. Courtesy of DHF chairman Dr. Sami Moubayed.

Figure 6 US Marine sits in a foxhole and points a machine gun toward Beirut, Lebanon, in the distance, 1958.
Source: Library of Congress. Public Domain.

Figure 7 American soldier reads a newspaper in the shade under a US Marine tank in Beirut, Lebanon, 1958.
Source: Library of Congress. Public Domain.

Figure 8 Picture collage of the Algerian War of Independence.
Source and Author: Madame Grinderche, Public Domain.

Figure 9 Arab Federation talks between Jordan and Iraq in early 1958, with King Hussein and King Faisal II present.
Source: Jordanian Archive, Public Domain.

Figure 10 US president Dwight D. Eisenhower meeting with Egyptian President Gamal Abdel Nasser during Nasser's visit to UN in New York, 1960.
Source: Bibliotheca Alexandrina and Gamal Abdel Nasser Foundation, Public Domain.

Figure 11 President Eisenhower meeting with Secretary of State John Foster Dulles at the White House, 1956.
Source: US National Archives and Records Administration, Public Domain.

Figure 12 Leaders of the July 14, 1958, revolution in Iraq, including Khaled al-Naqshabendi (front row, left), Abd as-Salam Arif (back row, second from left), Abd al-Karim Qassim (back row, third from left) and Muhammad Najib ar-Ruba'i (back row, fifth from left). Also included is Michel Aflaq (front row, first from right). The person between Aflaq and Naqshbandi is possibly Baba Ali al-Barzanji (front row); the person behind Aflaq and beside ar-Rubai'i is possibly Muhammad Mahdi Kubba (back row).
Source: Public Domain.

Figure 13 Seated from left to right: Chief of Staff of Arab Legion Glubb Pasha, King Hussein of Jordan, and Aide-de-camp Ali Abu Nuwar. Behind them are Jordanian officers of the Arab Legion (a British officer is standing in the middle of the Jordanian officers). *Source*: Ali Abunwar Memoirs, Public Domain.

Chapter 8

THE OUTSIDER INSIDE

TURKEY AND THE DOMINO EFFECT OF ARAB NATIONALISM IN 1958

Murat Kasapsaraçoğlu

As the ruling party of Turkey in the 1950s, Democrat Party (DP) was ambitious for political liberalization, economic development, and military modernization, which determined objectives of Turkish foreign policy in this decade. Turkey's political, economic, and military objectives were harmonized by the decision-makers, and the development of relations with the United States, which had already been started by the Republican People's Party (RPP) in the post–Second World War era, was regarded indispensable for the maximization of Turkey's interests.[1]

After Turkey's membership to the North Atlantic Treaty Organization (NATO) in 1952, the only area in which Turkey could prove its goodwill and loyalty to the United States for maximizing its interests was the Middle East. For the United States, in return, Turkey's role in the Middle East as a bridge between the West and the region was a priority, especially in the first half of the decade.[2] Accordingly, Turkey played a pivotal role in the formation of the Baghdad Pact with Iraq, which paved the way for deepening hostility and tension between the allies of the West and the followers of Arab nationalism in the region, and for the spread of Nasserist propaganda. Throughout the decade, DP government harmonized its Middle East policy with the United States and took a stance against Nasser's Egypt, blaming it for the infiltration of communism into the region because of its cooperation with the USSR, particularly in economic and military areas. The split and tension in the region ended up with crises and revolutions uprooting the region in 1958.

Developments in 1958 were revolutionary for the DP government in Turkey as well as the Middle East in the sense that the regime in Iraq, Turkey's closest ally in the region, changed and the Baghdad Pact collapsed after the withdrawal of Iraq. The collapse of the Baghdad Pact stood for the bankruptcy of Turkey's US-centric policy in the Middle East. Regarding Turkey's domestic politics, indicators of the military intervention in 1960 were seen in the horizon and the DP government carried out more oppressive policies toward the opposition and the press especially after 1958.

The Impact of the Baghdad Pact on Turkey

Developments in 1958 stemmed from the changing dynamics in the region in the second half of the decade, so the Baghdad Pact was a critical point in the analysis of the revolutionary year of 1958 and its impact on Turkey. The Baghdad Pact was established as a setback to Soviet expansion in the region, and Turkey played an active role in collaboration with the US interests. The Pact was signed between Turkey and Iraq in 1955, and then Iran, Pakistan, and the UK joined the establishment. The alliance was the keystone of Turkey's Middle East policy because it was used by the DP government to show its loyalty to the United States in order to get economic and military support from the latter. Similarly, the Pact was used by the member states as a leverage to reach their political, economic, and military objectives as they ambitiously negotiated with the US authorities who were joining Pact meetings.[3]

As time passed, the Baghdad Pact bolstered the split in the Arab world. Basic reasons for the deterioration of relations in the region were the intervention of big powers in regional politics, and the rivalry and hostility between regional states, particularly between Arabs and Israel. Great powers pushed hard for keeping these states under control, and, in return, the latter used their economic and military needs as leverage to maximize their interests. Therefore, the establishment of Baghdad Pact alliance influenced regional politics dramatically.[4] Throughout the process, Turkey acted in collaboration with the United States as it saw the Soviet infiltration into the region and the expansion of communism as a major threat. This shows how Turkish decision-makers misinterpreted the developments, specifically the rise of Arab nationalism and anti-Zionism under the leadership of Nasser. It can be argued that Turkey was the "outsider inside" the region throughout the decade. Shortly, the Pact deteriorated relations between pro-Western and nationalist governments in the region. Some scholars argue that tension among regional states stemmed from the intervention of outsiders such as the United Kingdom, France, and the United States in regional politics. On the other hand, some scholars argue that the tension resulted from the rivalry between Nasser's Egypt and Nuri Said's Iraq for the leadership of the Arab world.[5] Even if there was rivalry between Egypt and Iraq, obviously it was not among equals when the success and domination of Nasser in the region as the pioneer of Arab nationalism until the 1970s is taken into consideration.

Under these conditions, Turkey took side with Nuri Said's Iraq and pushed for the consolidation of Baghdad Pact alliance in vain. Similarly, in the crises erupted between 1955 and 1958 such as the Suez Crisis and border crisis with Syria, Turkey acted in collaboration with the United States. During the Suez Crisis Turkey acted as a mediator by joining London Conferences and denounced Israel for its attack on Egypt.[6] In the border crisis with Syria, Turkey acted as a hardliner against the USSR and Egypt with the support of the United States.[7] To the disadvantage of Western powers, after the Suez Crisis, the prestige and popularity of Nasser increased in the Arab world as the leader of Arab nationalism, which paved the way for the revolutionary year of 1958.[8]

All in all, Turkey played the US card between the establishment of the Baghdad Pact in 1955 and the high tide of Arab nationalism in 1958.[9] With the rise of Arab nationalism and the revolutionary year of 1958, the Baghdad Pact lost the power ascribed to it, and the pillar of Turkey's Middle East policy collapsed. The split widened by the Baghdad Pact resulted in the unification of Egypt and Syria in early 1958—an indicator of the impact of rising Arab nationalism and influence of Nasser as the leader of this movement in the region.

Turkey and the United Arab Republic (UAR) under Nasser Rule

With the establishment of the UAR, joining Egypt and Syria, in early 1958, Turkey's position toward Arab nationalism and Nasser began to change because the Communist Party was outlawed and Communists in the country were arrested.[10] As a result, the new state was recognized by Turkey, like the great powers and the other states in the region. However, despite the change in Turkish policy toward Nasser, the DP government did not understand the power and influence of Arab nationalism till the eruption of revolutions in the Arab world in the summer of 1958. After the recognition of the UAR by Turkey, the Turkish ambassador in Cairo met with Nasser in May 1958 and told him that the Turkish government was willing to establish friendly relations with the UAR. More importantly, he added that the Turkish government was happy with Nasser's efforts to eliminate communism in Syria. The DP government also forced the media in Turkey to end aggressive publications about the UAR.[11] In this meeting, Nasser stated that development of friendly relations between Turkey and the UAR was a reflection of his policy toward Turkey and that the problematic relations between them between 1955 and 1958 stemmed from "misunderstandings."[12] These developments were compatible with Turkey's approach to Middle East politics based on the prevention of Soviet influence and communism. After a while, the two states signed a trade agreement.[13]

After the formation of the UAR, the editor of the *Akis* journal, Metin Toker, criticized the developments in the region and the DP government's policy. He argued that after the establishment of this union, Iraq would leave the Baghdad Pact, so the Turkish government should be prepared for the collapse of the Pact. He added and urged the DP government to be more realistic and accept the reality of Arab nationalism. According to him, the USSR was more successful than the Western allies in understanding the realities of the Arab world. As a result, the region had become more open to the influence of the USSR, so the possibility of Iraq's withdrawal from the Pact should be considered because there was no common interest of the Pact members which might prevent Iraq from doing so.[14]

It can be argued that journalist Toker was more far-sighted than the DP government because shortly after the formation of the UAR, the summer of 1958 turned into a revolutionary period for Middle East politics. The dynastic rule in Iraq was overthrown by a military junta and the king, crown prince, and prime minister of Iraq were killed. In Turkey, the revolution in Iraq shocked and forced the DP government to take measures to save the Baghdad Pact. Turkey's Middle East policy in the 1950s, especially after 1955, had two pillars: the prevention of both the expansion of Arab nationalism as led by Nasser and the infiltration of the Soviet Union into the region. Therefore, successive developments in July 1958 represented the collapse of Turkey's US-centric Middle East policy.

Turkish Perception of Iraq

After radical and bloody developments in Iraq, the United States and United Kingdom expected an appeal from the Baghdad Pact members to take necessary measures to save the Baghdad Pact and prevent the threat to regional stability born out of the events in Iraq and Lebanon.[15] Turkey was the key actor in this scenario, and officials in the West were expecting a Turkish intervention in Iraq.[16] More importantly, some officials stated that Turkey was putting pressure on its Western allies for an intervention and that the latter prevented the former from taking an action.[17] According to the director of Central Intelligence Agency (CIA), Allan Dulles, the only impediment preventing Turkey from such an action was the lack of US support and assurance.[18] Similarly, the British ambassador in Washington said: "The Americans are confident that Turkey will not take any action in Iraq on their own without promises of US support."[19] Under these circumstances, the United States was trying to understand Turkish plans and estimates on the situation in Iraq. There wasn't any organized opposition against the new regime in Iraq, thus, if Turkey carried out a military operation in Iraq, it would most probably face opposition and resistance from the Iraqi population and military forces.[20] Upon these estimates, the US government decided not to encourage Turkey for such an intervention until they learned the Turkish government's plans and saw that there was no opposition in Iraq against Turkey's action.[21] While the possibility of a Turkish intervention was on the table, the US secretary of state urged President Eisenhower to recognize the new regime in Iraq as quickly as possible:

> Officials of Iran, Pakistan, and Turkey indicated their understanding of the advisability of US recognition, without delay so as to be in the best position to protect United States interests in Iraq and exert constructive influence upon the new regime. Lebanon and Jordan expressed similar appreciation privately. Other Arab states, such as Saudi Arabia and Tunisia, had already extended recognition.[22]

Despite the initial resentment and reaction against the military intervention and rumors about a Turkish intervention, the United States recognized the new regime in Iraq.[23] However, these rumors did not come to an end even after the new Iraqi regime was recognized by the states not only in the West but also in the Middle East, including Turkey. The British high commissioner in Pakistan said that in his meeting with the president of Pakistan, the president claimed that Turkey's prime minister, Adnan Menderes, offered to invade Iraq with some military divisions as soon as possible. Upon this suggestion, the president of Pakistan tried very hard to persuade Menderes that such an action would be foolish.[24] The British ambassador in Ankara approached the issue from a different angle. According to him, Turkey's main concern in Iraq was the possibility of the establishment of a Kurdish state in the north and the Turkish community in this area. Particularly, Mullah Mustafa Barzani's arrival in Iraq from the USSR after the coup caused anxiety and reaction in the DP government about the creation of a Kurdish state in northern Iraq.[25]

After the DP government had recognized the new regime at the end of July, it re-formulated its Iraq policy in a way that the Turkish consulate in Kirkuk which had been closed right after the coup is opened again. More importantly, Turkish government was following the developments in Iraq, and Turkey's ambassador in Baghdad reported that the USSR had delivered arms to the Iraqis at Basra and he "believed" that secret talks were carried out between the USSR and the new regime in Baghdad.[26] In other words, although the Turkish government gave up the idea of intervention, the possibility of "Communist threat" and support from the USSR to the new regime in Iraq were taken into consideration.

It can be argued that these expectations were groundless because although Qassim's regime in Iraq was based on Nasserist nationalists who had close ties with the Communists in the country, there was no proof that Nasser and the USSR provoked these groups, so the United States and Turkey were heavily influenced by their anti-Communist and anti-Nasserist sentiments in their analyzes rather than by the dynamics in the region. By the same token, unrest and disorder continued along the Iraqi border shared with Iran, Syria, and Turkey. Iraqi government argued that the tribes along its borders were provoked and supported by Turkey and Syria against the new regime. At the same time, Communists consolidated their power especially in the economic realm. Upon these developments, Turkey questioned its policy of rapprochement with Iraq.[27]

As a result, the military intervention in Iraq had a serious influence on Middle East politics: the regime in Iraq that was friendly with the West and Turkey was overthrown and it was regarded as the victory of Nasser's Arab nationalism, presumably supported by the USSR. Regarding Turkey, there were rumors and expectations for a military intervention and there were some indicators that the DP government was planning to do so. However, the lack of US support for this action prevented the DP government from intervening in Iraq. In a short while, and following the United States, the Turkish government recognized the new regime in Iraq and pushed hard for normalizing and developing its relations with the new regime. The power and role of communism influenced Turkey's relations with Iraq after the coup d'état. More importantly, Turkish government had to deal with two other crises in Lebanon and Jordan following the regime change in Iraq.

Turkish Perception of Lebanon and Jordan

Especially the US intervention in Lebanon following the events in Iraq was based on the Eisenhower Doctrine aiming to support friendly regimes in the region.

Crises in Lebanon and Jordan mainly stemmed from the political unrest and Civil War. The role of Turkey in the Civil War was mentioned in a report as follows: "Turkey has not been cut in any way because they are very leaky in security matters but the state department feels that they will help Lebanese if fighting begins."[28] In particular, Turkey might offer assistance if the Cyprus situation, the main problem in Turkish foreign policy in this period, permitted.[29]

The US ambassador in Lebanon reported that the commander of Lebanese gendarmerie forces, Colonel Zouein, had told him that "Chamoun intended to use the possibility of intervention by Turkey and Iraq as his last cartridge."[30] These rumors about Turkey were proved wrong and the United States had to take action and intervene in Lebanon on July 15, 1958. The US forces landed on Lebanese soil to protect the regime of Chamoun, and, in the joint message of the president of Turkey, Celal Bayar, the shah of Iran, and the president of Pakistan to US president Eisenhower, the three leaders emphasized that before the US intervention in Lebanon, the conditions were serious.

The Turkish position during the British intervention in Jordan was supportive of King Hussein. The British ambassador in Amman stated that his Turkish counterpart in Amman, Mahmut Dikerdem, had been instructed by the Turkish president to declare Turkey and the DP government's support to the king of Jordan. In this crisis, Turkey was not in favor of a government change, and the Turkish ambassador told his British colleague that the Turkish government was strongly supporting the view and action of the UK: the protection of Jordan's independence.[31] Moreover, Dikerdem argues that King Hussein was planning to cooperate with Turkey in order to protect its rule by putting military pressure on Syria with the help of Turkey, while Turkey was not willing to conduct an independent policy from its Western allies. Therefore, Turkey and Jordan did not form any alliance against Syria.[32]

The Impact of Summer 1958 on Turkey's Domestic Politics

The crises in the Middle East had some repercussions in Turkish domestic politics, particularly in relations between the DP government and the parliamentary opposition and the press. Especially in the second half of the 1950s, relations between the government and the opposition were full of problems and tension. The DP government intensified its pressure on the press, criticizing its policies. After the coup in Iraq, the opposition in the parliament, mainly the RPP, repeatedly point out a possibility of a "revolution" (*ihtilal*) in Turkey and such declarations disturbed the DP government. Rulers of the DP government began to approach possible sources of revolution with suspicion and they implemented more oppressive policies toward the opposition, in the parliament and society, so as not to share the same fate as the Iraqi rulers. For example, the Fatherland Front (Vatan Cephesi) was established by the DP to show the public support behind the party. However, the most critical point in the way to "revolution" was the Commission of Investigation (Tahkikat Komisyonu) putting pressure on the opposition in the parliament which inflamed the reaction in the society and gathered all dissident groups—opposition parties, intellectuals, university students, and ultimately soldiers—as a united front against the government. Despite all these measures and oppression, Turkey fell into turbulence and the DP rule ended with a military intervention on May 27, 1960.[33]

Regarding the reflection of foreign policy on domestic politics, successive developments in Iraq, Lebanon, and Jordan in 1958 were closely followed and debated by the opposition in the parliament and the press. Turkey's Middle East policy was harshly criticized by the opposition after the collapse of the Baghdad Pact right after the revolution in Iraq. In an article right before the successive crises, Toker analyzed the developments in the Middle East and criticized the DP government for government's failure in analyzing the realities in the region. For him, the leaders in the region were competing with each other and seeking allies to reach their goals, so the Turkish government should be alert and not become involved in the struggles between Arab states. On the contrary, Turkey should be more objective regarding the developments in the region.[34] It can be argued that the position of Toker was deeply influenced by İsmet İnönü: "to act realistically and not to be engaged in and not to be a part of struggles and conflicts in the region."

Rumors about a Turkish intervention in Iraq and the DP government's policy during the crisis in general were harshly criticized by the main opposition party, RPP, in the parliament. İnönü, as the leader of the party and the former president of Turkey, stated that successive rumors about a Turkish military intervention in Iraq were disturbing and harmful. According to him, such an intervention by Turkey might invite more serious military actions. In addition, İnönü criticized "off-the-record" statements of the Turkish minister of foreign affairs, Fatin Rüştü Zorlu, for sending volunteers to save the regime in this country. He also touched upon the fact that the United States prevented Turkey from carrying out such an intervention.[35] After İnönü's speech and criticisms, Minister Zorlu replied to these accusations and rejected all the rumors about Turkey's intervention in Iraq.[36] Therefore, rumors about a Turkish intervention in Iraq were heavily criticized by the leader of the main opposition party.

Upon the coup d'état in Iraq and crises in Lebanon and Jordan, İnönü made another speech in the parliament evaluating these developments and the DP government's policy in general. According to him, the Arab world was politically and domestically in turmoil and Turkey welcomed the independence of some Arab states and had tried to establish friendly relations in the last forty years. The RPP desired the development of relations with the neighboring Arab states. On the contrary, Turkey should not interfere with the conflicts between the Arab states, and the Arab states, in return, should respect Turkey's noninvolvement policy as well as its rights and interests. Only under these circumstances was it possible to start a new age in the region.[37] Shortly, İnönü and his party were against the DP's efforts to be involved in the successive crises in the Middle East, because Turkey had nothing to gain from being part of such developments within or among the states in the region.[38] Therefore, Turkey had to formulate and conduct its foreign policy according to its own interests.[39]

Like the opposition, the press was closely following and hotly debating the developments in the Middle East in 1958 while there was a split between the supporters and opponents of the DP government. For example, in the newspapers closer to the government, the military intervention in Iraq and the crises in Lebanon and Jordan were regarded as the intervention and provocation of outside forces, implying President Nasser and the USSR. Accordingly, their main objectives were destabilizing the region, benefiting from the instability, and undermining the Baghdad Pact. Therefore, for the writers in these journals, the United States and the United Kingdom had intervened in Lebanon and Jordan, respectively, to prevent the region from falling into instability and unrest; so, the DP government's policy in support of the Western powers was right and legitimate. On the contrary, the possibility of a Turkish military intervention in Iraq was criticized because of the public support behind the new regime.[40]

Writers in the *Forum* journal, which was known as a leftist journal, emphasized the necessity of policy change by the government and criticized the government's Middle East policy. According to the editorial board of the journal, Middle East policy of the DP government had been proved wrong with the successive events in Iraq, Lebanon, and Jordan. The DP government should have cooperated with the key figures of Arab nationalism rather than with the pro-Western notables and rulers, who had lost their legitimacy and public support, and should have persuaded its Western allies to do the same. The military intervention in Iraq would decrease the prestige and popularity of the West in Asia, Africa, and the Middle East, so Turkey and its allies should change their policies. However, the US intervention in Lebanon did not imply such a policy change.[41]

On the contrary, the press closer to the opposition strongly criticized the government's Middle East policy in general and its policy during the crises in particular. After the regime change in Iraq, journalist Bülent Ecevit, who would become the prime minister and carry out the Cyprus intervention in 1974, wrote that the developments in Iraq were not surprising because Middle East policies of the Western powers and Turkey were wrong. Moreover, the DP government did not take warnings on its Middle East policy into consideration. He also claimed that the Baghdad Pact would continue without Iraq and the new regime might establish a federation with the UAR.[42] By the same token, he criticized the US intervention in Lebanon in the sense that it did not ameliorate the situation, but would deepen the resentment and hostility in the Arab world against the West. If mandate regimes were established in these Arab states, this would force the Arabs to make a choice between Western and Eastern blocs, and, the Arabs would most probably choose the Communist East.[43] Toker's article on the US intervention in Lebanon shows his position toward the Middle East policy of the government. According to Toker, the US intervention in Lebanon was not legitimate and it was in conflict with the principles of justice that the United States had pioneered. This action would decrease the prestige of the United States in the eyes of the Arab world and it would be a "fiasco" and, more importantly, it would be better for Turkey to try and prevent the United States from intervening rather than to support its action immediately.[44]

In addition, *Forum* writer Mümtaz Soysal stated that the government should change its Middle East policy, but there was no indicator of a change in this direction. He referred to İnönü and stated that the best policy for Turkey would be to stay out of the regional problems and to implement a policy aiming to protect the security of the region and Turkey against the USSR.[45]

DP government's policy after the coup d'état in Iraq was also discussed during budget discussions in February 1959. RPP member Kasım Gülek criticized government's policy on Iraq and stated that the developments in Iraq were not "bloody events supported from abroad" and criticized the claims of DP government. Moreover, for him, Turkey's aggressive stance toward the new regime in Iraq at the beginning had been criticized throughout the world.

To sum up, DP government's policies and approach to successive crises in the Middle East, which were harmonious to those of the Allies, particularly the United States, were strongly criticized by the opposition in the parliament, mainly RPP and its leader. According to İnönü, Turkey should have stayed out of the problems in the Arab world to protect the regional status quo in order to preserve Turkey's independence and sovereignty. For him, the DP government took some risks by involving in these crises, and Turkey's position in the region weakened due to rumors about a military intervention in Iraq. The press which was critical of government's Middle East policy suggested that the government should change its West-centric Middle East policy and act more realistically in the region.

Having taken the approaches of the government and opposition into consideration, it can be concluded that regarding the crises in Iraq, Lebanon, and Jordan; DP government's position was in harmony with the United States and that Turkish decision-makers approached these successive events with the lenses of Western powers: anti-communism and anti-Nasserism. On the contrary, the opposition was stressing the necessity of noninvolvement in these crises and the protection of Turkey's country-specific interests and regional status quo, so the revolutionary year of 1958 widened the gap between the government and the opposition. Ultimately, as the domino effect of Arab nationalism and revolutions in the region, the military intervention took place against the ruling government in 1960.

Conclusion

The Middle East was a battleground for big powers in the 1950s and this rivalry, together with inherent problems in the region such as Arab nationalism and rivalry among states, caused tension and crises especially in the second half of the decade. Developments in 1958 were revolutionary for the DP government in Turkey as well as for the Middle East in the sense that the regime in Iraq, Turkey's closest ally in the region, changed and the Baghdad Pact collapsed after the withdrawal of Iraq. The collapse of the Baghdad Pact stood for the bankruptcy of Turkey's US-centric policy in the Middle East. In the following period until 1980s, Turkey would not try to step in the region and be as active as in the 1950s.

Regarding Turkey's domestic politics, feeling the anxiety of a coup d'état forced DP rulers to conduct more oppressive policies toward the opposition and the press, so relations between the government and the opposition were ill-poised by the problems and tension, especially in the second half of the 1950s. Moreover, DP's Middle East policy was heavily criticized by the opponents of the DP regime after the collapse of the Baghdad Pact following the revolution in Iraq. As a result of this tension and polarization in the society, indicators of the military intervention in 1960 were seen in the horizon. As the DP government intensified its pressure on the opposition and the press criticizing its policies, opposition in the parliament and society, mainly the RPP, repeatedly point out a possibility of a revolution (*ihtilal*) in Turkey and such declarations and demonstrations disturbed the DP government. Rulers of the DP government began to approach possible sources of revolution with suspicion, so as not to share the same fate as the Iraqi rulers. Despite all these measures and suspicion, the DP period ended with a military intervention on May 27, 1960.

Notes

1 Murat Kasapsaraçoğlu, "Harmonization of Turkey's Political, Economic and Military Interests in the 1950s: Reflections on Turkey's Middle East Policy," *Turkish Studies* 16, no. 3 (2015): 344; Oral Sander, *Türk-Amerikan İlişkileri 1947–1964* (Ankara: İmge Kitabevi, 2016). For more details about social and economic dynamics that shaped the DP's foreign policy see Korkut Boratav, *Türkiye İktisat Tarihi 1908–2015* (Ankara: İmge Kitabevi, 2018), 110–21; Şevket Pamuk, *Türkiye'nin 200 Yıllık İktisadi Tarihi* (İstanbul: Türkiye İş Bankası Kültür Yayınları, 2014), 225–34; Oktay Yenal, *Cumhuriyet'in İktisat Tarihi* (İstanbul: Türkiye İş Bankası Kültür Yayınları, 2013), 98–104; Gülten Kazgan, *Tanzimat'tan 21.Yüzyıla Türkiye Ekonomisi* (İstanbul: Bilgi Üniversitesi Yayınları, 2006), 78–84; For more on Turkey's nation building process and definition of national interests during the 1950s see Reem Abou-Fadl, *Foreign Policy as Nation Making: Turkey and Egypt in the Cold War* (Cambridge: Cambridge University Press, 2019).
2 FRUS 1951.v.5.i.8, 51–2.
3 For a detailed analysis of the Baghdad Pact see Behçet Kemal Yeşilbursa, *The Baghdad Pact: Anglo-American Defense Policies in the Middle East* (London: Frank Cass, 2005). See also John Ghazvinian, "Creating the Island of Stability: Iran, the Cold War, and American Cultural Diplomacy at the End of the 1950s," in *The Middle East in 1958: Reimagining a Revolutionary Year*, ed. Jeffrey G. Karam (London: I.B. Tauris, 2020), for an analysis of the instrumentalization of the Pact by Iran, similar to Turkey, for its own interests.
4 For the impact of the Baghdad Pact on regional states in detail see Caroline Attie, "The Crisis of 1958 in Lebanon: Political Rivalries," in *The Middle East in 1958*; Hupp, "Evolution and Revolution: Jordan in 1958," in *The Middle East in 1958*; Romero, "The Iraqi Revolution of 1958: Its Historic Significance and Relevance for the Present," in *The Middle East in 1958*.
5 For the first group of scholars see Rashid Khalidi, *Sowing Crisis: The Cold War and American Dominance in the Middle East* (Boston: Beacon Press, 2009), 73; Yakup

Halabi, *US Foreign Policy in the Middle East* (Surrey: Ashgate, 2009), 35–40; Mehran Kamrava, *The Modern Middle East* (Berkeley, CA: University of California Press, 2005), 109; Robert McNamara, *Britain, Nasser and the Balance of Power in the Middle East 1952–1967* (London: Frank Cass, 2003), 40–2. For the second group see Philip Robins, *Turkey and the Middle East* (London: Royal Institute of International Affairs, 1991), 25–6; George Lenczowski, *The Middle East in World Affairs* (New York: Cornell University Press, 1980), 145, 780–1; Sander, *Türk-Amerikan İlişkileri 1947–1964*, 132.

6 FO 371.119147. JE 14211-1951.
7 FRUS 1955-57. v.24.i.13.,704-706; FO 371.128242.VY 10344; Sander, *Türk-Amerikan İlişkileri 1947–1964*, 164–5.
8 Roger Louis and Roger Owen, *A Revolutionary Year: The Middle East in 1958* (London: I.B. Tauris, 2002), 16–17.
9 Ömer Kürkçüoğlu, *Türkiye'nin Arap Ortadoğusu'na Karşı Politikası 1945–1970* (Ankara: Ankara Üniversitesi Yayınları, 1972), 33–128; Sander, *Türk-Amerikan İlişkileri 1947–1964*, 200–25; Baskın Oran, *Türk Dış Politikası* (İstanbul: İletişim Yayınları, 2006), 627–32.
10 For more details about the UAR see Dina Rezk, "Egypt's Revolutionary Year: Regime Consolidation at Home, Pragmatism Abroad, and Neutralism in the Cold War," in *The Middle East in 1958*; Fadi Esber, "No Turning Back: Syria and the 1958 Watershed," in *The Middle East in 1958*.
11 FO 371.131338. JE 10344-1. See also Mehmet Gönlübol, *Olaylarla Türk Dış Politikası* (Ankara: Siyasal Kitabevi, 1996), 300; Oran, *Türk Dış Politikası*, 631.
12 Ibid.
13 FO 371.130196. RK 11316.
14 *Akis*, February 22, 1958.
15 Michael Cohen, *Strategy and Politics in the Middle East 1954–1960* (London: Frank Cass, 2005), 198.
16 Although we lack any evidence to assess whether Turkey would have been successful in any intervention, especially since it did not occur, one must keep in mind that Turkish military capabilities were not sufficiently extensive or vast to pull off a successful operation without the support of the great powers and probably could have sparked a wider confrontation between the United States and the Soviet Union in the Middle East.
17 Cohen, *Strategy and Politics in the Middle East 1954–1960*, 199.
18 FRUS 1958-60. v.12.i.9., 308–11. See also Oran, *Türk Dış Politikası*, 632; Sander, *Türk-Amerikan İlişkileri 1947–1964*, 166.
19 FO 371. 134212. VQ10344-2.
20 Romero's arguments support the public support behind the military intervention and the new regime. See Romero's chapter in this volume.
21 FO 371. 134212. VQ10344-2.
22 FRUS 1958-60. v.12.i.9., p. 334. See also Oran, *Türk Dış Politikası*, 632; Gönlübol, *Olaylarla Türk Dış Politikası*, 301–3.
23 Ibid.
24 FO 371. 134212. VQ 10344-4.
25 FO 371. 134212. VQ 10344-3.
26 FO 371. 133085. EQ 10344-7.
27 FRUS 1958-60. v.12.i.9., 443–5.
28 FRUS 1958-60. v.11.i.8., 58–9.
29 Ibid.

30 FRUS 1958-60. v.11.i.8.Footnote 2., 204–5.
31 FO 371. 134020. VJ 10344-1. See also Gönlübol, *Olaylarla Türk Dış Politikası*, 304.
32 Mahmut Dikerdem, *Ortadoğu'da Devrim Yılları: Bir Büyükelçinin Anıları* (İstanbul: Cem Yayınevi, 1990), 186–7.
33 For the relations between the government and the opposition see Erik J. Zürcher, *Modernleşen Türkiye'nin Tarihi* (İstanbul: İletişim Yayınları, 2013), 323–41. For the rumors about a military intervention in Turkey see Şevket Süreyya Aydemir, *Menderes'in Dramı* (İstanbul: Remzi Yayınevi, 2007), 271–9; Cem Eroğul, *Demokrat Parti: Tarihi ve İdeolojisi* (Ankara: İmge Kitabevi, 2003), 222–7; Ümit Özdağ, *Menderes Döneminde Ordu-Siyaset İlişkileri ve 27 Mayıs İhtilali* (İstanbul: Boyut Kitapları).
34 *Akis*, July 10, 1958.
35 Republic of Turkey, t.11, s.1, v.4, 843–4.
36 Ibid., 848.
37 Republic of Turkey, t.11, s.3, v.12, 498.
38 Metin Toker, *Demokrasimizin İsmet Paşalı Yılları 1954–1957* (Ankara: Bilgi Yayınevi, 1990), 220.
39 Republic of Turkey, t.11, s.1, v.4, 844 and t.11, s.3, v.12, 498.
40 *Cumhuriyet*, 15-16-23 July 1958; *Son Posta*, July 19, 1958.
41 *Forum*, July 15, 1958.
42 *Ulus*, July 16, 1958.
43 *Ulus*, July 17, 1958.
44 *Akis*, July 19, 1958.
45 *Forum*, August 1, 1958.

Chapter 9

CREATING THE "ISLAND OF STABILITY"

IRAN, THE COLD WAR, AND AMERICAN CULTURAL
DIPLOMACY AT THE END OF THE 1950s

John Ghazvinian

Placed next to some of the other states in the region, Iran at the end of the 1950s often comes across as a relative oasis of peace, pro-Western sentiment, and political tranquillity—and this is generally how the country was portrayed at the time in the annals of official Washington as well.[1] In 1955, Iran's youthful pro-Western monarch, Muhammad Reza Pahlavi Shah, had joined the Baghdad Pact, and in 1957 endorsed the Eisenhower Doctrine, signaling his country's unambiguous alliance with the United States in the Cold War.[2] And in March 1959, the United States repaid the shah's friendship by signing a landmark defense agreement with Iran.[3] But this cozy pro-Western alignment did not emerge from nowhere. From the perspective of Washington, much of the impression that Iran was an "island of stability in a troubled region" (the phrase that would become commonplace among American officials by the 1970s) was the result of a carefully calculated program of cultural diplomacy aimed at convincing Iranian public opinion that the future of the country lay with the United States. From the perspective of Tehran, however, it was also a direct, defensive response to the revolutionary developments taking place elsewhere in the region.

This chapter looks at the mechanisms of Cold War alignment and mythmaking in Iran—in particular the importance of the cultural dimension. And it examines the ways in which these mechanisms overlapped with Iran's own internal drift toward authoritarianism in the late 1950s, resulting in a decisive and critical shift in Iranian public opinion by the end of the decade. But it also attempts to do what has traditionally not been done by scholars of Iranian political history, which is to situate the shah's domestic political posture within the context of the broader revolutionary moment that was transforming the Middle East in 1958.

In many parts of the Middle East, 1958 represents a caesura, an irruptive force, or a dramatic break from the past in one form or another (a republican revolution in Iraq; a US military intervention in Lebanon; and the creation of the Egyptian-Syrian United Arab Republic, under the juggernaut of Gamal Abdel Nasser's "Arab socialism"). Iran, by contrast, has frequently been presented by Western historians as a paragon of continuity and stability during this period.[4] Nevertheless, despite this outward veneer of immutability, a subtle and ultimately critical transition was underway in the years around 1957–9. By the end of the decade, Iran would play host to the largest and most intricate US overseas aid mission in the world—a vast network of military and agricultural projects that steadily fanned out across every corner of the kingdom.[5] But it would also find itself engaged in numerous educational, artistic, and cultural exchanges with the United States—all of which played a critical role in creating a generation of Iranian and American officials deeply embedded in mutually reinforcing cycles of ideological codependence. The years around 1958 were thus an inflection point for Iran. Though the term "island of stability" was not yet widely used in Washington parlance about Iran, the groundwork was laid during this revolutionary year. Whether it was "leader grants" that sent promising young Iranians to the United States to study, visits by the Harlem Globetrotters to Iran, or lectures about Persian carpets in New York, the shah and his American allies successfully cultivated an image of Iran as a reliable, stable counterweight to the Nasserite socialism of the Arab world—setting the stage for two decades of official complacency and the steady transformation of the "island of stability" myth into an article of faith in Washington.

All of this was a striking contrast to the way US-Iranian relations had looked just a generation earlier. In the 1930s and 1940s, the United States was still taking the same aloof and largely disinterested attitude toward Iran that it had taken since the establishment of official relations in the 1850s.[6] And, as I have argued elsewhere, this long-standing tradition of foreign-policy neutrality and aloofness toward Iran—coupled with occasional but important demonstrations of support for Iranian sovereignty and constitutionalism—had earned admiration for the United States from the growing numbers of educated, progressive, and "modern" middle classes in Iran.[7] Among this rapidly expanding and influential demographic, the United States enjoyed a widespread reputation for integrity, altruism, neutrality, and noninterference in other countries' affairs. Almost by accident, and largely as a result of its own passivity, Washington had left many Iranians with the impression that the United States was a fundamentally "anti-imperialist" power that quietly sympathized with their century-long struggle against British and Russian interference.

By the late 1950s a crucial transition had begun to take place. As Washington looked for ways to instrumentalize this reservoir of goodwill, US policy began moving away from the organic credibility that the United States enjoyed among Iran's "modern middle classes" and toward what we would today call the conscious consolidation of "soft power"—accompanied by a more explicit association of US officialdom with the shah's regime. This shift, in turn, coincided with the shah's creeping authoritarianism. The result is by now well known: the United States in the 1950s and 1960s increasingly became associated in Iran with the rule of technocrats, status-quo politics, and Cold War imperatives, and began to move away from its traditional passive, ideological identification with the grassroots Iranian nationalism of the early twentieth century. And, though US-Iran relations were only one of many factors that shaped internal Iranian politics in the direction of iron-fist rule during these years, the visibility of this relationship meant that it played an outsized role in public perception.

Traditionally, this shift in orientation is identified as taking place as a result of Operation Ajax—the CIA-sponsored coup of August 1953 that overthrew the popular liberal-nationalist government of Prime Minister Muhammad Mosaddegh and helped pave the way for the shah's long period of authoritarian rule. And indeed, there is no question that the shah's regime took a decisive turn toward autocracy in the immediate aftermath of the coup.[8] But in fact, the dramatic events of 1953 were only one part of a larger, subtler, and more complex transition taking place throughout the 1950s—a transition which picked up pace in the middle years of the decade, but which would only fully come to fruition as a result of the revolutionary events of 1958.

US-Iran Relations in the 1950s

It is far too easy to idealize the image of the United States in Iran before 1953, and we must be careful about falling too readily into that trap. By no means was the United States a purely benevolent power in Iran in the early part of the twentieth century, and by no means did Iranians have a uniformly positive (or even particularly clearly articulated) view of the United States during those years. Nevertheless, for a certain generation of progressive, educated, mostly urban and Western-oriented Iranian nationalists—the generation that would later form the core of what historians have called Iran's "modern middle class"—the United States held a special kind of allure. Prosperous, dynamic, and democratic, but also visibly uninterested in imperial domination of the Middle East, it was almost the platonic ideal of the perfect Western nation.[9] For decades, Iranian elites had admired and even sought to emulate the technical and political achievements of the European powers, but had also resented the way these same powers sought to extend their imperial or quasi-imperial domination over Iran.[10] The United States, which was generally held to have come into existence by overthrowing the yoke of imperial monarchy, and had pursued an isolationist foreign policy for most of its history—while simultaneously building itself into an economic and political powerhouse—seemed to embody the best of both worlds.

By 1953, of course, all that was over. It was impossible, after Operation Ajax, for Iran's modern middle classes to maintain the belief that the United States was a neutral, disinterested power that respected the aspirations of the Iranian people, or that it pursued a foreign policy appreciably different from that of the European powers.[11] And as the shah set about consolidating his power after the coup, the United States became irrevocably associated with his particular brand of authoritarian rule. Internally, the new Iranian government, now led by military generals, declared martial law, stationed soldiers on street corners throughout the country, closed dozens of newspapers, sent tanks into the Tehran bazaar to suppress a protest and launched a massive anti-Communist crackdown in the armed forces.[12] Externally, it directed its foreign-policy orientation much more visibly toward the United States. In December 1953, just four months after the coup, US vice president Richard Nixon paid a high-profile visit to Tehran to bolster the shah and cement Washington's relationship with his regime.[13] Nixon's visit touched off a storm of protests at Tehran University that culminated in three students being shot dead by security forces.[14]

There is perhaps no better way to appreciate the effect this shift in the reputation of the United States had on Iran's modern middle classes than to study the example of Allahyar Salih, Iran's ambassador in Washington. In September 1953, just a month after Operation Ajax, Salih quietly resigned from his position, despite being urged informally by the US State Department to continue in the post. "How could I?" Salih protested to his American counterparts. "When I have so often walked up and down the stairs of the State Department in service to the noble principles of Mosaddegh, how could I now traverse the same stairs on behalf of a hated government—the nature of whose ringleaders I am all too familiar with?"[15]

In the early 1950s, it would have been hard to find a more pro-American figure among the Iranian political elite than Salih. As a young boy, he had attended the American School in Tehran (later Alburz), and attentively absorbed the lessons on American democracy—becoming so enamored of the Samuel Jordan ethos that he later became president of the school's alumni association. One of his first jobs after graduation was at the US Legation in Tehran, where he and his brother worked as clerks from 1918 to 1922—translating documents, and generally soaking up the atmosphere of can-do American officiousness.[16] He was, in many ways, the epitome of the young and idealistic generation of liberal nationalists that had come to adore the United States and everything it stood for during the first half of the twentieth century—a man perfect in every way for the job of ambassador to Washington. And yet, like so many of his compatriots in 1953, Saleh felt deeply betrayed by America.

For the rest of the 1950s, the relationship between Iran and the United States moved steadily in the direction of clientelism. Every time Iran did what it was asked, or performed some sort of service or favor for the United States, it was rewarded with a swift and substantial injection of cash. In 1954, when an agreement was reached to give control of Iran's oil to an international consortium that included US companies, the shah received $127 million in fresh aid commitments. In 1955, when Iran joined the Baghdad Pact (a regional anti-Soviet alliance championed by John Foster Dulles), another tranche of money landed in the shah's lap. In 1957, the shah endorsed the Eisenhower Doctrine, and the following year Iran joined Cento (the successor to the Baghdad Pact). Both decisions were rewarded with fulsome financial payments.[17]

By the end of the decade, this merry-go-round of blandishments and favors was becoming a source of great resentment to the modern, educated, and increasingly restless middle class. The same people who had rallied round Mosaddegh from the late 1940s to 1953, and who deeply resented the way he was being left to rot away under house arrest in Ahmadabad, now lapsed into a mood of disillusionment and cynicism as they watched their country turn into something vaguely resembling an American protectorate. For years, these modern middle classes had believed that their country was about to embark on a free and independent future, in which its actions were not constrained by lopsided arrangements with foreign powers. Instead, it seemed, the shah had merely traded the British lion for an American eagle.[18]

This growing mood of cynicism and disillusionment with the United States was most visible on the cultural front. The American Library in Tehran, which had been one of the US Embassy's great success stories at the end of the 1940s, recorded a steep drop in visitor numbers during the first half of 1953—largely in response to the Eisenhower administration's increasingly critical stance toward Mosaddegh—and never bounced back.[19] Just three years earlier, as the first lending library in Iran, it had been heaving under the weight of its own popularity—frequently turning people away for lack of space. More than 4,000 Iranians a month were dropping in during the early 1950s, eager to improve their English, or to learn about the latest in agricultural techniques, nursing, psychiatry, and science—or just, in the words of one embassy official, to flick through magazines full of ads depicting "a dream-world beyond their imagination."[20] The chamber music concerts held on Wednesday evenings were a big draw—attracting large crowds of excitable urbanites, dressed in stylish suits and sporting the latest Western hairstyles. But by 1953, even before the coup, it felt like the times were changing. In the minds of educated Iranians, the image of America as a purely benevolent force in the Middle East—committed to the struggle of oppressed peoples against European imperialism—was beginning to look decidedly quaint, and the American Library was no longer the "in" place to see and to be seen in.[21] After the coup, of course, such cultural symbols of American friendship became even more socially toxic. The American Library in Tehran never regained the social cachet it had held in the late 1940s and was eventually shuttered.

None of this is to say that Iran's modern middle classes had an inherent or reflexive dislike of the United States, or that the latter was even the main target of their frustrations. What Iran's middle classes resented much more than the United States, in fact, was the shah himself. The removal of Mosaddegh by the CIA in 1953, and America's direct intervention to restore him to the throne, appeared to have put a spring in the step of the King of Kings—and the result was particularly distasteful to middle-class democrats. Reassured that he had, at least for the moment, the firm backing of the United States and Britain, the shah set about consolidating his position in the late 1950s—expanding his constitutional powers, stifling dissenting voices, and surrounding himself with men he could count on to be unflinchingly loyal to his personal rule. In the Majlis elections of 1954 and 1956, the voting process was blatantly rigged—with many of the same south Tehran thugs who had helped to overthrow Mosaddegh wheeled out again to intimidate voters (the legendary "Sha'ban the Brainless" alone was said to have hospitalized fifty people in 1954).[22] The result was a parliament dominated by old-guard aristocratic landowners and conservative politicians—all with an unshakable loyalty to the shah.

In 1955, General Fazlullah Zahidi, who had led the coup against Mosaddegh at the behest of the CIA and had been rewarded with the job of prime minister, was given the sack. His government, like Mosaddegh's before it, had lasted only two years—a victim of the shah's traditional lack of comfort with prime ministers who appeared to be stronger than him. Zahidi was replaced by the elderly courtier Husayn 'Ala', and then in 1957 by Manuchihr Iqbal—an obsequious politician who famously signed his letters to the shah with the words "Your Majesty's house-born slave." History has generally regarded Iqbal as the politician most responsible for introducing a culture of extreme sycophancy to the Royal Court—the atmosphere of bowing and scraping and empty obedience that would eventually rot out the regime from within. It was Iqbal who, as prime minister, first declared that matters of foreign policy should be left entirely to the shah's discretion, and Iqbal who helped create a secret police force to monitor Iranians perceived as disloyal to the shah—the notorious SAVAK.[23]

In 1957, the shah banned all political parties and announced that anyone who wanted to participate in politics would have to do so through one of two newly created parties—the Milliyun (Nation Party) and the Mardum (People's Party). The idea, ostensibly, was to create a two-party system in Iran, based loosely on the American model of Democrats and Republicans, but it degenerated into a mockery. Able and sincere young politicians made attempts to work within the confines of the two parties, but quickly discovered that the whole thing was a vehicle for sycophancy, favoritism, and royal control of the political process. The Milliyun and the Mardum became a laughingstock among the Tehran intelligentsia—membership in the party ranks a radioactive label for anyone who aspired to a measure of credibility. A popular joke summed up the difference between the two parties' ideologies as "Yes" and "Yes, Sir."[24]

The US-Iran Alliance and the New Phase of Authoritarianism

As the shah drifted steadily toward authoritarianism in the late 1950s, he also began to attach his regime's fortunes more explicitly to Iran's alliance with the United States. Although he explored a range of foreign-policy orientations, and remained pragmatic in his management of Iran's external relations, there was, by 1957–8, a growing range of very visible cultural and educational links with the United States. And these links interacted with Iran's increasingly authoritarian political history to cement an image in the minds of many Iranians of American complicity with the shah's regime. Though this was a long-term trend in the 1950s, and might have continued regardless of external developments in the region, it was, ultimately, the events of 1958 that most clearly cemented Iran's pro-American, anti-Soviet and authoritarian foreign-policy orientation.

With a newly invigorated bilateral relationship between Iran and the United States came a wealth of opportunities for cultural, professional, and educational exchanges. Beginning in the mid-1950s, many prominent Iranians were sent to the United States on so-called leader grants funded by the State Department, thus helping a rising generation of political elites to become familiar with American methods of journalism (at the University of Virginia), agriculture (Utah State

University), and business administration (the University of South Carolina). In November 1957, the Fulbright program in Iran was fully activated, following an eight-year funding delay.[25] On the artistic front, popular American plays, such as Thornton Wilder's *Our Town*, were translated into Persian and performed in Tehran; and in 1956, the Martha Graham Dance Company played to packed houses across the country. There was even a visit by the Harlem Globetrotters, which helped to popularize basketball (or at least some version of it) in Iran.[26]

Educational reform was a particularly important area of bilateral cooperation. Traditionally, Iran's universities had been modeled after the French system, but from the late 1950s this began to change. In 1956, Manuchihr Iqbal, while he was still chancellor of Tehran University, traveled to the United States on a leader grant and returned "bubbling over with enthusiasm for the United States." He was particularly struck by the American concept of a university "campus," where all social, residential, and educational needs were met, and made attempts to introduce the idea to Tehran University. Although he had been educated in France and was married to a French woman, Iqbal returned from the United States convinced that America was now the "leading light of the Western World," and before long, teams of American experts were being brought over to advise Iran on how to create and run a university.[27] Amid the oilfields of the Persian Gulf, the Abadan Institute of Technology was set up with the help of a team from Lafayette College of Easton, Pennsylvania.[28] And in 1960, the shah invited University of Pennsylvania (Penn) president Gaylord Harnwell to Shiraz—determined that the newly established Pahlavi University there would be transformed into the only institution in the Middle East to offer an American-style university education.

The choice of Penn was, in many ways, a logical one, given the many years that the university's archaeologists had spent digging through the ruins of Riyy and Turang Tappih. But it also marked the beginning of a new and robust relationship between Penn and the Pahlavi regime—an era in which the faculty and administration became highly influential in the shaping of educational policy in Shiraz, and, perhaps unwittingly, also served as unofficial cultural ambassadors for the shah in the United States. Harnwell was neither the first nor the last American to turn up in Iran knowing very little about the country, spend time only with the shah and a few of his loyal politicians, and return preaching the gospel of an enlightened monarch who was trying to pull his nation out of its backwardness. In 1961, he described Iran as a place where "ignorance is orthodox, education is feared, and obscurantism is rife" but noted with pleasure that "today an enlightened and democratic ruler is endeavoring to leap many centuries of poverty and ignorance in order to assimilate our modern civilization and achieve a distinguished position among the growing nations of the Middle East and of the world."[29]

This pattern of American advisers returning from Iran to become unofficial spokesmen for the shah in the United States was often repeated in other areas of cultural and commercial "cooperation" between the two countries in the late 1950s. In 1956, for example, the shah brought in David Lilienthal and Gordon Clapp from Development and Resources Corporation of New York to finance and build a series of dams and irrigation networks for Khuzestan Province. Famed for their work at the head of the Tennessee Valley Authority, Lilienthal and Clapp were two of the most influential and well-connected Americans around. But their understanding of Iran was limited, and they quickly became pawns in a complex political rivalry between the shah and the head of the Plan Organization, Abul-Hasan Ibtihaj. Rather than act as neutral outside contractors, the Americans became fierce defenders of the shah—both in Iran and in the United States, where they helped to shield his regime from media criticism and congressional scrutiny. The Khuzestan dam project was wrapped up in 1962, after it failed to achieve many of its goals. But for the next twenty years, Lilienthal would continue to act as one of the shah's most important surrogates in the United States.[30]

As the 1950s progressed, enormous amounts of American aid money and American technical advice began to make its way into Iran—most of it channeled through the Point Four agreement that Truman had signed into law in 1950. In 1953, Iran received $23 million in Point Four assistance, but the following year that figure was increased to $85 million. Whereas in 1952, there had been only ten "technical advisers" employed by the US Embassy in Tehran, by 1956, that number had ballooned to 207. A further 100 or so technicians were employed by American professional and educational organizations, and between them, these Americans had a staff of some 3,800 Iranian employees.[31] And yet, perhaps inevitably given its size and complexity, the aid effort was badly managed. Americans had little awareness of the intricacies of Iranian politics and culture, and often came across as brash and wealthy upstarts, full of patronizing attitudes and an unwillingness to listen or adapt their technical expertise to the needs of the local population. On the Iranian side, meanwhile, dishonest actors were happy to take advantage of American inexperience, and quickly found ways to channel US aid money into their own pockets. In 1956, a lengthy investigation carried out by the US House of Representatives found that American assistance programs in Iran had been administered "in a loose, slipshod, and unbusinesslike manner," and that it was often impossible to tell exactly what had happened to the funds.[32]

What all of this added up to was a growing perception, in the minds of many Iranians, that the United States was enabling and abetting an increase in corruption and decadence in Iranian society, as well as propping up a dictatorial government that was depriving them of their rights. Already unpopular for the way it had undermined Mosaddegh and brought an end to the period of national aspiration and political pluralism, the United States now appeared to have moved in, in a forceful way, behind a regime that did not seem to care about the well-being of its people. As the shah's ministers enriched themselves, and as critical, constructive voices were frozen out of a political system that seemed to have no use for their talents, America became an obvious focal point for people's frustrations.

The cultural manifestations of this trend were visible on both the US and Iranian sides of the relationship. At the Iranian Embassy in Washington, for example, there was little to suggest that the shah's regime viewed cultural "exchange" with the United States as anything other than a one-way street. In 1956, the new ambassador, 'Ali Amini, set up an "Iranian Information Center" in Washington, but it didn't seem particularly geared toward educating Americans on Iranian arts, culture, or history. In charge of the Center was ʻAliquli Khan, a silver-haired veteran of the Washington party circuit who had risen to prominence in the early 1900s after his marriage to the Boston heiress Florence Breed—one of the most talked-about society events of the age.[33] ʻAliquli had spent the last forty years in the United States, giving lectures on Persian art and antiquities, and was in a good position to foster an interest in Iranian culture among the American public.[34] But the Center's mission statement made it clear where the priorities lay. It was instructed by Tehran to "familiarize the American people with conditions in Iran and to make them rally behind their government in extending our country immediate and generous financial and economic aids to bolster up [sic] our ailing economy."[35] The point, in other words, was to milk more money out of America—one of the shah's evergreen preoccupations.

Ultimately, though, it was the July 1958 revolution in Iraq that added an entirely new level of urgency to the shah's already visible drift toward pro-Western autocracy. Iranian archives demonstrate clearly that following the coup in Baghdad, the shah experienced a heightened level of fear about both internal and external threats to his regime. Anecdotal reports suggest a significant increase in domestic surveillance and interrogation by SAVAK, particularly in Iranian towns close to the Iraqi border, such as Kirmanshah.[36] Even before July, Ambassador Amini was recalled from Washington following rumors that he was involved in a plot to overthrow the Iranian government.[37] The breakdown of negotiations with the USSR on a nonaggression pact in 1959, and the presence of Soviet ships carrying weapons to the new Iraqi regime via the Shatt al-ʻArab, only added to the shah's urgent desire to draw closer to the United States.[38]

The growing bond between the United States and the Pahlavi regime in the late 1950s was also reflected in the frequency of official visits by the two countries' leaders. In 1954, the shah and his queen spent two months in the United States, where they had the opportunity to meet Eisenhower and thank him personally for his assistance the previous year.[39] In January 1958, John Foster Dulles visited Tehran, and six months later, the shah and his twin sister Ashraf came to Washington, hoping to convince the Eisenhower administration to increase military support to Iran. Disappointed not to be receiving more from the United States, the shah had spent much of 1956 and 1957 cultivating closer ties with the Soviet Union—making a state visit to Moscow and signing a number of treaties and trade agreements.[40] The whole thing had been a transparent bluff, designed to ensure that the United States did not take Iran's friendship for granted, but it left Eisenhower distinctly unamused. In no uncertain terms, the president informed the shah that his "friends would be unhappy" if he signed a treaty with the Soviet Union. "I am confident," Eisenhower wrote, "that you would not knowingly take a step which would imperil your country's security."[41]

In the end, however, the shah got most of what he wanted from America—mostly thanks to the unexpected turn of events in neighboring Iraq. On July 14, just as the shah was getting ready to leave Washington, word arrived that a bloody revolution had broken out in Baghdad, and that the pro-British monarchy had been replaced by a democratic republic committed to taking a neutral position in the Cold War. American minds quickly became concentrated on the possibility of something similar happening in Iran, and the Eisenhower administration began stepping up its financial and military commitments to the shah. In March 1959, the shah showed his appreciation by signing a landmark defense agreement with the United States—cementing Iran's status as an important American client state in the Middle East, and ending the short-lived flirtation with Moscow.

In December of that year, Eisenhower rewarded his newfound friend with an official visit to Tehran. For the American president, Tehran was merely a five-hour stopover on a goodwill tour of eleven regional capitals, from Karachi to Casablanca, but the shah wasted no time milking the visit for everything it was worth. A national holiday was declared to mark the occasion, and thousands of schoolchildren ordered to school at 6:00 a.m. so they could be on hand to cheer Eisenhower's arrival.[42] As the president stepped off the plane, fighter jets flew overhead and spelled out the word "Ike" in the sky, as nearly a million people lined his route into Tehran—dutifully cheering and waving.[43] Eisenhower's motorcade passed under sixteen decorative arches hung with American flags and slogans like "We Like Ike Too—Welcome to Iran!" before finally arriving at the Marble Palace—where he was greeted by representatives of Iran's thirty provinces, each dressed in traditional costume and bearing lavish gifts. Once inside the Palace, the president had twenty minutes to rest and refresh himself, before beginning two hours of talks with the shah, followed by an address to a special session of the Majlis. To ensure his maximum comfort during these twenty minutes, Eisenhower was given the bedroom once used by Reza Shah. Sixty typewriters and eight direct phone lines were put at the disposal of his staff.[44]

A week before Eisenhower's arrival, the shah had declared triumphantly at a press conference that "our relations with the United States have never been so strong."[45] During his five-hour stay in Tehran, the president said nothing to contradict this—only praising the shah for his "wise leadership" and reaffirming America's commitment to a future of mutual cooperation between America and Iran. In his address to the Majlis, however, Eisenhower included a line that many interpreted as a direct swipe at the shah and his obsession with military hardware. "In the long term," he stated bluntly, "military strength alone will not bring about just and permanent peace."[46]

This was a gentle word of warning, from an old friend who, six years earlier, had quietly intervened to restore Muhammad Reza Shah to his troublesome throne. But it was also a harbinger of things to come. Eisenhower was a realist—a hard-bitten man of war who was slowly coming to accept the limitations of conventional military firepower in the atomic age. America's next president, however, would (at least in his initial rhetoric) turn out to be an idealist—a young and energetic Massachusetts senator with a powerful new vision for the projection of American leadership in the world. And his presidency would mark the first serious rift between the shah and his American patrons. From 1961 to 1963, Washington would press the shah to enact liberalizing reforms and expand the political process to a wider swathe of Iranians as part of an attempt to prevent the possibility of Communist revolution.[47] The Kennedy interlude would not last long, and would be followed by more than a decade of robust official US patronage of the shah's regime that would culminate, in the late 1970s, in an earth-shattering anti-American backlash.

Conclusion

The political dimensions of this late Pahlavi US-Iranian relationship of the 1960s and 1970s and its collapse are by now well known and much dissected. However, the seeds for this relationship were in many respects sown in 1958. And it is this subtle but unmistakable shift that makes 1958, in unexpected ways, a revolutionary year in Iran. Though Iran might not have experienced the kind of outward signs of upheaval that other regional states experienced during this dramatic year, it nevertheless can be said to have made a radical break from the past during the final two or three years of the 1950s. Furthermore, it is in the realm of cultural diplomacy with the United States that this radical break is most evident. Though historians of the 1950s, 1960s, and 1970s have traditionally focused their analyzes on the political decision-making in Washington and Tehran that led up to the Iranian revolution, the cultural dimension provides an equally important backdrop—particularly in the formative years following Operation Ajax, when Iranian and US officialdom were undertaking their first really high-level interactions since the establishment of relations a century earlier.

Perhaps most importantly, a close study of US-Iranian cultural diplomacy carries significant implications for the periodization with which historians approach the political history of Iran in the twentieth century. While the folk memory of US-Iranian relations often treats 1953 as the decisive year in the transformation of the shah's relationship with Washington, in fact—in subtler but more important ways—the revolutionary year of 1958 might hold a stronger claim to that dubious mantle.

Notes

1 Traditional diplomatic histories of US-Iran relations, all of which discuss official American attitudes to the shah in the 1950s, include James Bill, *The Eagle and the Lion: The Tragedy of American-Iranian Relations* (New Haven: Yale University Press, 1988); Mark Gasiorowski, *US Foreign Policy and the Shah: Building a Client State in Iran* (Ithaca: Cornell University Press, 1991); James Goode, *The United States and Iran: In the Shadow of Mosaddegh* (New York: St. Martin's Press, 1997); Richard Cottam, *Iran and the United States: A Cold War Case Study* (Pittsburgh: University of Pittsburgh Press, 1988); Barry Rubin, *Paved with Good Intentions: The American Experience in Iran* (New York: Oxford University Press, 1980); Gary Sick, *All Fall Down: American's Tragic Encounter with Iran* (New York: Random House, 1985); Kenneth Pollack, *The Persian Puzzle: The Conflict between Iran and America* (New York: Random House, 2004). Two recent studies illustrate well the attitude of Washington: Matthew Shannon, *Losing Hearts and Minds: American-Iranian Relations and International Education during the Cold War* (Ithaca: Cornell University

Press, 2017); David Collier, *Democracy and the Nature of American Influence in Iran, 1941–1979* (Syracuse: Syracuse University Press, 2017).

2 For a good discussion of these developments, see Bill, *Eagle and the Lion*, 116–19.
3 Bill, *Eagle and the Lion*, 119ff.
4 See, e.g., Rubin, *Paved with Good Intentions*, 92–105; Pollack, *Persian Puzzle*, 72–80.
5 See, e.g., Peter Avery et al. eds., *Cambridge History of Iran*, vol. 7 (Cambridge: Cambridge University Press, 1991), 444; Rubin, *Paved with Good Intentions*, 100.
6 There exists no good, recent, general overview of US-Iran relations in the early twentieth century written in English. Aspects of the relationship have been covered in, among others, Michael Zirinsky, "A Panacea for the Ills of the Country: American Presbyterian Education in Inter-War Iran," *Iranian Studies* 26, no. 1–2 (1993): 119–37; Louise Fawcett, *Iran and the Cold War: The Azerbaijan Crisis of 1946* (Cambridge: Cambridge University Press, 1992); Adrian O'Sullivan, *Espionage and Counterintelligence in Occupied Persia (Iran)* (London: Springer, 2015), 195–230; Mohammad Gholi Majd, *Oil and the Killing of the American Consul in Tehran* (Lanham: University Press of America, 2006). An informative and well-researched overview of the period in Persian is Rahim Rezazadeh Malek, *Tarikh-i Ravabit-i Iran va Mamalik-i Muttahidih-i Amrika* (History of Relations between Iran and the United States of America) (Tehran: Tahuri, 1972). A shorter but serviceable treatment in English is Mansour Bonakdarian, "US-Iranian Relations, 1911–1951," in *The United States and the Middle East: Diplomatic and Economic Relations in Historical Perspective*, ed. Abbas Amanat (New Haven: Yale University Press, 1999), 13–32. An older book that looks at the Middle East generally but deals in part with Iran is John DeNovo, *American Interests and Policies in the Middle East, 1900–1939* (Minneapolis: University of Minnesota Press, 1963), 275–317.
7 John Ghazvinian, *America and Iran: A History, 1720 to the Present* (New York: Knopf, 2020).
8 See, for example, Ervand Abrahamian, *The Coup: 1953, the CIA and the Roots of Modern US-Iranian Relations* (New York: New Press, 2013).
9 This is visible, for example, in the writing of Allahyar Salih, who served as ambassador to Washington during the Mosaddegh government. Saleh, a graduate of US mission schools had worked, along with his brother, in the US legation in Tehran in the 1920s, and had spent a lifetime enamored of the American way of life. Khusrau Saʿidi, ed., *Allahyar Salih (Zindigi Namih)* (Tehran: Muhammad Ibrahim Shariʿati Afqanistani, 1382/2003), 207. Also Salih to Cornelius Engert, November 7, 1921, and August 8, 1922, Engert papers, Georgetown University, Box 2, folder 46.
10 Mid-nineteenth-century reformist prime minister Amir Kabir is a good example of this phenomenon.
11 The extent to which educated Iranians knew about US involvement in the coup at the time is a complex one, but it is fairly clear that suspicions about American involvement, at the very least, were widespread. The process is perhaps best articulated by Abrahamian, *Coup*, passim.
12 Bill, *Eagle and the Lion*, 98; Homa Katouzian, *Mosaddegh and the Struggle for Power in Iran* (London: I.B. Tauris, 1991), 208.
13 Bill, *Eagle and the Lion*, 115–16.
14 This was the first episode in what would eventually become a long and important history of anti-shah activism on the part of Iranian students. It would culminate, in the 1970s, in a major international network of student activists, many of whom became radical leftists.
15 Saʿidi, ed., *Allahyar Salih*, 207.

16 Salih to Engert, November 7, 1921 and August 8, 1922, Engert papers, Georgetown University, Box 2, folder 46.
17 Bill, *Eagle and the Lion*, 115–19.
18 Abrahamian, *Coup*; Ghazvinian, *America and Iran*.
19 United States National Archives and Records Administration (hereafter NARA), 511.88/9-1253—USIS semi-annual evaluation report December 1, 1952—May 31, 1953; September 12, 1953.
20 NARA 511.88/5-1550—memo from Embassy to State, May 15, 1950.
21 The American Library recorded a sharp drop in visitors in first half of 1953 (NARA 511.88/9-1253—USIS semi-annual evaluation report December 1, 1952—May 31, 1953; September 12, 1953).
22 "Brainless and the Ballots," *Time*, March 22, 1954.
23 Abbas Milani, *Eminent Persians*, vol. 1 (Syracuse: Syracuse University Press, 2008), 126.
24 Ali Ansari, *Modern Iran: The Pahlavis and After* (Harlow: Longman, 2007), 174.
25 Rouhollah Ramazani, *Iran's Foreign Policy 1941–1973* (Charlottesville: University Press of Virginia, 1975), 289.
26 Tim Kelly, *The Legend of Red Klotz: How Basketball's Loss Leader Won Over the World—14,000 Times* (Margate: ComteQ Publishing, 2013), 11–23.
27 NARA 511.883/6-656—Chapin to State, June 6, 1956.
28 "Lafayette in Persia," *Lafayette Magazine*, Spring 2013.
29 Gaylord Harnwell, *Educational Voyaging in Iran* (Philadelphia: University of Pennsylvania Press, 1962), 16, 18.
30 A good summary of the DRC Khuzistan project and its shortcomings is in Bill, *Eagle and the Lion*, 120–4.
31 Ibid., 124–5.
32 Ibid., 126, n. 46.
33 Marzieh Gail, *Arches of the Years* (Welwyn: Ronald, 1991), 328.
34 For more on Aliquli Khan, see Karim Soleimani, *Ulqab-i rijal, dawrih-i qajariyyih* (Tehran, 1379/2000), 195; "Appointed Consul General," *New York Times*, September 22, 1915, 22; "Persia in America," *New York Observer and Chronicle*, July 27, 1911, 111.
35 NARA 601.8811/12-1955—G. Lewis Jones to State, December 19, 1955.
36 Author interviews with Iranian political activists of the time.
37 NARA 601.8811/3-2458—memo for Brig-Gen A. J. Goodpaster, White House, from Fisher Howe, director of executive secretariat, March 24, 1958.
38 Ramazani, *Iran's Foreign Policy*, 400.
39 Bill, *Eagle and the Lion*, 115.
40 Ibid., 118.
41 *Foreign Relations of the United States, 1958–1960*, vol. 12, 628–9.
42 "Tehran to Give All-Out Greeting," *New York Times*, December 13, 1959, 35.
43 "Shah Welcomes President in Iran," *New York Times*, December 14, 1959, 1; *Kayhan*, 22 Azar 1338 (December 14, 1959), 1.
44 *Kayhan*, 21 Azar 1338 (December 13, 1959), 1.
45 *Arizu*, 13 Azar 1338 (December 5, 1959), 1.
46 "Texts of Eisenhower's Talks in Athens and Tehran," *New York Times*, December 15, 1959, 16.
47 Bill, *Eagle and the Lion*, 133ff. For more on Kennedy and Iran, see Collier, *Democracy* and Roland Popp, "Benign Intervention? The Kennedy Administration's Push for Reform in Iran," in *John F. Kennedy and the "Thousand Days": New Perspectives on the Foreign and Domestic Policies of the Kennedy Administration*, ed. Manfred Berg and Andreas Erges (Heidelberg: Winter Verlag, 2007), 197–219.

Part 3

Connecting the Local to the Global

Revolutions, Wars, and Coups in the Middle East

Chapter 10

HOW ABOUT 1958 IN ALGERIA?

A TRANSNATIONAL EVENT IN THE CONTEXT OF THE WAR OF INDEPENDENCE

Sylvie Thénault

On May 13, 1958, in Algiers, a huge crowd of French people, who were living there, protested against the execution of three French soldiers by the Algerian nationalist movement, the Front de Libération Nationale (FLN; National Liberation Front). They provoked nothing less than the collapse of the Fourth Republic in Paris. After four years of a bloody war, the FLN, which had launched the fight for independence in 1954, gained support, and the French authorities proved their incapacity to defeat it. Once again after the Second World War, General de Gaulle appeared as a savior. He returned to power and founded a new regime: the Fifth Republic that survived many crises until now. For that reason, 1958 represents a fundamental break in the history of contemporary France.

Would de Gaulle be able to keep Algeria French? The millions of French living in Algeria, who had been in the colony for one or two generations in their overwhelming majority, hoped so, but the war lasted four more years. The conflict ended in 1962, resulting in exactly that which the French of Algeria feared: independence. The year 1958 then saw the man who finally negotiated the independence of the Algerian colony arriving at power. For that reason, French historiography has long viewed 1958 as a turning point in the Algerian War of Independence.[1] This idea, however, is debatable, based on an account that overlooks the FLN as an actor in this story and reduces its role.[2] Additionally, neither Mohamed Teguia's Algerian overview nor John Talbott's English-language discussion, both of which appeared in the 1980s, agree with this position.[3]

What changed then in 1958 in the history of the Algerian War of Independence? Was 1958 a revolutionary year in the course of that War? Nothing is less sure, as the chapter demonstrates. It analyzes three crucial moments that brought three underlying issues into play: February 1958 and the internationalization of the conflict;[4] May 13, 1958, at the heart of tensions around the status of combatants between the two camps;[5] and autumn 1958, with General de Gaulle's pronouncements and the FLN's decision to form a Gouvernement provisoire de la République algérienne (GPRA; Provisional Government of the Algerian Republic).

February 1958: Sakiet-Sidi-Youssef, the "Good Offices," and the Internationalization of the War

The events of the winter of 1958 demonstrated the repercussions of the Algerian War of Independence on its Maghreb neighbors.[6] Tunisia was hit hard by the situation. On February 8, 1958, in response to Algerian combatants firing shells that landed on Tunisian soil, the French Air Force bombed the village of Sakiet-Sidi-Youssef.[7] The outcome (70 dead and 150 injured, including children) was unanimously condemned. On that day, tensions between France and the very young Tunisian Republic were high. Just previously, in January 1958, four French soldiers had been taken prisoner in Tunisia by the Algerian army: the Armée de Libération Nationale (ALN; National Liberation Army). The French government therefore approved the exercise of its right to follow the enemy across the Algerian border. Habib Bourguiba, the Tunisian president, promised to act to curb the Algerians, and offered to mediate, but the French authorities, viewing his initiative as interference, refused. In February, following the bombing of Sakiet, Bourguiba responded by blocking the military base at Bizerte, which was still in French hands, expelling French nationals and closing consulates. He also demanded the evacuation of the French troops that were still in Tunisia and appealed to the UN.

What happened next bears testimony to the geopolitical challenge the Maghreb represented for the United States and Great Britain. They feared that the region would go up in flames or that the Maghreb leaders would seek Soviet support, like Nasser in Egypt. They also wanted to rescue their French ally from this quagmire. From their point of view, not only did the French military resources invested in Algeria act to the detriment of the Atlantic Alliance in Europe, but France was also exhausting its credibility in this colonial war. After the bombardment of Sakiet, therefore, they offered their services (their "good offices") to resolve the crisis. Robert Murphy, an American diplomat and President Roosevelt's former envoy in Algiers during the Second World War, and Harold Beeley, on behalf of the British Foreign Office, were charged with this task.

This intervention is an illustration of France's international isolation, which had been weakening its position for two years. On October 22, 1956, France intercepted a Moroccan plane that was carrying four Algerian leaders—Ahmed Ben Bella, Hocine Aït Ahmed, Mohammed Boudiaf, and Mohammed Khider—and the writer Mostefa Lacheraf. They were travelling from Rabat to Tunis to take part in a conference on a possible association among the three nations of the Maghreb. The five men, victims of a true aerial kidnapping, would remain detained in France until the end of the conflict. Then, barely two weeks later, the Suez Crisis, which had been interrupted by the joint condemnations of the Soviet Union, America, and the United Nations, accentuated the deterioration of France's situation on the global scene.

The FLN, conversely, played the internationalization card successfully. Its representatives in New York worked effectively at the UN. There, the FLN found the support of the Afro-Asian and nonaligned countries, which fought for recognition of UN jurisdiction over Algeria's destiny. On July 2, 1957, Senator John Kennedy pronounced himself in favor of an acceleration of the "movement towards Algerian political independence."[8] This event illustrates the progress made by the Algerian cause during this period. In February 1958, the bombardment of Sakiet naturally strengthened this trend. For France, it meant the hostility of countries, such as those in Scandinavia, that had avoided overwhelming it up to that point.[9]

The FLN wanted to break its adversary. During the Fourth Republic, the French authorities had stood by a three-point plan, called in French "triptych," like a painting made of three panels: "ceasefire, elections and negotiations." That plan was unacceptable to the Algerians. The ceasefire was designed to be without any conditions, while the FLN demanded that there should first be an "official declaration repealing the edicts and laws that make Algeria a French territory."[10] It therefore required recognition of independence before a laying down of arms. There was also total disagreement on the elections to be held after the ceasefire as the French authorities saw them. The vote count was, in fact, intended to designate qualified representatives for the negotiations, while the FLN claimed to speak on behalf of all Algerians. Finally, in the absence of prior acknowledgment of independence, the negotiations could lead to a completely different solution (autonomy, for example). The FLN could not accept this either.

Through internationalization, the FLN made the French position untenable: How could the French authorities refuse discussions with the representatives of an organization some of whose members were present at the UN, had been received by officials from other countries, and had been invited to international conferences? How could they reject a claim for independence when the UN wanted discussions to be held? The offers of mediation in 1958, by Bourguiba in January and by the Anglo-Saxons following the bombing of Sakiet, increased this pressure. For the historian Matthew Connelly, the FLN's strategy would serve as a model: the Algerian War of Independence would be a true "diplomatic revolution."[11]

The internationalization of the war also had another dimension, however: material and logistical.[12] It primarily involved Morocco and Tunisia. Training camps were established there, tens of thousands of refugees fleeing the war went there, and the Algerian leaders went into exile there. In addition, the aid came from the Arab world: Libya, Egypt, and Saudi Arabia supplied and transported arms. They all collected funds. Over in Europe, Czechoslovakia, Yugoslavia, the DDR, and the USSR, above all after their rapprochement with Nasser, provided concrete assistance to the Algerians. In the Atlantic bloc, support was more prudent, out of respect for its French ally. Solidarity came from anti-colonialist movements and humanitarian organizations. The United States disappointed the FLN, because while it was holding back its interests in the Maghreb and working for a negotiated solution, it went easy on the French by refraining from making any material commitments.

Although the Arab world was a major area of support for the Algerian cause, it did not suffer from dissent any the less. Cairo competed with Tunis as the place to host the Algerian leaders. The challenge here was nothing less than Nasser's hegemony over the Arab world.[13] Egyptian aid was also contested within the FLN; it strengthened those who viewed Algerian identity as Arabic-Muslim compared to those who took a pluralist view that was open to Berber languages and cultures as well as Francophonie. Within the Maghreb, tensions grew. In the first place, in its proclamation issued on November 1, 1954, the FLN had stated the objective of "North African unity," associating Morocco, Algeria, and Tunisia. However, after France proposed negotiations to its two protectorates, Morocco and Tunisia gained independence separately in 1956. Thereafter, Morocco and Tunisia had to manage the flow of refugees, the presence of armed Algerian forces on their territory and any kind of convergence between their opponents and certain Algerian nationalists. In the case of Morocco, the conflict also affected the borders. In 1958, a conference organized in Tangier between April 27 and 30 reaffirmed the desire for a federation among the three countries of the Maghreb, but it appealed above all for the formation an Algerian government. A second Maghreb conference followed in June. The Tunisians then agreed to a French pipeline being installed across their territory for the export of oil from Algeria, and the crisis with the FLN reached its apogee in the summer. At that moment, Egypt appeared to be a better ally.[14]

May 13, 1958: The Power Struggle on the Status of Combatants and Prisoners

The internationalization of the conflict was directly behind the government crisis that proved fatal for the Fourth Republic. On April 15, 1958, Félix Gaillard's government lost the confidence of the National Assembly following a meeting with the diplomats charged with the "good offices," Harold Beeley and Robert Murphy. France found itself without a government. The chain of events that led to the fall of the regime was, however, triggered by the execution of Algerians some days after the overthrow of Félix Gaillard's government.[15]

On April 24, 1958, Abderrahmane Taleb, a young chemist who had made bombs for the FLN in Algiers during the famous "battle" of the previous year, and who had been sentenced to death three times by the Military Tribunal of Algiers, was guillotined. Six other Algerians who had been condemned to death were guillotined between April 24 and 30. The FLN organ *El Moudjahid* announced reprisals: "The execution of the student Taleb and other patriots obliges us to act. The blade of the guillotine must stop. French public opinion is warned: from tomorrow, for every Algerian patriot who climbs on to the scaffold a French prisoner will be executed."[16] On May 10, the FLN made the execution of three French soldiers it had taken prisoner public: "On April 25, 1958, the special tribunal of the National Liberation Army, sitting on national soil, condemned three French soldiers to death for torture, rape and assassination against the civil population of Rame Souk *mechta* in the La Calle region. The sentence was carried out at dawn on April 30, 1958."[17] In the opinion of the historian Raphaëlle Branche, there is nothing to prove that the three soldiers were executed on this date. It is even possible that they died during detention, as other French prisoners did.[18]

Whatever the facts may be, the FLN decided at that moment to raise the question of the application of international law. By responding to the execution of Algerians who had been sentenced to death for taking part in urban terrorism with the execution of French soldiers, the FLN placed both on the same footing. They were all combatants prior to being subjected to the same treatment: if one side were to be brought before the courts for their actions, condemned to death, and executed, the other side also had to be, or else everyone had to have the right to protection by international law when they fell into enemy hands. By taking this position, the FLN applied pressure for the application of the 1949 Geneva Conventions. The newspaper daily *France-Soir* was not mistaken when it commented on the announcement of the execution of the three soldiers thus: "France, which is legally sovereign in Algeria, executes terrorists, who are not covered by the Geneva Conventions."[19] Conversely, in the opinion of the paper, which was expressing a widely shared opinion, "the FLN ignores all the laws and customs of war" and the French soldiers should have had the benefit of the protection offered by the Conventions. There was no question of reciprocity. As for the French authorities, when questioned by the International Committee of the Red Cross, they adopted a restrictive interpretation of the text of the Conventions so as to avoid their being applied in full in Algeria. At most, they granted the ICRC the right to visit their detention centers.[20]

In Algeria, the "ultras," the pro-French Algerian activists, arranged protests against the execution of the three soldiers. Demonstrations were organized in a number of towns on May 13, the day on which Pierre Pflimlin, who was expected to form a new government, was scheduled to appear before the National Assembly. In Algiers, the authorities attempted to channel the demonstrators by organizing a ceremony to pay tribute to the three soldiers in front of the monument to the dead in the presence of General Salan, who was the commander of the French Army in Algeria. It was all in vain. The demonstrators invaded the general government building, the seat of French power in Algeria. Activists, Gaullists, and generals like Salan, who was the commander of the French Army in Algeria, then founded a Comité de Salut Public (Public Safety Committee).

Two days later, on May 15, Salan made the crowd acclaim General de Gaulle, who declared that he was "ready to assume the powers of the Republic." Other Public Safety Committees were formed throughout Algeria. Some Algerians, closely supervised by the army, joined the demonstrations. On May 17, Gaullist Jacques Soustelle, who had been governor general of Algeria, arrived from France. In Paris, on May 28, Pierre Pflimlin resigned. There was a power vacuum. General de Gaulle then assumed the leadership of a new government on June 1.

On the right, the presence of "Muslims" among French people in the demonstrations in Algiers was interpreted as a sign of a promising "fraternization." "Be in no doubt, there is hope among all those people who by a large majority currently prefer integration to independence," wrote *Le Figaro* in its May 28 edition. This "fraternization" was a limited phenomenon, however, and had been managed by specialists in crowd manipulation. The spectacular unveiling of a few young women was sometimes based on threats, and sometimes on strict management of the Algerian people by military bodies specializing in crowd manipulation.[21]

For General de Gaulle, however, the re-establishment of state authority, which had been weakened by the institutions of the Fourth Republic and by the war, took priority over other tasks. He oversaw a new Constitution that reinforced executive power, and took over control of Algerian policy. After approval of the Constitution in a Referendum on September 28, the first government of the Fifth Republic was formed on January 8, 1959. As far as Algeria was concerned, the new Head of State raised conflicting expectations: Would he restore the authority of power from Paris over the army and the Algerian activists, or would he serve their purposes?

Autumn: What's New with de Gaulle?

A man of providence, de Gaulle had without doubt been the hero of the French Resistance during the Second World War. In 1944, he was in Algiers where he had formed and assumed the leadership of the Comité Français de Libération Nationale (CFLN; French Committee of National Liberation) and then the Gouvernement Provisoire de la République Française (GPRF; Provisional Government of the French Republic). After the Second World War, he had retired from political life because he disapproved of the institutions of the Fourth Republic that suffered from chronic instability.

There were six successive governments between the start of the Algerian War of Independence in 1954 and 1958. This instability did not, however, prevent a relative degree of continuity as regards the policy toward Algeria. All these governments sought to maintain two objectives: to repress the insurgents and to develop economic, social, and administrative reforms. This policy was the result of an analysis that associated the desire for independence with the blatant inequalities in Algerian colonial society.[22] Algeria, which was the only settlement colony in the French Empire, had a French minority of nearly a million people in 1954 and a demographic majority of 8 million Algerians. They were in an inferior situation from every standpoint: economic, social, political, and legal. When confronted with the mobilizations and claims of the Algerians, who drove toward independence, the French governments viewed reform as a solution.[23]

After 1954, however, French policy first manifested itself in widespread repression: it was necessary to re-establish order before it would be possible to act effectively. Repression was a priority that took precedence over everything else, and mobilized the energy and resources that had been reserved for the Algerian colony.[24] In addition, the development of reforms encountered disagreements in the French political class, and above all the objections of the representatives of French citizens in Algeria, who were able to foresee nothing other than maintaining the status quo. Most of them had no ties to mainland France; it was unthinkable that they should leave Algeria.[25] They were also opposed to any reforms at all out of a fear that they would lose their supremacy in a context in which the demographic ratio was extremely unfavorable toward them. In 1958, General de Gaulle was called to power to unblock the situation.

The evidence of General de Gaulle's intentions is contradictory. In addition to the general himself in his memoirs, many leading personalities have said that he was in favor of Algerian independence prior to 1958.[26] Other accounts attribute a preference for "the Association" of Algeria with France in the form of a federal tie between the two countries. An analysis of his policies bears witness to considerable pragmatism and relative continuity, even though he began by announcing a measure of immense significance.[27] His first speech in Algiers on June 4, 1958, remains famous: "I understand you! I know what has happened here. I see what you wanted to do. I see that the road you have opened up in Algeria is one of renovation and fraternity,"[28] he proclaimed at the time. He then announced a measure that broke from over a century of political inequality in the Algerian colony: a single electoral college to replace a dual-college system that separated French people who had full citizenship from those who did not: that is, virtually all of the Algerians who were then known as "Muslims."

Following this measure, which led to a true break, he reconnected with the logic of his predecessors who, as mentioned below, tried to develop economic, social, and administrative reforms.[29] On October 3, de Gaulle announced a plan to develop the country that included measures aimed at industrialization, increasing wages, homebuilding, and schooling: the Constantine Plan. Nonetheless, the development of the plan made use of previous studies that had inspired the reform projects under the Fourth Republic.[30] The Constantine Plan also resembles an echo of the previous reformist policy. Then, on October 23, General de Gaulle called on the "men of the insurrection," who "have fought courageously" to cease fire and return "without humiliation to their families and their jobs."[31] This offer is known as the "peace of the braves." Clearly, for the Algerians, this looked like the unconditional ceasefire the governments of the Fourth Republic previously defended.

At the same time, General de Gaulle freed thousands of Algerian internees.[32] Above all, after he became the first president of the Fifth Republic in January 1959, he decided to pardon the 200 to 300 men who had been condemned to death while awaiting a decision on their fate.[33] In this way, he was ostensibly breaking with previous policy: there had been dozens of executions in the months leading up to May 13, 1958, and they would start up again a few months after the collective pardon of January 1959, in the spring. At the time it was made, however, General de Gaulle's gesture fit into the context of regime change, and was seen as an appropriate means of creating a "new climate" on his terms: "I wanted a new climate to be installed before I became President of the Republic," he declared to *L'Écho d'Oran*. In his opinion, the pardon given to the men who had been condemned to death "was very favourably welcomed among the Muslim population."[34] In fact, his clemency cornered the nationalists, who were obliged to welcome the policy. While the FLN's organ, *El Moudjahid*, expressed the opinion that "these decisions" were "proof that the legitimacy of the Algerian cause was imposing itself more and more," it also noted that they "rectify the inhumane and absurd policy of the previous governments."[35]

A single college, the Constantine Plan, a call for the "peace of the brave," a pardon for men condemned to death—was there a pause in the war? In reality, the fight against the ALN was reinforced by the Challe Plan, from the name of the new commander-in-chief in Algeria in 1959. Accordingly, in 1958, de Gaulle's strong announcements mask a certain continuity.

The Delayed Impact of 1958

De Gaulle's break came later, following a speech on September 16, 1959, when he announced "recourse to self-determination" to seal Algeria's destiny.[36] For the first time since the beginning of the war, a French official admitted that independence might happen. The Algerian policy was only truly modified fifteen months after the regime change because before defining it and potentially giving it a new tone, it was necessary, among other things, to acquire information, place confidants in key positions, test the reaction of the adversary and Algerians, assess the state of the forces on the ground, and gauge the reactions of the international community. The announcement of self-determination was neither a sudden turnaround nor the general's implicit aim following his return to power. It was the deferred effect of the regime change, which involved a redefinition of the Algerian policy within a period of time that was, in fact, not so long: fifteen months.

The existence of a turning point in the course of the war, cannot, however, be demonstrated without taking developments on the Algerian side into account. In the Algerian camp, 1958 saw the FLN form a Provisional Government of the Republic of Algeria, on September 19, in Cairo, under the presidency of Ferhat Abbas: the GPRA. The aim of the creation of the GPRA was to give the FLN new legitimacy.

At the very outset, when it triggered the insurrection that would finally end in victory and lead to independence, the FLN was nothing more than a small group. Its founders had come from the existing independence party, the Parti du Peuple Algérien (PPA; Algerian People's Party).[37] Messali Hadj was its charismatic and historical leader. Within the PPA, since 1945 and the massacres of Algerians that marked the end of the Second World War in the colony, a new generation of militants had been making the case for resorting to an armed struggle. The PPA had also equipped itself with a military branch, the Organisation Spéciale (OS; Special Organization). In 1954, however, the PPA experienced a serious crisis, and it was during this period that some of its members decided to form a new organization in order to launch their action. This was the FLN. Practically all the nine historic heads of the FLN came through the OS, and two of them (Hocine Aït Ahmed and Ahmed Ben Bella) had also led it. After the beginning of the insurrection, the FLN obtained the alliance of two other movements that had marked Algerian political life since the interwar period: the *ulama*, these Muslim scholars, who promoted Algeria's Arabic-Muslim identity and were organized under the aegis of Abdelhamid Ben Badis;[38] the republican movement, which defended equal rights, represented by Ferhat Abbas.[39]

For Messali Hadj, the creation of the FLN represented a real coup d'état. He rejected the legitimacy of this new organization and formed another, competing one: the Mouvement National Algérien (MNA; Algerian National Movement). In 1958, the FLN gained supremacy over the MNA and succeeded in imposing itself as the exclusive representative of the Algerian people. The formation of the GPRA completed this evolution; however, it was also conceived as a response to the return to power of General de Gaulle. The creation of the GPRA mimicked the French Resistance led by de Gaulle. The name "Gouvernement Provisoire de la République Algérienne"[40] was chosen to evoke the GPRF of the Liberation, which de Gaulle led at the time. Revealing this unconscious reference to the vocabulary of resistance that sparked the formation of a representation in exile of an occupied country, the newspaper daily *Le Monde* even announced the creation of a "free Algerian government,"[41] using a term that was directly inspired by the former "Free France" of the French Resistance. From a legal standpoint, Mohamed Bedjaoui, the FLN's jurists based his argument in favor of the GPRA's legality on a number of historical precedents, including France: "The examples of the creation of the GPRF in 1944 and the GPRA on September 19, 1958 follow the same direction," he wrote.[42]

One year later, in September 1959, the GPRA delayed its reaction to the announcement of self-determination, although it did make it possible to envisage negotiations. The struggle for independence was not suspended with the announcement of self-determination, however. As mentioned below, 1959 was marked by the Challe Plan. Practically speaking, a series of French offensive actions led to the destruction of the armed groups that composed the ALN, but Algerian attacks in the cities persisted: "Let us concentrate all our efforts on intensifying attacks in cities. Aim above all at SAS officers, pilots and other specialists whom it is very difficult for the enemy to replace," suggested the ALN's instructions in Wilaya 3.[43] Also, the networks and cells created by the FLN on the ground were gradually recreated just as they were being dismantled by the French who regularly arrested their members. Through these networks, the FLN remained active. As the French army was powerless to stamp out the commitment of the Algerians in the nationalist networks, there was no French victory on the ground. Algerian victory was also, as mentioned below, a diplomatic one. The problem was that at the time the announcement of self-determination was made, however, the GPRA was suffering from a grave internal crisis. A second GPRA developed out of this deep crisis in January 1960. This new GPRA was in a position to respond to the French self-determination proposal but in 1960 only.

Conclusion

This chapter has argued that historiographical developments over the past twenty years or so allow us to suggest another narrative of 1958 which appears to be not only the year of de Gaulle's return to power. The FLN's internationalization strategy has been considerably reconsidered and has now been given a decisive place in the conduct of the conflict. The issue of the status of combatants and prisoners during this war, which lies at the heart of the events of 1958, has also seen the benefit of in-depth studies. *Last but not least*, the narrative of the war can't ignore the internal history of the Algerian camp that contributed also to define the chronology of the conflict. Nineteen fifty-eight was therefore a revolutionary year in both camps, with strong institutional evolution: the collapse of the Fourth Republic and the creation of the Provisional Government of the Algerian Republic.

What was then 1958 in the history of the Algerian War of Independence? Ultimately, while not apparent at the time, 1958 was not a turning point in the course of the war but a part of its central segment. Before, between 1954 and 1956, the conflict expanded in favor of the Algerian initiatives. Then, between 1957 and 1959, the war reached its apogee with the episode for which it is most famous: the "Battle of Algiers," which Gilbert Meynier logically suggested to rename the "Great Repression of Algiers," from an Algerian, rather than a French, standpoint.[44] After, between 1960 and 1962, the major issue for the two combatants was to find a way to bring this cruel, long-lasting conflict and the lengthy colonial period of more than a century to an end.

Notes

1. As witnessed by Bernard Droz and Évelyne Lever, *Histoire de la guerre d'Algérie (History of the Algerian War)* (Paris: Seuil, 1991). The first edition dates from 1982. The translation of the titles of books and articles published in French, as demanded by the editor, are my own.
2. For a renewed viewpoint of 1958, see: Sylvie Thénault, "1958, Algiers and the Collapse of the Fourth Republic," in *France in the World: A New Global History*, ed. Patrick Boucheron and Stéphane Gerson (New York: Other Press LLC, 2019), 771–7.
3. Mohamed Teguia, *L'Algérie en guerre (Algeria at War)* (Alger: OPU, 1988). John Talbott, *The War Without a Name* (New York: Alfred A. Knopf, 1980).
4. The international aspects have been very widely analyzed in Gilbert Meynier's reference work, *Histoire intérieure du FLN (1954–1962) (Internal History of the FLN (1954–1962))*, (Paris: Fayard, 2002). See also Matthew Connelly, *A Diplomatic Revolution: Algeria's Fight for Independence and the Origins of the Post-Cold War Era* (Oxford: Oxford University Press, 2002). On that point see in the volume: Sofia Papastamkou, "France and the Near East in 1958: Continuity and Change though Crisis."
5. On the status of combatants in the war and the events of 1958: Sylvie Thénault, *Une drôle de justice. Les magistrats dans la guerre d'Algérie (Strange Justice: The magistrates in the Algerian War)* (Paris: La Découverte, 2004), 166–8. See also: Raphaëlle Branche, *Prisonniers du FLN (Prisoners of the FLN)* (Paris, Payot, 2014).
6. This section is taken in part from Chapter 8 of my book *Histoire de la guerre d'indépendance algérienne (History of the Algerian War of Independence)* (Paris: Flammarion, 2012).

7 On the bombing of Sakiet-Sidi-Youssef and its consequences, see Samya El Machat, *Les États-Unis et la Tunisie. De l'ambiguïté à l'entente. 1945–1959 (United States and Tunisia: From Ambiguity to Agreement. 1945–1959)* (Paris: L'Harmattan, 1996).
8 Cited by Samya El Machat, *Les États-Unis et l'Algérie. De la méconnaissance à la reconnaissance. 1945–1962 (United States and Algeria: From Ignorance to Recognition. 1945–1962)* (Paris: L'Harmattan, 1996), 181.
9 Maurice Vaïsse provides an accurate description of the state of affairs in "La guerre perdue à l'ONU?" (The War Lost at the UNO?), in *La Guerre d'Algérie et les Français (The Algerian War and the French)*, ed. Jean-Pierre Rioux (Paris: Fayard, 1990), 451–62.
10 According to the wording of the proclamation issued on November 1, reproduced by Mohammed Harbi in *Les Archives de la révolution algérienne (Archives of the Algerian Revolution)* (Paris, Jeune Afrique, 1981), 101–3.
11 Connelly, *A Diplomatic Revolution*.
12 Gilbert Meynier provides a detailed summary by each major region of the world in *Histoire intérieure du FLN (Internal History of the FLN)*.
13 On Nasser see also in this volume: Dina Rezk, "Egypt's role in the Arab revolutions: Reconceptualizing Nasser from 'nationalist ideologue' to 'reluctant pragmatist.'"
14 This is based on the complete and detailed analysis by Meynier in *Histoire intérieure du FLN (Internal History of the FLN)*.
15 This part of the text is based on my own research. See: Thénault, *Une drôle de justice (Strange Justice)*, 166–8.
16 Quoted by *France-Soir* on May 12, 1958, and by *Le Monde* in its May 11–12 issue.
17 This communiqué was reproduced in particular by *Le Figaro* on May 10–11, 1958.
18 Branche, *Prisonniers du FLN (Prisoners of the FLN)*, 153.
19 In its May 21 issue.
20 Raphaëlle Branche, "Entre droit humanitaire et intérêts politiques: les missions algériennes du CICR" ("Between Humanitarian Law and Political Interests: The Algerian Missions of the ICRC"), *Revue historique*, January–March 1999, no. 609, 101–25.
21 Neil MacMaster, *Burning the Veil. The Algerian War and the "emancipation" of Muslim Women, 1954–62*, (Manchester University Press: Manchester, 2009).
22 The reforms are presented in minute detail by Harmut Elsenhans in *La guerre d'Algérie, 1954–1962 (The Algerian War, 1954–1962)* (Paris: Publisud, 1999).
23 Some great specialists of French colonization in North Africa defended reforms not only in Algeria, like the famous Charles-André Julien in 1952 in *L'Afrique du nord en marche (Moving North Africa)* (Paris: Omnibus, 2002). See: Sylvie Thénault, "The End of Empire in the Maghreb: The Common Heritage and Distinct Destinies of Morocco, Algeria and Tunisia," in *The Oxford Handbook of the Ends of Empire*, ed. Martin Thomas and Andrew Thompson (Oxford: Oxford University Press, 2018), 299–316.
24 See: Daniel Lefeuvre, *Chère Algérie (Dear Algeria)* (Paris: Flammarion, 2005).
25 Among the extensive bibliography relative to the French of Algeria, see Yann Scioldo-Zürcher, *Devenir métropolitain. Politique d'intégration et parcours de rapatriés d'Algérie en métropole, 1954-2005 (Becoming a Mainland French: Integration Policy and Algerian Returnees' Paths in Mainland France, 1954–2005)* (Paris: Editions de l'EHESS, 2010).
26 See Mahfoud Kaddache in "De Gaulle et les nationalistes algériens" *(De Gaulle and the Algerian Nationalists)*, *De Gaulle en son siècle (De Gaulle and His Century)*, t. VI, *Liberté et dignité des peuples (Freedom and Dignity of People)* (Paris: Plon/La Documentation Française, 1992), 100.

27 The sense of continuity is underlined by John Talbott in *The War without a Name*.
28 See the text of this speech in Charles de Gaulle, *Discours et messages (Discourses and Messages)*, t. III, *Avec le renouveau (The Renewal), 1958-1962* (Paris: Plon, 1970), 43-4.
29 On that, see the Chapter 8 of Thénault, *Histoire de la guerre d'indépendance algérienne (History of the Algerian War of Independence)*.
30 See Lefeuvre, *Chère Algérie (Dear Algeria)*. Harmut Elsenhans also provides us with details of the reformist policy in its continuity throughout the war in *La guerre d'Algérie, 1954-1962 (The Algerian War 1954-1962)*.
31 See the text of the press conference during which he launched this appeal in Charles de Gaulle's *Discours et messages (Discourses and Messages)*, 66-71.
32 On internment during the Algerian War of Independence, see Sylvie Thénault's research: *Une drôle de Justice (Strange Justice)* and *Violence ordinaire dans l'Algérie coloniale. Camps, internement, assignation à residence (Ordinary Violence in Colonial Algeria: Camps, Internment and House Arrests)* (Paris: Odile Jacob, 2012).
33 See Thénault, *Une drôle de justice (Strange Justice)*, 173.
34 Interview with the editor of *L'Écho d'Oran*, reproduced by *Le Monde*, May 2, 1959.
35 Quoted by *Le Monde*, January 17, 1959.
36 See the text of this speech in de Gaulle's *Discours et messages (Discourses and Messages)*, 142-5.
37 For a history of Algerian nationalism, before 1954 and during the Algerian War of Independence, see Meynier, *Histoire intérieure du FLN (Internal history of the FLN)*.
38 In addition to Gilbert Meynier's work, on the *Ulama*, see: James MacDougall, *History and Culture of Nationalism in Algeria* (Cambridge: Cambridge University Press, 2006).
39 In addition to Gilbert Meynier's work, on Ferhat Abbas and his movement, see Malika Rahal's research. For example: "Algeria: Nonviolent Resistance Against French Colonialism, 1830s-1950s," in *Recovering Nonviolent History: Civil Resistance in Liberation Struggles*, ed. Maciej Bartkowski (Boulder: Lynne Rienner Publishers, 2013), 107-24.
40 Provisional Government of the Algerian Republic.
41 In its issue dated September 19, 1958.
42 Mohamed Bedjaoui, *La Révolution algérienne par le droit (The Algerian Revolution and the Law)* (Bruxelles, Éditions de l'Association internationale des juristes démocrates, 1961), 79.
43 Directive from the General Staff of Wilaya III, zone 3, region 3, May 11, 1959, in Mohammed Harbi and Gilbert Meynier, *Le FLN, documents et histoire, 1954-1962 (The FLN, Documents and History, 1954-1962)* (Paris, Fayard, 2004), 97.
44 In his *Histoire intérieure du FLN (Internal History of the FLN)*, 322.

Chapter 11

THE IRAQI REVOLUTION OF 1958

ITS HISTORIC SIGNIFICANCE AND RELEVANCE FOR THE PRESENT

Juan Romero

The year 1958 was the culmination of a decade of unrest in the Arab world and the Iraqi Revolution one of the most important events of that year. Unlike some scholars who have consistently portrayed the overthrow of the Iraqi monarchy as a purely military coup which later turned into a revolution, this chapter reveals that it was a much more complex event—simultaneously a military coup, a plot within a larger conspiracy, a joint venture with political parties, and a genuine revolution.[1] Furthermore, the reactions to the revolution demonstrate that its impact was not limited to the Middle East, but that it was an event of global significance, influencing political and military decisions in North America, Europe, Africa, and Asia, and contributing to heightened Cold War tension between the superpowers. The Western powers were completely taken by surprise at the loss of a staunch ally in Baghdad.[2] Concurrently, there was great apprehension in Washington and European capitals that radical Arab nationalist regimes and, presumably, the Soviet Union would seize control of much of Middle Eastern oil.[3]

Conversely, Moscow perceived the revolution as a great victory for the Soviet bloc[4] despite the fact that the new Iraqi leader, ʿAbd al-Karīm Qassim, was not a Communist.[5] The overthrow of the Iraqi monarchy also had an unexpected effect—the revolution caused a drastic deterioration in Egyptian-Iraqi relations over pan-Arab policies.[6] The chapter examines the reasons for the subsequent domestic political instability in Iraq. Finally, this chapter demonstrates that the revolutionary year of 1958, despite the passage of sixty-one years, still is of great importance in the twenty-first century.

The Ills of Monarchic Society

A brief review of political, economic, and social conditions in monarchical Iraq will reveal why the revolution should have been anticipated by the regime and Western observers alike. The monarchic regime and British and American diplomats in Iraq were all aware of the ills of Iraqi society.[7] These three parties pinned their hopes on oil revenues, contending that if these gradually began to trickle down to the poorer strata of the population, stability would ensue, and political and social unrest would cease.[8] The authoritarian regime, wishing to maintain a firm grip on political activity in the country, was convinced that a disaster could be averted by launching large-scale infrastructure and development projects. A major problem with such an approach, however, was that the positive effects anticipated would take several years to materialize.[9] A second significant problem, as demonstrated by the political and social unrest in the country, was that the regime was running out of time. Its citizens, particularly students, intellectuals, workers, the impoverished rural population, and opposition politicians, had made it clear to domestic and foreign observers alike during the last decade preceding the regime's collapse that it enjoyed very little credibility among an overwhelming majority of Iraqis.[10]

Iraqis were very active in their opposition to the regime during the last decade of monarchic rule despite the repression. As a result, the opposition joined forces in the National Front in 1954,[11] later demanding the abolition of feudal estates, elimination of foreign economic control, departure of foreign troops, and adoption of a neutralist foreign policy.[12] The intensive legal and illegal activities of the opposition during the last decade of the monarchy constitute clear and compelling evidence of the regime's unpopularity.[13] Most Iraqis lived in small villages as tenant farmers or agricultural laborers. Landlords could remove the former from the land at will.[14] A British diplomat reported that the standard of living in rural areas was extremely low and that conservative sheikhs had a detrimental influence on the peasantry.[15] Reformist officials could not do much about the situation, however, because of strong resistance on the part of conservative landowners, their influence in the capital, and the opposition of Prime Minister Nuri al-Said to a redistribution of land.[16] Uprisings in several parts of Iraq—a result of poor living conditions in the countryside and unpopular government policies during the Suez Crisis of 1956—testify to the tense situation. One uprising was quelled only with the assistance of the army.[17] Late in 1957 British and American diplomatic communications confirm the volatile situation in rural areas and widespread peasant discontent with feudal landlords.[18] Finally, the discontent among civilians was also matched by similar sentiments in the army. However, despite the serious situation in the country, intelligence reports of plots in the military between 1956 and 1958 were disregarded by the regime.[19]

Following the Egyptian Free Officers' overthrow of the monarchy in 1952 tension between Iraq and Egypt increased exponentially. The Egyptian leader Gamal Abdel Nasser rejected military alliances with extra-regional powers,[20] whereas, the Iraqi monarchic regime considered the Soviet Union the foremost threat to the security of the Middle East.[21] This conviction led to the formation of the Baghdad Pact in 1955, an initiative sharply condemned by the Iraqi opposition and Egyptian leadership.[22] Furthermore, the Iraqi Fertile Crescent project envisioned an Arab federation comprising Iraq, Syria, and Jordan for the realization of which Baghdad was prepared to resort to violence in Syria.[23] For this purpose, the Iraqi prime minister transferred arms and money to the Syrian opposition.[24] Unfortunately for Nuri, Syrians elected a pro-Egyptian president, Shukri al-Quwatli, in 1955, ushering in closer ties with Cairo and intensifying an Arab cold war between Cairo and Baghdad.[25]

Egyptian-Iraqi tension continued in 1956 and 1957, resulting from the Suez Crisis and Iraqi and American attempts to bring about regime change in Syria. In 1956 the Iraqi government conspired with former Syrian president Adīb al-Shishakli to overthrow the government in Damascus. By June 1956 the United States and British officials had joined forces with the Iraqi conspirators. The plot involved some Iraqi saber-rattling along the border with Syria, but nothing came of this, since the conspiracy was betrayed to Syrian authorities who broke the news in late 1956.[26] Despite the Anglo-French-Israeli Suez Crisis debacle of 1956, Washington continued its unsuccessful attempts to unseat the Syrian government in 1957, arguing that Syria was about to be taken over by communism.[27] These clandestine American efforts to prevent a Communist "takeover" were exposed to the world in August 1957, when Damascus expelled three American diplomats.[28]

The closer ties between Cairo and Damascus paved the way for the formation of two competing Arab unions—the Egyptian-Syrian United Arab Republic (UAR)[29] and the Iraqi-Jordanian Arab Union. At a Baghdad Pact meeting in January 1958, a month before the proclamation of the UAR, Nuri had made his hostility to the project clear, by arguing that it was a Communist initiative and that the Pact needed to intervene to prevent the formation of the UAR, if the leftist Syrian government refused to change course.[30] The proclamation of the UAR on February 1, 1958, was followed two weeks later by the formation of the Arab Union.[31] Only one state, Yemen, joined the UAR and no other state joined the Arab Union.[32] Furthermore, there was opposition among Palestinians in the West Bank and Kurds, Shi'is, and intellectuals in Iraq to the formation of the Arab Union.[33] The Union lasted a mere five months until July 15, 1958.[34] The Syrians and Egyptians parted ways in 1961. However, despite their brief existence, these unions had a profound impact on Middle East politics—they contributed greatly to exacerbating already existing divisions and tensions in the region, and the Arab Union ironically offered an opportunity to the Iraqi military to overthrow the monarchy.

The Free Officers

The Free Officers who toppled the Iraqi monarchy in 1958 were a loosely structured organization of anti-regime military officers. The name of the organization suggests that its founders had been inspired by their Egyptian namesake Al-Ḍubbāṭ al-Ahrār (The Free Officers) who had put an end to the Egyptian monarchy in 1952, but the Arab defeat in the first Arab-Israeli war in 1948 and the perceived lack of support of the Iraqi government for its troops in the Palestine theater appear to have been other reasons for the Free Officers to want the demise of the monarchic regime.[35] An important issue which was discussed at the meetings of the Free Officers' Supreme Committee was the question whether Iraq would accede to the United Arab Republic after the revolution. It was decided that Iraq would join Egypt and Syria in the UAR if the revolutionaries faced an existential threat.[36] The pan-Arabists accepted this compromise solution only to oppose Qassim's anti-union policies after July 14, 1958. However, the question of setting a date for the revolution proved much more divisive.[37] Also, there was friction between Qassim and some other Free Officers prior to the revolution,[38] an indication that cooperation and unanimity on divisive issues would not easily be achieved in the post-monarchic period.

In the early hours of July 14, 1958, the Free Officers entered Baghdad, seizing control of key targets in the capital within a few hours.[39] The military's overthrow of the regime was an operation more complex than a regular coup, since it can be described as a plot within a wider conspiracy. All Free Officers were involved in the latter, but only a select few under the command of ʿAbd al-Karīm Qassim were privy to the former.[40] An order to deploy to Jordan created the perfect opportunity to overthrow the monarchic regime, since the presence of troops near the capital would not raise suspicion. Two further circumstances made the takeover feasible—the simultaneous presence in the capital of the king, crown prince, and prime minister, all of whom constituted targets of the Free Officers, and the fact that some troops had been issued live ammunition.[41] The only target which offered token resistance was the royal Rihāb Palace, which was subjected to artillery fire until the royal guard surrendered.[42] The simultaneous presence of King Faisal II and Crown Prince ʿAbd al-Ilāh made the palace an important target. Both were killed.[43] Surprisingly enough, violence was limited despite the manner of death of two of the pillars of the regime.

As indicated above, the Iraqi Revolution was not the first involvement of the military in politics. Throughout Iraq's modern history military officers have played a prominent role and continued to do so, following the coup against Qassim in 1962. The military's role in the Revolution must thus be seen in a historical context beginning with the creation of Iraq, following the First World War and not as an isolated catalyst for the military's subsequent involvement in the political process of the country.[44]

A Coup or a Revolution?

The overthrow of the Iraqi monarchy constitutes compelling evidence that this event amounted to something more complex than a mere military coup, singlehandedly executed by the Free Officers. Prior to July 14, Qassim had contacted at least one civilian politician with respect to the fate of the king, crown prince, and the prime minister.[45] Furthermore, early in the morning on July 14 huge crowds of Baghdadis took to the streets in celebration of the military's takeover, converging on the Rihāb Palace where they played a role in the royal guard's surrender.[46] According to one eyewitness, the crowds were a spontaneous expression of the people's joy,[47] but another source contends that they had been organized by the United National Front at the request of the Free Officers.[48] Several party leaders seem to have been informed of the date of the military plot, at the initiative of individual Free Officers.[49] The fact that opposition leaders had been consulted by the Free Officers[50] is evidence of popular participation prior to and during the events of July 14, a fact which supports the argument that the toppling of the monarchy was not an ordinary military coup. This conclusion is confirmed by the American ambassador to Iraq, Waldemar Gallman, who states that the public and army had unhesitatingly lent their support to the conspirators.[51] The above discussion of the events of July 14 leads one to conclude that the purely military operation constituted a coup. Conversely, the presence of large crowds of Baghdadis in the streets, the Free Officers' contacts with the political opposition, and the officers' request that the opposition be prepared to mobilize its followers in support of the coup clearly suggest revolutionary elements. However, it should be emphasized that popular participation alone or a military coup which supplants a monarchy does not necessarily amount to a revolution, if the policies of the old regime largely remain in place.[52]

In addition to popular participation, there are other aspects of the July 14 overthrow of the Iraqi monarchy which, if analyzed in a comprehensive fashion, allow us to conclude that the military coup was just one element in a series of events and policies which, if considered conjointly, are tantamount to a revolution. The system of government changed from monarchy to republic, which in and of itself does not constitute a revolution as argued above, but was merely window dressing if not followed by a radical departure from previous policies. A temporary Sovereignty Council consisting of three members would fulfill the role of a president until one was elected by the people of Iraq.[53] A government was formed with a majority of posts occupied by civilians. Real power was, however, concentrated in the hands of the military. The Sovereignty Council appointed Qassim prime minister, minister of defense, and commander-in-chief of the armed forces.[54] The new government allowed political activity, but declined to issue licenses to political parties, which did not prevent Qassim from reassuring Iraqis that the country was "heading towards healthy democratic rule."[55]

Notwithstanding the revolutionary changes, the new republican system of government shared one important characteristic with the old regime—it was authoritarian. This suggests that Qassim placed no trust in political parties or other Free Officers as to their ability to take the country in the right direction.[56] At least one scholar concurs in this assessment, doubting that opposition politicians could have formed a government based on cooperation, had the military turned over power to them. He rejects the notion that Qassim was the source of division, contending that he actually encouraged cooperation among the different political parties.[57] Nonetheless, Qassim's authoritarian leanings made him a dictator, albeit a lenient one.

The above discussion reveals that the new system of government entailed change and continuity at the same time, but it was the actual policies of the new regime which departed radically from those of the monarchy. Unlike the monarchic regime, the republican government strove initially to improve the situation of the Kurdish minority, declaring that Arabs and Kurds are partners in Iraq.[58] Efforts were also made to redistribute land in rural areas, but these attempts were not very successful due to the lack of resources and land surveyors.[59] By contrast, progressive labor legislation and housing programs for the poor greatly improved the situation of workers and Iraqis living in the slums—segments of the population which the monarchic regime had neglected.[60] The replacement of many foreign oil experts with Iraqi professionals and regaining of control over several oil concessions also set the new regime apart from monarchic governments.[61]

Relations with foreign powers and international trade were other areas in which the revolutionary government's policies radically departed from those of the monarchic regime. The new regime in Baghdad had early on informed the British ambassador, Michael Wright, that it had adopted a policy of genuine neutralism toward foreign powers.[62] This meant a fundamental change in the close ties between the Iraqi monarchy and the Western powers, as testified to by Iraq's withdrawal from the Baghdad Pact in March 1959, access to Soviet intelligence reports, barter trade with the Soviet bloc, and Soviet arms transfers to Iraq.[63] It should be emphasized, however, that cooperation with the USSR did not turn Iraq into a Soviet satellite and did not prevent Qassim from taking resolute steps to curb Communist influence in Iraq.[64]

International Repercussions

The Iraqi Revolution of 1958 had a far-reaching global impact. Britain lost access to two important air bases, Iraq discontinued all cooperation with the Baghdad Pact, and the revolutionary regime seceded from the pro-West Arab Union.[65] Cairo initially welcomed the revolution as demonstrated by a defense agreement between the two states,[66] but relations soon deteriorated when Qassim showed little enthusiasm for adhering to the United Arab Republic and Nasser supported the pan-Arab opposition in Iraq.[67] The weakened Western position in the region was also reflected in an emergency meeting of the US government on July 14, 1958, at which officials discussed concerns about possible Soviet and radical pan-Arab control over the region's oil fields, if political instability spread to Saudi Arabia.[68] This fear precipitated the US intervention in the Lebanese Civil War on July 15, 1958, the intention of which was to preempt such a scenario.[69] The British undertook a similar operation in Jordan to shore King Hussein up.[70] The American and British interventions testify to the international significance of the Iraqi Revolution.

The Middle Eastern members of the Baghdad Pact, and Israel and Jordan generally took a more aggressive stance on intervention in Iraq than the United States and Britain, with Soviet leaders representing a completely different position. Both Washington and London had early on recognized the futility of an intervention to restore the old regime to power in Baghdad, concluding that such an operation was a doomed undertaking for lack of domestic support in Iraq.[71] By contrast, Israeli prime minister David Ben-Gurion argued that intervention was necessary to stop the Iraqi Revolution,[72] and so did Turkish, Pakistani, and Jordanian leaders.[73] States in the region thus took a more militant position on regime change in Iraq, to a degree where Washington had to express its concern to Ankara.[74] Not surprisingly, the Soviet Union interpreted the Iraqi Revolution as a victory for the socialist camp, partly because of the anti-imperialist rhetoric of the new regime.[75] Interestingly enough, reactions in Moscow to the regime change in Baghdad reveal that Soviet and American leaders interpreted the revolution in a similar way, namely, as a victory for the Soviet bloc.

Conclusion

This chapter has argued that Iraq played a major role in a revolutionary year of great historical significance. The authoritarian rule and economic disparities of Iraqi monarchic society caused the overthrow of the *ancien régime*. The partial dismantling of the monarchy's institutions and the fundamental change in policies under the new regime especially testify to the fact that the collapse of the monarchy was tantamount to a political and social revolution.[76] The Western powers were taken by surprise despite obvious ills of Iraqi society and their initial primary concern was that radical Arab nationalists and the Soviet Union would seize control of the region's oil resources. The result of the revolution was a weakened Western position in the Middle East. Furthermore, the Qassim regime's replacement of the monarchy's pro-West policies with neutralist policies resulted in closer political and economic ties with the Soviet bloc, without, however, turning the country into a Soviet satellite.

This chapter has revealed that the impact of the Iraqi Revolution was not limited to Iraq or the Middle East; it had global repercussions due to the involvement of the superpowers, European, and regional powers in developments following the July 14 events. Also, evidence has been presented in support of the argument that the revolution was not the direct cause of the military's role in Iraqi politics following the overthrow of Qassim, since the military has played a central role in Iraqi society since the creation of the modern state.[77] Finally, a revived interest in the events of more than sixty years ago is evidence that the Iraqi Revolution matters in the twenty-first century, not just for nation-building efforts and future developments in Iraq, but for the Middle East in general.[78]

Notes

1 Neither Thabit A. J. Abdullah in *A Short History of Iraq* (Harlow, UK: Pearson Education, Ltd., 2011), 119, nor Phebe Marr in *The Modern History of Iraq* (Boulder, CO: Westview Press, 2012) discuss the contacts between some officers on the Supreme Committee of the Free Officers and political leaders prior to the overthrow of the monarchy.
2 This is evidenced by the confusion regarding the role of the Communists in the Iraqi Revolution and lack of reliable intelligence on the leading military officers of the new regime, National Archives (NA), UK, Wright to the Foreign Office, July 20, 1958, No. 15, Secret, FO371/134200. It was not until nine days after the revolution that the British ambassador to Iraq reported that the ministers of the revolutionary

government were "liberal reformers," Wright to the Foreign Office, July 23, No. 24, Secret, FO371/134200.
3 Juan Romero, *The Iraqi Revolution of 1958: A Revolutionary Quest for Unity and Security* (Lanham, MD: University Press of America, 2011), 151–2.
4 *Pravda*, August 2, 1958, 3.
5 Samira Haj, *The Making of Iraq 1900–1963: Capital, Power, and Ideology* (Albany, NY: State University of New York, 1997), 108. Qassim himself claimed that he was above political affiliation and that he was the leader of all Iraqis, Shamīl ʿAbd al-Qādir, *Al-Ightiyāl biʾl-Dabāba: Asrār al-yawmai 8 wa 9 shubāṭ 1963 fī ḥayāt al-zaʿīm ʿAbd al-Karīm Qassim* (Assassination by Tank: Secrets of February 8 and 9, 1963 in the Life of ʿAbd al-Karīm Qassim) (Baghdād: Dār al-Jawāhiriyy, 2011), 41. *Foreign Relations of the United States* (FRUS) 1958–1960, Vol. XII, No. 144, Cumming to Dulles, November 25, 1958, 353–4, referred to in Stephen Blackwell, "A Desert Squall: Anglo-American Planning for Military Intervention in Iraq, July 1958-August 1959," *Middle Eastern Studies* 35, no. 3 (July 1999): 5.
6 The difference between the strained Egyptian relations under the monarchy and the Qassim regime was that monarchic leaders had a pan-Arab alternative of their own to that of Gamal Abdul Nasser, *Al-Zamān* (Baghdad), August 17, 1958, 1; *Al-Nahār* (Beirut), August 30, 1958, 1; *Al-Zamān*, August 17, 1958, 1; *The Iraq Times* (Baghdad), August 26, 1958, 2. Conversely, the tension between Egypt and Iraq under Qassim was caused by the lack of such a plan on the part of Qassim and Nasser's support for the pan-Arab faction in the Iraqi military, Romero, *The Iraqi Revolution*, 206–7; Majid Khadduri, *Republican Iraq: A Study in Iraqi Politics since the Revolution of 1958* (London: Oxford University Press, 1969), 87, 92; 14 July Celebration Committee 1958–1959, *The Iraqi Revolution: One Year of Progress and Achievement* (Baghdad: The Times Press, 1959), 9.
7 National Archives and Records Administration (NARA), College Park, Maryland. W. Clyde Dunn, Chargé d'Affaires, July 26, 1956, Secret, Despatch No. 67, Enclosure, 787.5-MSP/7-2656.
8 NARA. Gallman to the Department of State, April 26, 1955, Despatch No. 522, Top Secret, 787.5/4-2655, Subject: Threat of Communist Subversion in Iraq and Recommendations Re Possible Steps to Support Indigenous Counter-Measures.
9 Muḥammad Fāḍil al-Jamāliyy, *Al-ʿIrāq al-Ḥadīth: Arāʾ wa Mutalaʿāt fī Shuʾūnihi al-Masīriyya* (Modern Iraq: Views on and Studies in Its Decisive Affairs) (n.d., n.p.), 67; Michael Ionides, *Divide and Lose: The Arab Revolt of 1955–1958* (London: Geoffrey Bles, 1960), 120; James Arthur Salter, *The Development of Iraq: A Plan of Action* (London: Caxton Press, 1955), no page reference, referred to in Ionides, *Divide and Lose*, 121.
10 NARA. Gallman to the Department of State, April 26, 1955, Despatch No. 522; NA, Kew, United Kingdom. Wright to the Foreign Office, Confidential, January 11, 1956, FO371115759. See also Nathan Citino, *Envisioning the Arab Future: Modernization in US-Arab Relations 1945–1967* (Cambridge, UK: Cambridge University Press, 2017).
11 Hanna Batatu, *The Old Social Classes and the Revolutionary Movements of Iraq: A Study of Iraq's Old Landed and Commercial Classes and of Its Communists, Baʿthists and Free Officers* (London: Saqi Books, 2004) (first published by Princeton University Press in 1978), 686–7.
12 Fāḍil Husain, *Suqūṭ al-Niẓām al-Malakiyy fīʾl-ʿIrāq* (The Fall of the Monarchic Regime in Iraq) (Al-Qāhira: Jamiʿat al-Duwal al-ʿArabiyya, al-Munaẓẓama al-ʿArabiyya liʾl-Tarbiya waʾl-Thaqāfa waʾl-ʿUlūm, Maʿhad al-Buḥūth wa al-Dirāsāt al-ʿArabiyya, Qism

al-Buḥūth wa'l-Dirāsāt al-Tarīkhiyya, 1974), 51; *Al-Fihā*', January 19, 1956, referred to in Aleksei Fedorovich Fedchenko, *Irak v Bor'be za Nezavisimost' 1917-1969* (Iraq in the Struggle for Independence 1917–1969) (Moskva: Izdatel'stvo Nauka, 1970), 206.
13 Fedchenko, *Irak*, 205.
14 NARA. W. Clyde Dunn, Chargé d'Affaires, Baghdad to the Department of State, Despatch 67, Secret, July 26, 1956, 787.00/7-2656; Rony Gabbay, *Communism and Agrarian Reform in Iraq* (London: Croom Helm, 1978), 25.
15 NA. Wright to Selwyn Lloyd, Foreign Office, Confidential, December 31, 1957, FO371/134197, report by Oriental Counselor Samuel Falle.
16 NARA. Nicholas G. Thacher, First Secretary of Embassy, Baghdad (for the ambassador) to the Department of State, Confidential, October 17, 1957, 787.00/10-1757; Uriel Dann, *Iraq Under Qassim: A Political History, 1958–1963* (New York, NY: Frederick A. Praeger, Inc., Publishers, 1969), 10; NA. Wright to Selwyn Lloyd, Foreign Office, Confidential, December 31, 1957, FO371/134197, report by Oriental Counselor Samuel Falle.
17 *Sovremennii Vostok*, 1957, No. 8, 15–16, referred to in Fedchenko, *Irak*, 209–10.
18 NARA. Nicholas G. Thacher, First Secretary of Embassy, Baghdad (for the ambassador) to the Department of State, Confidential, October 17, 1957, 787.00/10-1757; NA, Wright to Selwyn Lloyd, Foreign Office, Confidential, December 31, 1957, FO371/134197, Report by Oriental Counselor Samuel Falle.
19 Khadduri, *Republican Iraq*, 32; Tawfīq al-Suwaidiyy, *Mudhakkirāt* [Memoirs] (n.p.: Dār al-Kitāb al-ʿArabiyy, 1969), 594–7, referred to in Marr, *The Modern History of Iraq*, 77–8.
20 Magnus Persson, *Great Britain, the United States, and the Security of the Middle East: The Formation of the Baghdad Pact* (Lund: Lund University Press, 1998), 212.
21 NA. Wright to the Foreign Office, February 8, 1957, No. 43, Confidential, FO371/128038, Iraq: Annual Review for 1956; Walīd Muḥammad Saʿīd al-Aʿzamiyy, *Nūri al-Saʿid wa'l-Sirāʿ maʿa ʿAbd al-Nāsir* (Nūri al-Saʿid and the Struggle with Abdul Nasser) (Baghdād: al-Maktaba al-ʿĀlamiyya, 1988), 83–4.
22 Waldemar J. Gallman, *Iraq Under General Nuri* (Baltimore: Johns Hopkins Press, 1964), 56; Persson, *Great Britain*, 212.
23 *Al-Zamān*, August 17, 1958, 1.
24 *Al-Nahār*, August 30, 1958, 1; *Al-Zamān*, August 17, 1958, 1; *The Iraq Times*, August 26, 1958, 2.
25 For a detailed discussion of the Arab Cold War, see Malcolm Kerr, *The Arab Cold War: Gamal ʿAbd al-Nasser and His Rivals, 1958–1970* (Oxford: Oxford University Press, 1971).
26 Patrick Seale, *The Struggle for Syria: A Struggle of Post-War Arab Politics 1945–1958* (New Haven, CT: Yale University Press, 1986), 271–6. Also, see Sofia Papastamkou, "France and the Middle East in 1958: Continuity and Change through Crisis"; Jeffrey G. Karam, "Cautious Revisionism and the Limits of Hegemony in 1958: A Revolutionary Year for the United States in the Middle East"; and Fadi Esber, "No Turning Back: Syria and the 1958 Watershed"; Chapters 3, 4, and 12 in this volume.
27 Kerr, *The Arab Cold War*, 6.
28 Seale, *The Struggle for Syria*, 291.
29 For a discussion of the formation of the United Arab Republic see Fadi Esber, "No Turning Back: Syria and the 1958 Watershed," Chapter 12 in this volume.
30 Muhsin Muḥammad al-Mutawalliyy al-ʿArabiyy, *Nūrī Bāshā al-Saʿīd: min al-bidāya ilā al-nihāya* (Nūri Pasha al-Saʿīd: From the Beginning to the End) (Bairūt: Al-Dar

al-ʿArabiyya liʾl-Mawsūʿāt, 2005), 373–4. The Syrian Communist Party's opposition to the Egyptian-Syrian merger seems, however, to undermine Nūri's argument, John Major, "The Search for Arab Unity," *International Affairs* 39, no. 4 (October 1963): 556. For a detailed discussion of the UAR, see Robert McNamara, "The Point of Departure: The Impact of the Revolutionary Year of 1958 on British Policy," Chapter 2 in this volume.

31 Nasser had expressed misgivings about an Egyptian-Syrian union, but had relented to pressure from Syrian Baʿath military officers, James Jankowski, "Arab Nationalism in 'Nasserism' and Egyptian State Policy, 1952-1958," in James Jankowski and Israel Gershoni, eds., *Rethinking Nationalism in the Arab Middle East* (New York: Columbia University Press, 1997), 162, 164; Egypt, Ministry of National Guidance, *Majmūʿat Khutub wa Tasriḥāt wa Bayānāt al-Raʾis Jamāl ʿAbd al-Nāsir* (Collected Speeches, Statements, and Communiques of President Gamal Abdul Nasser) (Al-Qāhira: n.p., n.d.), multivolume, 1:771, referred to in Jankowski, "Arab Nationalism," 164.

32 King Hussein of Jordan made great but unsuccessful efforts to attract Saudi Arabia to the Arab Union, Alan de Lacy Rush, ed., *Records of the Hashemite Dynasties: A Twentieth Century Documentary History, Jordan*, Vol. IX (Cambridge: Cambridge University Press, 1995), 6. Baghdad shared Amman's hopes that other Arab states would join the union, particularly Saudi Arabia and Kuwait, Rush, RHD, Vol. XIV, Embassy, Baghdad to the Foreign Office, No. 151, Secret, February 3, 1958; Politisches Archiv (PA), Auswärtiges Amt, Berlin (Archive of German Ministry for Foreign Affairs), B12, Band 813, 316.83.00-490, Baghdad, No. 20, February 25, 1958; Ibrāhīm Fāʿūr al-Sharʿa, *Al-Ittiḥād al-ʿArabiyy1958* (The Arab Union 1958) (ʿAmmān: Al-Lajnā al-ʿUlyā li Kitābat Tārīkh al-Urdunn, 2004), 270–1. Also, see Jeffrey G. Karam, "Cautious Revisionism and the Limits of Hegemony in 1958: A Revolutionary Year for the United States in the Middle East," Chapter 4 in this volume.

33 Al-Sharʿa, *Al-Ittiḥād al-ʿArabiyy*, pp. 205, 210; PA B12, Band 813, 316.83.00-483, Embassy, Amman to the Ministry of Foreign Affairs, Bonn, February 19, 1958; NA. Ambassador Trevelyan, Baghdad to Selwyn Lloyd, January 29, 1959, FO371/40896, Subject: Annual Report 1958, Iraq; Edward C. Keefer, ed., *Foreign Relations of the United States, Near Eastern Region; Iran; Iraq; Arabian Peninsula* (Washington, DC: United States Government Printing Office, 1993), Vol. XII, Special National Intelligence Estimate 30–58, February 20, 1958, Secret, 41; ʿAbd al-Razzaq al-Hasani, *Tarīkh al-Wizārāt al-ʿIrāqiyya* (History of Iraqi Ministries) (Saidā: Al-ʿIrfān, 1968), Vol. X, 1955–1958, 212; Fathī Shahāda al-Dīb, *ʿAbd al-Nāṣir wa Taḥrīr al-Mashriq al-ʿArabiyy* (Abdul Nasser and the Liberation of the Arab East) (Cairo: Markaz al-Ahrām liʾl-Dirāsāt al-Siyāsiyya waʾl-Istrātijiyya, 2000), 299.

34 For a detailed discussion of the Arab Union, see Juan Romero, "Arab Nationalism and the Arab Union of 1958," *British Journal of Middle Eastern Studies* 42, no. 2 (April 2015).

35 ʿAbd al-Khāliq Husain, *Thawrat 14 Tammūz 1958 al-ʿIrāqiyya wa ʿAbd al-Karīm Qassim* (The Iraqi Revolution of July 14, 1958 and ʿAbd al-Karīm Qassim) (Dimashq: Dār al-Ḥaṣād, 2003), 15; Nūrī Ṣabīh, ed., *Istiʿādat al-zaʿīm: hiwārāt wa arāʾ ʿirāqiyya ʿan al-zaʿīm ʿAbd al-Karīm Qassim, maʿa bāhith ʿAqīl al-Nāṣiriyy* (Recollections of the Leader: Iraqi Conversations about and Views on ʿAbd al-Karīm Qassim with Collaboration of ʿAqīl al-Nāṣiriyy) (Bairūt: Matbaʿat al-Baṣāʾir, 2013, third edition), 68.

36 Husain, *Suqūt al-Niẓām al-Malakiyy*, 72. Muhsin al-Rufaiʿiyy, Qassim's director of intelligence, has stated that ʿAbd al-Salām ʿĀrif, Qassim's second in command and

subsequently his arch-enemy, demanded, but was not serious about, immediate unity with the UAR, Sattar Jabbār al-Jābariyy, ed., *Anā wa'l-za'īm: mudhakkirāt al-'aqīd Muhsin al-Rufai'iyy, mudīr istikhbārāt fī 'ahd al-za'īm 'Abd al-Karīm Qassim* (The Leader and I: Memoirs of Lieutenant Colonel Muhsin al-Rufai'iyy, 'Abd al-Karīm Qassim's Director of Military Intelligence) (Baghdād: Majmū'at al-'Adāla li'l-Ṣaḥāfa wa'l-Tab'a wa'l-Nashr, 2010), 37.

37 Batatu, *The Old Social Classes*, 797.
38 Husain, *Suqūt al-Niẓām al-Malakiyy*, 76.
39 *Al-Zamān*, July 25, 1958; *The Iraq Times*, July 26, 1958.
40 Romero, *The Iraqi Revolution*, 109; al-Jābariyy, ed., *Anā wa'l-za'īm*, 31.
41 Ṣabīḥ 'Alī Ghālib, *Qiṣṣat Thawrat 14 Tammuz wa'l-Ḍubbāṭ al-Ahrār* (The Story of the July 14 Revolution and the Free Officers) (Bairūt: Dār al-ṭalī'at li'l-tabā'āt wa'l-nashr, 1968), 52–62; Batatu, *The Old Social Classes*, 796.
42 Fāliḥ Ḥanẓal, *Asrār Maqtaliyy al-'Ā'ila al-Malika* (The Secrets of the Murder of the Royal Family) (n.p., second and revised edition, 1992), 98–9.
43 Marr, *The Modern History of Iraq*, 85; Muhammad Husain al-Zubaidīyy, *Thawrat 14 Tammūz 1958 fi'l-'Irāq: Asbābuhā wa Muqaddamatuhā wa tanẓīmāt al-Ḍubbāṭ al-Ahrār* (The July 14 Revolution 1958: Its Causes and Origins, and the Free Officers Organizations) (Baghdād: Dā'irat al-Shu'ūn al-Thaqāfiyya wa'l-Nashr, 1983), 455–9.
44 Ṣabīḥ, ed., *Isti'ādat al-za'īm*, 125. Also, see Batatu, *The Old Social Classes*, 319–61.
45 Husain, *Suqūt al-Niẓām al-Malakiyy*, 70.
46 Ḥanẓal, *Asrār*, 112.
47 Norman Daniel, "Contemporary Perceptions," in *The Iraqi Revolution of 1958: The Old Social Classes Revisited*, ed. Robert A. Fernea and Wm. Roger Louis (London and New York: I.B. Tauris & Co. Ltd., 1991), 11.
48 NARA, Robert C. F. Gordon, Second Secretary of Embassy (For the Ambassador) to the Department of State, Confidential, August 7, 1958, Despatch No. 60, 787.00/8-758. Subject: Some Observations on Baghdad Mob Action, July 14–16, 1958; al-Zubaidīyy, *Thawrat 14 Tammūz*, 481–2.
49 Al-Zubaidīyy, *Thawrat 14 Tammūz*, 481–2.
50 Qassim had informed the leaders of the National Democratic Party and the Communist Party of his plans, and 'Arif had contacted Ba'ath leaders, al-Jābariyy, *Anā wa'l-za'īm*, 35.
51 NARA, Gallman to the Department of State, Secret, July 14, 1958, 10:00 p.m., 787.00/7-1458; NARA, Gallman to the Department of State, Secret, August 4, 1958, 787.00/8-458. His conclusion is also echoed in the coup leaders' first proclamation to the nation, in which they stated that the country had been liberated with the assistance of the Iraqi people, Iraq, 14 July Celebrations Committee 1958–1959, *The Iraqi Revolution: One Year of Progress and Achievement* (Baghdad: The Times Press, 1959), 7.
52 For a detailed discussion of revolutionary criteria, see Romero, *The Iraqi Revolution*, 138–50 and 171–87.
53 Al-Zubaidīyy, *Thawrat 14 Tammūz*, 500.
54 Khadduri, *Republican Iraq*, 49.
55 'Abd al-Karīm Qassim, *Principles of the 14 July Revolution* (Baghdad: The Times Press, n.d.), 13.
56 Ibid., 5.
57 'Abd al-Khāliq Husain, "Mi'a 'ām 'alā milād al-za'īm 'Abd al-Karīm Qassim," (One Hundred Years since the Birth of 'Abd al-Karīm Qassim), '*Mawqi*' '*Abd al-Khāliq Husain*, http://www.abdalkhaliqhussein.nl/?news=694 (accessed February 11, 2018).

58 Khadduri, *Republican Iraq*, 64; al-Zubaidi, *Thawrat 14 Tammūz*, 505–6.
59 Muhammad Kāẓim ʿAli, *Al-ʿIrāq fī ʿAhd ʿAbd al-Karīm Qassim: Dirāsāt fi'l-Quwa al-Siyāsiyya wa'l-Sirāʿ al-Idiūlujiyy 1958-1963* (Iraq in the Era of ʿAbd al-Karīm Qassim: A Study in Political Power and Ideological Struggle) (Baghdād: Maktab al-Yaqẓa al-ʿArabiyya, 1989), 107; *Al-Ahrām*, October 2, 1958, 1–2; Rony Gabbay, *Communism and Agrarian Reform in Iraq* (London: Croom Helm, 1978), 113–14, 116; Batatu, *The Old social Classes*, 837.
60 Batatu, *The Old Social Classes*, 841–2; Qassim had more than 250,000 houses built for the poor, a unique record in Iraq's history, Ṣabīḥ, *Istiʿādat al-zaʿīm*, 10.
61 14 July Celebrations Committee, *The Iraqi Revolution*, 53; Ibrāhīm Kubba, *Hādha Huwa Tarīq 14 Tammūz* (This Is the Way of July 14) (Bairūt: Dār al-Talīʿa, 1969), 42–4. Furthermore, a number of Soviet experts filled advisory positions, *The Iraq Times*, September 1, 1959, 7. Also, for a detailed discussion of domestic reforms introduced by the Qassim regime, see Romero, *The Iraqi Revolution*, 131–50.
62 NA, Wright to the Foreign Office, August 9, 1958, No. 1346, Confidential, FO371/134201.
63 NARA, A. Guy Hope, GTI, the Department of State, Memorandum of Conversation, April 3, 1959, NATO ministerial meeting April 2–4, 1959. Secret, 787.00/4-35. Subject: Iraq and Iran; 14 July Celebrations Committee, *The Iraqi Revolution*, 103–4; Kubba, *Hādha Huwa Tarīq 14 Tammūz*, 78; Blackwell, "A Desert Squall," 9.
64 Marr, *The Modern History of Iraq*, 94.
65 14 July Celebrations Committee, *The Iraqi Revolution*, 103–4; al-Zubaidīyy, *Thawrat 14 Tammūz 1958*, 80.
66 NARA, Hugh S. Cumming to Mr. Reinhardt, Department of State, the Director of Intelligence and Research, July 20, 1958, Secret, 787.00/7-2058. See also *Al-Nahār*, July 20, 1958, 1.
67 Seale, *The Struggle for Syria*, 314; Qassim, *Principles*, 5, 13; Marr, *The Modern History of Iraq*, 91.
68 NARA, J. Bruce Hamilton, IRA/DFI, United States Government, Office Memorandum, July 14, 1958, Secret, 787.00/7-1459.
69 J. P. Glennon, ed., *Foreign Relations of the United States, 1958–1960*, Vol. XI, Lebanon and Jordan (Washington, DC: United States Government Printing Office, 1992), Document 49, Telegram from the Department of State to the Embassy in Lebanon, Washington, May 23, 1958, 8:14 p.m.
70 Kerr, *The Arab Cold War*, 7.
71 NARA, Hugh S. Cumming to Mr. Reinhardt, Department of State, Director of Intelligence and Research, July 20, 1958, Secret, 787.00/7-2058.
72 Sannān Ṣādiq Husain al-Zaidiyy, *Siyāsat al-Wilāyāt al-Muttaḥida al-Amrīkiyya tujāha al-ʿIrāq fī ʿahd ʿAbd al-Karīm Qassim 1958-1963* (US Policy Toward Iraq in the Era of ʿAbd al-Karīm Qassim 1958–1963) (Dimashq: Ahl al-Jadīd, 2013), 61.
73 NARA, Secretary of State Dulles to the American Embassy, Tehran, July 23, 1958, Top Secret, 787.00/7-2358; James M. Langley, Karachi to the Secretary of State, July 18, 1958, No. 178, Secret, 787.00/7-1958; Ambassador Edward T. Wailes, Tehran to the Secretary of State, July 19, 1958, No. 191, Confidential, 787.00/7-1958. See also Murat Kasapsaraçoğlu, "The Outsider Inside: Turkey and the Domino Effect of Arab Nationalism in 1958," Chapter 8 in this volume.
74 NARA, Secretary of State Dulles to the American Embassy, Tehran, July 23, 1958, Top Secret, 787.00/7-2358.
75 *Pravda*, August 2, 1958, 3.

76 See Marr, *The Modern History of Iraq*, 97.
77 Ṣabīḥ, ed., *Istiʿādat al-zaʿīm*, 125.
78 See al-Jābariyy, ed., *Anā waʾl-zaʿīm*; ʿAbd al-Qādir, *Al-Ightiyāl biʾl-Dabāba*; Husain, *Thawrat 14 Tammūz 1958*; Husain, "Miʾa ʿām ʿalā milād al-zaʿīm"; al-Zaidiyy, *Siyāsa al-Wilāyāt al-Muttaḥida al-Amrīkiyya tujāha al-ʿIrāq*; Ṣabīḥ, ed., *Istiʿādat al-zaʿīm*, 125.

Chapter 12

NO TURNING BACK

SYRIA AND THE 1958 WATERSHED

Fadi Esber

On January 12, 1958, fourteen officers from the Syrian military command arrived in Cairo to demand union between Syria and Egypt.[1] They left behind them in Damascus 'Abd al-Hamid al-Sarraj, the powerful chief of Syria's intelligence service, and Ahmad 'Abd al-Karim, the deputy chief of staff, to deliver the news to Syria's political leadership.[2] In Cairo, Gamal Abdel Nasser, a hero in the eyes of many Syrians for having defeated the old colonial empires of France and Britain in Suez, accepted the call for union.[3] The officers were elated to hear him utter the words. The Egyptian leader, however, had four nonnegotiable conditions: the union should be a total merger, it must be approved in a plebiscite, political parties in Syria had to dissolve themselves, and the Syrian military should no longer intervene in politics. The officers accepted the terms and the paralyzed political leadership in Damascus acquiesced.[4] On February 1, 1958, Abdel Nasser stood alongside the Syrian president, prime minister, and cabinet members to announce the birth of the United Arab Republic (UAR) to cheering crowds in Cairo. By the month's end, Abdel Nasser, now president of the UAR, arrived in Damascus for his first-ever visit to the ancient capital. The union he and his Syrian allies crafted, despite its short and turbulent life, entailed long-lasting consequences for Syria.

This chapter aims not to write a history of the events of the 1958 watershed in Syria, but to understand the political order which emerged from it. This chapter argues that the year 1958 was a revolutionary watershed in Syria's modern history. The rush to union, the circumstances surrounding its inception, and its immediate aftermath drastically transformed the Syrian body politic. First, the majority of political parties and leaders who had dominated the political scene in postindependence Syria made their exit from politics in 1958—an exit which, for the most part, was not voluntary, as the following sections of this chapter will show. Second, the elimination of nearly all other political forces in 1958 enabled the Arab Socialist Ba'ath Party to emerge as the dominant political power in Syria not long after the breakup of union and to, eventually, capture the state in 1963. Third, the Ba'ath itself witnessed revolutionary changes in its leadership, structure, and modus operandi in the aftermath of 1958; it transformed from an organization led by intellectuals and civilian cadres to one commanded by a nucleus of restless and disillusioned military officers.

The first section of this chapter looks at the period leading up to the merger between Syria and Egypt. It identifies the key events and dynamics that shaped political life in Syria between independence from France in 1946 and merger with Egypt in 1958. It also provides the reader with necessary background information on the main political actors in Syria and the transformations they went through prior to 1958. The second section delves into the first two months of 1958. It attempts to reconstruct the succession of events that lead to the Syrian-Egyptian union and analyzes the motives of different involved Syrian factions by cross-referencing different, at times conflicting, historical accounts. The third, concluding section, examines the impact of the Syrian-Egyptian union on the Syrian body politic beyond 1958.

In Syria, archival sources on the events of 1958 are not open to the public. In contrast to the poverty of archives, in the years that followed the 1958 watershed dozens of manuscripts were penned and published by Syrian witnesses to the era; a significant number of such publications, however, were written by individuals not directly involved in the making of events. The main primary source employed in this chapter is the memoirs of Syrian politicians, government officials, and military officers who were directly involved in the making and the aftermath of 1958. These political memoirs and autobiographies were largely left unexamined by the scholarly literature on the period, despite being crucial to understanding the Syrian side of events.[5] These testimonies were not unbiased and were, therefore, always taken with a grain of salt; the claims they made were cross-referenced with other sources to discern their accuracy—to the best degree possible. Reports and other correspondence, in particular daily summaries of the press in Syria and Lebanon, and detailed descriptions of events unfolding in Damascus, produced by British diplomats in Ankara, Beirut, Cairo, Damascus, and Washington, DC, and found at the British National Archives, supplemented the research effort for this chapter. These sources were also treated carefully given that Britain had no diplomatic representation in Damascus at the time and was deeply involved in Syrian affairs in the lead up to 1958.[6]

The regional and international struggle for Syria in the 1950s has generated ample scholarly literature, which provided much-needed context for this chapter.[7] Scholars, however, paid only scant attention to the political order that emerged in the country after 1958, with most studies actually stopping at the moment union with Egypt was announced. Although many scholars had studied post-1963 "Ba'ath Syria," they seldom examined the role of the 1958 watershed and the political disorder that emerged from it in preparing the ground for the rise of the Ba'ath Party to power in Syria in 1963. This chapter is a modest attempt to bridge this particular gap in the historiography of Syria.

Prelude to 1958

Shortly after gaining independence from France in 1946, Syria was thrown into political turmoil. The five years that followed the Arab defeat in the 1948 Arab-Israeli

War saw several coups, counter-coups, and failed attempts at establishing a military dictatorship in Damascus. Parliamentary life was only restored in 1954. The People Party and the National Party—heirs to the National Bloc that led the political struggle against France—and independent parliamentarians allied to them dominated the newly elected Chamber of Deputies.[8] The Arab Socialist Ba'ath Party (ASBP) gained 22 out of the 142 seats in the 1954 Chamber (up from one seat in the 1947 parliament)— the ASBP was only formed two years earlier when the Arab Ba'ath Party, led by Michel Aflaq and Salah al-Din al-Bitar, merged with Akram al-Hawrani's Arab Socialist Party.[9] Khalid Bakdash, leader of the Syrian Communist Party, recovered from having followed Stalin's dictates to not condemn the 1947 partition of Palestine and won a seat in the Chamber—representing Damascus.[10] Also in the years following independence, the economic landscape of Syria underpinning the political scene witnessed significant changes. Allied demand for Syrian grain and other produce during the Second World War resulted in an economic boom that benefited the old landed notables and a new class of capitalists who ventured into industry and invested in modern agricultural machinery.[11] Very little of the new wealth trickled down to the peasantry, which made up two-thirds of the population and produced half of Syria's GDP, and to the emerging working class, while both groups were hit hard by the resulting inflation.[12] Furthermore, living conditions throughout rural Syria remained dismal and feudalistic practices persisted, which only aggravated centuries-old grievances and created much fertile ground for political agitation. The Ba'ath capitalized on these grievances to spread its influence in rural areas and, most importantly, among young military officers of rural extraction.[13]

The regional and international struggle for Syria escalated after the Baghdad Pact came to life in early 1955.[14] In late 1956, the increasingly influential Syrian *Deuxième Bureau* (military intelligence), headed by Colonel 'Abd al-Hamid al-Sarraj, foiled a British and Iraqi backed regime-change attempt in Damascus.[15] The fact that the "plot" coincided with the Suez Crisis and the involvement of members from the People Party in it gave opposition factions great ammunition against the traditional political class. What remained of the latter not tarnished by the revelations, mainly President Shukri al-Quwatli, joined forces with the Ba'ath and Khalid al-'Azm, an independent politician and wealthy industrialist. The new political coalition was dubbed the National Front, which adopted, as a result of pressure from the Ba'ath, union with Egypt as a national objective in its charter. Al-'Azm, now minister of defense, successfully negotiated an economic agreement with the Soviet Union in the summer of 1957. Al-'Azm had ambitious plans for the economic development of Syria that required foreign capital, which the West refused to provide without political strings attached.[16] Furthermore, as the United States dumped wheat into traditional Syrian markets such as Greece and Italy, al-'Azm looked to export Syria's excess grain production to the Eastern Bloc.[17] Most importantly, in the aftermath of Suez and repeated Israeli attacks on Syrian territory, he sought military equipment from the Eastern Bloc because the West categorically refused to supply arms to Syria.[18] Despite being motivated by practical calculations, al-'Azm's overture toward Moscow drew Syria deeper into the complexities of the Cold War.

Less than a week after the Syrian-Soviet agreement was signed, al-Sarraj foiled another plot against the political coalition ruling Syria—sparking another purge in the Syrian military targeting officers close to the traditional political class. This time, the coup attempt was spearheaded by the Central Intelligence Agency.[19] Consequently, the Eisenhower administration concluded that Syria was drifting into the Soviet orbit, and an international crisis ensued.[20] This episode of the Cold War is the subject of numerous studies; one aspect of the crisis, however, merits examination here. The Soviet Union's response to American and Turkish threats against Syria increased its prestige in the country—already bolstered by the economic agreement. Abdel Nasser, unnerved by Soviet moves, summoned al-Sarraj and Afif al-Bizri, the Syrian military's chief of staff, to Cairo, where they agreed to form a joint command for the Syrian and Egyptian armies and to deploy Egyptian forces in Syria.[21] Egyptian troops arrived in Latakia two weeks after two Soviet destroyers had visited the Syrian port city as a show of force.[22] Abdel Nasser's intervention, despite being insignificant in military terms, helped maintain his popularity and influence in Syria, which had been running high since his triumph in the Suez Crisis.[23] It also enabled him to outflank King Saud's US-supported bid for Arab leadership, after the latter had tried to mediate between Syria and Turkey.[24]

As the international crisis receded in the closing weeks of 1957, political factions in Syria became embroiled in yet another struggle for supremacy. Al-'Azm and Bakdash rode high on the Soviet stance during the crisis.[25] Both flew to Moscow in December to follow up on the economic agreement, and al-'Azm—now also minister of finance—started work on establishing a political party that could enter the upcoming parliamentary elections set for August 1958.[26] Consequently, the Ba'ath leaders became increasingly worried about losing ground to al-'Azm and Bakdash.[27] The municipal elections set for November that year were canceled, as the Ba'ath joined Quwatli and Prime Minister Sabri al-'Asali in a bid to deny the SCP and al-'Azm an expected electoral victory.[28] This meant that the National Front was effectively dissolved. The military was also simmering; its high command was made up of twenty-four officers divided by personal ambitions and loyalties. The powerful al-Sarraj was loyal to Abdel Nasser; Mustafa Hamdun led a significant Ba'ath faction; Ahmad 'Abd al-Karim and Amin al-Nafuri, both deputies to the chief of staff and former protégés of military dictator Adib al-Shishakli (1949–54), commanded a group of "independent officers." All were presided over by General al-Bizri, whom the Ba'ath—and others—suspected of colluding with al-'Azm and the SCP.[29] It is in these troubled waters that Syria drifted in the closing days of 1957 and the first weeks of 1958 toward the fateful union with Abdel Nasser's Egypt.

Syria in 1958

The relationship between Abdel Nasser and the Ba'ath had been bourgeoning for years. His envoys in Damascus, Ambassador Mahmud Riad and the military attaché 'Abd al-Muhsin Abu al-Nur, had worked to lobby Syrian politicians and officers—especially members of the Ba'ath.³⁰ Egypt also funded the Ba'ath Party's official newspaper and helped arm its partisans during the 1957 crisis.³¹ The leaders of the Ba'ath Michel Aflaq, Salah al-Din al-Bitar and Akram al-Hawrani, on their part, were seldom a united front. 'Aflak and al-Bitar, despite preaching a "popular revolution," were opposed to military coups and had engaged in the parliamentary politics.³² Al-Hawrani, on the other hand, was a political firebrand who had a significant following in the army and had had a hand in most of the coups that rocked the country since 1949.³³ However, by the end of 1957, all three agreed that union with Abdel Nasser's Egypt was the best available solution to avoid losing ground to al-'Azm and the SCP and to break out of their own disagreements, which at the time were threatening to undo the Ba'ath itself.³⁴ The Ba'ath leaders had also thought of using Abdel Nasser's Egypt to achieve their grand ideological objective: Arab unity.³⁵ They, nevertheless, had envisaged a federal union rather than a total merger, with the Ba'ath in control of Syria.³⁶

Salah al-Din al-Bitar, the then foreign minister, met Abdel Nasser in December 1957 and suggested initiating talks for a federal union. Abdel Nasser, however, had serious doubts regarding the position of the Syrian military command on union with Egypt. Upon hearing this from al-Bitar, the twenty-four-officer-strong military command decided to impose a fait accompli on both Abdel Nasser and Syria's political leadership.³⁷ The officers drafted a memorandum calling for union, with the Egyptian military attaché 'Abd al-Muhsin Abu al-Nur present in the meeting; they, however, did not specify the political form the union would take.³⁸ Subsequently, fourteen of the officers, with al-Bizri at the helm, flew to Cairo on January 12, 1958.

Abdel Nasser accepted the officers' request but had four nonnegotiable conditions: the union should be a total merger, it must be approved in a plebiscite, Syria's political parties must be dissolved, and the Syrian military must refrain from intervening in politics. Meanwhile in Damascus, al-Sarraj and 'Abd al-Karim delivered a copy of the memorandum to Syria's political leadership. Al-Quwatli, al-'Asali, and al-'Azm rejected what they considered to be a coup attempt by the military.³⁹ They dispatched al-Bitar after the officers without a mandate to negotiate a union, but he only joined them in welcoming the merger despite Abdel Nasser's harsh conditions.⁴⁰ When the officers returned to Damascus with Abdel Nasser's dictates, al-'Azm tried to resist, while al-Quwatli and al-'Asali surrendered to the fait accompli.⁴¹ Al-Bizri allegedly warned the politicians that they had only two options: they could either go to Cairo, to sign off on the union, or go to Mazza, the infamous military prison in Damascus.⁴² Al-Quwatli, al-'Asali, al-'Azm, al-Hawrani, the entire cabinet, and the officers all traveled to Cairo where the union was announced on February 1, 1958.

Abdel Nasser arrived in Damascus on February 24, 1958, as president of the United Arab Republic (UAR). It was his first visit to the country he now ruled.⁴³ Abdel Nasser was "elected" president through a plebiscite that took place in both "regions" of the UAR, with 99 percent of the votes cast in his favor—his was the only name on the ballot paper. In Syria, al-Sarraj's Deuxième Bureau manipulated the results.⁴⁴ From the balcony of his residence, Abdel Nasser addressed cheering crowds that flocked from all corners of Syria to greet him. After more than a decade of persistent instability, many Syrians were relieved. They no longer feared a foreign invasion or another military coup, for now they were in the trusted hands of the "hero of Suez." Beside Abdel Nasser stood al-Sarraj, al-Hawrani, al-'Asali, and al-Quwatli, who had voluntarily given up presidency and was given an honorary title: "the first Arab citizen." The UAR constitution, approved in the same aforementioned plebiscite, granted Abdel Nasser full executive and legislative powers.[45] From thereon, Syria, the country that had been the focal point of regional politics for a decade, would be subsumed under Cairo's clout as the "northern region" of the UAR. Syria no longer had foreign and defense policies, while in all other matters Syrians would enjoy the mere illusion of control, for the new constitution had made Abdel Nasser the final arbiter in all UAR affairs.

The motives behind Abdel Nasser's quest to absorb Syria were numerous, but they remain understudied, and are not the subject of this chapter.[46] For Syria, the factors that made the union inevitable, regardless of the unplanned form it took, were many. The country was under real and present threats of invasion from abroad and subversion from within throughout the 1950s. The turbulent decade after independence saw constant political bickering that exhausted the Syrian people, body politic, and military, paralyzing their ability to handle continued pressures. Even al-Quwatli, joined by conservative figures and the business class, saw in union with Egypt a way to avoid a Communist or Ba'ath takeover in Damascus.[47] Last but not least, many ordinary Syrians believed in Abdel Nasser's leadership and in Arab unity as a noble objective—regardless of constitutional formalities. It is true that the plebiscite was manipulated by al-Sarraj but the overwhelming popular welcome that Abdel Nasser received in Damascus was genuine.

The union, at least in its initial phase, despite its harsh terms, benefited the Syrian factions that pursued it. The Ba'ath successfully eliminated its main political rivals: Khalid al-'Azm and the Syrian Communist Party—the latter's partisans were ruthlessly persecuted.[48] Afif al-Bizri was removed little over a month after the union despite having been reappointed commander of the Syrian Army by Abdel Nasser—which was renamed the "First Army" of the UAR.[49] Sabri al-'Asali was made vice president of the UAR alongside Akram al-Hawrani, who also became head of the "regional executive council" in the northern region, which ostensibly made him de facto ruler of Syria. Al-Sarraj was appointed minister of interior in the northern region with near absolute power over the Syrian populace. Al-Bitar became a minister of state in the UAR's central cabinet in Cairo, while 'Aflak genuinely believed that the Ba'ath would dominate the National Union—an inclusive political organization that was to be formed in both regions of the UAR.[50] Ba'ath ministries were a majority in the northern region's first cabinet.[51] As for the officers, Mustafa Hamdun, 'Abd al-Karim, and Amin al-Nafuri were appointed ministers in the northern region's first cabinet.[52] All of them were in their thirties and had only made it to the top ranks as a result of the many coups, power struggles, and subsequent purges in the Syrian military. They could have been discharged, or even killed, in the aftermath of a pro-Western or pro-Communist coup, or in a power struggle with their comrades—all were possible scenarios in 1957 and early

1958. After union with Egypt, they assumed high civilian posts in a regime that they had helped usher in; it was not a bad trade-off at the time, despite many of them eventually turning against Abdel Nasser.

Syria after 1958

The union between Syria and Egypt survived for three and a half years. Eventually, the Egyptian drive to dominate Syria politically and economically generated a wave of grievances that culminated in a coup which brought down the union on September 28, 1961.[53] The people of Syria were by then deeply disillusioned with Abdel Nasser, reacting to the coup with great apathy.[54] By the time the union came to an end, all the Syrian protagonists that helped bring it about had been politically eliminated. Shukri al-Quwatli voluntarily retired from political life. Sabri al-'Asali's complicity in the 1956 Iraqi plot was exposed during the trials that followed the July 1958 revolution in Baghdad, and he resigned as vice president of the UAR.[55] Al-Hawrani fell out with Abdel Nasser; the Ba'ath was kept out of the National Union; and Ba'ath ministers resigned from the UAR government in late 1959.[56] Some Ba'ath officers even contemplated a coup against UAR rule in Damascus.[57] Consequently, the Ba'ath was weeded out from the government bureaucracy and many Ba'ath officers were either discharged or transferred to Cairo.[58] Ahmad 'Abd al-Karim and Amin al-Nafuri also resigned from office in 1959. Eventually, even 'Abd al-Hamid al-Sarraj was pushed out of office by the Abdel Nasser's representative in Damascus, Field Marshal 'Abd al-Hakim Amir.[59]

The economic reorganization of Syria under UAR rule proved irreversible. The Agrarian Reform Law passed in September 1958 broke up large agricultural estates and with them the power of the landed notables of Damascus, Aleppo, Homs, and Hama, who had formed the backbone of the Syrian body politic for centuries and were the main pillars of the People and National parties.[60] Abdel Nasser's 1961 nationalization laws brought all banks, insurance companies, and industrial ventures in Syria under state ownership.[61] The weak regime that ruled Syria for the eighteen months between the breakup of union and the 1963 Ba'ath takeover failed to overturn these laws.[62] Between 1963 and 1965, the Ba'ath nationalized what remained of the Syrian private sector, eliminating once and for all any political influence the business class had enjoyed. Most capitalists, relentlessly targeted by the state, fled the country.

The 1958 watershed turned the Syrian body politic on its head. With its leader Khalid Bakdash on the run and its cadres captured, exiled, and killed, the Syrian Communist Party was never able to recover its pre-1958 position in Syrian political life.[63] Khalid al-'Azm briefly returned as prime minister in 1962, but was greatly weakened and was soon overthrown by the Ba'ath in 1963—he died in his Beirut exile two years later.[64] As a consequence of 1958, al-'Azm's "middle way" vision that emphasized both capitalist development and a fair redistribution of wealth remains one of the biggest "what-ifs" of modern Syrian history. Akram al-Hawrani was another political victim of the 1958 watershed. For the first few months of union, al-Hawrani seemed to have emerged a winner. His political rivals, al-'Azm and Bakdash, were neutralized. His grand vision for Syria was becoming a reality, especially with the passing of the Agrarian Reform Law, which broke the back of the feudal lords he had battled against for his entire political life.[65] But after doing away with his traditional rivals, al-Hawrani soon clashed with Abdel Nasser, resigning from the UAR government as a result. Al-Hawrani went on to support the coup that ended the union. Ba'ath cadres never forgave him for doing so, and his faction, the Arab Socialists, split from the party in 1962.[66] Al-Hawrani, with his political influence undermined, was also ousted by Ba'ath takeover in 1963, leaving Syria to never return.

After clashing with Abdel Nasser, the leaders of the Ba'ath realized the gravity of their decision to dissolve the party and decided to reorganize, holding two congresses in Beirut in 1959 and 1960.[67] Ba'ath cadres were disillusioned with their leadership for rushing them into union.[68] Fragmentation ensued, facilitated by the lack of consensus on clear definitions of the party ideology and objectives—a deficiency lamented by many members of the Ba'ath at the time.[69] Aflaq and al-Bitar were able to retain only nominal authority, but real leadership of the party they had founded in 1947 soon moved into the hands of a faction of officers that Abdel Nasser had transferred from Syria to Egypt during the lifetime of the UAR in order to keep them away from politics.[70] In Cairo, exiled officers Muhammad 'Umran, Salah Jadid, 'Abd al-Karim al-Jundi, Ahmad al-Mir, and Hafez al Asad formed the "military committee."[71] They returned home after the UAR collapsed to find the Syrian body politic in disarray. They, alongside many civilian B'ath cadres, criticized the party's participation in the "hypocritical" parliamentary life before 1958, which kept it from achieving the "popular revolution" its original manifesto had preached.[72] Therefore, they refused to revert to the old methods and instead sought to swiftly capture the state and from there proceed to realize the party's grand political vision.[73]

Conclusion

In the decade following independence from France in 1946, the young, weak Syrian state was drawn into a myriad of regional and international struggles, which only compounded the ever-growing internal political strife between a traditional political class, a restless military, and the emerging, youth-driven ideological parties—especially the Arab Socialist Ba'ath Party. The fateful merger with Abdel Nasser's Egypt in 1958 represented a climax of these trends. Although Syria did not witness a revolution, in the textbook definition of the word; however, the drastic—and irreversible—changes in the nature of the country's body politic and economic organization were perhaps more revolutionary in their impact, and more long-lasting, than those that unfolded elsewhere in the Middle East during the same historical period.

The *ancien* political forces made one last attempt to regroup and recapture the political scene between 1961 and 1963, but to no avail. When the military committee finally made its move to capture the state on March 8, 1963, it found the Syrian body politic nearly void of meaningful opposition as a result of the 1958 watershed and its aftermath. Unchallenged by serious political opposition from other Syrian factions, the committee entered into a vicious internal power struggle that lasted until November 16, 1970, when Hafez al Asad emerged triumphant and went on to rule Syria for the remainder of the twentieth century.

Notes

1 Muhammad Hasanayn Haykal, *Sanawat al-Ghalayan (vol. 1)* (Years of Boiling, vol. 1) (Cairo: Al-Ahram, 1988), 273.
2 Khalid Al-'Azm, *Mudhakarat (vol. 3)* (Memoirs, vol. 3) (Beirut: Dar al-Muttahida, 1973), 126.
3 Al-Baghdadi, 'Abd al-Latif. *Mudhakarat (vol. 2)* (Memoirs, vol. 2) (Cairo: Al-Maktab al-Masry al-Hadith, 1977), 38.
4 Al-'Azm, *Mudhakarat (vol. 3)*, 126–8.
5 Syrian accounts surveyed in this chapter were those of Ahmad 'Abd al-Karim (independent officer; head of the Syrian Army's operations command in 1958; minister of municipal affairs in the executive council of the northern region of the UAR; minister of municipal affairs in the central UAR cabinet); Shibli al-'Aisami (Ba'ath Party; vice president of Syria, 1965–6); Khalid Al-'Azm (independent; Syrian minister of defense, 1956–1958; prime minister, 1962–63); Bashyr al-'Azma (Ba'ath Party; minister of health in the central UAR government 1958–60; prime minister of Syria, 1962); Akram al-Hawrani (co-leader of the Ba'ath Party, 1954–8; vice president of the UAR, 1958–59); Sami al-Jundi (Ba'ath Party; Syrian minister of information, 1963–4); Munif al-Razzaz (secretary general of the National Command of the Arab Socialist Ba'ath Party, 1965–6); Sami Jum'aa (independent; senior officer in the Syrian military intelligence, 1946–61); and Muhammad 'Umran (Ba'ath Party officer and founder of the "military committee"). Egyptian accounts also surveyed in this chapter were those of 'Abd al-Muhsin Abu al-Nur (Egyptian military attaché in Damascus, 1958; vice commander of the First Army of the UAR, 1958–61); 'Abd al-Latif al-Baghdadi (speaker of the Egyptian National Assembly, 1956–8; vice president of the UAR, 1958–61); and Muhammad Hasanayn Haykal (editor in chief of Egyptian daily al-Ahram, 1957–74).
6 The National Archives (TNA). "Series reviewed: FO 371: Foreign Office: Political Departments: General Correspondence from 1906-1966"; FO 407: "Foreign Office: Confidential Print Egypt and the Sudan"; and FO 552: "Foreign Office: Confidential Print United Arab Republic (Egypt and Syria)."
7 David W. Lesch, *Syria and the United States: Eisenhower's Cold War in the Middle East* (Boulder: Westview Press, 1992); Sami Moubayed, *Syria and the USA: Washington's Relations with Damascus from Wilson to Eisenhower* (London: I.B. Tauris, 2012); William Roger Louis, and Roger Owen, *A Revolutionary Year: The Middle East in 1958* (London: Tauris, 2002); Tabitha Petran, *Syria* (London: Ernest Benn Ltd., 1972); Andrew Rathmell, *Secret War in the Middle East: The Covert Struggle for Syria, 1949–1961* (New York: Tauris Academic Studies, 1995); Bonnie F. Saunders, *The United States and Arab Nationalism: The Syrian Case, 1953–1960* (Westport, CT: Praeger, 1996); Patrick Seale, *The Struggle for Syria: A Study of Post-war Arab Politics,*

1945–1958 (London: Oxford University Press, 1965); Gordon Torrey, *Syrian Politics and the Military* (Ohio: Ohio University Press, 1964); and Salim Yaqub, *Containing Arab Nationalism: The Eisenhower Doctrine and the Middle East*. The New Cold War History (Chapel Hill: University of North Carolina Press, 2004).

8   Seale, *The Struggle for Syria*, 182–5.
9   Ibid.
10 Tareq Y. Ismael and Jacqueline S. Ismael, *The Communist Movement in Syria and Lebanon* (Gainesville: University of Florida, 1998), 39 and 45.
11 Petran, *Syria*, 82; and Seale, *The Struggle for Syria*, 130–1.
12 Petran, *Syria*, 82; and Nahid 'Abd al-Karim, *Al-Hayat al-Iktisadiyya wa al-Ijtima'iyya fi Suriyya* (Economic and Social Life in Syria, 1946–58) (Damascus: Dar Tlass, 1996), 35.
13 Al-'Azm, *Mudhakarat (vol. 3)*, 37; and S. Jum'aa, *Awrak min Daftar al-Watan* (Pages from the book of the homeland, 1946–61) (Damascus: Dar Tlass, 2002), 157.
14 Elie Podeh, "The Struggle over Arab Hegemony after the Suez Crisis," *Middle Eastern Studies* 29, no. 1 (1993): 91–110, 91–2.
15 Jum'aa, *Awrak*, 237.
16 Al-'Azm, *Mudhakarat (vol. 3)*, 7–13, 30–1.
17 Petran, *Syria*, 120.
18 Al-'Azm, *Mudhakarat (vol. 3)*, 30–1.
19 Douglas Little, "Cold War and Covert Action: The United States and Syria, 1945–58," *Middle East Journal* 44 (1990): 51–75, 71; for further analysis of American policy vis-a-vis Damascus in 1957–8 see Jeffrey G. Karam, "Cautious Revisionism and the Limits of Hegemony in 1958: A Revolutionary Year for the United States in the Middle East," in this volume.
20 Lesch, *Syria and the United States*, 156–7; and Philip Anderson, "'Summer Madness' the Crisis in Syria, August-October 1957," *British Journal of Middle Eastern Studies* 22, no. 1–2 (1995): 25.
21 Haykal, *Sanawat al-Ghalayan (vol. 1)*, 266–7; and Torrey, *Syrian Politics and the Military*, 363.
22 TNA. FO 371/134381: Middleton (Beirut) to Foreign Office, "Review of Events in Syria (1957)," February 6, 1958.
23 TNA. FO 371/134382: Chancery (Ankara) to Foreign Office, "Internal situation in Syria," January 3, 1958; Podeh, "The Struggle over Arab Hegemony after the Suez Crisis," 106; and Al-'Azm, *Mudhakarat (vol. 3)*, 41.
24 Seale, *The Struggle for Syria*, 305; Lesch, *Syria and the United States*, 179–86; and A. Abu al-Nur, *Al-Hakika 'an Thawrat Yulu* (The Truth about the July Revolution) (Cairo: Maktabat al-Usra, 2002), 104; for more information on Saud's US-supported bid to challenge Abdel Nasser see Nathan Citino, "Saudi Arabia in the Crucible of 1958," in this volume.
25 Patrick Seale noted that Soviet policy at the time aimed at "setting up a 'bourgeois' regime friendly to the Soviet Union, manipulated behind the scenes by the [SCP]." It was in this context that Bakdash and al-'Azm found each other. The former saw in al-'Azm a rogue bourgeois and, therefore, the perfect ally. The latter did not have a political party to lean on and could not count on support from the traditional political class for his progressive platform, which included cooperation with the Soviet Union (Seale, *The Struggle for Syria*, 315).
26 TNA. FO371/128241: Reilly (Ankara) to Foreign Office, "Syrian delegation in Moscow," December 21, 1957; Al-'Azm, *Mudhakarat (vol. 3)*, 121.

27 Jum'aa, *Awrak*, 280; and Al-'Azm, *Mudhakarat (vol. 3)*, 36.
28 TNA. FO 371/134381: Middleton (Beirut) to Foreign Office, "Review of Events in Syria (1957)," February 6, 1958; Jum'aa, *Awrak*, 277; and Seale, *The Struggle for Syria*, 317.
29 Jum'aa, *Awrak*, 277–9; A. al-Hawrani, *Mudhakarat (vol. 3)* (Memoirs, vol. 3) (Cairo: Madbouli, 2000), 2568; and Seale, *The Struggle for Syria*, 321.
30 Seale, *The Struggle for Syria*, 314–15; Petran, *Syria*, 120; Zuhair al-Mardini, *Al-Ustaz* (The Teacher: The Life of Michel Aflaq) (London: Riad el-Rayyes, 1988), 229–30; and A. 'Abd al-Karim, *Adwa'a 'ala Tajrubat al-Wihda* (On the Union Experience) (Damascus: Al-Ahali, 1991), 94.
31 Al-Hawrani, *Mudhakarat (vol. 3)*, 2564–6.
32 M. Al-Razzaz, *Al-Tajruba al-Murra* (The Bitter Experience) (Munif al-Razzaz Foundation for National Studies, 1986), 31–2; al-Mardini, *Al-Ustaz*, pp. 225–6; S. al-'Aisami, *Hizb al-'Ba'th al-'Araby al-Ishtiraky* (The Arab Socialist Ba'ath Party, 1949–1958) (Baghdad: Afaq Araiyya, 1987), 292; and S. al-Jundi, *Al-Ba'th* (The Ba'ath) (Beirut: Dar al-Nahar, 1969), 68.
33 Al-Razzaz, *Al-Tajruba al-Murra*, 31–2.
34 Al-Mardini, *Al-Ustaz*, 231; and al-Jundi, *Al-Ba'th*, 76.
35 Seale, *The Struggle for Syria*, 311; al-Hawrani, *Mudhakarat (vol. 3)*, 2615.
36 Seale, *The Struggle for Syria*, 318.
37 'Abd al-Karim, *Adwa'a 'ala Tajroubat al-Wihda*, 95–6.
38 Abu al-Nur, *Al-Hakika 'an Thawrat Youlu*, 108.
39 Al-'Azm, *Mudhakarat (vol. 3)*, 125–6.
40 Ibid., 128.
41 Ibid., 128–36.
42 Moubayed, *Syria and the USA*, 172.
43 Haykal, *Sanawat al-Ghalayan (vol. 1)*, 281.
44 Bashir Al-'Azma, *Jyl al-Hazimah* (The Generation of Defeat) (London: Riad el-Rayyes Books, 1991), 191.
45 TNA. FO 552/1: Middleton (Beirut) to Foreign Office, "The Provisional Condition of the United Arab Republic," March 10, 1958.
46 For an in-depth analysis of Abdel Nasser's motives to takeover Syria in 1958 see Dina Rezk, "Egypt's role in the Arab revolutions: Reconceptualizing Nasser from 'Nationalist Ideologue' to 'Reluctant Pragmatist,'" in this volume.
47 Al-Mardini, *Al-Ustaz*, 237; and al-Hawrani, *Mudhakarat (vol. 3)*, 2562.
48 Ismael and Ismael, *The Communist Movement in Syria and Lebanon*, 52–3.
49 Afif al-Bizri's motives for supporting merger with Egypt have always been a subject of controversy. The head of Egypt's National Assembly 'Abd al-Latif al-Baghdadi argued that al-Bizri, following the same SCP tactic, tried to outsmart Abdel Nasser by proposing total merger, thinking he would refuse it (Al-Baghdadi, *Mudhakarat (vol. 2)*, 36). Patrick Seale offers a different explanation: "Unable to stop the union taking place, the communists may have preferred to have their man [al-Bizri] at the centre of power than to see him eliminated by openly adopting their line" (Seale, *The Struggle for Syria*, 321). Alas, al-Bizri never left a written account of his role in delivering the union and the depth of his ties to the SCP was never revealed; he did, however, tell journalist and author Tabitha Petran that he was "deceived by Abdel Nasser's assurances as to the nature of the union" and, therefore, "refused to heed the advice of Bakdash and other friends" who counseled him against it (Petran, *Syria*, 126).
50 Al-'Aisami, S. *Hizb al-'Ba'th*, 293.

51 Al-'Azm, *Mudhakarat (vol. 3)*, 176.
52 Ibid.
53 TNA. FO 407/331, Lord Home (Damascus) to Foreign Officer, "Review of the situation in Syria resulting from the coup d'etat," October 17, 1961.
54 Ibid.
55 TNA. FO 371/134385: Scott (Beirut) to Foreign Office, "Weekly letter on Syria," September 3, 1958; Sami Jum'aa claims that Abdel Nasser ordered the publication of documents implicating al-'Asali in order to force him out of politics (Jum'aa, *Awrak*, 301).
56 TNA. FO 552/3: Crowe (Cairo) to Foreign Officer, "United Arab Republic: Annual Review for 1959," January 31, 1960; Haykal, *Sanawat al-Ghalayan (vol. 1)*, 559–63; Al-'Azma, *Jyl al-Hazimah*, 206–10; Jum'aa, *Awrak*, 346; al-Mardini, *Al-Ustaz*, 238; Abu al-Nur, *Al-Hakika 'an Thawrat Youlu*, 150; and al-Jundi, *Al-Ba'th*, 78–84.
57 Al-Hawrani, *Mudhakarat (vol. 3)*, 2786–7.
58 FO 552/3. Crowe (Cairo), "United Arab Republic: Annual Review for 1959," January 31, 1960.
59 Haykal, *Sanawat al-Ghalayan (vol. 1)*, 564–5; and Al-Baghdadi, *Mudhakarat (vol. 2)*, 65.
60 TNA. FO 371/141890: Chancery (Beirut) to Foreign Officer, "Syria: Annual Economic Report for 1958," February 10, 1958.
61 TNA. FO 407/331: Beeley (Cairo) to Foreign Officer, "Extension of government ownership and control over the UAR economy," August 2, 1961; TNA. FO 407/331: Clarke (Damascus) to Foreign Officer, "Syria Region," August 22, 1961.
62 Al-Jundi, *Al-Ba'th*, 100.
63 For details on the campaign against the Communist Party and the murder of Farjallah al-Hilu, see Sami Jum'aa, *Awrak*, 322–40; and Naddaf, 'Imad. *Khalid Bakdash Yatahadath* (Khaled Bakdash Speaks). Damascus, 1993, 37–8.
64 Al-'Azm, *Mudhakarat (vol. 3)*, 199.
65 For more information on Al-Hawrani's political activism and the Agrarian Reform project see Hanna Batatu, *Syria's Peasantry, The Descendants of Its Lesser Rural Notables, and Their Politics* (Princeton, NJ: Princeton University Press, 1999), 124–30.
66 Al-Razzaz, *Al-Tajruba al-Murra*, 55–7; and Jum'aa *Awrak*, 80.
67 Al-Razzaz, *Al-Tajruba al-Murra*, 55; and al-'Aisami, *Hizb al-'Ba'th*, 301.
68 Al-'Aisami, *Hizb al-'Ba'th*, 299; and Muhammad 'Umran, *Tajrubati fi al-Thawra* (My Experience in the Revolution) (Beirut: Dar al-Jyl, 1970), 16.
69 Al-Razzaz, *Al-Tajruba al-Murra*, 59–60; al-Jundi, *Al-Ba'th*, 68.
70 Al-Razzaz, *Al-Tajruba al-Murra*, 55–7; 'Umran, *Tajrubati*, 17; for more information on the "old Ba'th" (1947–1963) see Batatu, *Syria's Peasantry*, 133–43.
71 'Umran, *Tajrubati*, 18–19; and al-Jundi, *Al-Ba'th*, 85–6; for more information on the "transitional Ba'th" of the 1960s, see Batatu, *Syria's Peasantry*, 144–75.
72 Al-Razzaz, *Al-Tajruba al-Murra*, 30–1.
73 Ibid., 32.

Chapter 13

THE CRISIS OF 1958 IN LEBANON

POLITICAL RIVALRIES

Caroline Attie

The crisis of 1958 in Lebanon was the first of several that would test the resilience of the multi-confessional state that had been independent for a mere fifteen years. In order to reconcile their differing political loyalties to Western powers and Arab states Lebanon's Christian and Muslim political elites had reached a modus vivendi on the eve of independence in 1943. This was the unwritten agreement of the National Pact. In a deeply penetrated state system,[1] foreign intervention is intertwined with domestic politics and the regional and global polarization in the 1950s accentuated the divided loyalties of Lebanon's communities. In light of the brutal fifteen-year-long Civil War from 1975–90 and the unresolved debate of causation, a reassessment of the 1958 crisis raises the issue of the agency of President Chamoun in leading the country to the brink of civil war within the constraints of regional polarization and the confessional political structure of Lebanon.

Chamoun's political ability to play off his adversaries and friends was evidenced by his alienation of political elites in the aftermath of the Suez war in 1956 as well as his ability to get Anglo-American support for his reelection. His ambition and subordination of foreign policy to these ends divided the country and led to the three-month-long insurrection against his presidency. His successor's (Fuad Chehab) ability to accommodate Nasser's Arab nationalism and provide Lebanon with more than a decade of regional and domestic stability reflects the decisive role of presidential leadership in Lebanon in those years.

How do we classify the events of 1958? The literature refers to 1958 as an insurgency, a civil war, a rebellion, an insurrection, or even a revolt of the pashas.[2] The conflict that broke out in May 1958 and destabilized the country for a three-month period did not lead to irreversible change in Lebanon's political system as the commercial, landowning, and political elite retained their privileges.[3] However, there were changes in politics and politicians as the new president and former army commander General Fuad Chehab relied on technocrats and trusted officers to strengthen the state and enhance national integration through state building and socioeconomic development later known as Chehabism. Chehab asked French experts in 1959 to prepare a detailed study of the development needs of Lebanon. His state-led planning challenged the ultra-liberal economic policies of his predecessors and concentrated on developing hitherto neglected regions of the country as well as creating institutions such as the Central Bank, Social Insurance, the Civil Service Board, and other new state bureaucracies that would formalize state employment and decrease patronage appointments. Chehabism constituted an interlude in Lebanon's political development where administrative reform was implemented with more equitable economic expenditure by the state on infrastructure in hitherto neglected regions of Lebanon.

In that sense, 1958 marked a watershed in Lebanon's political development and was "revolutionary" in the state-led development championed by Fuad Chehab. What was the main cause of the 1958 crisis? Was it the grievances of politicians who had lost their seats in the 1957 elections or socioeconomic injustice unmet by inadequate reforms or a tilted foreign policy that violated the National Pact? This chapter will review these three issues and will argue that the primary cause of the 1958 crisis in Lebanon was President Chamoun's ambitions on one hand and the refusal of Muslims to be marginalized within the sectarian structure of the Lebanese state, on the other.

Personal Political Grievances: The 1957 Elections

In early July 1956 a US State Department intelligence report on political trends in Lebanon forecast political stability and attributed it to the country's economic prosperity as well as its confessional system and stated:

> Confessionalism precludes development of a genuine sense of national unity, yet paradoxically promotes stability since government in Lebanon is perforce government by compromise.... The 2 main influencers that shape the course of Lebanon—confessionalism and commercialism militate against radical change.[4]

Three weeks later, Egyptian president Gamal Abdel Nasser nationalized the Suez Canal Company and set in motion a series of events with momentous consequences for the stability of Lebanon and the Middle East.

Although sectarian polarization was not as serious in 1958 as in 1975, sectarian rhetoric obscured the personal power struggles of Lebanese politicians and divided the country as seen in public attitudes toward figures such as the Maronite patriarch Boulos Meouchi and Prime Minister Sami al Sulh who were politically aligned against the majority of their co-religionists. The Maronite patriarch broke with many of his clergy and the majority of the Maronite community. His visit to the opposition stronghold in the Basta quarter of Beirut earned him the title "Patriarch of the Arabs" among the Lebanese Muslims but he was reproached by Maronites and called "Muhammad al Meouchi."[5] In February 1958, funeral bells were tolled in Deir al-Qamar, Chamoun's hometown, in protest to an alleged statement by the patriarch that "the Maronites were a drop in the sea of Muslims and must therefore support Muslim Arab nationalism or pack up and leave."[6] The patriarch's statements in the years leading up to 1958 were controversial within the Maronite community and this indicated the predominantly sectarian alignments of communities in 1958. Prime Minister Sami al Sulh's support for Chamoun effectively ended his political career. His house was burned down, and he was boycotted by his community at events such as the traditional Ramadan iftar held at the Dar al Fatwa on April 19, 1958.[7] At the end of the crisis he left the country to Turkey for a long vacation. These examples indicate the extent of widespread populist sectarian alignments of communities in 1958 despite cross-sectarian alliances among the elites.

The political system in Lebanon allocates political office and parliamentary representation to sectarian communities, enabling them to coexist within a political framework while enhancing communal differences. Hence, political divisions in Lebanon are often sectarian, which preempts the formation of class-based alliances, and socioeconomic and political conflict is often manifested as a confessional struggle.[8]

Unlike the crisis of 1952 where a similar coalition of politicians forced President Bechara al-Khuri to step down, a domestic resolution of the crisis in 1958 was not possible due to regional polarization and the outreach of Lebanese politicians to external patrons such as Nasser's Egypt and the United States.[9] The irony of Lebanese politicians' sectarian rhetoric to mobilize their constituents in Lebanon in support of Nasser was that Nasser himself shunned religious symbolism in his secular Arab nationalist discourse. There was support for Nasser among some Christians in Lebanon as well as the overwhelming majority of Muslims in secular parties such as the Arab nationalist movement founded at the American University of Beirut.

Camille Chamoun was the central political figure in Lebanon in 1958 and was charismatic, handsome, and articulate. While assigned to Lebanon's first diplomatic mission in London in 1944 he had established a reputation as an effective spokesman for the Palestinian cause at the UN in 1947 which earned him the title of "fata al uruba al aghar" (the preeminent youth of Arabism).[10] Chamoun was elected president in 1952 by a broad coalition of the political elite and with a mandate to reform the administration and to rehabilitate a presidency tainted with corruption. His constant reshuffling of prime ministers alienated Muslims who had no figure comparable to Riyad al Sulh to somehow balance the president's high-handed policies.

The "revolt of the pashas" in 1958 was prompted by traditional politicians who had been sidelined by Chamoun and lost their access to state patronage and hence power.[11] The main grievance expressed by politicians throughout the 1950s was that of underrepresentation in political institutions of the Lebanese state and not the need to reform the institutions of the "Merchant Republic" that had served the commercial and political elite.[12] These "pashas" were both Christian and Muslim political leaders whose opposition was often based on individual ambitions such as Hamid Frangieh's opposition to Chamoun as a rival Maronite contender to the presidency in 1952. The rivalry of the Frangieh and Duwaihi families was another example and was manifested in the Miziara church shooting a month before the

1957 elections. Fawzi al Huss and Saeb Salam, cofounders of the national Middle East Airlines, were engaged in a fierce personal and legal dispute, and in 1958 Salam was a key opposition leader while al Huss was close to Chamoun and was engaged in mediation of the 1958 crisis.[13] Chamoun also had Muslim support from families such as al-Khalil and al Sulh as well as lawyers and businessmen such as Jamil Makkawi, Fawzi al Huss and Khalil Hibri, all of whom were elected in 1957.

The cross-sectarian cooperation of the elite that had brought Chamoun to the presidency broke down due to a number of tactical errors such as the overwhelming defeat of political opponents in the 1957 parliamentary which gave his disparate opponents an opportunity to join forces against him in a loose coalition that would ensure their return to power and access to patronage. Chamoun's domestic and foreign policies alienated his former allies. As the only Arab country to openly endorse the Eisenhower Doctrine and have it ratified in parliament, Chamoun sought US approval for his reelection bid.[14] The pace of events leading to the crisis of 1958 was quickened by Chamoun's undeclared bid for reelection. Prominent politicians who lost the 1957 parliamentary elections were left with no choice but to resort to open revolt in the street in order to preempt another six years of a Chamoun presidency that would keep them out in the cold. Prior to the elections they had sought the president's goodwill in order to safeguard their interests and access state benefits. Their opposition was prompted neither by a reform agenda nor political principle as evidenced by their published documents, political manifestos, and speeches.[15] Chamoun, on the other hand, sought to benefit from regional and international polarization to seek reelection to the presidency and proceeded to weaken his adversaries using Anglo-American support.[16]

A cross-sectarian coalition of politicians formed an electoral bloc called the National Front in order to preempt Chamoun's reelection. Predominantly, traditional politicians, some of whom had lost their parliamentary seats in the 1957 elections, included Saeb Salam, Abdallah al Yafi, Hussein Oueini, Hamid Frangieh, Nasim Majdalani, Philippe Takla, Henri Pharaon, Rashid Karami, Kamel al Assad, and Kamal Junblat. Former president Bechara al-Khuri, and the Maronite patriarch Boulos Meouchi also opposed Chamoun's policies. Political ambition for leadership of the Sunni Muslim community led Yafi and Salam to support Chamoun against Frangieh in the 1952 presidential election, for according to Saeb Salam

> Hamid Frangieh insisted on sticking to the Al Sulh family Takyeddine and Kazim—cousins of Riyad al Sulh—and we had grown tired of seeing Riyad al Sulh as Prime Minister during Bechara Al Khoury's tenure.[17]

In the Shuf region Kamal Junblat had supported Chamoun's foreign policy until he lost the June 1957 elections.[18]

Chamoun amended the electoral law in April 1957 and used American funds[19] to counter expected Syrian and Egyptian aid to his opponents.[20] His high handedness was demonstrated in disregarding opposition politicians whose preference for eighty-eight deputies was ignored in favor of sixty-six.[21] Opposition leaders Kamal Junblat, Saeb Salam and Ahmad Al-As'ad lost their seats while Sabri Hamade, Rashid Karami, and Hamid Frangieh held on to theirs. Invoking the threat of communism, Chamoun urged US president Eisenhower to take action against communism in this region and received US funding for that purpose.

The argument that the domestic issue of Chamoun's reelection was of greater significance than foreign policy to Lebanese politicians in 1958 is reinforced by the willingness of prominent Beirut deputies Saeb Salam and Abdallah al Yafi to compromise with Chamoun even after their unexpected defeat in the June 1957 elections. They agreed to cease their opposition to the government on the condition that the election results be invalidated and Chamoun declare that he would not seek reelection. The offer was made via the mediation of King Saud in early July 1957; however, it was short-lived and nothing came of it as Nasser stepped up his campaign attacking the Eisenhower Doctrine, and Lebanon's opposition leaders supported it.[22]

Socioeconomic Grievances

The 1950s was a period of growth and prosperity for the Lebanese economy as it attracted capital flight, political exiles, and pipelines. The beneficiaries were the politicians, bankers, merchants, and a rising middle class. One indicator of prosperity was the fourfold increase in the number of tourists between 1952 and 1955 from 216,000 to 901,464.[23] However, job creation and development projects in the agricultural or "peripheral" regions beyond Beirut and Mt. Lebanon were neglected and many of these Lebanese emigrated to Africa, the Americas, and later to the Arabian Gulf.

Socioeconomic grievances were of secondary importance[24] as a cause of the crisis, as evidenced by opposition documents and statements that reflected the sentiments of their constituents.[25] One of these is the pamphlet issued by the newly established Mu'tamar al Hay't al Islamiyya al Da'im (Permanent Commission of Islamic Associations) in 1953, entitled *Moslem Lebanon Today*. The pamphlet reflected the public mood of resentment toward the perception of a Lebanon dominated by Christians who distorted its Arab identity:

> The Maronite sect of Lebanon and some of the other Christian groups in our country do not feel or sympathize with the Arab national spirit, but to the contrary are prepared to fight it in every possible way and to impose by force their own Christian civilization on all of Lebanon and to violently separate Lebanon from the rest of the Arab world.[26]

Muslim discontent was voiced again in a sermon by the chief Shari'a judge of Beirut, Sheikh Shafik Yamut, at the Omari Mosque on March 13, 1953.[27] He outlined grievances such as the nationality law, inaccurate population census, distorted history textbooks, the Department of Tourism's presentation of Lebanon to tourists as a Christian country, and the National Museum's emphasis on pre-

Islamic pagan and Christian artifacts to the exclusion of Muslim ones. The sermon emphasized social and cultural alienation rather than economic deprivation although it alluded to the government's unequal allocation of aid such as that of the US Point IV program and the lack of rural development of predominantly Muslim-inhabited areas.

Five years later and a week into the three-month-long crisis of 1958, Shaikh Nadim al-Jisr, member of parliament and close adviser to Tripoli's preeminent politician and former prime minister Rashid Karami, reiterated Muslim grievances at a press conference on May 17, 1958.[28] Although he referred to the economic hardship suffered by the people of Tripoli due to its separation from its natural hinterland, he emphasized that the suffering on the foreign policy front was greater. Al-Jisr was critical of the lukewarm attitude of the Lebanese government toward the formation of the UAR and called for a foreign policy of positive neutrality and better relations with the UAR, including the restoration of economic relations with Syria-the historic economic hinterland of Tripoli.[29]

Foreign Policy

The two turning points in Chamoun's foreign policy were the Suez War and Lebanon's endorsement of the Eisenhower Doctrine.[30] However, his foreign policy alone may not have led to the three-month-long insurrection from May to July 1958 had he maintained the political alliances that had won him the presidency and refrained from repeating the former president's mistake to seek another presidential term.

The Suez Crisis greatly enhanced Nasser's influence and shifted the focus of the Arab-Israeli conflict from one of the repatriation of Palestinian refugees to a struggle for the regional balance of power.[31] The polarization of the Arab World into pro-Nasser and pro-Western alignments, starting with the Baghdad Pact and intensifying with the Suez war and the union of Syria and Egypt into the United Arab Republic (UAR), increased the pressure on Chamoun to shift his overtly pro-Western orientation.

Nasser never forgave Lebanon for maintaining diplomatic relations with Britain and France during the Suez Crisis[32] and publicly said so: "The rulers of Lebanon stabbed us in the back during our time of stress, at the time when Britain, France and Israel were attacking us."[33] Prime Minister Al Yafi and Minister of State Saeb Salam resigned on November 16, 1956 in protest at Chamoun's policy. Chamoun replaced Yafi with Sami al Sulh and the pro-American and longtime Lebanese Ambassador to the United States Charles Malik was appointed minister for foreign affairs. The distinguished academic had earlier been considered for the post of president of the American University of Beirut in order "to forestall neutralist and nationalistic trends in the area which might endanger the University."[34] Chamoun's appointment of Charles Malik was a declaration of a pro-American policy in the polarized Arab world after the Suez Crisis, especially in view of Malik's antipathy toward communism and Arab nationalism[35] His influence on Chamoun and on

Lebanon's adherence to the Eisenhower Doctrine may have been substantial due to his personal ties to John Foster Dulles and others in the State Department.[36]

As the "Arab Cold War" intensified, Nasser's populist message of Arab nationalism resonated with Arab populations and forced their leaders to toe the line.[37] Henceforward, Lebanon's Muslim leaders would be dependent on Nasser's goodwill to maintain their leadership as their constituents were swept up in the fervor of Nasserism.[38] However, Lebanese opposition leaders were selective as they emphasized the Arab nationalist component of Nasserism and not the socialist rhetoric for they, together with their Christian counterparts, were beneficiaries of Lebanon's liberal service economy and were committed to preserving it.[39]

The Eisenhower Doctrine was introduced in January 1957 to enable countries in the Middle East to call for US economic and military assistance to counter the threat of communism, a threat that was dubious at best in Lebanon as evidenced in US Department of Defense reports.[40] Nasser himself repressed Communists in Egypt and this would extend to Syria with the formation of the UAR as the dissolution of political parties was one of Nasser's conditions.[41] Moreover, Communist parties in Syria and Lebanon had lost popularity after the Soviet vote at the UN supporting the partition of Palestine in November 1947 and the consequent recognition of the new state of Israel in May of the following year.[42] Popular interest in the Arab world centered on the question of Palestine and Arab nationalism as expressed by Nasser. Israel was the threat, not the Soviet Union.[43] Nasser perceived the Eisenhower Doctrine as yet another attempt to contain Arab nationalism and not communism as claimed.[44]

Chamoun sought to benefit from international and regional polarization to seek reelection to presidency and proceeded to weaken his adversaries using Anglo-American support. He promoted himself as the champion of the West against an exaggerated threat of communism and that of Nasserism. Lebanon's adherence to the Eisenhower Doctrine signaled a break with the country's previous foreign policy that had maintained a guarded neutrality in accordance with the National Pact agreement of 1943. Lebanon was the only Arab country to formally accept the terms of the Doctrine in a joint statement announced at the end of US special envoy James Richard's visit on March 16, 1957.[45] Political tensions increased with vitriolic attacks against Chamoun and the al Sulh government by Cairo Radio's Voice of the Arabs program.[46] Nasser's charisma and popular appeal across socioeconomic groups was manifested in schools of the Makassed Charitable Society[47] among other venues as his portrait was hung in every classroom and his heroic exploits against the British as well as his land reforms were recounted.[48]

The opposition initially split over the Eisenhower Doctrine with Kamal Junblat, Bechara al-Khuri as well as the pro-Saudi politician Hussein Oueini refusing to oppose it. The ratification of the Eisenhower Doctrine in parliament on April 5, led to the resignation of seven deputies.[49] Although they had expressed support for US economic aid, Rashid Karami and Abdallah al Yafi resigned when the government insisted on a parliamentary vote of confidence for its foreign policy. As Egyptian pressure increased, Karami, Yafi, and others needed to fall in line with their constituents in view of the upcoming parliamentary elections in June 1957.

The opposition politicians were not anti-American, and they later expressed their regret to the US ambassador after the burning down of the US Information Centre in Tripoli in May 1958. Kamal Junblat explained that Chamoun's motivation for accepting the Eisenhower Doctrine was reelection for "he was willing to sign a pact with the devil if that would enable him to attain this goal."[50] Junblat informed the American Embassy that he would join the opposition but not oppose Lebanon's pro-Western policy that Chamoun was using to eliminate his political rivals.[51]

The formation of the United Arab Republic in February 1958 polarized the situation further in Lebanon. While Nasser assured numerous visitors such as the US ambassador to Cairo and the Maronite patriarch[52] that he did not seek a subservient Lebanese government, Chamoun sought to capitalize on the popular excitement generated by the union and to present himself as the defender of Lebanon's independence.[53] He discouraged rapprochement with Nasser, and Prime Minister Sami al Sulh threatened to resign when faced with reservations by Chamoun and Malik for his proposal to head an official delegation to visit Cairo and congratulate Nasser on the formation of the UAR.[54] The prime minister eventually visited Cairo accompanied by Selim Lahoud, minister of foreign affairs and Chamoun's close friend.

To celebrate the birth of the UAR, Al Makassed declared the first day of February a national holiday. When Nasser visited Damascus on 24 of that month, 65,000 persons crossed the Lebanese Syrian border in that week chanting "al Sha'b al lubnani al tha'ir badduh al wihdah 'ajjil ajjil" (the Lebanese people in revolt want the union right away). Many Lebanese Christians saw these events as expressions of disloyalty to Lebanon. However, despite the popular outburst of support for Nasser very few appeals for unity were made by opposition members. Secretary general of the Muslim National Organization Abdul Wahab Rifa'i expressed the views of his co-religionists thus:

> While the United Arab Republic appeals strongly to their emotions . . . yet the majority of Lebanese Moslems recognize the advantages to be derived from cooperation with the Christian elements of the population and from maintenance of the sovereignty and independence of Lebanon.[55]

Lebanese army commander General Fuad Chehab attributed the crisis to Chamoun's selfish ambitions.[56] Chamoun and Malik's strategy to identify the crisis in Lebanon with US regional interests was reinforced by their insistence that the crisis was generated by an external threat of the Soviets and of Nasser and hence Lebanon could invoke the Eisenhower Doctrine and call upon US support.[57]

After US funding of the 1957 elections, American and British policy-makers went a step further in responding to Chamoun's electoral ambitions. On May 7, 1958, they reluctantly assured the Lebanese president of their support for his reelection "should he decide to follow that course."[58] Anglo-American support was withdrawn a week later when violence broke out on May 9 following the assassination of opposition journalist Nasib al Metni. Street barricades were set up in Beirut and elsewhere with calls for Chamoun's resignation. Notwithstanding cross-sectarian alliances and intra-sectarian divisions among political elites, regions with Muslim majorities and Nasserist sympathies joined the insurgency that had spread to the northern city of Tripoli, the western area of the Beqaa and southern Lebanon.[59] US ambassador Robert McClintock advised Chamoun to publicly renounce intentions of reelection. Eleven days later on May 27 Prime Minister Sulh declared that his government did not intend to amend the constitution.[60] A US-Nasser rapprochement was underway.

In agreement with UN secretary general Dag Hammarskjold for a watered down UNOGIL report, Nasser had pledged to end assistance to the opposition on June 24.[61] The UN observer force had been requested by the Lebanese government to investigate infiltration of arms across the Syrian border. The political impasse in Lebanon had already been resolved before the Iraqi revolution of July 14, as evidenced by the US-Egyptian diplomatic correspondence of May and June 1958. The US marine landing in Lebanon was prompted by regional events and strategic considerations beyond Lebanon.[62] Chamoun's earlier request for US military intervention on June 18 had been turned down by the US secretary of state Dulles who had informed Charles Malik that the United States would not fight Nasser and the forces of Arabism to please Chamoun.[63]

The US military intervention set a precedent for interventions in other parts of the world and reinforced an unrealistic perception by some Lebanese policy-makers of seeking future US protection.[64] The landing of marines in Lebanon was prompted by the revolution in Iraq, fear of the disruption to oil supplies flowing to Lebanon's refineries from Iraq and Saudi Arabia, as well as the need to demonstrate that the United States would support its friends. Lebanon's intrinsic value to Anglo-American policy-makers was deemed as "not very important in itself"[65] and was secondary to regional and Cold War considerations.

In discussions with the US and British ambassadors, Chamoun had endorsed General Chehab as his successor and plans were underway to convene parliament to elect the president. Since the Syrian crisis of August 1957 events in the Arab world had effected a change in strategy by US policy-makers after a series of setbacks for Western powers including the July revolution in Iraq.[66] This policy shift was evidenced by the "Statement of US Policy toward the Near East" adopted by the US National Security Council on November 4, 1958. Nasser and his ideology of Arabism was to be accommodated and the resource of oil was classified as a US interest of "critical importance" while "the military and commercial transit facilities of the Near East were less essential."[67]

Conclusion

In Lebanon the political ambition of President Chamoun and his weakening of political opponents was a principal cause of the crisis. The tense internal situation was magnified by regional polarization that provided the international context for the three-month-long civil strife in 1958 and the outreach of Lebanon's political elites to regional and international patrons. The multilayered conflict with personal elite rivalries reflected the alliances of the "Arab Cold War."[68] President Chamoun had tilted Lebanon's foreign policy by accepting the Eisenhower Doctrine and resisting Nasserism and identifying Lebanon's independence with his presidency. He underestimated the popular outcry, that his policies would engender, and he failed to provide for the contingency of an Egyptian-American rapprochement which ultimately defused the crisis and brought General Fuad Chehab to the presidency.

Sectarian rhetoric widened the rift among communities despite some intra-communal rivalries as well as cross-sectarian alliances such as the Maronite patriarch's opposition to Chamoun's policies. The president's attempts to capitalize on popular fears of Lebanon's subversion by the UAR and secure the endorsement of regional and Western powers for a second presidential term failed as widespread violence broke out to preempt this. The middle class managed to benefit from the extraordinary prosperity in the 1950s as Lebanon was a safe haven for capital flight in the Arab world and the banking capital for the new wealth of the oil-producing Gulf. There was no spokesman for the underprivileged populace. The urban underprivileged merely voiced their discontent by supporting Nasser while their leaders continued to support the status quo.

While the 1958 crisis resulted from a myriad of causes at the local, regional, and international levels, its eruption was not inevitable. The actions of political elites, their political ambitions and overreach did play a role in the intensification and militarization of the crisis. The structure of the political system enabled the agency of the politicians to undermine the delicate sectarian balance in order to mobilize their constituents and enhance their respective positions. Chamoun ended his presidency to the sound of church bells. He had remained in office until the last day of his term, rejecting the opposition's demands in May that he step down immediately. His supporters had celebrated the arrival of American troops to Lebanon's shores with the same gesture, as church bells rang in Beirut. He was now a Christian hero who had stood up to the threat of Nasser and would be a pivotal partner in the Tripartite Alliance formed in 1968 to defeat Chehabism.[69] In the Civil War of 1975, he would be a central figure in the "Christian Front" whose ideologue was Charles Malik and the two would again request American military intervention in 1976 in the midst of the 1975 Civil War and frame it in similar terms of bipolarity by depicting the opposition as Communists.[70]

The events of 1958 constituted a watershed in Lebanon's socioeconomic development as they led to the election of President Chehab, who restored political stability, established state structures to enhance accountability in administration, weed out corruption, and promote economic development in the rural areas of the country.[71] His administration was revolutionary in its shift away from the politics of the zuama and their patronage networks. The zuama were the traditional political leaders of their community and acted as intermediaries between their constituents and the state by providing patronage in return for political support. Chehab's neutralist foreign policy that repaired ties with Nasser's Egypt was also a major shift from his predecessor's foreign policy. In another departure from the politics of former presidents and political elites who sought foreign patrons and support for their internal rivalries in Lebanon, Chehab was able to detach Lebanon's internal politics from regional polarization. He accommodated Nasser and the Lebanese who supported him and shifted the state narrative from foreign policy to one of reform and social justice. However, the revolutionary moment of Chehabism in Lebanon was short-lived, for unlike other Arab countries whose traditional politicians had been swept away by the aftermath of Suez and the rising tide of Arab nationalism, Lebanon's politicians were resilient and regrouped to defeat Chehabism in the 1968 parliamentary elections.

The resolution of the 1958 crisis with the oft-repeated slogan "No Victor, No Vanquished" maintained the self-serving political system for Lebanon's political elites for another seventeen years when the opportunity to challenge the status quo presented itself once again in 1975 and led to a brutal fifteen-year-long civil war. In 1989 at the Taif Conference ending the Lebanese Civil War, new players would challenge the political establishment and revise the power-sharing agreement in Lebanon thirty years after the events of 1958, but the sectarian structure of the political system remained unchanged and perpetuated an unstable sociopolitical order. The new elite of warlords and merchants would thrive in postwar Lebanon.[72]

Notes

1 L. Carl Brown, *International Politics and the Middle East: Old Rules, Dangerous Game* (Princeton, NJ: Princeton University Press, 1984), 3–5.
2 Fahim Qubain, *Crisis in Lebanon* (Washington, DC: Middle East Institute, 1961); M. S. Agwani, *The Lebanese Crisis, 1958: A Documentary Study* (Bombay: Asia Publishing House, 1965); Nawaf Salam, *L'Insurrection de 1958 au Liban* (Paris: Sorbonne, 1979); Erika G. Allin, *The United States and the 1958 Lebanon Crisis* (Lanham, MD: University Press of America, 1994); Irene Genzier, *Notes from the Minefield: United States Intervention in Lebanon and the Middle East 1945–1958* (New York: Columbia University Press, 1997). For the official historical record of declassified US government documents on the 1958 events in Lebanon see John P. Glennon, ed., *Foreign Relations of the United States, 1958–1960, Lebanon and Jordan, Volume XI* (Washington, DC: United States Government Printing Office, 1992).
3 Kamal Salibi maintains that the objective the leaders of the insurrection was simply a change of government not the yearning for an Arab union expressed by their constituents in demonstrations. *The Modern History of Lebanon* (London: Caravan Books, 1977), 202.
4 *Political Trends in Lebanon* in Paul Kesaris, ed. The Middle East 1950–1961 Supplement, O.S.S/State Department Intelligence and Research Reports, Secret, July 5, 1956.
5 For an analysis of the political and personal conflict between President Chamoun and Patriarch Meouchi in 1958, see Sami E. Baroudi, "Divergent Perspectives among Lebanon's Maronites during the 1958 Crisis," *Middle Eastern Studies* 15 (2006): 13.
6 Ibid., 5–28.
7 Najla W. Atiyah, "The Attitude of the Lebanese Sunnis towards the State of Lebanon" (unpublished D. Phil thesis, University of London, 1973), 287.

8 Michael Johnson, *Class & Client in Beirut: The Sunni Muslim Community and the Lebanese State 1840–1985* (London: Ithaca Press, 1986). Johnson reinforces this argument with the example of the 1944 property law in Beirut that was presented by Muslims as benefiting Christian landlords and disregarding the substantial number of Sunni Beiruti landlords, 129–30.
9 For Egyptian educational, political, press, and propaganda activities supported by the Egyptian Embassy's press attaché in 1958 see an "Untitled Report about Egyptian activities in Lebanon" Emir Farid Chehab Collection, GB165-0384, Box 8, File 29F/8, Middle East Centre Archive, St. Antony's College, Oxford.
10 For Chamoun's personal account of these years see Camille Chamoun, *Marahil al Istiqlal* (Beirut: 1949). See also the memoirs of Nadim Dimechkie, the economic attaché in London and later Ambassador to the US during the 1958 crisis, *Mahattat fi hayati al Diplumasiyyah* (Beirut: Dar Al Nahar, 1995), 56–66.
11 The term was used by Tabitha Petran in *The Struggle over Lebanon* (New York: Monthly Review Press, 1987).
12 For an insightful review of the emergence of the Merchant Republic and its beneficiaries see Carolyn L. Gates, *The Merchant Republic of Lebanon* (London: I.B. Tauris, 1998), 134–5, 137, and 151.
13 In his autobiography Najib Alamuddin discusses the management rift between the two men and the dismissal of al Huss as technical manager at MEA by Chairman Saeb Salam in 1951 and the ensuing events. Salam resigned the chairmanship of MEA in 1956 in conjunction with his Nasserist politics as BOAC had bought MEA, and he did not want to be seen as working with a British company. *The Flying Sheikh* (London: Quartet Books, 1987), 35–7, and 58–9.
14 American support for Chamoun's reelection was maintained until the outbreak of the crisis on May 9 and was rationalized by policy-makers as necessary to maintain a Western-oriented Lebanon and that failure to support Chamoun would have a demoralizing effect on America's friends in the Middle East. See McClintock to Dulles, Foreign Service Dispatch No. 3674, Top Secret, Department of State, Central Files, 783A.00, May 4, 1958, *FRUS, 1958-1960*, Vol. XI, pp. 28–30.
15 Johnson in *Class & Client in Beirut* argues that as beneficiaries of the economic system the Sunni leaders did not want to risk jeopardizing it by pressing for a redistribution of wealth and preferred to maintain the status quo of a multi-confessional Lebanon. p. 127.
16 See Caroline Attie, *Struggle in the Levant* (London: I.B. Tauris, 2004), 133–7 for references to British Foreign Office and American State Department Central Files archives revealing Chamoun and Malik's request for military assistance to resist communism as well as American funding for the parliamentary elections.
17 Elias al Deiry, *Man Yasna' al-Ra'is?* (Beirut:nd) Saeb Salam in an interview with Deiry, p. 57.
18 Kamal Junblat, *Haqiqat al-Thawrah al-Lubnaniyya* (Beirut: Dar al Nashr al 'Arabiyyah, 1959), 91.
19 In his account, "Ropes of Sand" (New York: Norton, 1980), CIA agent Wilbur Crane Eveland gives a detailed account of his role as a special envoy of CIA director Allen Dulles. Eveland's account is reinforced by archival evidence in a veiled reference to the US role in the Lebanese elections: "where we played an active role" Top Secret Memo from Waggonner to Rockwell, Dept. Of State Central Files 783A00, January 17, 1958, *FRUS, 1958-1960*, Vol. XI, pp. 5–7.

20 References to Embassy assistance for the opposition in a report entitled "The Electoral Race" dated January 1, 1957, by Intelligence Chief Emir Farid Chehab in the Emir Farid Chehab Collection, GB 165-0384, Box 13, File 14/13 Middle East Centre Archive, St. Antony's College, Oxford.
21 Atiyah, "The Attitude of Lebanese Sunnis," 267.
22 The mediator representing the king was the veteran pro-Saudi Husayn al Oueini. Atiyah, "The Attitude of Lebanese Sunnis," 275.
23 Gates, *The Merchant Republic*, 118.
24 Ibid.; Gates argues that "although the available evidence shows no tidy relationship between Lebanon's economic model and political stability, conventional wisdom holds that it contributed to sociopolitical disharmony." p. 150. Hence President Chehab's emphasis on a more equitable economic development in Lebanon to areas that had received little government attention since independence.
25 Basim al-Jisr maintains that socioeconomic conflict first became an issue in Lebanese politics in the 1950s but was muted by the political and national crises that Lebanon faced in 1956, 1957, and 1958. See Basim al-Jisr, *al -Sira'at al Lubnaniyah* (Beirut, 1981).
26 FO 1018/93.
27 A General Review of the Political Situation" by Wadih Malouf, a Lebanese employee of the British Embassy, Confidential, November 26, 1953, FO 1018/93, cover page and p. 3.
28 As reported in McClintock to Dulles, Foreign service Dispatch No. 4006, Department of State, Central Files, 783A.00, May 18, 1958.
29 As reported in McClintock to Dulles, Telegram No. 4006, May 18, 1958.
30 Salim Yaqub, *Containing Arab Nationalism: The Eisenhower Doctrine and the Middle East* (Chapel Hill: University of North Carolina Press, 2004).
31 Albert Hourani, in Wm. Roger Louis and Roger Owen, eds., *Suez 1956* (Oxford: Clarendon, 1989), 407.
32 Nasser's displeasure was personally conveyed to Ambassador Nadim Dimechkie who was visiting Cairo. Dimechkie, *Mahattat*, 113.
33 From a speech by Nasser in Cairo on May 16, 1958 in Agwani, *The Lebanese Crisis*, 101.
34 Attie, *Struggle in the Levant*, 107.
35 Kamal Salibi makes this point in "The Lebanese Crisis in Perspective," *The World Today* (London: Chatham House), vol. 14, no. 9, September 1958.
36 In his memoirs veteran diplomat Nadim Dimechkie who had been Lebanon's ambassador in Cairo and was appointed to the United States in January 1958 maintains that it was Malik's zealous anti-communism that influenced Chamoun to adopt the Eisenhower Doctrine and also convinced Chamoun to seek a second term as president in order to combat Nasserist expansionism after the formation of the UAR. Dimechkie, *Mahattat*, 237 and 120.
37 For the press coverage of Nasser's popularity in Lebanon and the photo opportunities he provided for Lebanese politicians who visited him in Cairo, see Atiyah, "The Attitude of the Lebanese Sunnis," 280-1.
38 Johnson, *Class and Client in Beirut*, 134. The threat of Nasserism to the Lebanese state and the Sunni commercial financial elite with vested interests in maintaining the status-quo key prompted an attempt by Muslim businessmen led by Fawzi al Hoss to buy off key supporters of the Beiruti opposition leaders and neutralize the movement. The attempt failed as the insurgents were prompted by an ideology that transcended ties of

patronage and clientelism and hence businessmen and politicians had to identify with the ideology of the day. Johnson attributes this episode to Copeland who in his own book *The Game Player* does mention countless meetings with Fawzi al Huss.

39 Michael Hudson, *The Precarious Republic* (New York: Random House, 1968), 111.
40 See Chapter 4 in this volume by Jeffrey G. Karam on the establishment of US dominance in the Middle East in 1958 as a status-quo power.
41 Patrick Seale discusses the exaggerated American view of the Communist threat in Egypt and Syria and attributes it to the error of viewing a local struggle in Cold War terms. Patrick Seale, *The Struggle for Syria: A Study of Post-War Arab Politics 1945–1958* (Yale University Press, 1965), 196 and 286–94. See also Chapter 12 in this volume by Fadi Esber, "No Turning Back: Syria and the 1958 Watershed."
42 For a detailed discussion of the competition of home grown ideological parties such as the Ba'ath Party with the Communist party in Syria and Lebanon whose members were accused by their rivals of conflicting loyalties and of being foreign agents of the Soviet Union, see Seale, 156–63.
43 The former CIA Damascus chief and stationed in Beirut in 1957 critiqued the Eisenhower Doctrine as a document that was ill timed and "infuriated those Arab states which our political action campaigns were trying to bring into line" in view of the fact that "at the time, there were no Middle Eastern nations controlled by international Communism, and no nations threatened by Communist aggression." Miles Copeland, *The Game Player: Confessions of the CIA's Original Political Operative* (London: Aurum Press, 1989), 204.
44 Miles Copeland, the CIA agent with close ties to Nasser and who claims that he helped Nasser with anti-American propaganda to assist him with enhancing his new regime's "hold on the country" in the early 1950s.
    pp. 167–8 lamented the "lack of expertise behind the Eisenhower Doctrine" and "the influence that Nasser was gaining as a result of the Eisenhower Doctrine." For some in the intelligence community, "if a government was anti-American it was Communist." Copeland, *The Game Player*, 216–17.
45 For the text of the joint communique, see Heath to Dulles, Foreign Service Dispatch No. 2225, Department of State, Central Files, 783A.00, March 16, 1957.
46 Radio Cairo's inflammatory broadcasts by Ahmad Said called on the Lebanese people more than once to overthrow Chamoun. Attie, *Struggle in the Levant*, 103 and 222.
47 For a detailed report of Egyptian propaganda activities in Lebanon in 1958 coordinated by the Egyptian Embassy, see Emir Farid Chehab. Influence included schools of Al Makassed, the press, distribution of portraits of Nasser, and contacts with political figures. The Emir Farid Chehab Collection, GB 165-0384, Box 8, File 29F/8 Middle East Centre Archive, St. Antony's College, Oxford.
48 Desmond Stewart, *Turmoil in Beirut: A Personal Account* (London: Allan Wingate, 1958), 15.
49 *Mahadir Majlis al Nuwwab* (Parliamentary Minutes of Meeting) Meeting of April 5, 1957, pp. 960–8.
50 Junblat, *Haqiqat al-Thawrah*, 78.
51 Heath to Dulles, Foreign Service Dispatch No. 3115, Department of State, Central Files, 783A.00, June 21, 1957.
52 Baroudi, "Divergent Perspectives," p. 20.
53 Hare to Dulles, June 7, 1958, No. 3241, FRUS 1958-1960, Vol. XI, p. 101.
54 Sami al Sulh, '*Lubnan al 'abath al Siyasi wa al masir al majhul*' (Beirut: Dar al Nahar, 2000), 280–1. He attributes their reservations to the fear of projecting weakness.

55 McClintock to Dulles, March 27, 1958, Foreign Service Dispatch No. 547.
56 *FRUS 1958-1960, Lebanon and Jordan*, 36.
57 Ibid., 153.
58 McClintock to Dulles, No. 3709, May 7, 1958, and London to Secretary of State, No. 6892, May 28, 1958. See also telegram No. 4346 from McClintock to Dulles, May 30, 1958, where he notes: "We have never indicated our support for Chamoun's re-election except to him alone."
59 For intra-sectarian divisions in 1958 within the Shiite sect in both southern Lebanon and the Bekaa' see Omri Nir, "The Shiites during the 1958 Lebanese Crisis," *Middle Eastern Studies* 40, no. 6 (November 2014), 109–29.
60 FRUS *1958-1960, Lebanon and Jordan*, 76.
61 Dag Hammarskjold talk with President Nasser on June 22, 1958, Secret, Hammarskjold Collection, National Library of Sweden. I am indebted to Salim Yaqub and Nathan Citino for this document.
62 The greater value attached by Nasser to a rapprochement with the United States than expanding Egypt's influence in Lebanon is reflected in US-Egyptian diplomatic correspondence in May and June 1958 and in Murphy's account, Robert Murphy, *Diplomat Among Warriors* (Garden City: Doubleday and Co. Inc., 1964), 483–4.
63 *FRUS 1958-1960, Lebanon and Jordan*, 153–4.
64 As related by the DCM in Beirut, George Basil Lambrakis, Perception and Misperception in Policymaking: The US Relationship with Modern Lebanon, 1943–1976" (Unpublished dissertation, The George Washington University, 1989), p. 117. For a wider discussion of the impact of the US intervention in Lebanon as a model for "limited wars" see Jeffrey G. Karam, "Cautious Revisionism and the Limits of Hegemony in *1958*: A Revolutionary Year for the United States in the Middle East," in *The Middle East in 1958*.
65 This is clearly stated in the declassified British and US diplomatic documents. To Eisenhower, No. 4477, "Top Secret" July 15, 1958, FO 371/134130. See also Attie, *Struggle in the Levant*, 201.
66 See Chapter 11 in this volume by Juan Romero, "The Iraqi Revolution of 1958."
67 National Security Council NSC 5820/1 November 4, 1958 Statement of US Policy toward the Near East. Declassified Documents Quarterly Catalog, 1980, 386B.
68 Malcolm Kerr first coined the term in his book *The Arab Cold War: Gamal Abdel Nasser and His Rivals, 1958–1970* (Oxford: Oxford University Press, 1965).
69 Chamoun remained popular after leaving office as evidenced in a 1972 survey. According to the authors: "When asked which two persons they most admire, 43% of the Christian respondents named a Christian Lebanese political figure, with former President Camille Chamoun being the individual most frequently cited." David R. Smock and Audrey C. Smock, *The Politics of Pluralism* (New York: Elsevier, 1975), 136.
70 George Basil Lambrakis, "Perception and Misperception in Policymaking: The US Relationship with Modern Lebanon, 1943–1976" (Unpublished dissertation, The George Washington University, 1989), 235.
71 For a review of Chehab's reforms see Kamal Salibi, "Lebanon under Fuad Chehab 1958–1964," *Middle Eastern Studies* 4 (1968): 221–6. See also Nicholas Nassif, *Jumhuriyyat Fuad Chehab* (Beirut: Dar al Nahar, Institute of Fuad Chehab, 2008).
72 The supreme role of the families that constitute the warlord-merchant establishment in Lebanon's politics is the thesis of Kamal Dib's, *Warlords and Merchants: The Lebanese Business and Political Establishment* (London: Ithaca Press, 2004).

Chapter 14

EVOLUTION AND REVOLUTION

JORDAN IN 1958

Clea Hupp

1958, a revolutionary year in Iraq, did not bring an end to the Hashemite monarchy in Jordan. Internal and external threats to the monarchy existed both before and after 1958; the events surrounding the coup in Iraq, while destabilizing in Jordan, were not atypical for this perpetually unstable monarchy. Although the year did not result in regime change, a notable evolution in Jordan's relationship with the United States and Great Britain occurred during the years around 1958; the year can justifiably be viewed as a transformational period for Jordan's foreign relations. King Hussein bin Talal successfully negotiated the transition from an old patron (Great Britain) to a new one (the United States), in large part due to the disruptive events of 1957 and 1958. Remarkably, the twenty-three-year-old king survived a period that destroyed the monarchy in Iraq and eroded government stability in Lebanon. To understand how the monarchy endured this tumultuous time, it is important to look at the background to 1958 and recognize the internal and external entities that threatened the king's reign.[1]

The Baghdad Pact Crisis

King Hussein came to power in 1952 at the age of seventeen due to the consensus of the Jordanian parliament, a body that orchestrated his father's abdication when Hussein was still studying at school in Great Britain.[2] The boy king was extremely vulnerable in a culture that valued age and experience over bloodlines. His first significant diplomatic challenge occurred due to the creation of the Baghdad Pact in 1955.[3] The Pact exacerbated animosities between governments that still embraced assistance from Great Britain—Jordan, Iran, and Iraq—and the revolutionary regimes of Egypt and Syria. Hussein, under severe pressure from Great Britain, entertained the idea of joining the Pact in late 1955.[4] Prime Minister Tawfiq Abul Huda, the Jordanian elder statesman who once struggled to maintain the monarchy during the mental illness of Hussein's father, resigned rather than consenting to the Pact, and Hussein attempted to replace him with the pro-Pact Hazza Majali.⁵ Reform-minded Jordanians chafed at Majali's appointment. Anti-regime demonstrations erupted in Amman and cities throughout the West Bank, the political opposition called for a general strike, and bombs exploded at the French and Turkish consulates in Jerusalem.⁶ Hussein, faced with his first major domestic crisis, realized that the Pact was a tremendous political liability and reversed course.⁷ The domestic dissent created by the issue of the Baghdad Pact represented one of the most dangerous political crises of Hussein's reign. But the public outcry forced the king to recognize that his relationship with Britain, although financially necessary, alienated the Jordanian population.⁸

The popular pro-Nasser Egyptian radio program *Sawt Al-Arab* (Voice of the Arabs) portrayed Hussein as a tool of imperialism, and opposition leaders in Jordan echoed the charge.⁹ This accusation forced King Hussein into a defensive posture; the king needed to placate his Arab nationalist opponents. On March 1, 1956, he abruptly dismissed the British commander of the Arab Legion, John Glubb, and requested that Glubb leave the country at once.¹⁰ As a result of Arab pressure and Glubb's humiliating exit, Britain and Jordan negotiated the termination of the Anglo-Jordanian Treaty and the British subsidy of approximately $84 million in US dollars.¹¹ American officials believed that Glubb's dismissal spelled the end for Hussein's regime.¹²

Replacing British officers with Jordanian natives seemed to soothe Hussein's opponents for a time; however, many Jordanian citizens viewed pan-Arabism as the best route to victory over Israel.¹³ Within a few months, the Suez Crisis enhanced Nasser's regional prestige and divided the Middle East nations into pro-Western and pro-Soviet blocs.¹⁴

Coup or Counter-Coup?

As the Suez Crisis developed through the summer of 1956, Hussein faced growing criticism for failing to join Nasser. In October 1956, while Nasser stood in defiance of Great Britain and the UN, Jordanian voters elected Suleiman Nabulsi, an openly pro-Nasser politician, to serve as prime minister. Nabulsi announced his intention to improve ties with Nasser's Egypt and the Soviet Union, an action that jeopardized Hussein's relationship with Western powers.¹⁵ Hussein requested Suleiman Nabulsi's resignation in early April 1957.¹⁶ When Hussein removed Nabulsi, the opposition plotted another method to re-align the government. On the afternoon of April 14, 1957, a junior officer requested a private meeting at the palace with Hussein. He informed the king that a coup was in progress, although he was not privy to significant details.¹⁷ That same night, the king became aware of a coup instigated by the army's chief of staff Ali Abu Nuwar and his cousin Ma'an. Fighting erupted in Zerqa, about 30 miles from Amman, between loyalist ground troops and the junior officers who were accused of plotting against the king.¹⁸ The troops apparently feared that the king had been assassinated by the plotters. Hussein drove to Zerqa to reassure his loyalists. The troops greeted him with cheers and widespread support. The next day, Abu Nuwar and his family, along with other alleged plotters, fled across the Syrian border.[19]

This event displays some similarities to the shah's CIA-supported counter-revolution in Iran.[20] When asked about this accusation, Hazem Nuseibeh, a Palestinian former member of Hussein's government, stated that the accused conspirators were seeking change: "They were patriotic, nationalistic, and sometimes unruly; they were dissatisfied with the status. We were all hoping we could do something to recover the lost land—let's face it. We would go together every night and drink scotch. Some of them had nationalist feelings and felt we were not doing enough, even though (Jordan) did a great deal to save the West Bank."[21] British ambassador Charles Johnston characterized the coup and counter-coup as "a confused triangular affair" and not the work of "two well-knit teams led respectively by masterminds." Johnston believed that Hussein was genuinely shocked by Abu Nuwar's betrayal: the man had been his protégé. In addition, Hussein tended to brag to the ambassador about his clever political maneuvers and yet said nothing of a preemptive move against Nuwar and Nabulsi.[22] One transcript of a call between John Foster Dulles and Allen Dulles mentioned that Kermit Roosevelt was in Amman at the time, but no other documents or interviews confirm or add to this statement.[23] If the CIA manufactured this crisis to bolster support for Hussein, American officials were either unaware or made a deliberate display of indifference to the fate of the king.[24]

We may never know if the Zerqa crisis was manufactured, real, or a mix of both, but it gave Hussein the perfect excuse to crack down on dissent.[25] He imposed martial law for an eighteen-month period, outlawed political parties, and imposed censorship on the Jordanian media.[26] A former prime minister of Jordan, Fayez Tawraneh, said of this event, "There were some Nasserists in Jordan who became prime minister, but King Hussein gave them the premiership for them to commit suicide."[27]

The coup attempt brought about a notable change in President Eisenhower's view of Jordan.[28] Eisenhower eagerly promoted the king's version of the events. When John Foster Dulles received information that Abu Nuwar and his associates had traveled to Cairo for a secret meeting with Nasser, Eisenhower seized on this story, telling the secretary, "We should get out the real story—even if you can't prove every word. Picture these people and call them puppets of the Kremlin under secret orders."[29]

As the victor in this power struggle, Hussein depicted the events in a way that accentuated his courage and intelligence.[30] Eisenhower, who placed a great deal of emphasis on personal character, expressed his admiration and support for Hussein in correspondence with British prime minister Harold Macmillan at the end of April:

Right now, the young King of Jordan seems to be waging a gallant fight to eject subversive elements from his government and country. Of course, whatever support he gets from the West must be carefully handled because he could be ruined if his enemies falsely spread abroad the charge that he is acting as a puppet. He seems to be a courageous young man and I am sure that if he succeeds in establishing a stable government in that country, completely independent of Communist domination, the position of the West will be immeasurably strengthened.[31]

Subsequently, the United States granted Jordan $10 million in financial assistance to the king in his struggle.[32] Hussein clearly understood the importance of anti-Communist rhetoric when he thanked Eisenhower for his support, writing:

> Destructive elements and propagandists of sedition and international Communism have attempted to put an end both to the citadel of the state that we have built and to the pillars of government in order that the country might become the prey of the Communists and the opportunists. When their evil designs became known to us for certain and their bad intentions became clear, we hastened to set matters aright.[33]

The New Political Landscape

Syria joined Egypt to form the United Arab Republic on February 1, 1958.[34] The spread of Nasser's influence fueled Western fears that the Soviets intended to dominate the entire region with Nasser as a proxy ruler. Eisenhower worried about Nasser's objectives. "To realize his ambitions, he of course relies on Soviet help. As he gets deeper and deeper into debt to the Kremlin, the great danger is that he will set off an explosion of terrifying proportions," Eisenhower wrote to a friend.[35] In response to the creation of the UAR, Iraq and Jordan joined to form the Arab Union.[36] Shortly thereafter, President Eisenhower approved a subsidy of $25 million to meet the entire Jordanian share of the Arab Union budget for the coming year, thus strengthening the American commitment to Jordan, yet simultaneously undermining Hussein as an independent leader.[37] In a cable to Iraqi prime minister Nuri al-Said, Eisenhower stated: "We hope, too, that you will regard this as a further demonstration of our continuing interest in the Arab Union and our determination to do what we can to ensure its success."[38]

Nasser's continued animosity toward Hussein afforded the king additional credibility in Washington as suspicions of Egypt intensified.[39] When tensions grew between Egypt and Israel, the presence of a pro-American leader in Jordan became essential to maintaining a foothold in the region. Nasser thus played an important role in initiating the Jordanian-American friendship.[40] In addition, the British encouraged the United States' transition from detached observer to economic and military patron; they wanted to terminate their obligations while maintaining sympathetic rulers in the Middle East. British officials pressed Eisenhower to support Hussein and maintained an interest in his continued reign. Meanwhile, US development assistance to Jordan increased dramatically, rising from $1.6 million in 1957 to approximately $20 million in 1958, effectively replacing the British subsidy.[41]

The Last Hashemite Kingdom

The new power structure created by the Arab Union existed for less than six months. The end of Hashemite rule in Iraq was brutal, swift, and took members of the Washington intelligence community by surprise.[42] Intelligence officials of the United States viewed this as a pro-Nasser coup and doubted that other nations could resist pan-Arab nationalism. Speaking with Secretary of State Dulles, Eisenhower lamented that "it looks now as if you have a solid Arab world against us because Jordan can't stick."[43]

Hussein's intelligence services preempted a simultaneous plot in Jordan, but details of that conspiracy remain obscure.[44] In the days following the Iraqi coup, Hussein's position remained volatile and uncertain. Word of Feisal's death did not immediately reach the king, and he hoped that loyalists in Iraq would rally around his cousin.[45] Hussein claimed leadership of both Jordan and Iraq, but the revolutionary government of Iraq responded by announcing the dissolution of the Arab Union. When he learned of Feisal's assassination, the king felt a sense of personal loss; the two had been playmates as children and schoolmates as young men.[46] But Hussein had little time to grieve: the new Iraqi government ended shipments of petroleum to Jordan, leaving the government without a means to supply water or electricity to the people. Realizing the gravity of the situation, Hussein immediately called for assistance from Great Britain and the United States.[47]

In the early hours of July 14, it seemed that the violence of the Iraqi Revolution might spread through the entire Middle East.[48] Lebanese president Camille Chamoun sent a desperate message to the United States and Britain asking for troops to defend his government against alleged Communist aggression.[49] In a meeting with President Eisenhower, CIA director Allen Dulles emphasized the importance of prompt action, arguing that the Lebanese president could not hold his position for long. Eisenhower decided to assist Chamoun, believing that Nasser's influence threatened to subvert a pro-Western leader. After a brief discussion of the political repercussions of military action, Eisenhower decided to deploy Marines to Lebanon and move the Sixth Fleet to the Eastern Mediterranean.[50]

British prime minister Harold Macmillan called President Eisenhower to discuss possible joint British and American military operations in the Middle East, if instability spread to more countries.[51] The president told Macmillan that he intended to "implement the plan"—referring to an Anglo-American military plan—by sending troops into Lebanon. Macmillan argued that the Iraqi coup presented an opportunity for the United States and Britain to reshape the entire Middle East.[52] He pressed Eisenhower for an extensive commitment, stating: "If we do this thing with the Lebanese it is only really part of a much larger operation, because we shall be driven to take the thing as a whole."[53] Eisenhower resisted committing to anything but a limited action and countered, "Now just a minute so that there is no misunderstanding. Are you of the belief that unless we have made up our minds in advance to carry this thing on through to the Persian Gulf, that we had better not go in the first place?"[54] Macmillan replied, "I don't think that, but

I think that we have got to see it together, dear friend. There is no good in being in that place and sitting there a few months and the whole rest being in flames. As soon as we start we have to face it—we have probably got to do a lot of things."[55] After the phone call, the president turned to Secretary Dulles and said, "He talked about the destruction of oil lines, then we are really at war, then what do we do?"[56]

While Eisenhower and Macmillan wrestled with the implications of events in the Middle East, King Hussein actively lobbied for US and British assistance. He told the American chargé in Amman that he was counting on Washington to stand by Jordan as a "good and trusted friend."[57] British officials pressured Eisenhower to support the king; yet he limited American military commitments to Lebanon.[58] The presence of a monarchy in Jordan provoked suspicions in Eisenhower; he worried that the United States might interfere with the wishes of the Jordanian people.[59] Eisenhower supported Lebanese president Chamoun as a democratically elected leader; the taint of monarchy continued to influence his opinion of Hussein. Secretary Dulles similarly had little enthusiasm for Hussein's prospects—he believed that strong Arab nationalist sentiment in Jordan would inevitably cause Hussein to suffer his cousin's fate. Jordan also represented a large financial liability. "We are hooked for 30–40 million a year to pay the budget deficit of Jordan," Dulles told Eisenhower, "(I would) rather Nasser or the Soviets do that." In Dulles's view, the Lebanon operation was a face-saving move: "Our rationale was that this was not going to help but would prevent our friends from losing faith in us."[60] Thus, the president, despite his assurances to the king about Jordanian independence and integrity, did not intend to guarantee the security of the Hashemite regime. Eisenhower still considered the integrity of the state and the security of the monarchy to be separate matters—despite an increased financial commitment to Jordan.[61]

After Marine landing operations began in Lebanon on July 15, Eisenhower reconsidered the idea of pursuing a comprehensive plan for the Middle East, questioning whether the Iraqi Revolution was another Soviet-inspired civil war.[62] The president did not want to be guilty of standing by idly while an important region of the world fell to communism, yet he believed that military action should only be used for a great moral purpose.[63] He told the commanders of the Lebanon operation, "If, however, our only argument is economic—saying that the life of the western world depends upon access to oil in the Middle East—this would be quite different, and quite inferior a purpose that rests on the right to govern by consent of the governed."[64] Eisenhower told his generals that he was "giving deep thought to finding a moral ground on which to stand if we have to go further."[65]

Meanwhile, the situation in Jordan continued to deteriorate. Saudi Arabia prohibited British and American planes from using its airspace to supply Jordan with petroleum.[66] Rumors of an imminent coup circulated through Amman.[67] On the evening of July 16, Prime Minister Macmillan informed Secretary Dulles that Britain would land troops in Amman that night.[68] He asked for confirmation that the United States would provide support, if not militarily then morally and diplomatically. Britain subsequently began to supply Jordan by using Israeli airspace—initially without the government's permission.[69]

With British and Israeli assistance, the petroleum crisis in Jordan abated rapidly. King Hussein informed the State Department that he no longer needed US troops but would like a symbolic American military presence in Jordan.[70] Although the immediate crisis appeared to be over, the White House continued to doubt the viability of the Hashemite monarchy.[71] On July 23, a group of key US officials met to discuss the outcome of the Iraqi Revolution. In general, the administration viewed the revolution as a Nasser-inspired event; thus, the focus of the meeting was containing Egyptian influence.[72] John Foster Dulles compared Arab nationalism to a flood and stated, "We cannot successfully oppose it, but we can put up sand bags around positions we must protect—the first group being Israel and Lebanon and the second being oil positions around the Persian Gulf."[73] Eisenhower agreed, acknowledging that Israel was a key element of US policy. He compared the implementation of Western policies in the region to the imposition of prohibition in the United States: unpopular agendas inevitably failed. "If our policy is solely to maintain the Kings of Jordan and Saudi Arabia in their positions, the prospect is hopeless, even in the short term," Eisenhower ruefully admitted.[74] Specifically referring to Jordan, the president wondered

> what kind of outcome we can foresee in the long run if the government is kept in power simply by outside troops. Mr. Dulles recalled that we had not wanted the British to go in. The President saw difficulty in continuing to back Hussein since we do not have as strong a legal basis as we do in Lebanon. Mr. Dulles said that in a sense Jordan lies in the main stream of the flood of which he has spoken. However, we cannot abandon them. Also, we must think of what Israel would do if Jordan goes down. It is clear they would act, and would win initially. The Soviets probably would aid the Arabs, however, and the war would widen, with great pressure on the United States to support Israel.[75]

The president confronted the prospect that the Arab-Israeli conflict might burgeon into a wider war involving the United States and the Soviet Union. Supporting Jordan seemed futile; abandoning it, impossible.

Conclusion

This chapter sought to explain, in part, factors that kept the Jordanian monarchy intact during a time when other monarchies toppled. The Iraqi crisis revealed the complexity of relationships in the Middle East and clarified Jordan's precarious position in the center of the region.[76] By the end of Eisenhower's term in office, in June 1960, the National Security Council acknowledged the importance of Hussein's role as a pro-Western voice in the Middle East.[77] An NSC paper stated there was "little choice but to continue support of Jordan lest without it the state collapse and the peace of the Near East be severely endangered in the ensuing scramble for Jordan's territory among Jordan's neighbors."[78] The crisis of 1958 forced American officials to recognize the repercussions of an end to the Hashemite monarchy.

Similarly, the Iraqi Revolution exposed the frailty of Iraq's monarchy as Hussein scrambled to maintain power in Amman. By couching threats to his monarchy in the language of the Cold War, Hussein attempted to bolster American support for his rule. As luck would have it, American officials felt the need to support the Hashemite regime as a buffer against future regional conflict.

Notes

1. For a more comprehensive look at this transition, see Clea Lutz Hupp, *The United States and Jordan: Middle East Diplomacy during the Cold War, 1948–1973* (London: I.B. Tauris, 2013).
2. Interview with Zaid Rifai, May 27, 2008, Amman, Jordan. Hussein ibn Talal, *Uneasy Lies the Head* (New York: Bernard Geis Associates, 1962), 35–41; Robert B. Satloff, *From Abdullah to Hussein: Jordan in Transition* (New York: Oxford University Press, 1994), 73–7.
3. Nigel Ashton, *Eisenhower, Macmillan and the Problem of Nasser* (London: Macmillan Press Ltd., 1196), 37–60.
4. Elie Podeh, *The Quest for Hegemony in the Arab World: The Struggle over the Baghdad Pact* (New York: E.J. Brill, 1995), 185–94; Joel Gordon, *Nasser's Blessed Movement: Egypt's Free Officers and the July Revolution* (New York: Oxford University Press, 1992), 170–4; Ashton, *Eisenhower, Macmillan and the Problem of Nasser*, 26–7.
5. Interview with Amjad Majali (son of Hazza Majali) May 27, 2008, Amman, Jordan; Telegram from Amman to the Foreign Office, December 10, 1955, Foreign Office File 371/115533, The National Archives (TNA), Kew, UK; Richard B. Parker, "The United States and King Hussein," in *The Middle East and the United States*, ed. D. Lesch (Boulder: Westview Press, 1996), 105.
6. Kamal Salibi, *The Modern History of Jordan* (New York: I.B. Tauris, 2006), 183–7.
7. Uriel Dann, *King Hussein and the Challenge of Arab Radicalism: Jordan, 1955–1967* (New York: Oxford University Press, 1989), 22–30.
8. Author Elie Podeh argued that Jordan played a pivotal role in the Baghdad Pact. After the debacle in Jordan, no other Arab leader felt free to join. Podeh, *The Quest for Hegemony in the Arab World*, 185–94.
9. Ibid.
10. Avi Shlaim, *Lion of Jordan: The Life of King Hussein in War and Peace* (London: Allen Lane, 2007), 100–5.
11. Ibid.
12. Record of the 279th meeting of the NSC, March 8, 1956, Papers of Dwight D. Eisenhower, NSC Series: 279th meeting, Dwight D. Eisenhower Library (DDEL), Abilene, USA.
13. Hazem Nuseibeh had a close relationship with King Hussein and claimed that the king was an Arab nationalist, albeit of a different type than Nasser. According to Nuseibeh, King Hussein did not like to use the term "refugee" because all Arabs should be at home in Jordan. In addition, some Jordanian officers credited the British with eliminating tribal rivalries within the army and establishing discipline. Interview with Hazem Nuseibeh, May 21, 2008, Amman, Jordan; Interview with Ahmed Yousef Al-Tal, May 20, 2008, Amman, Jordan.

14 For an in-depth look at the Suez Crisis, see *Re-assessing Suez 1956: New Perspectives on the Crisis and Its Aftermath*, ed. Simon Smith (New York: Ashgate, 2008).
15 Charles Johnston described the political rivalries within Hussein's government in a telegram to Selwyn Lloyd, March 20, 1957, AIR 812079/1051/136, TNA, Kew, UK.
16 Dann, *King Hussein and the Challenge of Arab Radicalism*, 55–60.
17 Hussein, *Uneasy Lies the Head*, 165–83.
18 Ibid.
19 Satloff, *From Abdullah to Hussein*, 166–9; Bonnie Saunders, *The United States and Arab Nationalism: The Syrian Case, 1953–1960* (Westport: Praeger, 1996), 58; Clinton Bailey, *Jordan's Palestinian Challenge, 1948–1983* (Boulder: Westview Press, 1984), 13.
20 Stephen Kinzer, *All the Shah's Men: An American Coup and the Roots of Middle East Terror* (Hoboken, NJ: John Wiley and Sons, 2003).
21 Interview with Fayez Tarawneh, May 17, 2008, Amman, Jordan; interview with Hazem Nuseibeh, May 21, 2008, Amman, Jordan. Adnan Abu Odeh, a Communist who later joined Hussein's government, agreed that there was a coup planned at the time. Interview with Adnan Abu Odeh, May 24, 2008, Amman, Jordan.
22 Report from Charles Johnston to the British Foreign Office, May 14, 1957, *Records of Jordan, 1919–1965 v.10*, ed. Jane Priestland (Chippenham, UK: Antony Rowe, Ltd., 1996).
23 Hugh Wilford, *America's Great Game: The CIA's Secret Arabists and the Shaping of the Modern Middle East* (New York, Basic Books, 2013), 266–7. Wilford indicated that Hussein's leniency to the plotters was evidence that the coup was not real, while many of Hussein's associates saw it as a sign of his adept handling of the opposition.
24 Telegram from Washington to Foreign Office, April 14, 1957, Foreign Office Files 371/127896, TNA, Kew, UK.
25 Dann, *King Hussein and the Challenge of Arab Radicalism*, 60–1.
26 Memorandum of discussion at the 320th meeting of the NSC, April 17, 1957, Ann Whitman file, NSC Series: 320th meeting of the NSC, DDEL, Abilene, USA.
27 Interview with Fayez Tawraneh, May 17, 2008, Amman, Jordan.
28 Letter from the British Embassy, Washington D.C. to R.M. Hadow, Foreign Office, October 13, 1958, Foreign Office Files 371/134021, TNA, Kew, UK.
29 Telephone call from Allen Dulles, April 26, 1957, Telephone call to Mr. Murphy, Papers of John Foster Dulles, Telephone Call Series: Memorandum of Telephone Conversations, White House, March 1957 to August 30, 1957, DDEL, Abilene, USA; for a detailed look at Eisenhower's goals in the Middle East, see Salim Yaqub, *Containing Arab Nationalism: The Eisenhower Doctrine and the Middle East* (Chapel Hill: University of North Carolina Press, 2004).
30 Letter from King Hussein to Dwight D. Eisenhower, May 12, 1957, Papers of Dwight D. Eisenhower, International Series: Jordan (4), DDEL, Abilene, USA.
31 Letter from Dwight Eisenhower to Harold Macmillan, April 28, 1957, Papers of Dwight D. Eisenhower, DDE Diary: April 1957, DDEL, Abilene, USA.
32 The $10 million was used to purchase 36 M-47 tanks, 40 British "Saracen" armored cars, 100 106mm recoilless anti-tank rifles, 18 155mm. US guns, transport vehicles, communications equipment and ammunition. In late 1958 the United States provided an additional $4.5 million for 12 British Hawker-Hunter jet fighter aircraft; letter from King Hussein to Dwight D. Eisenhower, May 12, 1957, Papers of Dwight D. Eisenhower, International Series: Jordan (4), DDEL, Abilene, USA.
33 Briefing Items, August 14, 1957, Papers of Dwight D. Eisenhower, DDE Diaries: August 1957, Memos on Appointments (2), DDEL, Abilene, USA.

34 Hussein, *Uneasy Lies the Head*, 184–5.
35 Letter from Dwight Eisenhower to Dr. Edward Elson, DDE Diaries Box 34, DDE Dictation, July 1958, DDEL, Abilene, USA.
36 Hussein, *Uneasy Lies the Head*, 184–5. Hussein lobbied King Saud to withhold recognition from the UAR: Hussein to Saud, February 7, 1958, Saudi Arabia File, Royal Hashemite Archives, Amman, Jordan.
37 Cable from Dwight D. Eisenhower to Nuri Said, June 12, 1958, Papers of Dwight D. Eisenhower, International File: Jordan(3), DDEL, Abilene, USA.
38 Ibid.
39 Letter from Dwight Eisenhower to Harold Macmillan, April 28, 1957, Papers of Dwight D. Eisenhower, DDE Diary: April 1957, DDEL; Letter from King Hussein to Dwight D. Eisenhower, May 12, 1957, Papers of Dwight D. Eisenhower, International Series: Jordan (4), DDEL; Briefing Items, August 14, 1957, Papers of Dwight D. Eisenhower, DDE Diaries: August 1957, Memos on Appointments (2), DDEL, Abilene, USA.
40 For more on the interplay of Hussein, Nasser, and Eisenhower, see Clea Lutz Bunch, "Supporting the Brave Young King: The Suez Crisis and Eisenhower's New Approach to Jordan, 1953–1958," in *Reassessing Suez*, ed. Simon Smith (New York: Ashgate, 2008).
41 MAP Sales to Saudi Arabia, another conservative regime, also increased dramatically during the same time period of the Eisenhower administration, from 1.5 million to 52 million. Financial Annex to Progress Report on the Near East, July 7, 1957, Disaster File: Near East (9) Box 64, DDEL, Abilene, USA.
42 Dann, *King Hussein and the Challenge of Arab Radicalism*, 88; Marion Farouk-Sluglett and Peter Sluglett, *Iraq since 1958: From Revolution to Dictatorship* (London: KPI Limited, 1987), 47–52; Said K. Aburish, *Saddam Hussein: The Politics of Revenge* (London: Bloomsbury, 2000), 38; and Jeffrey G. Karam, "Missing Revolution: The American Intelligence Failure in Iraq, 1958," *Intelligence and National Security* 32, no. 6 693–709.
43 For more details of the coup, see Juan Romero's chapter in this work. Telephone call from John Foster Dulles to Allen Dulles, July 14, 1958, Papers of John Foster Dulles, Telephone Call Series: Memorandum of Telephone Conversations, White House, April 1, 1958–August 1, 1958, DDEL, Abilene, USA.
44 Hussein, *Uneasy Lies the Head*, 193–5.
45 Ibid., 197.
46 Ibid., 198.
47 Dann, *King Hussein and the Challenge of Arab Radicalism*, 88.
48 Memorandum of Conference with the President, July 14, 1958, DDE Diary, Box 35, Staff Memos, July 1958(2), DDEL, Abilene, USA.
49 Burton Kaufman, *The Arab Middle East and the United States: Inter-Arab Rivalry and Superpower Diplomacy* (New York: Twayne Publishers, 1996), 27–30.
50 Memorandum of Conference with the President, July 14, 1958, DDE Diary, Box 35, Staff Memos, July 1958(2), DDEL, Abilene, USA.
51 Report of Telephone Call Between the President and Prime Minister Macmillan, July 14, 1958, DDE Diary Box 34, Telephone Calls—July 1958, DDEL, Abilene, USA.
52 Ibid.
53 Ibid.
54 Ibid.
55 Ibid.

56 Ibid.
57 Memorandum of Conversation: Foreign Secretary Lloyd's Visit, July 17, 1958, DDE Diary Box 35, Staff Memos July 1958(1), DDEL, Abilene, USA.
58 Synopsis—Intelligence and State Department Items Reported to the President, July 23, 1958, Papers of Dwight D. Eisenhower, DDE Diary: Goodpaster Briefings, July 1958, DDEL, Abilene, USA.
59 In reference to Jordan, Eisenhower later commented "Also, it is very questionable whether we should get into the position of supporting Kings against their people." Memorandum of Conference with the President, July 20, 1958, Papers of Dwight D. Eisenhower, DDE Diary: Staff Memos, July 1958(1), DDEL, Abilene, USA.
60 Telephone call from John Foster Dulles to the President, July 15, 1958, Papers of Dwight D. Eisenhower, DDE Diary: Telephone Calls-July 1958, DDEL; Memorandum of Conference with the President, July 16, 1958, Papers of Dwight D. Eisenhower, DDE Diary: Staff Memos, July 1958(2), DDEL; Telephone call to the President, July 19, 1958, Papers of John Foster Dulles, Telephone Call Series: Memorandum of Telephone Conversations, White House-April 1, 1958–August 1, 1958, DDEL, Abilene USA.
61 Memorandum of Conference with the President, July 20, 1958, Papers of Dwight D. Eisenhower, DDE Diary: Staff Memos, July 1958(1), DDEL, Abilene, USA.
62 Memorandum of Conference with the President, July 15, 1958, Papers of Dwight D. Eisenhower, DDE Diary: Staff Memos, July 1958(2), DDEL, Abilene, USA.
63 Ibid.
64 Ibid.
65 Ibid.
66 For a better understanding of Saudi leaders' political challenges in 1958, see Nathan Citino, Saudi Arabia in the Crucible of 1958 (full citation of this work).
67 Memorandum of Conference with the President, July 16, 1958, DDE Diary, Staff Memos 7/58(2), DDEL Library, Abilene, USA.
68 Memorandum of telephone conversation, July 16, 1958, Papers of John Foster Dulles, Telephone conversation Series: Memorandum of Telephone Conversations, General, June 2, 1958–July 31, 1958(3), DDEL, Abilene, USA.
69 Memorandum of Conference with the President, July 20, 1958, DDE Diary Box 35, Staff Memos July 1958(1), DDEL, Abilene, USA.
70 373rd Meeting of the National Security Council, July 24, 1958, Papers of Dwight D. Eisenhower, NSC Series, DDEL, Abilene, USA.
71 Ibid.
72 Memorandum of Conference with the President, July 23, 1958, DDE Diary Box 35: Staff Memos, July 1958 (1), DDEL, Abilene, USA.
73 Ibid.
74 Ibid.
75 Ibid.
76 Telephone Call to Mr. Berry, July 23, 1958, Papers of John Foster Dulles, Telephone Call Series Box 8: Memorandum of Telephone Conversations—General, June 2, 1958–July 31, 1958, DDEL, Abilene, USA.
77 NSC 6011, July 19, 1960, Disaster File: Near East (12), DDEL, Abilene, USA.
78 Ibid.

Chapter 15

REFLECTIONS AND CONCLUSIONS FROM THE REVOLUTIONARY YEAR OF 1958

Jeffrey G. Karam

The seminal events in 1958 ushered in new trajectories for states in the Middle East and North Africa, and ones outside the region. While the outcomes of different crises and developments differed, the previous chapters drew the linkages between major events to explain why and how some states weathered the revolutionary storm, while others could no longer evade calls for reform. All the authors analyzed sociopolitical developments in both studied and understudied cases by offering fresh interpretations of existing records to explain the connections between the local, regional, and global contexts of seminal developments as they unfolded at the time and in hindsight. Some of the chapters are breaking new ground, especially by shedding light on the experience of states outside the region that were affected by the revolutionary and transformative struggles in the Arab world and their wider repercussions.

Important Takeaways

The volume's theoretical and empirical findings suggest novel ways to analyze the experiences of different states, contribute new scholarship, and refine existing scholarly works. It is essential to highlight some key takeaways from different chapters. Each author provides an apt conclusion of their major findings, and I will now draw on three thematic highlights that cut across the volume.

The first centers on how both declining powers, especially Britain and France, and rising powers, mainly the United States, in the Middle East realized the dangers of vigorously opposing Arab revolutionary nationalism and other rising nationalist, anti-imperialist, and anti-colonial trends. This realization demonstrated the untenable foundations of the Anglo-French order in the Middle East after the Suez Crisis and War of 1956, and subsequently, the inability of the United States to create and sustain a new Western-led order in the region that would be supported by revolutionary states, particularly Egypt. Importantly, this compelled both rising and declining powers to readjust their strategies and policies in a "new" region that was undergoing decolonization, state formation, and development. However, this readjustment and realization was not only limited to Western powers. Egypt under Nasser soon realized the many inherent difficulties in achieving genuine Arab unity between different states.

In this context, Robert McNamara asserts that the revolutionary year of 1958 "significantly shifted British policy in the Middle East from an unrealistic policy of remaining, despite Suez, a significant actor in the regional struggles of the Arab Cold War (between the secular pan-Arabism of Nasser and the conservative pro-Western monarchies), and the Arab-Israeli conflict" (24). McNamara suggests that there is an implicit relationship between rapid decolonization in the global south and Britain's realization of its "new" status as a declining imperial power in the international system. Sofia Papastamkou concurs and equally argues that the revolutionary year of 1958 was an internally defining moment for France which brought about regime change and sparked a "painful process" of readjusting policy to self-recognize that it was a middle power in the international system rather than a colonial power. Papastamkou also demonstrates that France's declining status as an imperial power in the Middle East was clearly visible in the experience of decolonization in the *Maghreb* (in the West known as Northwest Africa), between 1955 and 1958.

In focusing on the United States, my chapter likewise contends that significant sociopolitical developments between the Suez Crisis of 1956 and specifically during the revolutionary year of 1958 "exposed the limits of the emerging US order and its restricted ability to use diplomacy, covert action, and economic assistance to achieve political goals" (47, 57). In fact, I argue that the revolutionary year of 1958 ushered in a new phase in US policy in the Middle East that centered on the use of coercion and military power, though dubbed at the time as "limited wars," to ensure favorable diplomatic outcomes. Elizabeth Bishop maintains the revolutionary year of 1958 and especially newfound and powerful transnational networks, such as the "Peace Partisans," a new nongovernmental organization, in different ways forced the USSR to adopt "new directions of Soviet policy in the Middle East" (73). Bishop asserts that these "new directions" became apparent with the support of "a series of Soviet-connected entities" and the role of Soviet diplomats in international organizations, such as the UN.

Drawing on the experience of Nasser and Egypt in 1958, Dina Rezk argues that the revolutionary year of 1958 and its aftermath of this revolutionary year "appeared to play out Nasser's private fears that neither Egypt nor his regional counterparts were ready for Arab unity in practice" (101). Despite the successful military-led revolution in Iraq, Rezk argues that Nasser failed to convince Qassim of the importance of a "pan-Arab union," and as a result, the Egyptian leader understood the limits of his state's power and influence in the region. In fact, Nasser was instead focused on maintaining Egyptian power and primacy above all else and was thus setting a limit on regional aspirations and goals.

The second thematic highlight centers on the varied and often limited sociopolitical opportunities that emerged during the revolutionary year of 1958, and consequently, how many political actors, especially in conservative regimes, sought assistance from foreign powers to quell opposition movements and stall significant change. The wider repercussions of the Suez Crisis and War of 1956, the failed Anglo-American attempts to deter Syria from titling closer to the Soviet Union, and the Egyptian-Syrian union in February 1958 reverberated across different states in the Middle East and North Africa. However, the direct effect of these significant sociopolitical developments played out differently across the region.

Against this background, Nathan Citino argues that the revolutionary year of 1958 "created potential but ultimately unrealized opportunities for political reform in Saudi Arabia" (87). Clearly, Citino asserts that Saudi rulers "successfully promoted modernization as a counter-revolutionary strategy with US support," and also utilized "Islamic institutions to counter" revolutionary nationalist currents, especially Nasser's ideological brand of pan-Arabism (88). John Ghazvinian likewise asserts that revolutionary year of 1958 did not spark "outward signs of upheaval that other regional states experienced" in Iran (135); however, the seeds of a closer relationship between the shah's regime and the United States "were in many respects sown in 1958" (135). In fact, the shah banked on US political and military support to shore up the regime and weather revolutionary currents for almost two decades after 1958.

Murat Kasapsaraçoglu likewise asserts that the revolutionary year of 1958, specifically the successful coup turned revolution in Iraq, forced the Turkish government to adopt harsher measures and "oppressive policies toward the opposition and the press" (113, 122). The shift in domestic strategy was focused on thwarting the possibility of a coup d'état; nonetheless and despite the heightened tension between the opposition and the ruling party, a group of Turkish officers staged a military coup on May 27, 1960. Similarly, in Jordan, Clea Hupp contends the Hashemite Kingdom of Jordan, and particularly Hussein, "scrambled to maintain power in Amman" after the successful coup turned revolution in Iraq swept the other Hashemite monarchy (200). Importantly, Hupp argues that Hussein couched threats to his monarchy "in the language of the Cold War" and thus, was successful in bolstering US support for his rule and the Hashemite regime as "a buffer against future regional conflict" (200). The increase in US aid to Jordan allowed the rulers to crack down on the opposition and quell any threats to the ruling regime.

The third important highlight underscores the varied success and positives of the revolutionary year of 1958 in various Arab and African states. The revolutionary current that swept across the Middle East and North Africa had both direct and indirect effects on the domestic politics of a handful of states at the time. It is vital to note that "varied success" and "positives" are couched in relative terms. Put differently, a reflection on positive developments in some states is in comparison to the experiences of others at the time, especially ones that were analyzed in the preceding chapters.

Juan Romero argues that "the partial dismantling of the monarchy's institutions and the fundamental change in policies under the new [Qassim and military-led] regime especially testify to the fact that the collapse of the monarchy was tantamount to a political and social revolution" (159). Importantly, Romero asserts that despite the trajectory of both positive and negative events after the coup on July 14, the revolution in 1958 "had global repercussions" and did in effect lead to the creation of the modern state in Iraq. In reflecting on Algeria in 1958, Sylvie Thénault demonstrates that beyond the Front de Libération Nationale's (FLN; National Liberation Front) internationalization strategy in the conduct of the revolutionary war of independence, 1958 was "a revolutionary year with strong institutional evolution" for both France and Algeria, which materialized in the form of the collapse of the Fourth Republic and the creation of the Provisional Government of the Algerian Republic (150). Thénault argues that this evolution occurred primarily between 1957 and 1959 and what is commonly known as the "Battle of Algiers" from the French perspective or more accurately, the "Great Repression of Algiers" from an Algerian standpoint.

In the Levant and specifically Lebanon, Caroline Attie asserts that the revolutionary year of 1958 "constituted a watershed in Lebanon's socioeconomic development" as it led to the election of President Fuad Chehab and sparked a transformational shift "from the politics of the *zuama* [traditional leaders] and their patronage networks" (187). Though Attie briefly highlights many of the positives that ensued under Chehab, including the shift from an overtly pro-Western foreign-policy orientation to one that advocated neutralism, she clearly emphasizes that "the sectarian structure of the political system remained unchanged and perpetuated an unstable sociopolitical order" that would benefit the traditional political elite and a new class of warlords and merchants (188). In neighboring Syria, Fadi Esber argues, the revolutionary year of 1958 and particularly the merger the creation of the United Arab Republic caused "drastic— and irreversible—changes in the nature of the country's body politic and economic organization were perhaps more revolutionary in their impact, and more long-lasting, than those that unfolded elsewhere in the Middle East" at the time (173). Esber suggests that the inability of "older" political factions to the recapture the state between 1961 and 1963 is rooted in the regime's (under the leadership of Nasser through the UAR) harsh repressive measures against the opposition that began in 1958 and continued afterward.

Future Avenues

The volume's theoretical and empirical findings suggest novel ways to analyze the experiences of different states, contribute new scholarship, and refine existing scholarly works. It is now important to reflect on how the present volume informs future avenues of research on the year 1958. I will highlight six important areas that deserve scholarly attention in future treatments.

The first area that deserves future scholarly attention is the impact of the revolutionary year of 1958 in Palestine and Israel.[1] In the Foreword, Salim Yaqub mentions that some of the book's chapters implicitly draw connections between significant junctures and the experiences of the Palestinian movement and Israel. However, it is vital, to the extent that records are declassified and available for a proper study, to examine and revisit the impact of the revolutionary year of

1958 on the trajectory of sociopolitical developments in Palestine, including the experience of the Palestinian Movement and different political factions, and Israel and their connections to states in the region and beyond.

The second area is the impact of the revolutionary year on Yemen, especially that it was an integral part of Egypt's foreign policy and a member state in the United Arab Republic.[2] A future examination of events in Yemen and the subsequent political competition turned proxy war between Saudi Arabia and Egypt deserve more attention and clearly have deep roots in important developments that occurred in the 1950s.

The third area will seek to study the role of China and the latter's diplomatic channels with various revolutionary, nationalist, and communist groups in the Arab world during the Cold War.[3] As a slowly emerging power during the Cold War, it is important to consider how the People's Republic of China interacted with various states and national movements during a period marked by both Cold War rivalry between the United States and the Soviet Union, and competition between different Arab and non-Arab states in the Middle East.[4]

The fourth possible area of exploration is the role of states in South Asia, including India and Pakistan, and some of the relationships between local groups and revolutionary and nationalist movements in the Middle East. Importantly, a focus on the broader connections between revolutionary struggles in the Middle East and Southeast Asia suggests how and why they shared similar concerns and the origins of such transformational events. Also, a focus on how many developing states in South America equally viewed their revolutionary struggles as part of a wider and international movement against colonialism, racism, and imperialism will undoubtedly highlight the many connections between the grievances of people living in different regions across the globe.

The fifth avenue of future research could examine the role of institutions and non-state actors in the 1950s and particularly in 1958.[5] While institutions such as the UN were limited in their ability to affect state behavior partly due to the nature of the international system, mainly bipolar rivalry between the United States and the Soviet Union, and the arms and space race between the two superpowers and the impact on their various allies, there are instances where institutions played an important role. Some of the functions of institutions in many states that were examined in this volume pertained to peacekeeping operations and developmental projects, and as a result, such a deep study could equally break new ground on the effectiveness of non-state actors during the Cold War and in the Middle East.

A sixth and final area for future exploration is the impact of revolutionary struggles and power alignments in the Middle East on states in the *Maghreb*, including primarily, but not exclusively, Tunisia, Libya, and Morocco. These North African states were certainly affected by the revolutionary war in Algeria and the rapid decline of France and Britain as imperial powers and the ascendancy of the United States and the Soviet Union in the Middle East. In parallel to an examination of North African states, a focus on the Horn of Africa, including Djibouti, Eritrea, Ethiopia, and Somalia, could equally broaden the scope of analysis and break new ground on the positive and negative repercussions of the events surrounding before, during, and after the revolutionary year of 1958.

All future avenues of research will widen the geographic scope of the volume and invite further scholarly investigation and discussion of connections between revolutionary movements within and beyond the Cold War. The preceding discussion of future research areas underscores the importance of events in the 1950s and the revolutionary year of 1958 in the Middle East and North Africa and its wider repercussions on and broader connections to other states outside the region. An initial assessment of where and how future scholarly works could build on this volume and break new ground will deepen the quality of scholarly conversations and by extension debunk and refute the exceptionalism that consistently characterizes sociopolitical developments in the Middle East and North Africa.

Lessons from the Past for Studying and Understanding the Contemporary Middle East

The chapters in the present volume suggest two important lenses for a contemporary understanding of sociopolitical developments in the Middle East and North Africa. The first relates to the pattern of relationships between local political actors in the region and foreign powers. While the geopolitical landscape changed after the end of the Cold War and has led to the decline and rise of powers in Europe and other regional theaters around the globe, successive administrations in the United States have leveraged their diplomatic and military power to shore up pro-Western and conservative regimes and monarchies in the region. Many of these regimes, including ones that have been analyzed and discussed in previous chapters, have been so far successful in insulating themselves from repeated calls for sociopolitical reform. Other regimes have been successful in receiving support from other powers in the system, such as the Russian Federation, to quell any opposition to the ruling regime. In other instances, many of the analyzed states in this present volume have experienced momentous changes in the aftermath of 1958, such as the consolidation of military-led authoritarian regimes or the resurgence of religion in politics, which has lingered for over sixty years. As the present volume suggests, the unresolved Arab-Israeli and Palestinian-Israeli conflicts, the active involvement of the Western and Eastern powers in several wars and domestic political crises across the Middle East, and the political bickering between Arab and non-Arab states over leadership in the region has deep roots in the transformational events that materialized in the mid-1950s and represented a climax of these trends in the revolutionary year of 1958.

The second relates to underscoring the agency of local political actors in the decisions that were taken after the revolutionary year of 1958. It is crystal clear that Arab and non-Arab officials have been extremely successful in banking on foreign support to contain any opposition to their regimes. However, the roots of this agency and the ability to "play off" Western and Eastern powers against one another in the region is directly connected to the period of decolonization, state formation, modernization, and rising authoritarianism in the 1950s. With the exception of a few states that witnessed varying degrees of success in the aftermath of the 2010–11 uprisings, many political regimes in the Middle East and North Africa have so far been able to stall any meaningful reform. As the recent protests in Iraq, Lebanon, Iran, and elsewhere across the globe demonstrate, the grievances and much of the demands that revolutionaries and protesters in the street are voicing have deep origins in the political and socioeconomic opportunities that failed to occur in the period of decolonization and state formation during the Cold War. In fact, they resemble similar struggles that many revolutionaries carried out during the twentieth century and into the twenty-first for better economic opportunities and social inclusion. Clearly, there is not a direct uninterrupted line between events in the 1950s and the ones that are presently unraveling in the Middle East and elsewhere across the globe. However, it is important to highlight the commonalities and the deep roots of political contestation and revolutionary struggle against injustice and tyranny, and the desired objective of reimagining and actively creating a better future.

The present volume strongly demonstrates that by inviting scholars and practitioners to widen the scope of their research and build broader connections between revolutionary movements across the world, this book, and future work that build on it, will join the rapidly growing ranks in academia that seek to refute the binaries, such as West versus East or capitalism versus communism, and simplified frames of reference that characterized the experiences of many states during the Cold War. Bipolar rivalry had an impact on the development and trajectory of many states in the global north and the global south. However, an accurate and inclusive examination of the experiences of various states needs to bring to the fore the voices and actions of different political actors and movements and their agency.

Only by drawing on multilingual sources, employing innovative methodologies that cut across disciplinary boundaries, and facilitating discussions between scholars and researchers in different corners of the globe, can one truly appreciate the complexity of state formation and revolutionary struggle. This book is a testament to the importance of bridging the many artificial boundaries that seek to constrain innovative scholarship in a world that should embrace much more diversity, inclusion, and tolerance.

Notes

1 For a discussion of the Palestinian National Movement see Yezid Sayigh, *Armed Struggle and the Search for State: The Palestinian National Movement, 1949–1993* (Oxford: Clarendon Press, 1997). For an overview of Israel in 1958 see Ilan Pappé, "The Junior Partner: Israel's Role in the 1958 Crisis," in *A Revolutionary Year: The Middle East in 1958*, ed. William Roger Louis and Roger Owen (London: Tauris,

2002); Avi Shlaim, "Israel, the Great Powers, and the Middle East Crisis of 1958," *The Journal of Imperial and Commonwealth History* 27, no. 2 (May 1, 1999): 177–92; D. Tal, "Seizing Opportunities: Israel and the 1958 Crisis in the Middle East," *Middle Eastern Studies* 37, no. 1 (January 2001): 142–58.

2 For a discussion of Yemen during the Cold War see Asher Orkaby, *Beyond the Arab Cold War: The International History of the Yemen Civil War, 1962–68* (New York: Oxford University Press, 2017); Saeed M. Badeeb, *The Saudi-Egyptian Conflict over North Yemen, 1962–1970* (New York: Routledge, 2019).

3 For an overview of some of these interactions see Muhamad S. Olimat, *China and the Middle East since World War II: A Bilateral Approach* (Lanham, MD: Lexington Books, 2014).

4 See Kyle Haddad-Fonda, "Revolutionary Allies: Sino-Egyptian and Sino-Algerian Relations in the Bandung Decade" (PhD Dissertation, University of Oxford, 2013) for a discussion of the relationship between China, Egypt, and Algeria in the 1950s and 1960s.

5 For a discussion of the United Nations and the United States in 1958 see Michael Fry, "The United Nations Confronts the United States in 1958," in *A Revolutionary Year*. For a brief discussion of the UN around important junctures see Amy L. Sayward, *The United Nations in International History* (London: Bloomsbury Publishing, 2017).

CONTRIBUTORS

Caroline Attie is Assistant Professor and Director of the Masters of International Relations Program at Dar al Hekma University, Jeddah, Saudi Arabia. She published a book based on archival research entitled *Struggle in the Levant: Lebanon in the 1950s* (2004).

Elizabeth Bishop is Associate Professor at Texas State University-San Marcos in the Department of History. Her research includes local and global aspects of the Cold War in the Arab world, including "American Atomic Policy and Hashemite Iraq" (2018), "'Atoms for Peace': Hashemite Iraq and the Baghdad Pact during the Cold War" (2017), "Golden Flies: Egypt's Pharaonic Past in Multiple Mirrors" (2017), and "'Dogs of Wall Street, Let Us Alone': Graffiti in Cold War Baghdad" (2016).

Nathan J. Citino is the Barbara Kirkland Chiles Professor of History at Rice University, Houston, Texas. He is the author of *From Arab Nationalism to OPEC: Eisenhower, King Sa'ud, and the Making of U.S.-Saudi Relations* (2002) and *Envisioning the Arab Future: Modernization in U.S.-Arab Relations, 1945-1967* (2017), which was awarded the Robert H. Ferrell Book Prize by the Society for Historians of American Foreign Relations.

Fadi Esber is a founding associate at the Damascus History Foundation. He is the managing editor of the upcoming *Dimashq Journal*, a Syria-based, peer-reviewed, interdisciplinary journal dedicated to studies on the history of Damascus. He is currently pursuing a PhD in International History at the London School of Economics and Political Science. His research interests focus on Syrian politics, economics, and society in the twentieth century. His article "The United States and the 1981 Lebanese Missile Crisis" was published in the *Middle East Journal* in 2016.

John Ghazvinian directs the Middle East Center at the University of Pennsylvania. He is the author of *Iran and America: A History* (forthcoming), and co-editor of *American and Muslim Worlds before 1900* (2020). He holds a doctorate in history from Oxford University.

Clea Hupp is the director of Leadership Volunteer Engagement at Syracuse University. Prior to her position at Syracuse, she served as Chair of the Department of History and Chair of Middle East Studies at the University of Arkansas in Little

Rock. Hupp is the author of *The United States and Jordan: Middle East Diplomacy during the Cold War* (2014), in addition to several book chapters and articles on US-Middle East diplomacy. Her work has been supported by several institutions, including the Society of Historians of American Foreign Relations, the American Center for Oriental Research, the Dwight D. Eisenhower Presidential Library, and other Presidential Libraries in the United States.

Jeffrey G. Karam is Assistant Professor of Political Science at the Lebanese American University, Lebanon. He is also an associate at the *Middle East Initiative* at Harvard University's Belfer Center for Science and International Affairs and Visiting Assistant Professor of International Relations at Harvard University's Summer School. He is the author of several articles, book chapters, and policy briefs on US intelligence and foreign policy in the Middle East. He is the recipient of the *Christopher Andrew–Michael Handel Prize* for the best article in *Intelligence and National Security* during 2017. His award-winning article is titled "Missing Revolution: The American Intelligence Failure in Iraq, 1958."

Murat Kasapsaraçoğlu is Assistant Professor in the Department of Political Science and International Relations at Antalya Bilim University, Turkey. His research interests are political history, diplomatic history, Cold War history, Middle East politics, Turkish foreign policy, and Turkish politics. He has several publications on Turkish foreign policy, political history, and diplomatic history, such as *Harmonization of Turkey's Political, Economic and Military Interests in the 1950s: Reflections on Turkey's Middle East Policy* (2015).

Robert McNamara is Senior Lecturer at Ulster University, Ireland. He is a graduate of the National University of Ireland, and has held research and teaching positions at University College Cork and Maynooth University. He is the author of a number of books on the end of empire in the Middle East and Southern Africa, including *Britain, Nasser and the Balance of Power in the Middle East* (2003) and with Filipe de Meneses, *The White Redoubt, the Great Powers and the Struggle for Southern Africa, 1960-1980* (2018).

Sofia Papastamkou is Research Engineer in the French National Centre for Scientific Research (CNRS) in the Institut de recherches historiques du Septentrion at the University of Lille, France. Her research focuses on the history of international relations in the Middle East and in the Mediterranean, and on digital history. She is also an editor for the *Programming Historian* journal. Her most recent publication is *Twitter, l'événement du temps présent et l'historien-moissonneur: quelques pistes pour interroger le référendum grec de 2015* (2019).

Dina Rezk is Associate Professor in Modern Middle Eastern History and Politics at the University of Reading, UK. She is currently researching popular culture and politics in Egypt since the overthrow of Mubarak, funded by the AHRC. She has also been funded as a "Rising Star" by the British Academy (2017–19) and was selected by the AHRC/BBC to be a "New Generation Thinker" in 2019. She has published in *Security Dialogue*, *International History Review*, and *Intelligence and National Security*. Her most recent book is *The Arab World and Western Intelligence: Analysing the Middle East 1958-1981* (2017).

Juan Romero is Associate Professor at Western Kentucky University, USA, in the Department of History. His research interests focus on Middle East social and political history. His first book is *The Iraqi Revolution of 1958: A Revolutionary Quest for Unity and Security* (2011). He has published on Arab nationalism and decolonization. His most recent book manuscript on transnational and transcultural terrorism is currently under review. He is presently working on a book-length project on the Lebanese Civil War of 1958.

Sylvie Thénault is Research Director at the French National Centre for Scientific Research (CNRS in French) in the Centre d'Histoire Sociale des mondes contemporains (CHS, Paris). She specializes in law and justice during the Algerian War of Independence, and has extended her research to the full colonial period. She has written or co-edited many books on the topic, notably *Histoire de l'Algérie à la période coloniale* (The History of Colonial Algeria) (2012/2014). Her last book was co-edited with Magalie Besse in 2019: *Réparer l'injustice : la disparition de Maurice Audin* (Redress the injustice: The Disappearance of Maurice Audin).

Salim Yaqub is Professor of History at the University of California, Santa Barbara, USA, and Director of UCSB's Center for Cold War Studies and International History. He is the author of two books, *Containing Arab Nationalism: The Eisenhower Doctrine and the Middle East* (2004) and *Imperfect Strangers: Americans, Arabs, and U.S.–Middle East Relations in the 1970s* (2016), and of several articles and book chapters on US foreign relations, the international politics of the Middle East, and Arab American political activism. He is now writing a post-1945 history of the United States.

INDEX

Note: Page numbers followed by "n" refer to notes.

Abadan Institute of Technology 131
Abbas, Abdul Majid 71, 72
Abbas, Ferhat 149
'Abd al-Karim, Ahmad 166
Abdullah, Amer 69
Abu Nuwar, Ali 194, 195
Aflaq, Michel 101, 168, 170, 173
Afro-Asian People's Solidarity
    Organization 72, 73
Ahmed, Hocine Aït 142, 148
'Ala,' Husayn 130
Algeria 6, 34, 38, 42, 51, 85, 96, 208
    Armée de Libération Nationale
      (ALN; National Liberation
      Army) 144, 148
    Challe Plan 148, 149
    Comité de Salut Public (Public Safety
      Committee) 145
    Comité Français de Libération
      Nationale (CFLN; French
      Committee of National
      Liberation) 146
    fraternization 145–6
    Front de libération nationale (FLN;
      National Liberation Front) 32,
      41, 141–5, 147–50, 207
    Gouvernement Provisoire de la
      République Française (GPRF;
      Provisional Government of the
      French Republic) 146, 149
    Mouvement National Algérien
      (MNA; Algerian National
      Movement) 149
    Parti du Peuple Algérien (PPA;
      Algerian People's Party) 148
    Organisation Spéciale (OS; Special
      Organization) 148
    War of Independence 3, 7, 9, 32, 35,
      37, 39–41, 106, 141–52
    bombardment of Sakiet-Sidi-
      Youssef village 142, 143
    de Gaulle and 146–9
    delayed impact of 1958 148–9
    internationalization of 142–4
    power struggle on status
      of combatants and
      prisoners 144–6
Ali Zade, Shaykh al-Islām 65–6
alliances 4, 15, 21, 34, 37, 40, 48, 53, 65,
    73, 81, 86, 92, 114, 118, 125, 128,
    130–5, 142, 148, 154, 180, 183,
    186, 187
ALN. *See* Armée de Libération Nationale
    (National Liberation Army)
Amer, Abdel Hakim 93, 94–5, 100
American Library, Tehran 129
American University of Beirut (AUB) 3,
    10 n.4, 183
    Arab nationalist movement at 180
Amery, Julian 15, 23
Amini, 'Ali 132–3
Amir, 'Abd al-Hakim 172
Anglo-American Syrian Working Group
    "containment plus" 17, 19
    "Elimination of Key Figures" 16
    "Preferred Plan" 18, 28 n.30
Anglo-French–Israeli Suez intervention,
    failure of 13, 155
Anglo-Iraqi Treaty of January 1948 68
Anglo-Jordanian Treaty 194
Al-Ani, Youssef 69
anti-imperialism 1, 6, 126, 159
anti-Zionism 114
Arab Bank of Riyadh 83
Arab Cold War 2–4, 13, 24–5, 26 n.9, 33,
    41, 42, 47, 50, 58, 93, 99–100,
    125, 134, 153, 168, 169, 184,
    187, 200, 205, 208–10

Arabian American Oil Company
    (Aramco)   79, 81, 82, 84
Arab-Israeli War (1948)   93, 167–8
Arab nationalism   14, 15, 18, 22–4, 26
    n.9, 41, 47, 81, 82, 86, 92, 93, 95,
    97–9, 178, 179, 183, 184, 188,
    197, 199
  domino effect of   113–24
  revolutionary   53, 54, 79, 81, 88
Arab Union   29 n.48, 54, 72, 83, 101, 155,
    158, 162 n.32, 196, 197, 205
  Article 51   71
  Iraqi-Jordanian Arab Union   155
  opposition to UAR   18–19
Arab unity   1, 14, 16, 23, 54, 71, 83, 93–6,
    98, 99, 101, 170, 171, 205
Arab uprising   1
Aragon, Louis   71
archival sources and archives   2, 4–6, 13,
    28 n.30, 68, 70, 133, 167, 189
    n.16, 189 n.19
Arif, Abd al-Salam   98
Armed struggle and war   3, 5, 23, 50,
    127, 144, 148, 157
Al-As'ad, Ahmad   182
Al Asad, Hafez   101, 173, 174
al-'Asali, Sabri   169–71
ascendancy   3, 6, 8, 208
al Assad, Kamel   181
Atlantic Alliance   37
AUB. *See* American University of Beirut
authoritarianism   5, 7, 125, 126, 130–5,
    210
Azerbaijan   65–6, 68, 70, 73
al-'Azm, Khalid   168–72, 175 n.25

Badis, Abdelhamid Ben   149
Baghdad Pact   13, 18, 33, 34, 49, 50, 70,
    73, 81, 96, 111 n.35, 116, 120,
    125, 128, 154, 155
  collapse of   119
  crisis   193–4
  formation of   113
  impact on Turkey   114–15
  Iraq's withdrawal from   158
Bakdash, Khalid   17, 168, 172
Bandung Conference (1955)   41
Barzani, Mullah Mustafa   117
"Battle of Algiers" (Meynier)   150

Bayar, Celal   118
Bedjaoui, Mohamed   149
Beeley, Sir Harold   96, 142, 144
Bella, Ben   96, 142, 148
Bevan, Aneurin   13
al-Bitar, Salah al-Din   96, 168, 170, 173
al-Bizri, Afif   16–17, 97, 169, 176 n.49
Borejsza, Jerzy   67
Boudiaf, Mohammed   142
Bourguiba, Habib   32, 40, 142, 143
Branche, Raphaëlle   145
Breed, Florence   133
Britain   3, 6–8, 33, 35, 38, 41, 46 n.65, 48,
    53, 81, 92, 129, 152, 158, 166,
    167, 183
  and Baghdad Pact   111 n.35, 193, 194
  British Foreign Office   23
  Cabinet committee system   27 n.14
  Central Intelligence Agency
    (CIA)   16, 52, 56, 83, 93, 97,
    99, 100, 116, 127, 129, 169, 189
    n.19, 191 n.43, 191 n.44, 195,
    197
  and Egypt, relation between   13
  foreign currency reserves   14
  Joint Intelligence Committee
    (JIC)   15, 20, 21, 25 n.1, 96
  Labor Party   13
  Operation Straggle   16
  revolutionary year of 1958 (*see* British
    policy, impact of revolutionary
    year of 1958 on)
  Secret Intelligence Service (SIS)   16
British policy, impact of revolutionary
    year of 1958 on   13–31
  Anglo-French–Israeli Suez
    intervention, failure of   13
  Arab Union opposition to UAR   18–
    19
  financial negotiations with Egypt   15
  hawks and doves   22–4
  Iraqi Revolution   20–2
  Lebanon crisis   19–20
  phases of relationship with Egypt   13
  pro-British Iraqi regime, collapse
    of   14
  Suez Crisis   13–15
  Syrian crisis   16–17
Brook, Norman   15, 23, 27 n.14

Bulgaria 72, 73
Bull, John 70
Al Bustani, Abdullah Ismail 69

Cabinet Committee on the Middle East 22
Caccia, Harold 19–20
Cento 128
Challe Plan 148, 149
Chamoun, Camille 19–21, 23, 30 n.59, 52, 55, 118, 178–87, 188 n.5, 189 n.14, 189 n.16, 190 n.36, 192 n.69, 197, 198
   "fata al uruba al aghar" (the preeminent youth of Arabism) 180
   foreign policy 183, 186
   Frangieh's opposition to 180
   and Lebanon crisis 34–5, 36
   military operation in the Middle East 37, 38
   1957 election 179–82
   political ability 178
Chehab, Fuad 20, 36–8, 178, 185, 187, 207
   Chehabism 178, 179, 187, 188
chief of the imperial general staff (CIGS) 15, 23
China 51, 92, 208
CIGS. *See* chief of the imperial general staff
civil war 97, 118, 198
   Lebanon 1, 9, 37, 55, 64 n.83, 158, 178–92
   Yemeni 24, 100
Clapp, Gordon 131, 132
Cold War 2–4, 13, 24–5, 26 n.9, 33, 41, 42, 47, 50, 58, 93, 99–100, 125, 134, 153, 168, 169, 184, 187, 200, 205, 208–10
communism 4, 14, 28 n.28, 67, 99, 113–15, 117, 155, 182–4, 189 n.16, 189 n.16, 198, 210
   anti-communism 121, 190 n.36
   International Communism 50, 51, 54, 55, 82, 100, 191 n.43
conservative regimes and monarchies 8, 14, 25, 47, 49, 57, 202 n.41, 205, 209

coups and coup d'états 1, 3, 5, 8, 9, 17, 19, 21, 22, 24, 27 n.13, 27 n.19, 34, 39, 47–8, 51–4, 56, 58, 65, 66, 71–3, 81, 86, 93, 98, 101, 103, 117–19, 121, 122, 126–9, 131, 136 n.11, 149, 153, 156–8, 163 n.51, 168–73, 193–8, 201 n.21, 201 n.23, 202 n.43, 206
covert operations and intelligence 16, 18, 21, 24, 27 n.13, 47, 49, 51–7, 82, 93, 205

decline 8, 13, 208, 209
declining and falling empires 3, 6–8, 22, 48, 58 n.2, 120, 144, 204, 205, 208, 209
decolonization and decolonized 1, 5, 6, 25, 32–4, 38, 41, 69, 204, 205, 210
de Gaulle, Charles 35, 37, 42, 145, 150
   and Algerian War of Independence 141, 146–9
   and Lebanon crisis 32, 34, 36, 38–40
   receptiveness to the Soviet proposal 41
de Murville, Maurice Couve 37
de Sébilleau, Pierre 35, 36
De Zulueta, Philip 23
Dikerdem, Mahmut 118
domestic politics 8, 69, 94–5, 113, 118–22, 178, 206
domino effect of Arab nationalism 113–24
Duce, James Terry 86
Dujaili, Kazem 69
Dulles, Allen 195
Dulles, John Foster 14, 26 n.8, 38, 83, 116, 186, 195, 197–9
   and Arab Union opposition to UAR 18, 19
   and Baghdad Pact 128
   and Lebanon crisis 19, 36, 40
   meeting with Eisenhower 108
   and regional politics 97–8
   and Syrian crisis 16, 17
   visit to Tehran 133

East Germany 72, 73
Eden, Anthony 14

Egypt   3, 6, 8, 13–15, 17, 20, 23, 32–4, 37, 39, 42, 47–53, 59 n.5, 66, 81–3, 86, 113–15, 142–4, 154, 155, 160 n.6, 166–73, 16 n.49, 180, 183, 184, 187, 191 n.41, 192 n.62, 193, 194, 196, 204, 205, 208
   Arab Solidarity Pact   15
   Aswan Dam project   50, 94
   and Britain, relation between   13
   revolutionary year of 1958 for   92–112
      Cold War politics   99–100
      domestic politics   94–5
      regional politics   95–9
   Suez Canal Company, nationalization of   1
   and Syria, union between   1
   Voice of the Arabs   73 (*see also Sawt el Arab* (Voice of the Arabs))
Eisenhower, Dwight D.   15, 27 n.13, 49, 50, 52, 55, 56, 83, 116, 118, 129, 134, 182, 196, 198
   Eisenhower Doctrine   15, 34, 57, 82, 84, 117, 125, 128, 181–4, 191 n.43
      foundation of   48–50
      policy in practice   50–1
      testing the limits and new US orders, 51–6
   and Iraqi revolution   21
   and Lebanon crisis   20
   and March 1958 crisis   82
   meeting with Dulles   108
   meeting with Nasser   107
   and Syrian crisis   16, 17
Europe, map of   102

Faisal II, King   66, 97, 104, 156
Faysal, Crown Prince   79, 83, 88, 156
   and March 1958 crisis   80, 82
   and modernization in Saudi Arabia   86, 87
Federation of Arab Trade Unions   82
France   3, 4, 6–8, 21, 26 n.4, 42, 46 n.65, 68, 69, 81, 114, 131, 141–7, 149, 166–8, 173, 183, 204, 205, 207, 208
   Communist Party   66
   Fourth Republic   3, 32, 34, 141, 43, 144, 146, 147, 150, 207
   in the Middle East, revolutionary year of 1958 for   32–46
      Lebanon crisis   34–7
      military operation   37–9
      normalization   39–41
      position up to 1958   33–4
Frangieh, Hamid   180–2
fraternization   145–6
Front for the Liberation of the Arabian Peninsula   84
Front of National Reforms   84

Gaillard, Félix   32, 144
Gallman, Waldemar   157
Geneva Conventions on the Laws of War (1949)   41, 145
Global South   13, 25, 205, 210
Glubb, John   194
"Good Offices Mission"   32
grand strategy   47, 52
Gülek, Kasım   121

Hadj, Messali   148
Hafez, Abdel Halim   94
Al-Hafiz, Safa   69
Hamade, Sabri   182
Hamdun, Mustafa   169, 171
Hammarskjold, Dag   20, 22, 36, 37, 72, 186
Hanna, George   69
Hare, Raymond   98–9
Harlem Globetrotters   131
Harnwell, Gaylord   131
Hasanli, Jamal   68
al-Hawrani, Akram   170–3
Haykal, Muhammad Hasanayn   97
Heikal, H. M.   98
Hibri, Khalil   181
Home, Lord   15
Horn of Africa and selection of African countries   208–9
Huda, Tawfiq Abul   193
Hussein bin Talal of Jordan, King   15, 19, 21, 22, 51, 52, 56, 84, 86, 107, 118, 158, 193–7, 200 n.13
Hussein Oueini   181, 184
Hussein, Taha   66
al Huss, Fawzi   181

Ibtihaj, Abu-l-Hasan 132
ICP. *See* Iraqi Communist Party
ICRC. *See* International Committee of the Red Cross
Illah, Abdul 66
imperialism and imperial 1, 5, 6, 13, 19, 24, 39, 47, 59, 57, 70, 85, 92, 93, 95, 100, 101, 111 n.35, 127, 129, 194, 205, 208
İnönüm, İsmet 119
interdisciplinary and multidisciplinary 1–10
International Committee of the Red Cross (ICRC) 145
internationalization 7, 34, 41, 141–4, 150, 207
internationalism 1
International Monetary Fund 82
Iqbal, Manuchihr 130, 131
Iran 3, 6–8, 16, 48, 51, 66–70, 114, 117, 118, 125–37, 193, 195, 206, 210
  educational reform 131
  Fulbright program 131
  Khuzestan dam project 132
  Mardum (People's Party) 130
  Milliyun (Nation Party) 130
  modern middle class 127
  relations with US 130–5
  in 1950s 127–30
Iranian Information Center, Washington 132–3
Iraq 1, 3, 6–8, 14–25, 38, 42, 47, 48, 51, 54, 56–8, 65–7, 70–3, 79, 81–4, 86, 87, 96–8, 100, 101, 107, 108, 113–22, 125, 133, 153–9, 163 n.51, 186, 193, 196, 197, 206, 207, 210
  British influence, maintenance of 15
  Iraqi Fertile Crescent project 154
  Law no. 51, 1938 penal code 67
  Revolution of 1958 153–65
    British policy and 20–2
    Free Officers 7, 47–8, 54, 56, 58, 81, 86, 96, 155–7
    ills of monarchic society 153–5
    international repercussions 158–9
    military's role 156–8
    Sovereignty Council 157

Supreme Committee of the Free Officers 155, 159 n.1
Turkish perception of 116–17
United National Front 156
Iraqi Communist Party (ICP) 98, 100
Islamic University of Medina (IUM) 87
island of stability 125–37
Ismail, Yusuf 67
Israel 14, 21–2, 37, 48, 49, 51, 81, 96, 114, 183, 184, 194, 196, 199, 205, 207–9
  access to the Gulf of Aqaba 82
  Ben-Gurion, David 158
  Anglo-French–Israeli Suez Crisis 13, 155
  Arab-Israeli War (1948) 93, 155, 167–8
  French–Israeli ties 34, 35, 39, 42
IUM. *See* Islamic University of Medina
I. V. Kurchatov Institute of Atomic Energy 71

Jadid, Salah 173
Jaudat, Ali 17
Jawad, Hisham 72
al-Jawad, Khalil Jameel 69
al-Jisr, Nadim 183
Johnson, Lyndon 58
Johnston, Charles 15, 195
Jordan 1, 3, 6, 8, 9, 14–19, 21–3, 37–40, 47, 48, 51–4, 56, 57, 67, 71, 73, 81–3, 86, 96, 97, 100, 107, 109, 117–21, 128, 154–6, 158, 162 n.32, 203 n.59, 206
  domestic crisis in 51
  exit from Arab Solidarity Pact 15
  military intervention in 19
  revolutionary year of 1958 for 193–203
    Baghdad Pact crisis 193–4
    coup and counter-coup 194–6
    last Hashemite Kingdom 197–9
    new political landscape 196
  Sawt Al-Arab (Voice of the Arabs) 194
  Turkish perception of 117–18
Jordan, Samuel 128
al-Jumayri, Sultan 86
Junblat, Kamal 181, 182, 185

Index

al-Jundi, 'Abd al-Karim   173

Karami, Rashid   181–4
Kennedy, John F.   86–7, 134, 143
Khalid, Umm   83
Khan, 'Aliquli   133
Khider, Mohammed   142
Khrushchev, N. S.   41, 65, 72, 73, 100
al-Khuri, Bechara   36, 180, 181, 184
Kuwait, protection of oil
　　resources in   15

Lacheraf, Mostefa   142
Lebanon   3, 6, 8, 15, 33, 38–40, 42, 47,
　　48, 51–8, 66, 69, 71, 81, 83, 86,
　　87, 96, 97, 105, 116, 119–21,
　　125, 167, 193, 197–9, 207, 210
　　Central Bank   179
　　Civil Service Board   179
　　crisis of 1958   1, 9, 37, 55, 64 n.83,
　　　　158, 178–92
　　　　British policies and   19–23
　　　　foreign policy   183–6
　　　　France policies and   34–7
　　　　socioeconomic grievances   182–3
　　　　Turkish perception of   117–18
　　　　US intervention in   37, 158
　　Department of Tourism   182
　　Moslem Lebanon Today   182
　　Mu'tamar al Hay't al Islamiyya al Da'im
　　　　(Permanent Commission of
　　　　Islamic Associations)   182
　　National Museum   182–3
　　National Pact   178, 179, 181, 184
　　1957 elections   179–82
　　Social Insurance   179
Lilienthal, David   131, 132
limited wars   48, 58, 59 n.3, 64 n.81, 192
　　n.64, 205
Lloyd, Selwyn   13, 15, 22–3
　　and Arab Union opposition to
　　　　UAR   18
　　and Iraqi revolution   22
　　and Lebanon crisis   20, 37
　　and Syrian crisis   17
Lodge, Henry Cabot   20

McClintock, Robert   37, 186
al-Machnouk, 'Abdullah   84

Macmillan, Harold   13–15, 23, 26 n.8, 27
　　n.13, 41
　　and Arab Union opposition to
　　　　UAR   18–19
　　and Eisenhower Doctrine   50
　　and Iraqi revolution   21, 22
　　and Lebanon crisis   20, 37, 40, 195–8
　　and Syrian crisis   16, 17
Mahmood, Abdulwahab   69
Majali, Hazza   194
Majdalani, Nasim   181
Makassed Charitable Society   184
Malik, Charles   183–4, 186, 187
Mansfield, Mike   50
　　Mansfield Amendment   55
Martha Graham Dance Company   131
Marwa, Hussein   67
al-Mashati, Sheikh Abdul Karim   69
Massu, General Jacques   37
al-Matni, Nassib   34, 55, 185
Menderes, Adnan   116–17
Mendès, Pierre   33
Meouchi, Boulos   179, 181
methodology and methodologies   2, 4,
　　5, 210
Meynier, Gilbert   150
Middle East, map of   102
Middleton, George   15, 20, 37
Mikoyan, Anastas   71
military intervention and operation   1,
　　3, 5, 7–9, 14, 16, 17, 19–23,
　　32–40, 47–53, 55, 56, 58, 65, 69,
　　79, 81–6, 93–7, 101, 113–22,
　　123 n.16, 123 n.20, 125–7, 133,
　　134, 142, 144, 146, 148, 153–9,
　　166–71, 173, 184, 186, 187, 189
　　n.16, 196–9, 205, 206, 209
al-Mir, Ahmad   173
Mohammed, Jassim   67
Mollet, Guy   36
monarchism and monarchy   1, 7, 14, 16,
　　22, 25, 39, 51, 52, 54, 56, 57, 73,
　　79, 81, 82, 84, 86, 88, 97, 125,
　　127, 131, 133, 153–9, 160 n.6,
　　193, 198–200, 205, 206, 209
Mosaddegh, Muhammad   66, 127–9
Mountbatten, Louis   15
Mu'ammar, 'Abd al-'Aziz ibn   82, 86, 87
multilingual sources, merits of   4–5

Munir, Tawfiq   69
Murphy, Robert   142, 144
Muslim World League   87

Nabulsi, Suleiman   51, 194, 195
Nahda (Renaissance)   1
Nasr, Salah   94
al-Nasser, Gamal Abdel   13–25, 27 n.13,
    28 n.28, 36, 37, 40, 46 n.65, 49–
    51, 53–5, 57, 79–88, 92–101, 110
    n.8, 113–17, 120, 121, 142–4,
    154, 158, 160 n.6, 162 n.31, 166,
    169–73, 176 n.49, 177 n.55, 179,
    180, 182–8, 190 n.32, 190 n.37,
    191 n.44, 192 n.62, 194–9, 207
  anti-Communist imperatives   100
  and Arab nationalism   18, 23, 81, 88,
    93, 95, 97, 98, 114, 117, 178, 184
  and Arab socialism   125, 126
  and Cold War politics   99–100
  and domestic politics   94, 95
  intervention in Yemen's Civil War   24
  and Iraqi revolution   20, 21
  leadership of Arab nationalism   23
  and Lebanon crisis   20
  meeting with al-Sarraj   103
  meeting with Eisenhower   107
  Nasserism   14, 23, 85, 87, 184, 187,
    190–1 n.38
  pan-Arabism   14, 24–5, 34, 35, 42, 93,
    98, 194, 205, 206
  positive neutralism   92
  and regional politics   95–9
  rule, Turkey under   115–16
  and Syrian Revolution   16, 17, 169,
    172
  and United Arab Republic   53, 83,
    115–16, 170–1
  visit to Damascus   104
  visit to Dammam   81
NATO. *See* North Atlantic Treaty
    Organization
North Africa, map of   102
North Atlantic Treaty Organization
    (NATO)   37, 40, 68, 69, 71, 93
North Korea   72
North Vietnam   72
al-Nur, 'Abd al-Muhsin Abu   169
Nuseibeh, Hazem   195, 200 n.13

Nuwar, Ali Abu   51

oil   1, 14, 15, 18, 24, 25, 47–9, 54, 55, 57,
    65, 79–81, 83, 84, 93, 96, 128,
    144, 153, 154, 158, 159, 186,
    187, 198, 199
Onassis, Aristotle   81
Operation Ajax   127, 135
Operation Straggle   16
Operation Wappen   16, 93
Order of Lenin for the "Hero Cities"   66
Organization of the Islamic
    Conference   87
Oueini, Hussein   181, 184
Our Town (Wilder)   131

Palestine and Palestinian National
    Movement   49, 85, 155, 168,
    184, 207, 208
pan-Arabism   14, 24–5, 34, 35, 42, 93, 98,
    194, 205, 206
Pasha, 'Azzam   86
Peace Partisans, "revolutionary year"
    among   70–1, 205
Pflimlin, Pierre   145
Pharaon, Henri   181
Philosophy of the Revolution (Nasser)   95
Point Four agreement   132, 183
postcolonial and postcolonialism   1–3,
    6, 33, 42
postwar petroleum order   80
"Preparatory Committee for Supporters of
    Peace"   69
protests   1, 69, 84, 85, 127, 141, 145, 179,
    183, 210

Al-Qaisi, Khaleda   69
Qandil, Mohammad   94
Qassim, 'Abdul Karīm   xii, xiii, 205, 206
  anti-union policies   156
  authoritarian leanings   157
  and Iraqi Revolution   97, 98, 100,
    117, 153
al-Quwatli, Shukri   93, 98, 99, 155,
    168–72

radical change   7
Radio Bagdad   71
Radio Moscow   67, 69, 71, 72

Rajab, Jassim Mohammed 67
reform 3, 5, 7, 58 n.2, 80, 94, 100, 134, 188, 204, 210
   administrative 146, 147, 179, 180
   constitutional 82
   educational 131
   economic 34
   institutional 180
   labor 84
   land 184
   political 79, 84–7, 206
   sociopolitical 209
regional politics 95–9, 114, 171
Republicanism and Republican 7, 56, 68, 113, 125, 130, 149, 157
revisionist and revisionism 47–64, 87
revolutionary Arab nationalism 53, 54, 79, 81, 88
revolutionary nationalism 1, 53, 79, 81, 82, 204
revolutionary struggles 2, 6–8, 208, 210
revolutionary year of 1958
   Algeria 141–52
   Britain 13–31
   Egypt 92–112
   France 32–46
   future avenues 207–9
   Iran 125–37
   Iraq 153–65
   Jordan 193–203
   Lebanon 178–92
   Saudi Arabia 79–91
   shift in political strategy and policy reassessment 7
   sociopolitical developments, contemporary understanding of 7, 209–10
   Soviet Union 65–76
   Syria 166–77
   takeaways 204–7
   transformative and critical events 7–8
   Turkey 113–24
   United States 47–64
Reza Shah, Muhammad 134
Riad, Mahmud 169
Richard, James 184
Rifa'i, Abdul Wahab 185

rising powers and empires 3, 7, 8, 47, 49, 57, 58 n.2, 115, 130, 167, 188, 204, 209
Roché, Louis 35
Rountree, William 23

Sadat, Anwar al 94
al-Sa'id, Nasser 82, 87
   Risala ila Su'ud min Nasser al-Sa'id (Letter to Saud from Nasser al-Sa'id) 84, 85
al-Said, Nuri 18–19, 20, 56, 66, 114, 154, 196
al-Salam, Khalid 67, 181, 182
Salam, Saeb 181, 183
Salan, General Raoul 37, 145
Salih, Allahyar 128
al-Samawi, Kazem 69
Sandys, Duncan 15
   and Syrian crisis 17
al-Sarraj, Abdel al-Hamid 16, 83, 103, 166, 168–72
Saudi Arabia 3, 6, 8, 14, 17, 51, 54, 143, 158, 186, 198, 199, 202 n.41, 203 n.66, 206, 208
   "Anglo-Hashemite encirclement" of 81
   dissidents 79, 80, 84, 85
   exit from Arab Solidarity Pact 15
   in the Middle East, revolutionary year of 1958 for 79–91
   fire beneath the ashes 83–6
   March crisis 80–2
   modernization 86–7
   National Council 86
Saud, 'Abd al-'Aziz ibn 79
   death of 81, 82
Saud, King, son of 'Abd al-'Aziz ibn Saud 17, 79, 82, 83, 182
   and March 1958 crisis 80–1
   and modernization in Saudi Arabia 86, 87
SAVAK 130, 133
Sawt el Arab (Voice of the Arabs) 96
Al-Sayyab, Bader Shaker 69
SCDP. *See* Soviet Committee for the Defense of Peace
sectarian and sectarianism and religion 55, 64 n.83, 179–81, 186–8, 207

"Sha'ban the Brainless" 129
Shah, Muhammad Reza Pahlavi 125
Sharaf, Sami 96
Shi'i International 66–70, 73
    diplomacy among 71–2
al-Shishakli, Adib 33, 155, 169
Six-Day War (1967) 42
Soustelle, Jacques 145
Soviet Committee for the Defense of Peace (SCDP). *See* Soviet Peace Committee
Soviet Peace Committee (SPC) 67, 68
Soviet Union/USSR 3, 4, 6, 8, 41, 47–54, 56, 57, 83, 94, 99, 100, 113–17, 120, 121, 123 n.16, 133, 142, 143, 153, 154, 158, 159, 168, 169, 175 n.25 184, 191 n.42, 194, 199, 205, 206, 208
    access to Gulf oil 48
    Communist Party 68, 71, 73
    in the Middle East, revolutionary year of 1958 for 65–76
    diplomacy among Shi'i International 71–2
    informal peace movement 68–70
    leaders in the gray zone 71
    origins 66–8
    Peace Partisans 70–1
    Operation Wappen 16, 93
Soysal, Mümtaz 121
SPC. *See* Soviet Peace Committee
Stalin, I. V. 65
state formation 1, 5, 6, 204, 210
Stevens, Sir Roger 24
"Stockholm resolution" 69, 73
Suez Crisis of 1956 13, 14, 33, 39, 47–50, 57, 93, 114, 142, 154, 155, 168, 169, 183, 204
Sukharno 92
al Sulh, Sami 179–81, 183, 185, 186
Sultaneh, Qavam es 68
superpowers 3, 4, 40, 41, 50, 153, 159, 208
Syria 6, 8, 9, 14, 16–20, 22, 28 n.28, 33, 34, 43 n.6, 48, 51–4, 57, 61 n.29, 67, 81–3, 93–101, 103, 114, 115, 117, 118, 154, 155, 183, 184, 191 n.41, 193, 196, 206, 207
    Agrarian Reform Law 172, 173

Arab Socialist Ba'ath Party (ASBP) 93, 97, 101, 166–8, 173, 191 n.42
Crisis of 1957 53, 186
Deuxième Bureau (military intelligence) 168
and Egypt, union between 1
National Party 168, 172
    after 1958 172–3
People Party 168, 172
revolutionary year of 1958 for 166–77
    British policy and 16–17
    prelude 167–9
Syrian Broadcasting Station 52–3
Syrian Communist Party (SCP) 169–71, 175 n.25, 176 n.49

Takla, Philippe 181
Talbott, John 141
Taleb, Abderrahmane 144
al-Tariqi, 'Abdullah 86
TASS. *See* Telegrafnoye agentstvo Sovetskogo Soyuza (Telegraph Agency of the Soviet Union)
Teguia, Mohamed 141
Tehran University 131
Telegrafnoye agentstvo Sovetskogo Soyuza (Telegraph Agency of the Soviet Union, TASS) 70–1
Templer, Gerald 15, 23
Thabet, Antoine 69
theocracy 7
Third World 3, 4, 41, 99
Toker, Metin 115, 119, 120
Tripartite Declaration 35
Truman, Harry S. 132
Turkey 3, 6, 8, 17, 48, 51, 67–70, 93, 111 n.35, 169, 180
    Baghdad Pact, impact of 114–15
    Commission of Investigation (Tahkikat Komisyonu) 118–19
    Democrat Party (DP) 113
    domestic politics, impact of summer 1958 on 118–21
    and domino effect of Arab nationalism 113–24
    Fatherland Front (Vatan Cephesi) 118

under Nasser rule   115–16
perception of Iraq   116–17
perception of Jordan   117–18
perception of Lebanon   117–18
Republican People's Party (RPP)   113, 118, 119

UAR. *See* United Arab Republic
Al-Uloum, Mohammed Saleh Bahr   69
'Umran, Muhammad   173
UN Charter   39, 69
United Arab Republic (UAR)   1, 3, 16, 20–2, 33, 35, 47, 48, 57, 83, 84, 86, 93, 95, 97, 98, 100, 101, 104, 120, 155, 158, 163 n.36, 166, 170–3, 174 n.5, 183–5, 187, 190 n.36, 196, 207, 208
    Arab Union opposition to   18–19
    "First Army" of   171
    formation of   92, 103, 166
    under Nasser rule   115–16
    new US order (1958) and   53–5
United Nations and international organizations   18, 20, 22, 40, 41, 72, 73, 142, 143, 180, 184, 186, 194, 205, 208, 211 n.5
United States (US)   3, 4, 6–9, 10 n.4, 14–17, 20–3, 25, 33–42, 46 n.65, 70, 79–88, 92, 100, 101, 113–21, 123 n.16, 125–35, 136 n.9, 136 n.11, 142, 143, 155, 158, 168, 169, 180–6, 189 n.19, 190 n.36, 192 n.62, 193, 194, 196–9, 204–6, 208, 209
    Congress   68
    covert operation   82
    Eisenhower Doctrine   15, 34, 48–56
    Information Centre   185
    and Iran, alliance between   130–5
    legacy of Suez   48–50
    in the Middle East, revolutionary year of 1958 for   47–64

military involvement in Vietnam   48, 59 n.3
National Security Council (NSC)   54, 83, 186, 199
New Look policy   33
Point Four agreement   132, 183
relations with Iran in 1950s   127–30
State Department   128, 130, 179, 199
    Beirut Embassy   38
"Statement of US Policy toward the Near East" (National Security Council)   186
and Syrian crisis   16
UN Resolution (1947)   49
UN Security Council   72
    resolution of June 11, 1958   20
US. *See* United States
use of force and coercion   16, 24, 48, 50, 56, 205
al-'Utaybi, Juhayman   87

Vietnam   48, 58, 59 n.3, 64 n.81, 64 n.85, 72, 73

Wahbi, Abdul Jabbar   69
"Wahhabi" Islam   79
war on terror   80
Wilder, Thornton   131
"Wings of Peace" (al-Jawahiri)   67
World Peace Committee   69
World Peace Congress   69
World Peace Council   66
Wright, Michael   15, 18, 20, 98, 158

al-Yafi, Abdallah   181–4
Yamut, Sheikh Shafik   182
Yasin, Yusuf   83, 85
Yemeni Civil War   24, 100
Yizraeli, Sarah   83

Zahidi, Fazlullah   129–30
al Zaim, Husni   33
Zorlu, Fatin Rüştü   119

www.ingramcontent.com/pod-product-compliance
Lightning Source LLC
Chambersburg PA
CBHW071827300426
44116CB00009B/1470